ANONYMITY

ANONYMITY

A Secret History of English Literature

JOHN MULLAN

PRINCETON UNIVERSITY PRESS

PRINCETON AND OXFORD

Published in the United States
by Princeton University Press
41 William Street
Princeton, New Jersey 08540

First published in 2007
by Faber and Faber Limited
3 Queen Square London WC1N 3AU

Library of Congress Control Number 2008927833

ISBN 978–0–691–13941–8

Typeset by RefineCatch Limited, Bungay, Suffolk

Printed on acid-free paper.

press.princeton.edu

Printed in the United States of America

2 4 6 8 10 9 7 5 3 1

For Harriet

CONTENTS

Acknowledgements ix

Introduction 3
1 Mischief 9
2 Modesty 41
3 Women being men 76
4 Men being women 114
5 Danger 138
6 Reviewing 181
7 Mockery and devilry 217
8 Confession 254
9 Epilogue 286

Notes 298
Bibliography 337
Index 353

ACKNOWLEDGEMENTS

Over the years, I have pestered many friends, and most of my colleagues in the English Department at University College London, for information about anonymous and pseudonymous publications. They may recognize shards of their own knowledge in this book. For particular advice I would like to thank Rosemary Ashton, Mary Aylmer, Juliet Barker, Matthew Bevis, Paul Davis, Lucy Dallas, Greg Dart, Alan Downie, John Dugdale, Lindsay Duguid, Giles Foden, Mark Ford, Mark Fox, Warwick Gould, Helen Hackett, Bruce Hindmarsh, Iona Italia, Danny Karlin, Ian Katz, Nigel Leask, Grevel Lindop, Aasiya Lodhi, Roger Lonsdale, Lucasta Miller, Charlotte Mitchell, Ruth Morse, John Morton, David Nokes, James Raven, Hermann J. Real, John Richetti, Isabel Rivers, Valerie Rumbold, Max Saunders, Peter Shillingsburg, John Sutherland, Keith Walker, Francis Wheen, Henry Woudhuysen, and Steve Zwicker.

I have made much use of contemporary reviews, and found the periodical holdings of the Senate House Library invaluable. I am grateful to its librarians, and also to the British Library, and the Library of University College London.

A Leverhulme Trust Research Fellowship in 2003–5 gave me the time to turn the examples and stories that I had been gathering over the years into a book. I gratefully acknowledge the Trust's support.

Finally, I am indebted to Julian Loose at Faber and Faber, first for his patience and then for his pointed advice.

ANONYMITY

INTRODUCTION

It is not obvious to today's readers that publication and secrecy might go together, but so they once did. When Alexander Pope published his five-canto version of *The Rape of the Lock* in 1714, he claimed that his satire of feminine mores was originally intended only for private amusement – 'to divert a few young ladies, who have good sense and good humour enough to laugh not only at their sex's little unguarded follies, but at their own'.[1] The private became public. 'But as it was communicated with the air of a secret, it soon found its way into the world': a paradox to amuse us. What is more publishable than a secret? *The Rape of the Lock* was a kind of 'secret history' – a story that had a 'true story' behind it. A certain Lord Petre had snipped a lock of the beautiful Arabella Fermor's hair, provoking a quarrel between their two high-born families. Pope's poem, a parody of epic conflict, was purportedly written to turn antagonism ('What dire Offence from am'rous Causes springs') into amusement ('What mighty Contests rise from trivial Things') (Canto I, ll. 1–2). 'An imperfect copy having been offered to a bookseller', supposedly without the author's say-so, Pope explains that he was 'forced' to publish his 'heroi-comical poem', before he had completed 'half my design'. This first appeared anonymously, in two cantos, in a miscellany published in 1712.

After Pope's death, his editor and all-round stooge William Warburton claimed that when it was published Arabella Fermor 'took it so well as to give about copies of it'.[2] In fact, there is evidence that some of the real-life characters were touchy about the glittering vanities of their counterparts in the poem. In a tone of mock-amazement, Pope wrote in a letter to a friend that 'the celebrated lady herself is offended, and, which is stranger, not at herself, but me'. The poem prompted speculation about authorship, and a few months after it was published an essay in polite society's leading journal, *The Spectator*, was admiringly attributing it to Pope.[3] Now an 'authorized', and appropriately elaborated, version of the poem was called for, and Arabella Fermor, sensibly enough, reconciled herself to her transformation into the self-regarding but enchanting Belinda of the poem:

> If to her share some Female Errors fall,
> Look on her Face, and you'll forget 'em all. (II, ll. 17–18)

Pope's story was a convenient fiction, which exploited the frisson of knowing that real people were intended. The poem's transformation from anonymous miscellany piece to signed text, which Pope pretended was forced on him, provoked and then satisfied the reader's interest in who was being mocked, and who was behind it.

Over the centuries, the first readers of many famous literary works have been invited to unravel their secret histories. A good proportion of what is now English Literature consists of works first published, like *The Rape of the Lock*, without their authors' names. These works are now collected in bookshops or libraries under the names of those who wrote them, but the processes by which they were attributed to their authors are largely forgotten. It is strange to think of *Joseph Andrews* or *Pride and Prejudice* or *Frankenstein* being read without knowing the identities of their creators, but so they once were. There is no single book giving you the history of anonymity, but if you want to glimpse the sheer bulk of anonymous publication down the centuries you can browse one of the great, but neglected, monuments to nineteenth-century scholarship: Halkett and Laing's *Dictionary of the Anonymous and Pseudonymous Literature of Great Britain.* In the 1850s, Edinburgh librarian Samuel Halkett began collecting materials for a dictionary of anonymous and pseudonymous publications. He died in 1871 and his editorship and all his notes were passed to another Edinburgh librarian, Rev. John Laing. Laing died in 1880, and editorial work was continued by his daughter, Catherine, who succeeded in completing the four volumes of the first edition, which was published between 1882 and 1888. (Her name has never appeared on the work's title pages.) Another Scottish clergyman, James Kennedy, helped Laing and his daughter, and set himself to produce a revised and expanded edition. He worked on the project for nearly fifty years, dying the year before the first volume of this new edition appeared in 1926. In 1934, its seventh and final volume was published. This edition, to which two supplementary volumes, edited by Dennis Rhodes and Anna Simoni of the British Museum, were added in 1956 and 1962, now resides in the reference section of most good academic libraries.

It is actually a dictionary of attributions. It includes only originally authorless works that have, since publication, been 'reliably' pinned on some particular writer or writers. Permanently anonymous publications are not there. It is a huge record of the activity of identifying authors that has preoccupied readers down the centuries. Nine massive volumes merely list works in English that were first published without their authors' names. They include books by almost every well-known English author from before the twentieth century. It is the accumulated evidence of a phenomenon that has never been plotted or explained. Attribution was for centuries the common habit of readers, the consequence of having to read in the absence of the author's name. That absence, the subject of this book, is not necessarily a matter of literal namelessness. What will provoke readers to look for an author? Not just anonymity, but also pseudonymity, if the author's name as printed seems, to some readers, evidently fictional. Often it is difficult to distinguish between an anonymous and a pseudonymous work, and it was inevitable that Halkett and Laing's dictionary had to include both types of publication. *Robinson Crusoe* was published in 1719 without an author's name, but its title page declared it to be 'Written by Himself', so we might say that it appeared under the pseudonym 'Robinson Crusoe' (not least as we are told, in the novel's first sentence, that this is not the narrator's real name). When Thackeray used a pseudonym like Michael Angelo Titmarsh on a title page he was advertising the fact of a disguise to his readers. If we are interested in how speculation about authorship was part of what it was to read, then the distinction between anonymity and pseudonymity will often be indistinct or even immaterial. If a pseudonym signals that the true author is in hiding, you might say that the work is anonymous.

The compilers of 'Halkett and Laing' (as it has come to be called) seemed somewhat mystified themselves as to why so many authors might have initially concealed themselves from their readers. The dictionary's Preface tries to categorize the types of anonymity or pseudonymity illustrated by the thousands of works listed in the seven volumes that follow. We should understand these in terms of authorial 'motive'. 'Generally the motive is some kind of timidity, such as (a) diffidence, (b) fear of consequences, and (c) shame.'[4] Motive (b) is interpreted narrowly as fear of persecution, imprisonment and the like, while (c) applies to pornography and spiteful personal attacks. 'The great majority of anonymous and pseudonymous books will be found to fall under these groups.' Only anxiety of some kind, including a proper 'diffidence', could explain an author's reluctance to be known. Yet much of the material gathered in Halkett and Laing exhibits anything but timidity or shamefacedness. What are the other reasons why authors have chosen anonymity? And what about readers? If we reopen once celebrated cases of anonymity, can we see how, for their first readers, an uncertainty about their authorship could give new and original works of literature a special voltage?

1

MISCHIEF

Sometimes the last thing that an anonymous author wants is to remain unidentified. Look at the lengths to which Jonathan Swift went to ensure that *Gulliver's Travels* was published anonymously and you might suppose that he was anxious to keep his authorship hidden. He arranged for a sample part of the manuscript, probably transcribed in another man's handwriting, to be dropped in secret by an intermediary at a publisher's house. It was accompanied by a letter purporting to be from Lemuel Gulliver's cousin, one 'Richard Sympson', which offered the whole of the *Travels* for publication in return for £200. The letter had been written by Swift but copied out for him by his friend John Gay. The publisher, Benjamin Motte, was told that, within three days, he should either return the 'Papers' or give the money 'to the Hand from whence you receive this, who will come in the same manner exactly at 9 a clock at night on Thursday'.[1] With only some cavils about being allowed time to raise the large sum of money that was being demanded, Motte bravely accepted the mysterious offer. A few nights later he duly got the rest of the book. Soon afterwards, Swift's friend and probable co-conspirator Alexander Pope discussed the business with the puzzled publisher, pretending to be quite as mystified as he was. He reported the conversation in a letter to Swift: 'Motte receiv'd the copy (he tells me) he knew not from whence, nor from whom, dropped at his house in the dark, from a hackney coach.'[2] The author himself had returned quietly to Dublin to resume his duties as Dean of St Patrick's Cathedral.

All Swift's satirical writings first appeared anonymously or pseudonymously, and it is possible to detect in the manoeuvres over *Gulliver's Travels* a playful, even childish, delight in surreptitiousness. The work came late in Swift's literary career, and he was already practised in the provoking tricks of authorial disguise. This was a man who published the first collection of his own works anonymously, and with as blank a title as possible: *Miscellanies in Prose and Verse* (1711) – as if he were challenging readers to discern, behind the absolute reticence, an imperious originality. Remaining unknown as the creator of *Gulliver's Travels* was not what he expected. He was renowned for his satirical writing and his association with fellow 'Scriblerians' like Pope, John Gay and John Arbuthnot. He was also known as a former political controversialist, a friend of the now disgraced Tory ex-ministers, Henry St John, Viscount Bolingbroke, and Robert Harley, Earl of Oxford. For the latter he had once written (anonymously) a political periodical, *The Examiner.* The political readings that the *Travels* invited – its picture of the Lilliputian régime, for instance, seemed in some particulars much like the ministry of Robert Walpole – as well as the mingled brilliance and darkness of the work were strong evidence to contemporaries of Swift's authorship. If he had been wanting to remain unguessed at, we would have to say that he was naive. Everything about his career as a satirist suggests that he had a strong feeling for the habits of interpretation of his readers. One of the strongest of these habits, as he knew, was the 'discovering' of a work's likely author.

Shortly after the appearance of *Gulliver's Travels*, Gay wrote to Swift with news of its almost immediate success and naturally mentioned readers' attempts to attribute the book: 'nothing is more diverting than to hear the different opinions people give of it, though all agree in liking it extreamly. 'Tis generally said that you are the Author, but I am told, the Bookseller declares he

knows not from what hand it came.'³ Surmises about the likely
writer were part of the stir that the book caused. Swift's friends
had always been in on the 'secret' of its authorship. His fellow
Scriblerians had seen a draft of part of it five years earlier. Gay
seems to have been particularly closely involved in preparations
for its launch, which took place while Swift was staying with him
at his Whitehall lodgings. It may well have been Gay who carried
the manuscript to Motte. Yet he, Pope and Arbuthnot all kept up
in their correspondence the fiction that they too were ignorant
of the *Travels'* authorship. 'About ten days ago a Book was publish'd here of the Travels of one Gulliver, which hath been the
conversation of the whole town ever since,' Gay begins his letter
to Swift about the book's initial impact. After much delighted
reporting of the mischief and amusement it has caused, he pauses
to consider that his topical chatter might be unintelligible to
Swift, over there in Dublin. 'Perhaps I may all this time be talking to you of a Book you have never seen, and which hath not yet
reach'd Ireland.' Facetiously, he adds that, if he were to read it
and to find the satire obscure, he could always return to England,
'where you will have the pleasure of variety of commentators,
to explain the difficult passages to you'. Arbuthnot, in the first
letter that Swift received after publication, writes as if Gulliver
himself were the true author (as the book's title page proclaims):
'*Gulliver's Travels* . . . will have as great a Run as John Bunian.
Gulliver is a happy man that at his age can write such a merry
work.'⁴ Pope makes the least effort to treat Swift as though he
were not the author, writing the day before Gay's letter,
'I congratulate you first upon what you call your Couzen's wonderful Book, which is *publica trita manu* at present, and I pro-
phecy will be in future the admiration of all men.' He adds that
none, bar 'the mob of criticks', 'accuse it of particular reflections' – by which he means attacks on identifiable individuals –
'so that you needed not to have been so secret upon this head'.⁵

Pope's comment gives the game away – or gives away the fact that it is all a game. It is true that all these men were used to the possibility that their letters might be opened and read by government agents, and were therefore used to being careful about what they wrote. Yet, in this case, no real sense of danger or caution attaches to their pretence. They are merely playing – extending into their own lives the fictional life of *Gulliver's Travels*. Less than six months separated the book's publication (on 28 October 1726) from Swift's next visit to England; his correspondence for this period is full of Gulliveriana. Part of the book's appeal was in its creation of alternative worlds whose inhabitants lived by rules that were mad or ridiculous, yet curiously familiar from the world in which its readers lived. The satire's admirers enjoyed treating Swift's imagined worlds as if they were real, and his friends, having privileged access to the ingenious deviser, especially enjoyed it. The Earl of Peterborough regretted not being able to master 'the fashionable new dialect' of Houyhnhnm-speak and being 'forced to write to you in the yahoo language', but was at least able to turn his news of the town into tales of 'mutations among the Lillyputians'.[6]

Lord Bolingbroke's French wife was gamely facetious, writing 'pour vous dire un mot de mon amy Mr Gulliver' and poohpoohing rumours of French preparations for a naval war by telling Swift that France was in fact sending its ships on an embassy to 'les Ouynhms'.[7] A new friend of Swift's, Henrietta Howard, sometime mistress of the Prince of Wales, lady-in-waiting and friend to the Prince's wife, entered into the business with particular enthusiasm, signing herself a 'Yahoo' and larding her letters with Gulliverian allusions. Swift was happy to reciprocate with his own Gulliverian jokiness. In one letter, he told her that 'this night, while I was caressing one of my Houyhnhnms, he bit my little finger so cruelly, that I am hardly able to write' – indignant, supposes Swift, that he should be corresponding with a

Yahoo courtier.[8] In another letter, signed 'Lemuel Gulliver', he enclosed 'the crown of Lilliput'. 'I found it in the corner of my wastcoat pockett into which I thrust most of the valuable furniture of the Royall apartment when the palace was on fire, and by mistake brought it with me into England.'[9] According to Sir Walter Scott, in his early nineteenth-century biography of Swift, this miniature coronet was passed on, with due family pride, to Mrs Howard's descendants.[10]

Penetrating the secret was one part of the pleasure of reading this book. So far from it being dangerous or difficult to be supposed the author of *Gulliver's Travels*, Swift's friends presumed that he would want to return to England and enjoy in person the book's success.[11] His satire had managed to be, as Gay said, 'the conversation of the whole town' – by which he meant the fashionable, the clever and the powerful. It was written to cause a fuss, to be talked about. In its early life, *Gulliver's Travels* was, above all, a topic of conversation, and some of this conversation was concerned with its authorship. Lady Mary Wortley Montagu, writing to her sister in November 1726, guessed, both shrewdly and inaccurately, at the company that had produced this work, which 'all our people of taste run mad about'. It was, she supposed, jointly composed by 'a dignify'd clergyman, an Eminent Physician, and the first poet of the Age' (i.e. Swift, Arbuthnot and Pope). 'Great Eloquence have they employ'd to prove themselves Beasts,' she added in a sardonic refence to the already infamous depiction of the Yahoos in Part IV.[12] As a particular foe of Pope, she was always alive to his possible involvement in satirical publications. Potential antagonists had strong motives for getting their attributions on target. Finding out the author was the equivalent of detecting the work's malign intent. The anonymous writer of one of the earliest hostile replies to the *Travels* had no doubts that it was written by the 'Dean', and provided a derogatory account of the 'Character of the Author'.

'The Doctor divests himself of the Gentleman and Christian entirely, and in their stead assumes, or if my Instructions are right, I should rather have said, discloses the reverse to them both.'[13] The writer of the pamphlet recognized the handiwork of one who had been denied preferment and political influence ever since his friends fell from power when George I came to the throne. 'Here's the most inveterate Rancour of his Mind, and a hoard of Malice, twelve Years collecting, discharged at once.'[14]

If the anonymity of *Gulliver's Travels* was a charade, why was it such an elaborate one? The leading biographer of Swift, Irvin Ehrenpreis, had a psychological answer:

> His passion for hoaxes involving various games with his own identity strengthened Swift's instinct for self-protection. But he also lived up to a pseudo-rational principle of his own, viz., that the true genius is too modest to risk the embarrassment of being known before his work has been judged. In Swift I think this principle is the outer aspect of his inner longing to be valued for his own sake.[15]

By this account, the author, pretending reticence, was but the hungrier for admiration; 'he hated to admit in public (though he did in private) how frantically he desired fame.'[16] Swift's anonymity was a kind of self-promotion – an incitement to his first readers to discover his 'genius'. But it was also a creative resource. Mischievousness – almost the opposite of fearfulness – was a good reason for a satirist leaving readers uncertain of a work's origins. Swift liked to make trouble, and anonymity helped him do so.

His satires were released without any marks of 'true' intent, 'true' authorship. They were presented as if they had been composed by the strange, deluded personae whom Swift invented for each occasion. The most famous of all these entertaining fakes is probably his *Modest Proposal*, which was let loose to argue its case to its readers. Anonymity was part of its deadly effect, enabling the murderous humility with which, after a few paragraphs lamenting the numbers of the Irish poor and their children, the proposal was made.

> I shall now therefore humbly propose my own Thoughts; which I hope will not be liable to the least Objection.
> I have been assured by a very knowing *American* of my Acquaintance in *London*; that a young healthy Child, well nursed, is, at a Year old, a most delicious, nourishing, and wholesome Food; whether *Stewed, Roasted, Baked*, or *Boiled*; and, I make no doubt, that it will equally serve in a *Fricasie*, or a *Ragoust*.[17]

The infamous shock of this idea, 'humbly' offered 'to *public Consideration*', is made by the tonelessness of the prose, a medium in which anything becomes thinkable. The piece has a horrible life because there is no trace of its author. The fictional proposer of the little scheme to solve both poverty and overpopulation in Ireland by making the Irish eat their own babies is too 'modest' ever to tell his public his name. He is but a well-wisher to the world.

> I profess, in the Sincerity of my Heart, that I have not the least personal Interest, in endeavouring to promote this necessary Work; having no other Motive than the *publick Good of my Country, by advancing our Trade, providing for Infants, relieving the Poor, and giving some Pleasure to the Rich*.[18]

He signs off with clinching proof of his disinterestedness.

> I have no Children, by which I can propose to get a single Penny; the youngest being nine Years old, and my Wife past Child-bearing.

Such severing of a text from the intentions and beliefs of an author is at its most perturbing in the case of *Gulliver's Travels*.

The object of its satire is its own narrator: Lemuel Gulliver. The story of the fourth of his voyages, to the land of the disgusting Yahoos and the virtuous Houyhnhnms, relied on this to cause its stir amongst his readers. After the ridiculous pride in his own country that has sustained him for three voyages, allowing him not to notice the parallels between the lands he visits and his own dear England, he is converted by living for a while with the inhuman Houyhnhnms. From these rational talking horses, who speak only the truth, and have few wants or passions, he learns a kind of self-disgust: 'The many Virtues of those excellent Quadrupeds placed in opposite View to humane Corruptions, had so far opened mine Eyes, and enlarged my Understanding, that I began to view the Actions and Passions of Man in a very different Light.'[19] The once prideful Gulliver has become all humility, looking up to his equine 'master' and despising the sly, bestial Yahoos, in whom he has learnt to see human nature in the raw. (There is always something wrong with those who call themselves 'humble' in Swift's satires.) Once punctured, pride readily becomes its opposite: misanthropy. Listening to his master describe the cowardly, filthy, malicious habits of the Yahoos, 'it was easy to apply the Character he gave of the Yahoos to myself and my Countrymen'.[20] Easy indeed. It would have been clearer to the first readers than it is to us that the ease of this conversion is all the greater because Gulliver has no religion to speak of. Godlessly self-reliant, there is nothing to warn him against pride or save him from despair. Undeceived from his previously complacent faith in modern civilization and in himself, Gulliver finally opts to live in a stable, with herbs stuck up his nose to keep off the stink of humanity.

Leaving the tale to Gulliver is its point. Swift might have wanted readers to be able to infer his authorship, but he would not let them hear his voice. It is Gulliver, not Swift, who speaks of himself as 'the author'. 'The Author's Veracity. His Design in publishing this Work' is the heading of his final chapter; 'my sole intention was the PUBLICK GOOD,' he professes, with the same self-important modesty as the projector of the *Modest Proposal*.[21] He leaves us with a lesson that is half plausible: 'Who can read of the Virtues I have mentioned in the Glorious *Houyhnhnms*, without being ashamed of his own Vices, when he considers himself as the reasoning, governing Animal of his Country?' That word 'Glorious' could only ever be Gulliver's, infatuation posturing as enlightenment, yet ever since 1726 the absent Swift has been tagged with the misanthropy that is the fate of his narrator. Some who have noticed the satire's Godlessness have suspected that it tells us of the satirist's own unbelief. This can only ever be a hunch. All the evidence is that Swift performed his religious – which were also his professional – duties without a flicker of heterodoxy, let alone scepticism. His surviving sermons are sternly and eloquently Anglican, and dismissive of all clever doubts. Those who knew him well spoke of his religious orthodoxy in private. Yet the man of religion is absent from his most famous book. He has given the tale over to Gulliver, who is too self-reliant to believe in anything more providential than his 'good Star' or his 'evil Destiny'.[22] In his satires Swift enacted what he disdained or despised or feared; he imagined what should not be. His best writing is entirely negative creation. Anonymity was at its root. The initially authorless life of *Gulliver's Travels* was part of its author's design.

The night-time journeys to Mr Motte's house, the peremptory letters from an invented character, the author's friends pretending ignorance – these shifts were more promotional than shy. The lengths to which Swift went were extreme, but it was not unusual for an author of his age to avoid responsibility for what he had written. In the seventeenth and eighteenth centuries, a satirical writer in particular might like to leave the impression that the very act of publication was inadvertent, and the publisher more like the author's antagonist than his or her collaborator. The social and literary convention of unwillingness to publish was surprisingly resilient. It was clearly still alive for Sheridan in the late eighteenth century, when he nicely catches the trouble-making it permits in an exchange in his *School for Scandal*:

> LADY SNEERWELL I wonder, Sir Benjamin, you never *publish* any thing.
>
> SIR BENJAMIN BACKBITE To say truth, ma'am, 'tis very vulgar to print; and as my little productions are mostly satires and lampoons upon particular people, I find they circulate more by giving copies in confidence to the friends of the parties.[23]

While Swift let loose his satires, without clue or comment, to vex the world, we have already seen that his friend Alexander Pope liked to return to once-anonymous writings to add layers of pseudo-explanation or pseudo-apology. His art was in the 'reclaiming' of his own work, repossessing what was once anonymous.

Pope used the strategy to trick his enemies out of their usual judgements.[24] In 1733 he began publishing, in parts, his 'philosophic' poem *An Essay on Man*. He was still smarting from the many accusations that in his *Epistle to Burlington* (1731) he had satirized the Duke of Chandos, a leading patron of the arts, in the character of the tasteless plutocrat 'Timon', master of 'huge heaps of littleness' (l. 109). While Pope was issuing a series of other satirical poems under his name through his regular book-sellers, he had *An Essay on Man* published anonymously, in parts, through a bookseller and printer whom he had never used before. Initially not even friends were informed. There was something formally appropriate about this poem's anonymity: its grand purpose was to 'vindicate the ways of God to Man' (Epistle I, l. 16), organizing into reasonable or witty couplets the puzzles of 'Man' and 'the Universe'. Pope was a Roman Catholic, but his poem was designed to satisfy the tastes and intellects of any educated eighteenth-century reader. It was also designed to make mischief. His foes dismissed the poems that bore his name, but, to his exquisite delight, some of them turned to one side to praise in contrast the *Essay on Man*. 'I am as much overpaid this way now as I was injured that way before,' wrote Pope to a friend.[25] Leonard Welsted, who had several times mocked Pope's poetry, wrote to 'the unknown author' of the *Essay* to congratulate him. Once he had said that Pope was a mere plagiarist, who

> Has sweat each Cent'ry's Rubbish to explore,
> And plunder'd every Dunce that write before.[26]

Now Welsted found a work which was 'above all commendation, and ought to have been published in an age and country more worthy of it'.[27] He made a point of contrasting it with 'the vilest and most immoral ribaldry' recently published: in other words, Pope's latest satires. His praise duly found its way into the (ever expanding) 'Testimonies of Authors' section of Pope's *Dunciad*, where he stored the more stupid judgements of his enemies. 'Of his Essay on Man, numerous were the praises bestowed by his avowed enemies, in the imagination that the same was not written by him, as it was printed anonymously.'[28] There Welsted kept company with another dunce, Bezaleel Morrice, who also had a record of attacking Pope, and who had also incautiously celebrated Pope's new, anonymous poem. Morrice's response was the more gratifying for coming in portentous verse, in an avowed imitation of Pope's poem called *An Essay on the Universe*:

> Auspicious bard! while all admire thy strain,
> All but the selfish, ignorant, and vain.

Just so.

As Swift was not trying to remain completely hidden from his readers, so other authors who have used anonymity and pseudonymity have expected to have their identities guessed at. Follow in any detail the use of anonymity by literary writers – satirists, poets, dramatists and novelists – and you will find that only rarely is final concealment the aim. Swift's use of anonymity to excite speculation about authorship, and about the author's designs, turns out to be typical rather than peculiar. Indeed, we will often find that the elaborateness of measures taken to preserve an incognito tells us nothing of any true desire to remain unknown. The lengths to which a writer might go to keep the public, or sometimes the publisher, or occasionally the writer's own friends or family, guessing about the authorship of a work is not in itself evidence of the author's modesty, or shamefacedness, or fear. Being guessed at might be a writer's ambition. Provoking curiosity and conjecture – highlighting the very question of authorship – can often be the calculated effect of authorial reticence.

It is not difficult to think of Swift and Pope, self-appointed excoriators of their age, as being up to mischief. Yet this can also be a motive for the most respectably reticent of authors. Literary history exhibits few more obstinate practitioners of anonymity than the author of the so-called 'Waverley novels'. In 1821 a young Fellow of St John's College, Oxford, John Leycester Adolphus, set out to show, by close critical analysis, that their author was Sir Walter Scott, lawyer, poet and baronet. This was no mere academic exercise. These novels were the best-selling books of the early nineteenth century, indeed the best-selling novels there had ever been. By 1821 there had been a dozen, including *Waverley* (1814) itself, *Rob Roy* (1817), *The Heart of Midlothian* (1818), and *Ivanhoe* (1819). No author's name had appeared on any of their title pages. There was feverish speculation about the identity of their author throughout Britain, and especially in

Edinburgh. The most widely admired novelist of his day was called 'the Great Unknown'.[29] The Postscript to *Waverley* had made it clear that the author was Scottish, and that his main ambition was to describe faithfully the 'habits, manners, and feelings' of the Scots.[30] Until *Ivanhoe*, the novels' plots had been drawn from Scottish history and their settings had been mostly in the Scottish Borders and in Edinburgh. The first edition of *Waverley* had the imprimatur of Edinburgh publisher Archibald Constable. Surely the author was an Edinburgh character? Scott was a highly successful poet before *Waverley* was ever published and was from the first named by some as the possible author. Francis Jeffrey's review of *Waverley* in the *Edinburgh Review* nicely hazarded the attribution without actually stating it. 'There has been much speculation, at least in this quarter of the island, about the author of this singular performance,' observed Jeffrey's article, adding that 'if it be indeed the work of an author hitherto unknown, Mr. Scott would do well to look to his laurels'.[31]

The author of the Waverley novels clearly took some relish in their anonymity, for he soon began to tease his readers about it. The third edition of *Waverley*, published in October 1814, invited them to wonder 'whether WAVERLEY be the work of a poet or a critic, a lawyer or a clergyman, or whether the writer, to use Mrs. Malaprop's phrase, be, "like Cerberus – three gentlemen at once".'[32] Subsequent Waverley novels began to construct increasingly elaborate stories about their origins. *Old Mortality*, for instance, begins with the account of Jebediah Cleishbotham, schoolmaster and parish clerk of the small Scottish town of Gandercleuch, who presents to the reader the researches of an amateur local historian, Peter Pattieson. Before his death Pattieson recorded the stories of Robert Paterson, known as 'Old Mortality' because he visited the graveyards of Lowland Scotland tending the graves of the Cameronians, a Protestant sect who had taken up arms against the forces of Charles II. The Waverley novelist enjoyed the business of pretending that the novel was made from real documents.

Adolphus's exercise in literary detection was published (anonymously) as *Letters to Richard Heber, Esq.: containing critical remarks on the series of novels beginning with "Waverley" and an attempt to ascertain their author* (1821). (Richard Heber was an Oxford don and MP for the University, who was also a good friend of Scott's.) Its Introduction describes a reading public possessed by the mysterious anonymity of these engrossing works of fiction. 'Days and months of expectation follow one another, and still the accomplished unknown inexorably persists in his concealment . . . what limits can be assigned to that man's taciturnity, who has already kept a secret nearly seven years?'[33] At last, 'public conjecture, which had long been unsettled and contradictory, has begun to take a more uniform and constant direction'. This book will settle all that public speculation, not by reference to literary gossip, but by 'proofs . . . derived from the characteristic beauties and blemishes of works deservedly admired'.[34] Scott might often have been talked of as the likely author of the novels, but Adolphus's book was to be above chat and rumour. The reader was to be presented with purely literary evidence: an 'essay of comparative criticism'.

This small volume is now an obscure curio of literary history. Yet it sets out to answer a question that is not in the least antique: what aspects of a group of books are distinctive of a particular author? It is decorous enough not actually to name that person. Instead, the Waverley novelist is said to be 'the Author of Marmion' (*Marmion* being a successful narrative poem published under Scott's name). The novelist had chosen anonymity and so, even in a book designed to settle the attribution of his novels, it would be ungentlemanly to handle his real name. Talking of the Waverley novelist as 'the Author of Marmion' was more than a matter of politeness. It was desirable for literary reasons to show that 'the author of Waverley possesses, in a high degree, the qualifications of a poet'.[35] Throughout the novels the critic found passages 'which betray the poet's hand'. *The Bride of Lammermoor*, for example, has 'that fervour and exaltation of mind, that keen susceptibility of emotion, and that towering and perturbed state of the imagination, which poetry alone can produce'. This was no ordinary novelist. The Waverley novelist may be the best-selling writer in Britain, but he transcends 'the professional cant of a vulgar novel-maker'.

The aspects of the novels identified as characteristic of both poet and novelist are wonderfully diverse. Some are qualities of education and upbringing:

Habitual residents in Edinburgh—Poets—Antiquaries—German and Spanish scholars—Equal in classical attainments—Deeply read in British history—Lawyers—Fond of field sports[36]

Others are matters of style, analysed under headings like 'Grave banter', 'Scoticisms', and 'Bookish air in conversation'. Even the author's faults ('Quaintness of language and thought', 'Unsuccessful attempts at broad vulgarity') are found distinctive, and almost admirable. To a Scott aficionado, some of the oddest insights are also the shrewdest. The analysis recognizes, for instance, how interested the author is in dogs: 'The importance given to the canine race in these works ought to be noted as a characteristic feature by itself.'[37] It gives us examples of how observant both the author of *Marmion* and the Waverley novelist are of the behaviour of dogs.

In short, throughout these works, wherever it is possible for a dog to contribute in any way to the effect of a scene, we find there the very dog that was required, in his proper place and attitude.[38]

Adolphus was pursuing to far greater lengths than most readers a common urge for attribution. It is clear from the hidden author's response that he was not exactly trying to remain hidden. Far from being irritated by the attempt to 'prove' that he had written all those novels, Scott was flattered and intrigued. In the Introduction of his next novel, *The Fortunes of Nigel* (1822), Captain Clutterbuck meets 'the Author of Waverley' in a cave-like secret room at the back of an Edinburgh publishing house and discusses *Letters to Richard Heber* with him. 'You are not now, perhaps, so impersonal as heretofore,' observes Clutterbuck.[39] In reply, the nameless author praises 'the wit, genius, and delicacy' of the critic who has guessed at his identity, but says, 'I shall continue to be silent on the subject'. Scott wrote to Richard Heber to find out who had written this study of authorship: 'If it is not a secret, I should like to know the author.'[40] He commended him for managing the matter 'so much like a scholar and a gentleman'. When Heber told him the identity of the critical detective, Scott wrote that it would be 'too ticklish' for him to contact Adolphus himself, but that Heber should let him know that he was 'much flatterd to see that he possesses a more exact acquaintance with my publications than I do myself' and appreciated 'his great personal delicacy'; 'I should like very well to know him.'[41] Heber put the two men in touch and Scott invited Adolphus to Abbotsford, the house near Melrose that he had bought and expanded on the proceeds of those anonymous novels.

We know about the visit because Adolphus later contributed his reminiscences to the official biography, *Memoirs of the Life of Sir Walter Scott*, written by Scott's son-in-law John Gibson Lockhart after the great man's death. Adolphus recalled feeling some trepidation, as the reason for his visit 'was one which could not without awkwardness be alluded to while a strict reserve existed on the subject of the Waverley novels'.[42] Though he had done his best to solve the mystery of the novels' authorship, it would have been improper to have breached the author's "reserve" in his company – even in private. Adolphus had no need to worry. When they met, Scott "entered into conversation as if any thing that might have been said with reference to the origin of our acquaintance had been said an hour before". Everything could remain implicit. Adolphus did find it strange not to mention the novels "in a scene where so many things brought [them] to mind".[43] One of the great achievements of the Waverley novels was to make the Scottish borders a territory of the imagination known to readers throughout Europe. But silence on the subject of these novels was a rule that Adolphus readily inferred. If "some topic in the novels" *was* accidentally mentioned, "conversation ... died a natural death".[44]

That Scott was playing a game was evident from his willingness to talk of his fiction tangentially. "Though Sir Walter abstained strictly from any mention of the Waverley novels, he did not scruple to talk, and that with great zest, of the plays which had been founded upon some of them, and the characters, as there represented". Thus was exhibited "the pleasure which their illustrious author thus received, as it were at the rebound".[45] You get a glimpse here, as Scott shows the young literary enthusiast around his grounds, of one reason why Scott might have found anonymity congenial. The commercial business of producing novels could be kept separate from the life of the Laird of Abbotsford – even if the Laird's estate was purchased by popular fiction.

We now know that Scott went to some of the same lengths as Swift to preserve his incognito. Believing that his handwriting would be well known in the print-house, he had collaborators copy out his novels before they were submitted to the publisher. When he wrote *Waverley*, his friend John Ballantyne copied it out as fast as Scott could produce it.[46] The measures which Scott took could be expensive. The publisher's accounts for the costs of producing *Rob Roy* in 1817 include an allocation of £378 (equivalent to an annual income for many a professional gentleman) just to cover the transcription of the manuscript in order to preserve anonymity.[47] Scott kept the circle of those who knew the secret as small as possible. When *Waverley* first appeared, only John Ballantyne, his brother James, whose printing company was to be responsible for most of Scott's subsequent work, William Erskine, a lifelong associate and fellow Edinburgh lawyer, and his friend and favoured correspondent John Morritt were told. Lockhart says that even five years after the publication of *Waverley*, Scott's wife was the only member of his family who knew that he was the novelist. When the subject of 'the Great Unknown' came up at breakfast one day, his sixteen-year-old daughter Anne made some ill-judged jokes that indicated her confidence that the hidden author was James Ballantyne.[48] An indication of the care with which Scott maintained his concealment was his claim thirteen years later, when he finally confessed his authorship, that even then only twenty or so people were 'participant of this secret', and that he did not know of a single one of them 'breaking the confidence required from them'.[49]

There are many stories about Scott's maintenance and mischievous enjoyment of his anonymity. One day in 1819 some American tourists turned up at Abbotsford and, in conversation with Scott's house guest John Ferguson, implied that they took the Laird to be the author of the novels. Later that evening, as they went in to dinner, Ferguson remarked to Scott that the tourists had been 'in quite a mistake' in their comments on the resemblance between Abbotsford and the baronial houses in the Waverley novels. 'They evidently meant all their humbug not for you,' he is reported as saying, 'but for the culprit of Waverley, and the rest of that there rubbish.'[50] The author was amused and Ferguson's blunder led to his 'formal initiation' into the mystery. Others had their hunches fended off. 'There was about Scott, in perfection, when he chose to exert it, the power of civil repulsion,' commented Lockhart.[51] This meant lying upon occasion. When the publisher John Murray wrote to Scott in 1816 as the author of *Tales of My Landlord*, which included *Old Mortality*, he replied, 'I do not claim that paternal interest in them which my friends do me the credit to assign to me.'[52] When questioned directly, Scott would always deny being the author of the novels.[53]

His anonymity fuelled the interest of readers. As Lockhart put it, 'his name loomed larger through the haze in which he had thought fit to envelop it'.[54] It was also a creatively useful reticence. Scott's novels have a first-person speaker who is ready with local history, geographical knowledge and antiquarian lore, a character whom the author was able to remove from himself. A characteristic passage near the beginning of *The Heart of Midlothian* describes the former site of the gallows in Edinburgh's Grassmarket. Recalling how the scaffold would be erected overnight before public executions, the narrator turns to personal observation. 'I well remember the fright with which the schoolboys, when I was one of their number, used to regard these ominous signs of deadly preparation.'[55] Officially this novel is another of Peter Pattieson's manuscripts, but everywhere the author is using his own recollection. 'If I were to chuse a spot from which the rising or setting sun could be seen to the greatest possible advantage, it would be that wild path winding around the foot of the high belt of semi-circular rocks, called Salisbury Crags.'[56] We are being shown a picturesque spot just outside Edinburgh for the meeting between Reuben Butler, suitor of the novel's heroine Jeanie Deans, and a mysterious man who turns out to have been the seducer of Jeanie's sister, Effie. Scott's achievement was, like Thomas Hardy, to make the places he knew seem known to his readers – to make locality universal. His anonymity was a way of turning his personal experience into impersonal fiction.

When he began as a novelist, anonymity was also a way of allowing the still controversial history in his fiction to come to life, divorced from the opinions of a particular author. *Waverley* concerned the Jacobite Rebellion of 1745, when 'Bonny Prince Charlie' invaded Scotland and attempted to topple the Hanoverian monarchy of George II. Though Scott was intensely loyal to the latter-day Hanoverians, George III and then, after 1820, George IV, readers still notice the emotional Jacobitism of his first novel. Its protagonist, Edward Waverley, has had an unmonitored tuition in 'Romance' through all the hours wandering in the 'ample realm' of his uncle's library.[57] He is thus made susceptible to the appeal of the rebels, with their high-flown ideals, their costumes, their love of Highland tradition and landscape. Half in love with the stern, beautiful Jacobite Flora MacIvor, he cannot help becoming caught up in the rebellion, as if it were an adventure from one of those books he has read. 'What a variety of incidents for the exercise of a romantic imagination,' exclaims the narrator, speaking for Waverley's excitement, but also his own. Anonymity allowed Scott to animate the romance of Highland Jacobitism without associating himself with it. From the first, he was decided about remaining hidden, telling Morritt in 1814, 'I shall not own Waverley . . . whatever I may do of this kind I shall whistle it down the wind to prey on fortune.'[58] His career as a novelist was built on this act of creative self-dispossession.

Scott owned up to his fiction in 1827. He did so in suitably dramatic style, at a Theatrical Fund Dinner in Edinburgh. Responding to a toast that named him as the author of *Waverley*, Scott confessed that he was the same. His avowal was reported in newspapers, and in turn a newspaper account was prefixed to his *Chronicles of the Canongate*, published later in the year. The decision to drop his disguise was not made suddenly. In 1826 the collapse of the publishing firm in which he had invested much of the profit from his novels had brought him close to financial ruin. Like the other partners, he was personally liable for the company's losses. He now needed his name to sell his way out of his acute financial difficulties. He confessed in his Introduction to *Chronicles of the Canongate* that 'it was my original intention never to have avowed these works during my lifetime.'[59] Circumstances compelled a change of mind. One of his money-making plans was to produce a collected edition of his works, and he had to claim those works as his own. 'The author, so long and loudly called for, has appeared on the stage, and made his obeisance to the audience.'[60] No one was exactly surprised; by now he was the only candidate ever put forward as the author of the Waverley novels. Yet only under extraordinary financial pressure did he finally give in to all the speculation. Even when he had owned up, he kept his sense of mischief. Discussing his anonymity in the General Preface to the 1829 collected edition of his novels, he offered only a mock-explanation. 'I can render little better reason for choosing to remain anonymous, than by saying with Shylock, that such was my humour'.[61]

Scott's resolute anonymity has many features that we will find again in the stories of anonymity in this book: the elaborate concealment of the author's handwriting; the initial deception even of publishers (Archibald Constable published *Waverley* without knowing its authorship) and family members; the willingness of the author to lie cordially when identified. Above all, Scott's case illustrates a paradox that we will find over and over again: the anonymous writer who does not truly attempt to remain unknown. For the most part, Scott enjoyed the speculation his anonymity attracted. 'I have seldom felt more satisfaction than when, returning from a pleasure voyage, I found Waverley in the zenith of popularity, and public curiosity in full cry after the name of the author.'[62] English (and Scottish) literature is full of similar cases – of authors who went to great lengths to maintain anonymity, but thereby promoted their readers' interest in the authorship of a work. The main lesson is a simple one: that anonymity is most successful when it provokes the search for an author.

In our own age of authorship, such provocation is rare. In many areas, notably fiction, the promotion of an author pre-exists the promotion of his or her book. Authors are always there in person, soliciting our attention. Yet in one notorious example from the 1990s, anonymity sealed the triumph of a work of fiction that reawakened habits of reading common before the twentieth century. *Primary Colors*, published in the United States in January 1996, was a *roman-à-clef*. In this type of fiction characters are recognizable, at least to some readers, as versions of certain real people. Those in the know are expected to work out the correspondences. The reader who knows that it is fiction 'with a key' will be admitted to a partly hidden world, described with an insider's knowledge. This was all certainly the case with *Primary Colors*, subtitled 'A Novel of Politics', which told the story of Jack Stanton, a Democrat contender for the American Presidency, as he fought his way through the primaries that would decide his party's nomination. Stanton – governor of a small Southern state, serial adulterer, barbecue addict and former draft evader – corresponded in every known detail to Bill Clinton. The novel, published in January 1996, was proclaimed on its jacket as 'a savvy insider's look at life on the stump' and was immediately recognized by all reviewers as an account of one phase of Clinton's 1992 Presidential campaign. What was most unusual about it was that its authorship was unknown. Its cover announced that it was 'by Anonymous'.

Primary Colors was on the American best-seller list almost from the moment it was published. It was a kind of *succès de scandale*, offering in the form of fiction an uncensored report on the misdeeds and machinations of the man who had indeed become President, and telling the satirical truth about the follies and vanities of his courtiers and his competitors. Its anonymity was a sign of its candour. It was as if the author needed to hide because he or she was well known to those who were depicted in the book – because he or she was breaking confidences and passing on secrets. Each character in the novel was taken to correspond to a real person, observed from close by. Some correspondences would be clear to any TV viewer: for Hillary Clinton there was Stanton's steely wife Susan, as powerful a figure as Stanton himself; for the pious Governor of New York and potential rival to Clinton, Mario Cuomo, there was the pious Governor of New York, Orlando Ozio (cordially despised by Stanton); for former mistress Gennifer Flowers there was former mistress Cashmere McLeod, like her original, possessor of tapes of amorous conversations with the would-be leader of the free world. And if you were a connoisseur, there was the implied promise that every minor character, each adviser and journalist, could be recognized by those with sharp enough eyes. The book invited the reader to write in their true identities. 'Only the identity of the author remains unknown to the reader,' observed one reviewer.[63]

Primary Colors is narrated in the first person by one Henry Burton, who has been charmed and pressurized by Stanton into working on his campaign. The invention of 'Henry' is crucial, for the novel aims to bring to life the seductive appeal of Stanton/ Clinton. 'Henry' is not only a witness to the deceitfulness of this consummate politician, he is also a bemused expert on his strange magnetism. 'Henry' keeps uncovering Stanton's squalid secrets, and keeps being seduced by him all over again. Much of the initial speculation about the book's authorship settled on the character of this narrator, who, despite being nominally black, was agreed by most American journalists to be closely based on Clinton's young adviser George Stephanopoulos. Soon Stephanopoulos found himself regularly having to deny his authorship as the book's success became inseparable from speculation about who had written it. By the end of January, influential broadcaster Larry King was devoting an hour-long CNN programme to the different possibilities. By February, Random House's initial print run of sixty thousand hardback copies had been increased to over half a million, and paperback rights had been sold to Warner Books for $1.5 million. It was widely publicized that not a single person at either publishing company knew the identity of the author. Negotiations were conducted through a literary agent, Kathy Robbins. Daniel Menaker, senior literary editor at Random House, told the press that his editorial discussions with the author took place via the agent's fax machine; no response to his suggestions were ever handwritten. When the book appeared, he and Harold Evans, head of Random House, duly received handsome acknowledgements in a note addressed to 'some people who don't know who I am'.

Journalists speculated about the author's identity on behalf of the readers. Who could have known enough to have written the novel? Its appalled yet fascinated depiction of the contradictory qualities of Stanton/Clinton – his sincerity and his duplicity, his moral fervour and his faithlessness, his political intelligence and his dangerous stupidity – could only be the creation of someone who had been very close to the man who became President. The closeness is where the book starts, with the narrator's first meeting with Stanton and Stanton's magical handshake.

I've seen him do it two million times now, but I couldn't tell you *how* he does it, the right-handed part of it—the strength, quality, duration of it, the rudiments of pressing the flesh. I can, however, tell you a whole lot about what he does with his other hand. He is a genius with it. He might put it on your elbow, or up by your biceps: these are basic, reflexive moves. He is interested in you. He is honored to meet you. If he gets any higher up your shoulder – if he, say, drapes his left arm over your back, it is somehow less intimate, more casual. He'll share a laugh or a secret then – a light secret, not a real one – flattering you with the illusion of conspiracy. If he doesn't know you all that well and you've just told him something 'important', something earnest or emotional, he will lock in and honor you with a two-hander, his left hand overwhelming your wrist and forearm. He'll flash that famous misty look of his. And he will mean it.[64]

Get close, and he will overwhelm your cynicism. The meaningless glad-handing of the politician somehow becomes seduction and Burton, a once-disillusioned political aide, is caught from the first touch. Given Stanton's 'follow-me nod' he is swept up in a visit to a Harlem adult literacy programme. Here dyslexic Dewayne, 'who weighed three hundred pounds easy and was a short-order chef', tells them of the boyhood humiliations suffered because of his illiteracy and Burton is embarrassed to find himself crying. 'I looked over at Jack Stanton. His face was beet-red, his blue eyes glistening and tears were rolling down his cheeks.'[65] Being in touch with his feelings is this politician's irresistible skill.

Intimacy with its leading characters, and therefore their real-life counterparts, is the novel's implicit boast. In one intimacy that reviewers and speculators seemed to pass by, the narrator – once again seduced – has sex, just once, with Susan Stanton. He recalls something to try to make it credible: 'She even *smelled* distant and formal, all soap and hair spray. I'd never, I realized, made love before to a woman who used hair spray. It made her hair feel stiff, and it preoccupied me.'[66] This is also anti-intimacy. (Nothing of the intensity or plausibility of that opening handshake with her husband.) The deed once done, the candidate's wife silently gathers her clothes and leaves. Unsurprisingly, the surprising sexual encounter was omitted from the film of *Primary Colors*. On screen, the novelist's fantasy might have been taken as a truth-claim. Readers were perhaps able to accept it as a wishful extension of the author's closeness to the leading couple. Yet 'Anonymous' was risking breaking his fiction's contract, which promised real secrets. Announcing 'the kind of truth that only fiction can tell', the dust-jacket proclaimed that the book was not fiction at all.

The unprecedented (but actually age-old) device of anonymity did not of itself guarantee the truth of the narrative, but it helped it come to life. A few months after publication this 'secret history' had a million readers, but, by the author's mischievous self-concealment, it was still 'secret'. *Primary Colors* had rediscovered the life of speculation that anonymity could fuel. Every new guess in the press as to the name of the novelist seemed to confirm his authority and help his sales (a month after publication, producer and director Mike Nichols was buying the film rights – off he knew not whom – for a million dollars). Here was a secret so successful that it just had to be uncovered. Less than two months after publication, *New York* magazine had a cover story declaring that the mysterious author was Joe Klein, a columnist with *Newsweek* magazine. Editors of *New York* had reached for literary expertise, asking Professor Donald Foster, a Shakespeare scholar specializing in computer analysis of the styles of individual writers, to give his verdict. Quantitative analysis of the otherwise insignificant verbal tics of particular writers has for some time been a small part of Shakespeare studies; scholars have wanted to know what proportions of particular plays are likely to have been written by Shakespeare or collaborators like Middleton, and have often had only stylistic evidence to go on. The professor applied his expertise to a computer analysis of the styles of thirty-five likely suspects and declared Klein the probable author. Almost simultaneously, the *Washington Post* commissioned a computer analysis which identified one of its own former writers, Sally Quinn, as the probable culprit. Both journalists strongly denied being 'Anonymous'. 'For God's sake, definitely, I didn't write it,' shouted Klein to fellow journalists in a New Hampshire press room, where he was reporting on voting in the 1996 Presidential primaries.

It was the more traditional method of handwriting analysis that finally solved the puzzle. The *Washington Post* had obtained an early draft of *Primary Colors* that included handwritten notes. An expert had compared these with samples of Joe Klein's handwriting and, on 17 July, the newspaper declared that this showed him to be the author. The same day, Klein called a press conference at the offices of Random House and announced, 'My name is Joe Klein and I wrote *Primary Colors*.' At first he seems to have expected other journalists to be amused – he arrived to make his announcement with a joke-shop fake nose and moustache. Instead he was greeted by something close to indignation, particularly when he revealed that the editor of *Newsweek*, Maynard Parker, had been in on the secret. *Newsweek* had joined in the speculation about the authorship of the novel, running an article in which several candidates, not including Klein, had been put forward as the person behind 'Anonymous'. Soon a contrite Klein was apologizing to other writers and editors at *Newsweek*, where his column was suspended. Anger was spreading amongst journalists. A portentous editorial in the *New York Times* solemnly declared that the behaviour of Klein and Parker 'violates the fundamental contract between journalists, serious publications and their readers'. Klein's was 'a duplicitous book-selling scheme . . . people interested in preserving the core values of serious journalism have to view his actions and words as corrupt and – if they become an example to others – corrupting.'[67] By the end of July, Klein's other employer, CBS News, had 'accepted his resignation'. Andrew Heyward, president of the television company, wrote in the memorandum to his staff announcing the resignation that he was 'deeply troubled to learn along with the rest of you that Joe had not been truthful with us or, more importantly, the public'.

The anonymity of *Primary Colors* was well judged because it encouraged the very curiosity that it seemed to frustrate. Even if the indignation of Klein's fellow journalists appears ridiculous, some of their irritation might be understandable. Klein's initial protest that he had hidden his identity because he was not sure how his fiction would be received was surely disingenuous. The anonymity of his 'secret history' was guaranteed to make mischief. The whole episode returns us to a lost world of novel-writing, when anonymity and pseudonymity were common. Many were shocked that Joe Klein had denied his authorship of *Primary Colors* on air to America's leading news broadcaster (and representative of media probity), Dan Rather of CBS. In a different age, that most respectable writer, Sir Walter Scott, publicly denied his authorship of the Waverley novels to the Prince Regent himself. Invited to dine with the heir to the throne, Scott politely rebuffed his host when he called for a toast to 'the author of *Waverley*', Scott's phenomenally successful first novel, while looking 'significantly, as he was charging his own glass, to Scott'.[68] According to his son-in-law, Scott denied the attribution (the elaborate form of words no doubt being invented by Lockhart himself): 'Your royal highness looks as if you thought I had some claim to the honours of this toast. I have no such pretensions.' Apparently, however, he promised to take good care that the true author 'hears of the high compliment that has now been paid him'.

In the mid-nineteenth century, Anthony Trollope clearly believed that barefaced denial was an anonymous author's right. In his novel *The Claverings* (1866–7), his hero, Harry Clavering, is talking to the Polish Count Pateroff about Lady Ongar, a young widow. Harry is trying to find out about her circumstances, but is warned in advance by the Count that he will not say 'any thing against any lady'.[69] Harry realizes that this means any subsequent assertions will be entirely unreliable.

> It was as when a man, in denying the truth of a statement, does so with an assurance that on that subject he should consider himself justified in telling any number of lies. 'I did not write the book,—but you have no right to ask the question; and I should say that I had not, even if I had.'

The readiness of the analogy implies that Trollope expects readers to recognize the situation – that an author's denial of an anonymous book might be as conventional, as respectable, as a gentleman's refusal to speak ill of a lady.

The supposed mendacity of *Newsweek*'s editor in allowing his magazine to perpetuate the mystery while knowing its solution is a small trick by the standards of other ages. Scott helped write an often biting anonymous review of one of his own novels, *Old Mortality*.[70] The review, which Scott composed with his friend Erskine, even drew attention to guesses about authorship.[71] Pronouncing *Waverley*, *Guy Mannering* and *The Antiquary* (Scott's first three novels) to be 'the work of the same author', it wondered about this author's motive for 'preserving so strict an incognito'.[72] It went on to handle him with a critical severity unmatched in most contemporary reviews. 'Probability and perspicuity of narrative are sacrificed with the utmost indifference to the desire of producing effect,' it grumbled. 'Against this slovenly indifference we have already remonstrated and we again enter our protest.' The dismissiveness was calculated: in Scott's day, a certain negligence could be thought the characteristic of a gentlemanly author, fiction's minutiae being beneath him. If we know that Scott was writing this, there is a droll mixture of parody and self-criticism in some of the comments. 'In addition to the loose and incoherent style of the narration, another leading fault in these novels is the total want of interest which the reader attaches to the character of the hero.' Critics have tended to go along with this: Scott's heroes are often characters who guilelessly wander through history, empty enough of characteristics or opinions to be shaped by what they encounter, like Edward Waverley, oscillating between Jacobites and Hanoverians.

Other aspects of the *Primary Colors* affair have their echoes in earlier times. In the stories in this book, publishers will sometimes be co-conspirators with authors, but often, as in the case of Harold Evans and *Primary Colors* – or Benjamin Motte and *Gulliver's Travels* – they are but willing instruments. In many cases publishers have put forth work whose authorship was hidden even from them. This might seem unsurprising where a writer writes for a coterie readership, or seems careless of commercial success. Yet there are prominent examples from the history of that most populist of literary genres: the novel. Thomas Lowndes, the publisher of Fanny Burney's *Evelina*, was made to conduct negotiations by letter to 'Mr King' at a London coffee house. When the final parts of the manuscript of the book were to be delivered, Burney sent her brother Charles heavily disguised. Walter Scott had his negotiations with publishers conducted by James Ballantyne. Awkward though this was, it gave the author a certain power: his ambassador was obliged to hand on demands to booksellers. Before her identity became known to John Blackwood, the publisher of her early fiction, George Eliot communicated with him only indirectly, through the letters of her lover, George Henry Lewes.[73] Blackwood initially had no idea that she was not a man. Only a year later, when Eliot was well into the writing of her first full-length novel, *Adam Bede*, was Blackwood put out of his misery of curiosity about the identity of his popular new writer. In an *éclaircissement* in the drawing room of Lewes's Richmond home, she was, literally, revealed to him.[74] It was, Blackwood confided in a letter to his wife the next day, 'the Mrs. Lewes whom we suspected'.[75] Now he was to share 'the profound secret'.

It is particularly satisfying that handwriting should eventually have given away the author of *Primary Colors*, for, in ages before the typewriter, it was this that was most likely to betray an incognito. When Swift wished to make corrections to *Gulliver's Travels* for its second edition he had them copied and submitted by his friend Charles Ford, on behalf of the still unnamed author. He was in the habit of dictating controversial works to 'a Prentice who can write in a feigned Hand', sending the finished work to the printer 'by a Black-guard Boy'.[76] It has often seemed necessary to keep publishers and printers, as well as readers, guessing, so writers have had to do something about their handwriting, the one true guide to attribution. Fanny Burney may have been an unknown when she wrote her first novel, *Evelina*, but she had been amanuensis for the *General History of Music* by her father, Charles Burney, which had recently begun to be published. Fearing her usual handwriting was known to printers and publishers she copied out her novel 'in a feigned hand'.[77] We have already seen that Walter Scott had his novels copied in another hand before being sent to the printing house. When he received the corrected proofs of one of these novels back from the author, his friend James Ballantyne would transcribe all alterations onto a clean set of proofs, so that Scott's handwriting would remain unseen by his compositors.[78] Scott later confessed that he had preserved the original manuscripts of his fiction 'with the purpose of supplying the necessary evidence of truth when the period of announcing it should arrive'.[79] When Charles Dodgson answered letters addressed to him, via his publisher, by his pseudonym, Lewis Carroll, he would have either a friend or the publisher copy out his response so that the admirer would not receive a specimen of his actual handwriting.[80] Handwriting has always been the truest proof of authorship.

2

MODESTY

⌒

Some famous authors have really not wanted to be known. When the first volume of Halkett and Laing's great *Dictionary of the Anonymous and Pseudonymous Literature of Great Britain* was published in 1882, one of the most famous literary pseudonyms of the age was missing. In November 1880, Rev. C. L. Dodgson had written to Catherine Laing, who had taken on the editing of the great reference work when her father died, imploring her 'most earnestly and urgently' not to identify him as 'Lewis Carroll' in the forthcoming book. 'I use a name, not my own, for writing under, for the one sole object, of avoiding *personal* publicity: that I may be able to come and go, unnoticed, to all public places.'[1] Dodgson wrote as if readerly interest in the true identities of authors was discourteous, even impudent. In a later letter he told Catherine Laing that he feared that the *Dictionary* would 'only serve to gratify impertinent curiosity'.[2] Dodgson was unusual in resenting that curiosity rather than wishing to exploit it. The convention of embarrassment at the mere fact of having one's writing published had passed.

Catherine Laing acceded to his request. For the man who, as 'Lewis Carroll', wrote two of the best-sellers of the age, works that eventually made him wealthy and allowed him to resign his Oxford mathematics lectureship, pseudonymity was a matter of privacy rather than concealment.[3] Dodgson acknowledged his authorship to a large circle of friends and acquaintances, yet strenuously refused to go public. All his efforts to preserve his incognito now look hopeless. Sometimes they amounted to attempts to erase common knowledge. He tried, for instance, to get the Bodleian, the library of his own university, to delete cross-references between his two names.[4] (The Library refused.) He protested to George's bookshop in Bristol when its catalogue named him as author of *Through the Looking-Glass*, demanding that they 'forbear from printing his name in connection with any books except what he has put his name to'.[5] He harassed various other writers of books about literature who published the old news of Lewis Carroll's true identity. In 1890, he printed a circular declaring that 'Mr. Dodgson ... neither claims nor acknowledges any connection with any pseudonym, or with any book that is not published under his own name'. Any correspondence addressed to 'Lewis Carroll' at Christ Church, Oxford, where he lived, would be returned unanswered accompanied by this notice.[6]

Over and over again he begged friends not to mention his real name in connection with the *Alice* books. When he wrote to the wife of the Professor of Divinity at Oxford asking her not to give away any specimen of his handwriting, he said of his request,

> It is a thing I often have to do – people seeming to assume that *everybody* likes notoriety, and scarcely believing me when I say I dislike it particularly. My constant aim is to remain, *personally*, unknown to the world.[7]

Remaining 'unknown to the world' meant not being recognized, literally not being seen. 'I cannot of course help there being many people who know the connection between my real name and my "alias",' he told his publisher Alexander Macmillan, 'but the fewer there are who are able to connect my *face* with the name "Lewis Carroll" the happier for me.'[8] When he begged Catherine Laing to omit him from Halkett and Laing's *Dictionary*, it was because 'it would be a real unhappiness to me to feel myself liable to be noticed, or pointed out, by strangers.'[9] Dodgson's special obsession was that some 'likeness' of himself might be attached to the name 'Lewis Carroll'. When the cartoonist Leslie Ward, the son of friends, proposed including a sketch of the writer in *Vanity Fair*, he wrote to 'beg and implore' that he would not do so. 'I would rather anything than that.'[10] The editors of the magazine, reconciling gentlemanliness with opportunism, agreed that no likeness would be published, provided that Dodgson wrote an article for them.

Dodgson's greatest horror was of the possibility that prying eyes would see any photograph of him. Few authors have been such lovers of photography as Dodgson, a man who confessed to seeing photographs in his very dreams.[11] Photography was perhaps the greatest passion of his life. He converted his rooms in Christ Church into a photographic studio with his own darkroom. He is now notorious for taking and collecting photographs of children, some '*sans habillement*', as he put it. He was once renowned for his photographs of celebrated men and women. He photographed Huxley, Tennyson, Millais and Ruskin, along with a small crowd of bishops and minor royals.[12] He collected celebrities. Perhaps it is not surprising that what he most feared, when he thought of the loss of his disguise, was photography. He tried to ensure that no 'photographs or autographs' became public property, begging close friends not to put either into albums where strangers might see them. He explained to a clergyman acquaintance, who had given him a book of his poems and had asked for a photograph in return, that he was always being 'bullied' by 'the herd of lion-hunters' who wished 'to drag him out of the privacy he hoped an "anonym" would give him'.[13] 'I so much *hate* the idea of strangers being able to know me by sight that I refuse to give my photo, even for the albums of relations.' He explained to another admiring clergyman that, while happy to send inscribed copies of his books to each of his three

daughters, he would not send photos. 'I don't give my photographs. I don't want to be known by sight! The "et dicier 'hic
est!' " [see, there goes so-and-so] has no attractions for me.'[14] In
fact, for many years he *had* given out photographs of himself,
though only to young girls who wrote to him. 'I make a rule of
not giving my picture to any but children,' he explained to the
aunt of one of his 'little friends'.[15] Often this involved an
exchange of photographs with them. He had 'cartes of myself'
specially printed and ready for despatch to young admirers.[16] He
knew that these gifts would not be seen only by children. When
he sent one to Adelaide Paine he asked in a covering letter to her
mother, 'Will you kindly take care, if any of your ordinary
acquaintances (I don't speak of intimate friends) see it, that they
are *not* told anything about the name of "Lewis Carroll".'[17]

'Lewis Carroll' was supposed to be a way of not being seen in
the public eye. Like many a pseudonymous disguise, it was not
a question of preserving any real secrecy about the authorship of
his books. When Catherine Laing replied to Dodgson's fevered
request that his true name be kept out of Halkett and Laing's
Dictionary, she observed that it was, after all, 'perfectly well
known'.[18] For Dodgson, however, a public announcement was
something different from common knowledge. In his sixties he
was congratulating himself that, 'For 30 years I have managed to
keep the 2 personalities distinct, and to avoid all communication,
in propria persona, with the outer world, about my books.'[19] He
had remained consistent to a principle, despite its practical awkwardness. Dodgson sometimes admitted that, though he did as
much as he could to 'keep the secret from the outer world', it
was unlikely to be a secret from any well-informed admirer.[20] Yet
he would never allow himself to be publicly recognized as Lewis
Carroll. 'I don't want to be known, except by *friends*.'[21] Invariably,
when Dodgson acknowledged to them that he was Lewis Carroll,
they were requested not to tell anyone. 'I wish my private name

to be as little known, publicly, as may be.'[22] He was quite happy to publish his works on mathematics, *Symbolic Logic* or *Euclid and His Modern Rivals*, under his own name. What he wrote as Lewis Carroll was for play.

Dodgson even required of friends and acquaintances that they should not embarrass him by mentioning his strange and wonderful inventions. 'Your friend Miss Collins was very kind and complimentary about my books,' he told Mary Manners, 'but may I confess that I would rather have them ignored? Perhaps I am too fanciful: but I *have* somehow taken a dislike to being talked to about them: and consequently have some trials to bear in Society.'[23] The two things he most hated, he told his friend Edith Blakemore, were 'having a tooth drawn' and being 'talked to about my books by a stranger'.[24] Dodgson himself wondered if his sensitivity might be unusual. After a visit to the mother of one of his 'child-friends' he wrote:

> . . . I was made *doubly* shy by your beginning to talk about my 'books'! I am quite sure you had not the least idea how I *hate* having my books, or myself, *en évidence* in the presence of strangers: but, also, I feel tolerably sure you will not mind my mentioning the fact. Possibly it is a morbid feeling: certainly it is not shared by *all* writers. I read, only the other day, an anecdote of somebody meeting, in society, for the first time, some writer or other, whose *first* question was 'Have you read my book?'
>
> If ever *I* ask such a question of a stranger, it will be due to 'temporary insanity'![25]

Beneath the self-deprecation is a disdain for immodesty, for the lack of sensitivity of any writer who should want to be addressed 'in society' as an author.

'Timidity' we might call this, if he had not been so untimid in his efforts to keep Charles Dodgson and 'Lewis Carroll' apart.

His 'shyness', as he liked to call it, was temperamental, but also had something to do with what he created in the role of Lewis Carroll. His brilliantly childlike nonsense grew out of his private world of 'child-friends', a world only posthumously invaded by biographers and academics. Carroll's preface to *Alice's Adventures in Wonderland* put into verse the famous story of the origins of a book that was first 'written for a child, with no thoughts of publication'.[26] On 4 July 1862, Dodgson had taken a boat trip up the Thames with his fellow don Robinson Duckworth and the three Liddell sisters, daughters of the Dean of Christ Church. To amuse Ina (aged twelve), Alice (aged ten) and Edith (aged eight) he had begun spinning 'the tale of Wonderland', and had promised Alice that he would write it out for her.[27] When he returned, he wrote notes of what he had imagined, and over the next few months turned these into 'Alice's Adventures Under Ground', a handwritten gift for Alice Liddell, illustrated with his own drawings. Friends persuaded him to extend and publish the work, 'my little dream-child'.[28] Whatever the sales of *Alice's Adventures in Wonderland*, finally published in 1865, and its sequel seven years later, *Through the Looking-Glass*, the works of Lewis Carroll were to be considered, by their author as well as by their readers, as taking their life from a special relationship with children. They hardly belonged to the realm of commercial authorship. In his preface to *Alice's Adventures Under Ground*, which Dodgson published in facsimile some twenty years after *Alice's Adventures in Wonderland*, Lewis Carroll explained that 'nothing of reward is hoped for' from his work 'but a little child's whispered thanks and the airy touch of a little child's pure lips'. Dodgson's obstinacy about his pseudonym was a proof of this claim – a proof as much to himself as to any friend or admirer.

'Modesty' would be a traditional word for his sense of the privacy of his authorship. And there is certainly a long tradition of 'modest' anonymity and pseudonymity in English literature. The

English literary renaissance is sometimes taken to have begun with a work, Edmund Spenser's *The Shepheardes Calender* (1579), that modestly appeared without its author's name. Its title page did have an important name on it: its patron's. The volume was dedicated to 'The Noble and Virtuous Gentleman most worthy of all titles both of learning and chevalrie M. Philip Sidney'.[29] Sidney was the model Elizabethan courtier: soldier, man of literature, and enthusiastic Protestant. A verse prologue was signed 'Immerito' and treated the book's anonymity as evidence of its author's proper humility.

> Goe little booke: thy selfe present,
> As child whose parent is unkent:
> To him that is the president
> Of noblesse and of chevalree. (ll. 1–4)

The author was in every sense 'unkent': hidden by his anonymity, but also an unknown – a person without distinction or fame who was presenting his poetic offering to Sidney, 'the president / Of noblesse'. A decade later in his *Arte of English Poesie*, the first major critical work on the writing of poetry in English, George Puttenham addressed himself to gentlemen, perhaps courtiers, and argued against the need for anonymity. He knew of 'very many notable Gentlemen in the Court' who have 'publisht without their own names to it: as if it were a discredit for a Gentleman, to seem learned, and to shew him selfe amorous of any good Art'. But he observes that 'Emperours, Kings, and Princes' have been proud of 'their Skils' in 'Poesie'. This being so, any 'meaner person' composing poetry should not be 'squeimish to let it be publisht under their names, for reason serues it and modesty doth not repugne'.[30] Yet Puttenham himself published *The Arte of English Poesie* anonymously. The book carried the name of a patron, or potential patron, Lord Burghley, to whom it was dedicated. The dedication was written in the voice of the book's printer, Richard Field, who talked of the book somehow 'coming to my handes, with his bare title without any Authours name or any other ordinarie addresse', and claimed the dedication to Burghley as his decision (with due apologies for offering a work on 'so slender a subject' to a person whose contemplations 'are euery houre more seriously employed upon the publicke administration and services').[31] Puttenham's anonymity, like Spenser's, acknowledged his humble status.

The anonymity of *The Shepheardes Calender* was suitable in another way. The prologue imagines the 'little booke' arousing curiosity about its authorship. 'And asked, who thee forth did bring, / A shepheards swaine saye did thee sing' (ll. 8–9). The sequence of pastoral verses is presented as a collection of shepherds' songs. The substance – lovesickness, a debate between youth and age, a shepherds' singing match – is often simple, though the collection is also a tour de force of different stanza forms and metrical patterns. It is elaborate contrivance (the author's artifice) masquerading as simplicity (these shepherds' lyrics).

The effect of the author's reticence is considerably complicated by the presence in the work of a mysterious commentator called 'E. K.', who provides glosses on the poems. (Debate continues amongst scholars as to whether these annotations were written by Spenser or not.) The glosses, perhaps especially when they seem pedantic or pompous, give the work the appearance of some antique, perhaps ancient, text, earnestly annotated by a dubious modern commentator. This illusion was further suggested by the book's typography: the poems themselves were printed in the Gothic so-called 'black letter' script, while the prose apparatus was produced in a modern Italian typeface. E. K.'s introductory Epistle celebrated the fact that the poetry made calculated use of 'olde and obsolete words', bringing 'great grace and, as one would say, auctoritee to the verse'.[32] The poet

had laboured to 'restore' archaic diction – 'such good and natu-
rall English words, as have ben long time out of use and almost
cleare disherited'.[33] The poems are indeed full of archaisms, the
vocabulary appearing to the modern reader often closer to
Chaucer than to Shakespeare. The whole work is carefully composed, but presented as if it were an old text rediscovered.

The author was 'shadowed' in the book as Colin Clout, the
shepherd whose lovelorn complaint begins the collection.
'COLIN Cloute is a name not greatly used,' observes E. K. in a
characteristically plodding note, 'and yet have I sene a Poesie of
M. Skelton's under that title. But indeede the word Colin is
Frenche, and used of the French Poete Marot (if he be worthy of
the name of a Poete) in a certain Æglogue.'[34] Spenser was certainly seeking recognition and advancement. The modesty of
'Immerito' is calculated to ambitious ends. The collection sets out
to remake English poetic language; 'our new Poete', as E. K. calls
him, is founding a new poetry. This becomes clear in the fourth
part, 'April', intended, as the Argument has it, 'to the honor and
prayse of our most gracious sovereigne, Queene Elizabeth'.[35] One
shepherd, Hobbinol, tells another, Thenot, how Colin Clout has
become distracted because of misfortune in love and recalls
his supreme poetic skills. This gives him occasion to repeat Colin's 'laye / Of fayre *Elisa*, Queene of shepheardes all' (ll. 33–4).
You can glimpse here that the poem was self-promotional – the
first move in a poetic career that was to culminate in the greatest
of all the poems celebrating Queen Elizabeth, *The Faerie Queene*.
It was in the 1590 edition of *The Faerie Queene* that Spenser
finally declared himself as author of *The Shepheardes Calender*.

There is evidence that Spenser's identity as the author of this
popular collection was carefully concealed yet guessed at. William
Webbe, a Cambridge contemporary, praised the work in his *A
Discourse of English Poetrie* (1586), saying that he did not know
whether the author was 'Master *Sp.* or what rare Scholler in

Pembroke Hall soever, because himself and his freendes, for what respect I knowe not, would not reveale it'.[36] Here is the trace of a mystery playfully kept up. Webbe was looking for confirmation of what he almost knew. Later in the book he was indicating his confidence by referring to 'Master *Sp*: Author of the *Sheepheardes Calender*'. In 1589 Thomas Nashe was celebrating 'divine Master *Spencer*, the miracle of wit' for his 'Pastorall Poemes'.[37] On the other hand, the circle of the knowing was limited. In the same year George Puttenham praised several contemporary authors by name, before including 'that other Gentleman who wrate the late *shepheardes Callender*'.[38] 'Gentleman' Puttenham called the nameless author, but in the sixteenth century a gentleman usually avoided print. Ambitious writers who did allow their work to be printed often exhibited reluctance or distaste.[39] Spenser's anonymity was a necessary sign of modesty, but the very publication of *The Shepheardes Calender* was the opening move in the pursuit of advancement as a writer.

Modesty has even more been a virtue associated with female authors. For many years there was even a standard pseudonym for the self-respecting woman writer: 'A Lady'. We are likeliest to know this pseudonym from its use (on just one occasion) by the most famous female author of all: Jane Austen. When her first published novel, *Sense and Sensibility*, appeared in 1811 it proclaimed itself, 'Sense and Sensibility. A Novel. In Three Volumes. By a Lady'. To today's readers this advertisement of modesty has a quaintly genteel ring. By the beginning of the nineteenth century, it was a long-established pseudonym. The earliest example of it dates from 1652: a collection of religious poems and meditations 'by a Lady, who only desires to advance the glory of God, and not her own'.[40] It was in the late seventeenth century that it became possible, even conventional, for female authors to publish works as being 'by a Lady'. These were likely to be books that seemed either earnestly – *The Whole Duty of a Woman* . . .

Written by a Lady (1696) – or wittily – *An Essay in Defence of the Female Sex . . . Written by a Lady* (1696) – appropriate for an elegant female author.

'A Lady', while venturing at a modest publication, refused to make herself public property as a few notorious female authors (Aphra Behn is the most important example) were willing to do. In Elizabethan and Jacobean England, it had been acceptable for a woman to publish under her own name, with the double proviso that she be of high social standing and that her writings be of an improving (preferably religious) as well as elegant cast. Women could be admired as prodigies of humanist learning. The exemplary female author in this respect was the Countess of Pembroke (Mary Herbert), younger sister of Sir Philip Sidney. Two of her translations from French were published in her lifetime: Robert Garnier's *Marc Antoine* and Philippe Du Plessis Mornay's *Discourse de la vie et de la mort*, works unfrivolously concerned with *ars moriendi* – the art of dying well. The title page proclaimed 'Both done in English by the Countesse of Pembroke'. However, her translations of Petrarch (his *Trionfo della Morte* – another work about death) and of the Psalms (the latter presented to Elizabeth I) remained in manuscript. Translation, an exercise of learning, was always likely to be safer than fiction. Her niece, Lady Mary Wroth, wrote the pastoral romance *Urania*, published under her name in 1621. It aroused controversy when it was read as a *roman-à-clef*, and Lady Mary claimed, probably untruthfully, that it had been published without her permission.

This kind of claim can rarely guide us. When some of the poems of Katherine Philips (the 'Matchless Orinda', as she became known) appeared in a poetic miscellany in 1663 as 'By a Lady', the author wrote to her friend Sir Charles Cottrell to tell him that she would soon be sending him a copy. The printer of it, she added, 'has thought fit, though without my consent or privity, to publish two or three poems of mine, that had been stolen from me'. As Germaine Greer, who quotes this letter in her chapter on Philips in *Slip-Shod Sibyls*, remarks, 'there is no hint here of outrage.' It would be reasonable to suspect that she was in fact delighted to appear in a volume which also included two poems (by men) celebrating her poetic achievements (both of them addressing her as 'Orinda' – Philips' name for herself in her poems).[41] Philips might well have been involved in the supposedly unauthorized *Poems by the Incomparable Mrs K. P.* announced the very next year and then withdrawn from publication at her request soon after it appeared (a number still found their way into circulation). Modesty could be an alibi as well as an obligation.

The poetic pseudonyms of woman writers were sometimes effective disguises: 'Ephelia', the author of *Female Poems on Several Occasions* (1679), remains as hidden from academics as she seems to have been from contemporaries. They could also, as in the case of Philips, be half-disguises, allowing other writers in the know to acknowledge them. The pious Elizabeth Singer (later Rowe) had her verse published in the early eighteenth century under the name 'Philomela', and was addressed and praised by this name by other writers who were well aware of her identity. Anne Finch, Countess of Winchelsea, first had her work appear in miscellanies as by 'Ardelia'. Male writers who addressed her by this name, including Nicholas Rowe, Jonathan Swift and Alexander Pope, all knew her true name. When she eventually published a collection of poems in her fifties, it was entitled *Miscellany Poems, on several occasions. Written by a Lady* (1713). Her high rank made it easier for her to allow her name to appear on the title page in the second edition, later the same year. Only from the mid-eighteenth century did non-aristocratic writers like Elizabeth Carter, Hannah More and Anna Seward make it respectable, one might say 'normal', for women to publish poetry under their own names during their lifetimes. Before this, they would commonly submit verse to magazines anonymously or under one of those feminine pseudonyms. The *Gentleman's Magazine* had a monthly section of poems submitted by readers: pseudonyms for contributors in one typical year, 1745, included Eugenia, Lavinia, Orinthia, Zephyretta and Belinda.[42] The latter purported to be a 'country damsel', who submitted a heartfelt lyrical encomium 'To the Author of Pamela'.[43] Only post-humously would collections be published under female poets' names.

Sometimes it is difficult to disentangle gender from class when encountering prejudices against publication. At a time when it was widely considered ungentlemanly for a man to publish under his own name, we should not suppose that clever women would have resented the requirement that they keep their names off what they write. Perhaps Lady Mary Wortley Montagu was being self-consciously aristocratic when, in the 1730s, she told Lord Cornbury, who was considering publishing his poetry, that 'it was not the business of a Man of Quality to turn author . . . he should confine himself to the Applause of his Friends and by no means venture on the press'.[44] But hers was a time-honoured aloofness. She was never caught authorizing the publication of any of her own writing. She took some care to preserve and bequeath her brilliant *Embassy to Constantinople*, an account in letters of a journey to Turkey, but it was only to be published posthumously half a century later. It was in bad taste for a *man* to publish what he had composed, and doubly unacceptable for a woman. Yet somehow Lady Mary's satirical poems did slip into print, hidden behind their anonymity, yet not hidden at all – her authorship never declared, yet guessed at by knowing readers. Her modesty was conventionally preserved, yet 'modest' does not seem to be the right word for what she wrote, or the ways in which her writing found its readers. In 1716, she had apparently suffered when the unscrupulous bookseller Edmund Curll

published *Court Poems*, which he puffed as being by Pope, Gay
and 'a Lady of Quality'. It included three of Lady Mary's privately circulated 'town eclogues', comic complaints about sexual
infidelity spoken by fashionable characters, some of whom could
easily be identified with particular courtiers. Curll's 'Lady of
Quality' tag mocked the convention of modesty and invited
readers to speculate as to her identity; those likely to be offended
by her poems would be most likely to know her authorship.
Pope responded by arranging a meeting with Curll at which he
tricked him into drinking an emetic, the consequences being
fully described in Pope's anonymous pamphlet *A Full and True
Account of a Horrid and Barbarous Revenge by Poison, On the
Body of Mr. Edmund Curll.*

Curll got hold of these satirical poems because their author
had been assiduously circulating them. As a poet she managed to
become 'the Fam'd Lady *Mary*', at least in the eyes of the select
readers who had access to her work, without putting her name to
anything in print.[45] One contemporary celebrated her writing
for its very anonymity in a poem 'To the Lady W—y M—e,
Upon Her Poems Being Publish'd without a Name'.[46] The qualities of her work, he declared, had to be known for themselves
because she cared nothing for the superficial prestige of authorship. In fact, Lady Mary seems to have connived at the publication of some acid satires. In reply to Swift's notorious poem 'The
Lady's Dressing Room', a catalogue of the fascinated and disgusted Strephon's findings in his beloved Celia's private chamber,
she wrote *The Dean's Provocation for Writing the Lady's Dressing
Room.* This explains Swift's misogyny as the bitter consequence
of his unhappy experience with a whore. His 'provocation' she
summarised in a couplet:

> It seems you have as little luck in
> The art of rhyming as the art of ****.[47]

Though she did not own up to *The Dean's Provocation*, she almost certainly arranged for its publication. So she probably did with her most infamous satire, *Verses Address'd to the Imitator of the First Satire of the Second Book of Horace*. This vicious, often ingenious, attack on Alexander Pope – once a friend, long since an enemy – was announced as being (that traditional badge of modesty) 'By a Lady'. It ruthlessly anatomises the inadequacies that have made Pope a satirist, not least his deformed and shrunken body, his 'wretched little Carcass' (l. 70).[48]

> But how should'st thou by Beauty's Force be mov'd,
> No more for loving made, than to be lov'd?
> It was the Equity of righteous Heav'n,
> That such a Soul to such a Form was giv'n. (ll. 48–51)

Pope was tiny and had a twisted spine as a result of childhood illness; Lady Mary was happy to imply in these lines that he was condemned to sexual frustration. Composed with the assistance of another of Pope's enemies, Lord Hervey, the poem was carefully released to the public, causing maximum controversy and amusement. It was universally attributed to Lady Mary, though there remains no tangible evidence of her authorship.[49] But then not leaving evidence, while exciting speculation, was itself a skill.

Late in her long life Lady Mary was still, if laughingly, denying the authorship of works on which she was complimented.[50] But she was old-fashioned. Amongst male writers, only the gentleman amateur remained squeamish. One such was the poet Thomas Gray, a Cambridge don who was highly sensitive to the identification of himself as a published author. The first of his works that appeared in print was his 'Ode on a Distant Prospect of Eton College', a poem rooted in his own schooldays. It appeared anonymously, and Gray told his confidante Horace Walpole that he denied his authorship in the face of attribution from Cambridge acquaintances.

It is said to be mine, but I strenuously deny it, and so do all that are in the secret, so that nobody knows what to think; a few only of King's College gave me the lie, but I hope to demolish them; for if *I* don't know, who should?[51]

A few months later it was reprinted in a volume of Robert Dodsley's genteel poetic miscellany *A Collection of Poems*, along with two of his other odes. All remained anonymous. Some of Dodsley's other poets had their names printed; some, like Walpole, did not. When he composed his 'Elegy Written in a Country Church-yard' some two years later, Gray sent a copy in manuscript to Walpole, only to find that copies were soon circulating more widely than he had expected.[52] He told Walpole that the editors of a magazine had written to him about 'an *ingenious* Poem, call'd, *Reflections* in a Country-Churchyard', saying 'that they are inform'd, that the *excellent* Author of it is I by name.'[53] Clearly they meant to publish it. Gray was left with 'one bad Way to escape the Honour they would inflict upon me': publish it himself. He told Walpole to issue Dodsley with the necessary instructions, stipulating that it must appear 'without my Name'. 'If he would add a Line or two to say it came into his Hands by Accident, I should like it better.'

This anonymity was clearly not playful; Gray's suggestion about Dodsley professing to have had the poem 'by Accident' looks more like the recommending of a lie. As if turning your poetry into a published work were mortifying. When the first edition of the 'Elegy' appeared in February 1751, a preface, written by Walpole but signed 'The Editor', duly declared that the poem 'came into my hands by Accident'.[54] Its author may have seemed to suffer by the necessity of making it public, but it soon became hugely popular. It went through at least nine editions in the next couple of years, as well as being widely pirated in magazines. Yet in none of the authorized editions did Gray's name appear. Though his fame was now wide, his 'Elegy' – destined to become the most frequently reprinted poem of the eighteenth century – was to remain officially anonymous.

Such pained self-effacement was not common in the mid-eighteenth century. The mere act of publishing your writing was no longer suspect, even for a woman. A book's declaration that it was 'by a Lady' was given new life by novels, on whose title pages it commonly appeared from the 1760s. About two thirds of more than 150 known publications 'by a lady' between 1750 and the appearance of Jane Austen's first novel in 1811 were novels. Sometimes they were even 'by a young lady'. What would once have been a gesture of self-deprecation – of modesty amounting to humility – had become an advertisement. In the eighteenth and early nineteenth centuries, the majority of novels published in Britain were anonymous.[55] In the lists of novels printed by booksellers or in the catalogues of circulating libraries, works were itemized alphabetically by title. Many who purchased novels or borrowed them from circulating libraries were women, and the novels advertised as 'by a lady' were often books about women: novels of courtship, of sentimental entanglement, of virtuous suffering in love. Frequently their titles were the names of their female protagonists: *Hortensia: or, the distressed wife. A novel. By a lady* (1769); *Aurulia: or the victim of sensibility. A novel, by a young lady* (1790).

By the 1750s it was usual to think of women as the likely readers and possible authors of novels. Critics began trying to detect the sex of unknown novelists. An anonymous critic commenting on Eliza Haywood's anonymous *History of Miss Betsy Thoughtless* (1751) condescendingly picked on the feminine details that critics would feature for the next century and more. 'The minute detail of particulars, and circumstantial descriptions of every thing relating to dress and equipage, and other little exteriors that too much attract the heart of a woman, sufficiently

confirm the voice of the public, as to the sex of our author.'[56]
When Fanny Burney published her first novel, *Evelina; Or, A
Young Lady's Entrance into the World*, anonymously in 1778, the
market for novels, most of them authorless, was established. It
was also becoming respectable for women to be 'literary ladies'.
Two of the male authors who most influenced Burney in her
youth, Samuel Richardson and Samuel Johnson, were known for
cultivating and encouraging women writers. There were established circles of 'bluestockings', sometimes satirized, but more
often celebrated as prodigies of modern womanhood. While it
might have been natural for Burney to publish her first novel
anonymously, she was not in the same situation as a female
author fifty years earlier. There was no necessary shame in a
woman being known as a published author, even of a novel.

Yet a myth of maiden modesty has attached itself to Burney's
debut as a writer, perhaps because virtuous bashfulness is a quality of her novel's heroine. It owes something to the story of her
father, Charles Burney, finding out the secret. Thanks to Fanny
Burney's own habit of retelling it, is the best-known remnant of
her original anonymity. Staying outside London in Chessington,
she received bulletins from her sister Charlotte in town, recount-
ing first his discovery of her authorship (he had been told by
another sister, Susanna) and then his reactions as he began reading the novel. Finally he visited her, their meeting preserved in a
tremulous journal entry.

> I was *almost* afraid—& *quite* ashamed to be alone with him—
> but he soon sent for me to his little Gallery Cabinet—& then,
> with a significant smile that told me what was coming, &
> made me glow to my very forehead with anxious expectation,
> he said 'I have read your Book, Fanny—but you need not
> blush at it.—it is full of merit—it is really extraordinary.—' I
> fell upon his Neck with heart-beating emotion, & he folded

me in his arms so tenderly that I sobbed upon his shoulder—
so delighted was I with his precious approbation.[57]

Her father's acknowledgement of her book was dreaded and
desired. Clearly she relished his pride. He was later to publish
anonymous verses in the *Morning Herald* celebrating her amongst
other women writers and would become a rather embarrassing
promoter of her fiction, buttonholing acquaintances to praise
her novels.[58] Reading of her modest trepidation at her father's
reaction, it is easy to forget that Burney was in a position to
enjoy her strategies of modesty. You can hear her mixture of
reticence and playfulness in her preface to *Evelina*. It is 'the
trifling production of a few idle hours'. Yet she points out wryly
that, while no writer is 'so much disdained by his brethren of the
quill, as the humble Novelist', novels do seem to be rather popular. This particular 'humble Novelist' writes with 'timidity and
confidence': 'trembling' because of the book's imperfections, yet
'happily wrapped up in a mantle of impenetrable obscurity'. Her
reticence is necessitated by the supposed lowness of novels, yet
Burney is surely making fun of just this idea. 'Perhaps were it
possible to effect the total extirpation of novels, our young ladies
in general, and boarding-school damsels in particular, might
profit from their annihilation.' Sadly, 'their contagion bids defiance to medicine of advice or reprehension', so best to produce
some novels that might be read 'if not with advantage, at least
without injury'.[59]

Burney had gone to great lengths to get her book into print,
while keeping her identity hidden. As her intermediary she used
her nineteen-year-old brother Charles, who first approached
the bookseller Thomas Lowndes 'in the dark of the evening',
disguised in hat and old greatcoat, and going by the name of
'Mr King'.[60] In her letters to Lowndes, Burney wrote as an
anonymous editor of the novel. Once Lowndes had accepted it,

her go-between became her cousin Edward, under the name
'Mr Grafton'. (She could no longer use Charles, who had disgraced himself by being caught stealing books from Cambridge
University Library and had been exiled to rural Berkshire.)
Lowndes had to write to him at Gregg's Coffee House in Covent
Garden, which was run by two of Burney's aunts. When the novel
was launched (according to Burney, she only knew of the publication when her stepmother read aloud a newspaper advertisement for the book) it was an almost immediate success.[61] There
seems to have been widespread speculation about its authorship. We have a record of some of this in Burney's own excited,
delighted journal entries.

> Lady Hales spoke of it, very innocently, in the highest terms,
> declaring she was sure it was written by somebody in high Life,
> & that it had all the marks of real Genius!—Miss Coussmaker
> carried her praise still higher; she was quite *bewitched* with it,
> & could talk of nothing else. The Writer, she said, was a great
> *acquisition to the World*, & Lady Hales added *he must be a man
> of great abilities!*—
>
> How ridiculous! But Miss Coussmaker was a *little* nearer
> the truth, for she gave it as *her* opinion, that the Writer was a
> *Woman*, for she said there was such a remarkable delicacy in
> the conversations & descriptions, notwithstanding the gross-
> ness & vulgarity of some of the Characters, & that all Oaths
> & indelicate Words were so carefully, yet naturally avoided,
> that she could not but suspect the Writer was a Female, but,
> she added, notwithstanding the preface declared the Writer
> never would be known, she hoped, if the Book circulated as
> she expected it would, *he*, or *she*, would be tempted to dis-
> covery. Ha! Ha! Ha!—that's my answer. They little think how
> well they are acquainted with the Writer they so much
> honour.[62]

Evelina, the comic and romantic adventures of a naive, virtuous seventeen-year-old girl, is now routinely praised for bringing to life her hopes and anxieties. We see London in the 1770s through her eyes. She has lived all her life in the country and now learns, as she puts it, to '*Londonize*' herself.[63] Evelina's letters detail her urban pleasures (it has one of the first uses in English of the word 'shopping') and the whirl of assemblies and entertainments that a respectable young woman can sample. It also shows us the risks she runs as a woman: she is endlessly embarrassed, often by male admirers, and twice narrowly escapes sexual assault. The fact that *Evelina* is in letters makes its anonymity especially appropriate. Evelina is excitable, callow, easily impressed: a novice with the goodness and insight to keep her from peril. So the book has these qualities too, charting the day-by-day excitements of London life. The letters are full of exclamations ('I am in ecstasy!' is a favourite) and, to the consternation of her aged guardian to whom she writes, they pulse with unworldly delight. Burney's triumph, which she was never to repeat, is to give over her book to her candid, enthusiastic young heroine. It is extraordinary to imagine contemporary readers not taking it for granted that the author was female. (Burney's cousin's nurse, Miss Humphries, was also sure that 'the Work was a *man's*', as was close family friend Samuel Crisp.[64]) Yet we should remember that probably the most influential novel of the century, Samuel Richardson's *Pamela*, had likewise fictionalized the experiences of an unworldly young woman, and was written mostly, like *Evelina*, in the very letters of the heroine.

You can hear in Burney's recording of Lady Hales' and Miss Coussmaker's comments her enjoyment ('Ha! Ha! Ha!') of the speculation that her novel aroused. Seven years later, when she first met and talked with George III, the King was intrigued by the details of the secrecy surrounding *Evelina*, presuming that Burney had been playful as much as retiring. He was particularly entertained to know that her father's friend Giuseppe Baretti, a well-known man of letters, had wagered that the novel must have been by a man, 'for no woman, he said, could have kept her own counsel'.[65] Even after this space of time, Burney found it painful to talk about how her authorship became public knowledge, but her copious letters and journal entries for 1778 are largely taken up with the book's reception, which she monitors closely and excitedly. Written 'simply for my amusement' and published 'merely for a Frolic' (as she told herself in her journal), the stir that *Evelina* made delighted her. Yet she was also properly nervous of her writing becoming public property. It was strange that 'it is in the power of *any* & *every* body to read what I so carefully hoarded even from my best Friends, till this last month or two.'[66] It was surely as a woman, rather than just as a first-time author, that she felt 'an exceeding odd *sensation*, when I consider that a Work which was so lately Lodged, in all privacy, in my Bureau, may now be seen by every Butcher & Baker, Cobler & Tinker, throughout the 3 kingdoms, for the small tribute of 3 pence.'

Burney's comments have all the more edge given the vein of snobbery that runs through the novel. One of the satirical high-lights of *Evelina* for contemporaries was its depiction of the irredeemably vulgar Branghtons. The family of a city silversmith, these distant cousins of the heroine torment her throughout the book with their loud impertinence and tasteless pursuit of urban sophistication. They are even vulgar enough to talk of people being vulgar. They are outdone by their tenant Mr Smith, who speaks of himself as 'a man who wishes to have things a little genteel'.[67] This '*Holbourn Beau*' particularly delighted Dr Johnson: 'such a *varnish* of low politeness!'[68] Vulgarity was Burney's theme because Evelina enters a world in which culture and plea-sure can be bought. The plays, assembly rooms, concerts, enter-tainments and pleasure gardens that she visits are open to those who can buy a ticket. Evelina and the reader must learn to enjoy them in the right way. When the genteel and the vulgar can so easily mingle, it has become more important than ever to distinguish them. Thus Burney's 'odd *sensation*'. The novel is another accessible pleasure of modern culture; the novelist cannot stop cobblers and tinkers from enjoying it.

There was pleasure accompanying her anxiety about her own 'entrance into the world'. She searched out the experience of hearing *Evelina* talked of by those who had no idea that she was its author. In her journal she admits prodding a Miss Humphries into praising it and reading aloud from it. 'I must own I suffered great difficulty in refraining from Laughing upon several occasions.' Anonymity could be an enjoyable game. 'I could not resist treating myself with a little *private sport* with Evelina,—a young lady whom I think I have some right to make free with,' she writes, as she records introducing Samuel Crisp to the novel without acknowledging her authorship.[69] Awkwardly for her, he asked her to read it out to him. Yet 'I had the satisfaction to observe that he was even *greedily* eager to go on with it; so that I flatter myself the *story* caught his attention.' Weeks later she was teasing him about the '*profound secret*' of the novel's authorship. She told him that she had heard a rumour about the author's identity, 'but I insisted upon his Guessing'.[70] He guessed first at Burney's father, then at Dr Johnson's friend Mrs Thrale, then at Burney's godmother Frances Greville, a noted intellectual and poet. 'I Grinned prodigiously . . . I sha'n't undeceive him, at least till he has finished the book.'[71] Meanwhile Hester Thrale herself recommended the book to Burney's own (still ignorant) stepmother, and even lent her a copy: 'how droll!' Burney exclaimed to her journal.[72] When she heard the 'Encomiums' of her cousin Richard she had a 'double pleasure' as they were 'totally unexpected'.[73] 'I was yet more satisfied, because I was sure they were sincere, as he convinced me that he had not the most distant idea of suspicion.' Through the spring and summer of 1778, she continued to collect the comments of unsuspecting readers, introducing the topic of the novel without owning up to it: 'there is no end of the ridiculous speeches perpetually made to me,' she told her sister and confidante Susanna.[74]

Burney knew that attribution was an activity of readers, and that the modesty of anonymous authors was commonly false. In her play *The Witlings* she satirized the mutual complacency that this allowed. Lady Smatter is a self-appointed patron of literature and head of a circle, including both men and women, calling itself the 'Esprit Party'. Cecilia is the play's orphan heroine, her good judgement neglected by Lady Smatter and her followers.

> LADY SMATTER Yes, yes, this song is certainly Mr. Dabler's, I am not to be deceived in his style. What say you, my dear Miss Stanley, don't you think I have found him out.
> CECILIA Indeed I am too little acquainted with his Poems to be able to judge.
> LADY SMATTER Your indifference surprises me! for my part, I am never at rest till I have discovered the authors of every thing that comes out; and, indeed, I commonly hit upon them in a moment. I declare I sometimes wonder at myself, when I think how lucky I am in my guesses.
> CECILIA Your Ladyship devotes so much Time to these researches, that it would be strange if they were unsuccessful.[75]

Lady Smatter is keen to prove her literary discrimination by finding the author, while Dabler hides his identity only in the hope that it will be discovered. Cecilia's 'indifference' implies that she knows that the witless Dabler's poems are not worth attribution.

An unknown author could not always expect to overhear praise. Soon after the anonymous publication of her first novel,

Sense and Sensibility, Jane Austen visited the local circulating library with her sister Cassandra, who knew of her authorship, and their niece Anna, who did not. Anna came across a copy of Austen's novel, 'which she threw aside with careless contempt, little imagining who had written it, exclaiming to the great amusement of her Aunts who stood by "Oh that must be rubbish I am sure from the title" '.[76] Like Burney, Austen would test out unsuspecting acquaintances with her own fiction. When *Pride and Prejudice* was first published, she and her mother read out a large part of it to a neighbour, Miss Benn, who had come for dinner, without ever telling her who the author was.[77] Austen was gratified to note the unsuspecting lady's admiration of Elizabeth Bennet.

Such pleasures were the prelude to 'discovery'. Burney's letters and journals give a close record of the becoming-public of an author's identity. The circle of those who know Burney as the author of the most fashionable book of the year widened; Burney called them them 'the *Evelina Committee*'.[78] Some ten months after the novel's publication, and a few weeks after it had appeared in a second edition, 'dear little Burney' was announced as the 'The Authoress of Evelina' in a satirical pamphlet. 'I can never express how extremely I was shocked,' she told her sister, 'it has quite knocked me up, for I have been in a state of utter lowness & vexation ever since.'[79] She had lost what she called her 'Snugship'. Her letters dwell on having to put up with being praised to her face by strangers. Nowadays, no author claiming to find this experience wearing would be believed. Indeed, Mrs Thrale accused Burney of affected delicacy ('if you *will* be an Author & a Wit,—you must take the Consequence!'), but perhaps we should not think her disingenuous. When she was first attracted to George Cambridge, a young man whom she began to imagine her suitor, she noted and appreciated his conversational grace in avoiding any reference to her writing.[80]

Burney's example quite naturally occurred to the Reverend George Austen, father of another modest lady novelist, when he wrote to the publisher Thomas Cadell in 1797 to offer him his twenty-one-year-old daughter's 'First Impressions'.

> I have in my possession a manuscript novel, comprised in three vols about the length of Miss Burney's *Evelina*. As I am well aware of what consequence it is that a work of this sort should make its first appearance under a respectable name, I apply to you. Shall be much obliged therefore if you will inform me whether you chuse to be concerned in it.[81]

He did not name the author of the work. The 'respectable name' on the title page of the novel would be Cadell's. Perhaps George Austen mentioned *Evelina* as a guide to the kind of book that he was offering, a comedy of courtship: 'First Impressions' was an early version of *Pride and Prejudice*. It is likely also that Burney's debut seemed a respectable precedent to him. His letter breathes sensitivity about the propriety of publishing 'a work of this sort'. No doubt he thought he was flattering Cadell, whose firm was not usually associated with novels. George Austen asked what would be 'the expense of publishing it at the author's risk'; he was prepared to pay the initial costs of publication. His offer was 'declined by return of post'. There is no evidence that any other publisher was approached. The work had been written as a kind of family entertainment. Both times that Austen mentions it in surviving letters, it is to speak of members of her family reading it. She read it out loud to them, as she did her later novels.[82] Unlike Charles Burney, George Austen was not ignorant of his daughter's 'writing passion'.

When Austen next approached a publisher it was again through a male intermediary, and without declaring her name. In 1803 her brother Henry persuaded his lawyer, William Seymour, to arrange the sale of 'Susan' (the early version of what became

Northanger Abbey) to the firm of Crosby & Co. Austen was paid £10 and the book was actually advertised by the firm. It never appeared. Six years later, exasperated by its non-publication, Austen wrote to the publishers to 'avow myself the Authoress' and to prod them into action.[83] She still kept her true identity secret. Demanding 'a Line in answer as soon as possible', she directed that any reply be directed to 'Mrs Ashton Dennis' at the Southampton Post Office. She signed the letter 'MAD'. Her efforts were unavailing, but two years later, in 1811, *Sense and Sensibility*, first drafted as 'Elinor and Marianne' in the 1790s, was published. Henry Austen was again active, later claiming that it was he who overcame his sister's reluctance to publish it at all.[84] Certainly he approached the publisher, Egerton's, and conducted all negotiations. Austen's sister Cassandra seems to have been much concerned that her authorship be kept secret.[85] We have the trace of her worry in a diary entry by her niece, Fanny Knight. Fanny, an avid novel reader who was clearly excited about the forthcoming publication, scribbled in her diary: 'Another letter from Aunt Cassandra to beg we would not mention that Aunt Jane Austen wrote "Sense and Sensibility".'[86] Cassandra did not mention the publication in letters to relatives who were not in on the secret.

Some sense of the amusement that family members could derive from the secret of Jane's authorship can be glimpsed in the anonymous poem (signed 'A Friend') that her clergyman brother James sent her, in disguised handwriting, soon after publication: 'To Miss Jane Austen the reputed Author of *Sense and Sensibility*'.

> On such Subjects no Wonder that she shou'd write well,
> In whom so united those Qualities dwell.[87]

'Oh then, gentle Lady! continue to write,' he exclaimed, seizing on that modest pseudonym. The 'gentle' is loyal and proper, but hardly fits the novel. Think only of its superbly ungentle second chapter, in which Mrs John Dashwood talks her husband down from giving his impecunious sister £3,000 to intending her the odd pheasant from his estate, in season. Those who knew of the 'gentle' lady's identity were soon in a position to enjoy their secret. The first edition sold out, received a good review and made its author over a hundred pounds. It was read in the Royal Family, the Duke of York telling his niece Princess Charlotte that its author was Lady Augusta Paget: a misprint in an advertisement had announced it as being not 'by a lady' but 'By Lady A—'. Later Austen's sister-in-law Mary was to inform her that, in the fashionable spa town of Cheltenham, 'it was very much admired' and attributed to the Scottish novelist and essayist Elizabeth Hamilton.[88] Hamilton had recently published the highly moralistic best-seller *The Cottagers of Glenburnie*. 'It is pleasant to have such a respectable Writer named,' commented Austen drily.

The success sent her back to revise 'First Impressions'. As *Pride and Prejudice*, it was accepted by Egerton, who gave her £110 for it. Henry Austen was again the go-between. It appeared in 1813, declaring itself to be 'by the Author of Sense and Sensibility'. The *British Critic*, which had briefly commended *Sense and Sensibility*, spoke favourably again of 'this author or authoress', while the *Critical Review*, in an enthusiastic piece, seemed sure that the 'fair author' was female.[89] Among readers, speculation grew about its authorship. Austen's brother Henry reported a literary acquaintance saying, 'I should like to know who is the author, for it is much too clever to have been written by a woman.'[90] Arabella Milbanke, later to be Lord Byron's wife, was told that the author was female; one rumour was that she was the sister of successful poet and novelist Charlotte Smith.[91] Margaret Mackenzie told her brother that the novel 'is said to be by Mrs Dorset, the renowned authoress of *The Peacock at Home*'.[92] Mary Russell Mitford, who had mutual acquaintances with the Austens, said that both Austen's novels were attributed to Lady Boringdon of Saltram, near Plymouth.[93] This attribution was still being credited a year later.[94] Austen herself eagerly collected reports from friends of the book's success and the accompanying curiosity about its author. 'I am read & admired in Ireland too,' she told Cassandra, some nine months after *Pride and Prejudice* had appeared. 'There is a Mrs Fletcher, the wife of a Judge, an old Lady & very good & very clever, who is all curiosity to know about me—what I am like & so forth—. I am not known to her by *name* however.'[95] She acknowledged that a pleasing sign of her popularity was widespread curiosity as to her identity. 'M[rs] Pole also said that no Books had ever occasioned so much canvassing & doubt, & that everybody was desirous to attribute them to some of their own friends, or to some person of whom they thought highly.'[96]

Austen records this amongst the 'Opinions of Mansfield Park' collected from family and friends. On the evidence of this document alone, the circle of those who knew of Austen's authorship was now wide. None of Austen's novels was published with her name on in her lifetime. It was only with the obituary notices that Henry Austen wrote for local newspapers that they were finally attributed to her in print. Yet there came a point, as with Burney, when the secret passed beyond Austen's immediate circle. While she was composing *Mansfield Park*, her third novel, she wrote to her brother Frank, a naval captain who was at sea, thanking him for allowing her to use in the novel the names of his old ships (Fanny Price's beloved brother William is in the navy). She realizes 'what I sh[d] be laying myself open to' by this: leaving clues as to her identity. However, she is reconciled to discovery: 'The Secret has spread so far as to be scarcely the Shadow of a secret now.'[97] When *Mansfield Park* appears, 'I shall not even attempt to tell Lies about it.—I shall rather try to make all the Money than all the Mystery I can of it.'

It is worth quoting at some length from this letter, which gives a strong impression of her family's involvement in her literary career, and of the secrecy that Austen required.

> Henry heard P. & P. warmly praised in Scotland, by Lady Robt Kerr and another Lady;—but what does he do in the warmth of his Brotherly vanity and Love, but immediately tell them who wrote it!—A Thing once set going in that way—one knows how it spreads—and he, dear Creature, has set it going so much more than once. I know it is all done from affection & partiality—but at the same time, let me here again express to you & Mary my sense of the *superior* kindness which you have shewn on the occasion, in doing what I wished.—I am trying to harden myself.—After all, what a trifle it is in all its Bearings, to the really important points of one's existence even in this World!—

Austen is clearly reconciled to her name spreading. With mock bravery, she prepares herself to be known by all and sundry. She sighs rather than despairs over Henry's flattering boastfulness. Her anonymity has become a matter of form. On the eve of the appearance of *Mansfield Park* she was still telling one of her brothers, 'Keep the *name* to yourself. I sh^d not like to have it known beforehand.'[98] If not to be avoided, discovery is at least to be delayed. Perhaps it is as if Austen has acquired a little of the vanity of successful authorship: 'beforehand' her identity should not be announced; afterwards knowledge of it will inevitably spread.

Mansfield Park was announced as 'By the Author of "Sense and Sensibility" and "Pride and Prejudice" '. It seems to have disappointed readers groomed on the previous books. Judging by the 'Opinions' that Austen collected (there were no reviews), this was for reasons that many would still recognize: after the intelligent audacity of Elizabeth Bennet, the virtuous reticence of Fanny Price seemed pallid to some. Publishers being sensitive to these matters, her next novel, *Emma*, was to have on its title page 'By the Author of "Pride and Prejudice," &c. &c.', which is also how it was advertised.[99] Speculation about the identity of the author was almost over; only the first two of Austen's novels truly excited some sense of mystery. A year after Mary Russell Mitford reported guesses as to their authorship, she was able to name Austen and know her for a friend of friends.[100] Most biographers have failed to note that Austen herself had taken a step that could be of great symbolic importance for successful women writers in the nineteenth century: she had met with her publisher. A couple of months after the appearance of *Mansfield Park* she visited the premises of Thomas Egerton in the company of Henry Austen, to discuss the prospects for a second edition of the novel.[101] This was one kind of coming out as an author. When Austen was negotiating with a different publisher, John Murray, over *Emma*, she was quite open about her authorship, writing to him herself under her own name. Before the novel had even appeared, Murray persuaded Walter Scott to review it (anonymously) for his own journal, the *Quarterly Review*. Observing the proprieties, Scott did not name her. By the time of her visit to London in October 1815 to make final arrangements for the publication of *Emma*, Austen's authorship was an 'open secret'. It was on this visit that the Prince Regent communicated his admiration of her fiction through an intermediary, and obliged her to dedicate her forthcoming novel to him. Appearances were maintained: the Dedication to the notoriously dissolute Prince that Austen reluctantly produced was signed simply 'The Author'.

For most readers, the first 'official' announcement of Austen's authorship was the 'Biographical Notice' by Henry Austen prefaced to the posthumous first edition of *Persuasion* and *Northanger Abbey*. Influenced by this attribution, the librarian of George III's wife Queen Charlotte listed two contemporary anon-

ymous novels in her collection, *Self-Control* and *Discipline*, as
being by Austen too.[102] The eager attributor could hardly have
been more mistaken. In fact, they were by Mary Brunton, and
the first of them, whose heroine is kidnapped to Canada by a
would-be seducer, and escapes by piloting a canoe down a wild
torrent, was the butt of Austen's mockery in her letters. 'I declare
I do not know whether Laura's passage down the American
River, is not the most natural, possible, every-day thing she ever
does.'[103] Brunton's name too was made public only after her
death, in 1819, when her husband included it on the title page of
a new collection of her writings.

In the memoir that he wrote half a century after her death,
Jane Austen's nephew James Edward Austen-Leigh celebrated his
aunt's literary modesty. Her secretiveness, by his account, is the
sign of a proper reticence, but also of the mystery of her peculiar
genius. Her fiction was miraculously forged in the ordinary gaps
of domestic life. He reflects, like later biographers, on the creative
hurry of her last five years at Chawton, during which she wrote
Mansfield Park, Emma and *Persuasion*. 'How she was able to effect
all this is surprising, for she had no separate study to retire to, and
most of the work must have been done in the general sitting-
room, subject to all kinds of casual interruptions.'[104] It was all
done without that 'Room of One's Own' which Virginia Woolf
memorably imagined as the space in which a woman could think
and create. Those who had known Austen wondered at her producing her novels without letting anyone outside the immediate
family glimpse all her activity. Her niece Caroline recollected,

> My Aunt must have spent much time in writing — her desk
> lived in the drawing room. I often saw her writing letters on it,
> and believe she wrote much of her Novels in the same way —
> sitting with her family, when they were quite alone; but I never
> saw any manuscript of *that* sort, in progress —.[105]

In 1999 this desk was bought for the nation and visitors to the British Museum could see how Austen wrote her novels without sequestering herself, and how her writing could be put aside. A small movable cabinet that sat on any flat surface, it lived amongst a household's other furniture and affairs.

To illustrate her wish to be unnoticed as a writer, Austen's nephew recorded what has become one of the best-known stories about her.

> She was careful that her occupation should not be suspected by servants, or visitors, or any persons beyond her own family party. She wrote upon small sheets of paper which could easily be put away, or covered with a piece of blotting paper. There was, between the front door and the offices, a swing door which creaked when it was opened; but she objected to having this little inconvenience remedied, because it gave her notice when anyone was coming.

Her secrecy is seen as a kind of considerateness. Authorship took second place to family affairs or routine hospitality. Looking back down the long years to his childhood, he thinks, like Caroline Austen, of the invisibility to him of his aunt's novel-making. 'I have no doubt that I, and my sisters and cousins, in our visits to Chawton, frequently disturbed this mystic process, without having any idea of the mischief that we were doing; certainly we never should have guessed it by any signs of impatience or irritability in the writer.'[106]

'Mystic' was the creativity of so unauthorlike a writer. Over and over again, Austen-Leigh stresses Austen's 'entire seclusion from the literary world'.[107] 'It is probable that she never was in company with any person whose talents or whose celebrity equalled her own.' Her 'obscurity' was complete. 'Whatever she produced was a genuine home-made article.' Austen-Leigh cannot think of 'any other author of note, whose personal obscurity was so complete'. Even Charlotte Brontë, who may have spent much of her life in 'a wild solitude compared with which Steventon and Chawton might be considered to be in the gay world', was drawn to London to be gazed at as the author of *Jane Eyre*. Austen remained hidden: 'Few of her readers knew even her name, and none knew more of her than her name.' For her family, Austen's anonymity was another sign of her modesty. For later critics, it has seemed something different: the veiling of a fierce creative ambition in order to meet a patriarchally imposed standard of reticence. Austen was joining the ranks of women required to conceal their talents, yet hungry to write and even to publish.

It is hard to disentangle the motives for anonymity and pseudonymity that might come from being a female novelist from those that might just come simply from being a novelist. In the early nineteenth century, as in the previous century, a woman was usually thought of as an entirely private person. Her writing would naturally be thought to reflect private circumstances. Austen's biographer Park Honan guesses that anonymity gave her a kind of 'freedom', protecting her from 'those who would accuse her of autobiography, of writing from experience, or of having lived through the ordeals of her characters'.[108] It also protected her from hunches about the originals of her characters. In an aside in a letter to Cassandra we glimpse the possible tiresomeness of this after a visit to the local Dusautoy family. 'Miss D. has a great idea of being Fanny Price, she & her youngest sister together, who is named Fanny.'[109] This is comedy, especially in its deadpan delivery, but such guesswork could be more embarrassing. Cassandra's defensiveness about her sister's fiction might well have been rooted in anxiety about possible 'identifications'. Defensiveness about 'identifications' would not be new. When Fanny Burney told the readers of *Evelina* that her characters were drawn 'from nature, though not from life', she was declaring that these characters were not matched with individuals whom she privately knew.[110]

Austen's relations did, however, occasionally enjoy the mischief her anonymity could make. Her niece Fanny Knight set her suitor James Wildman to read his way through her aunt's novels, but without letting him know the identity of their author. Believing that 'all young Ladies' should be perfectly good, he did not think well of them. Fanny reported his ridiculous opining to her aunt. 'Have mercy on him, tell him the truth & make him an apology,' wrote Austen, evidently amused.[111] It is the only time we hear her asking for her identity to be revealed. Fiction-loving Fanny, Austen's favourite niece, was using the novels to find her po-faced lover out. 'When he knows the truth he will be uncomfortable.—You are the oddest Creature!' exclaimed Aunt Jane, with what sounds as much like pleasure as disapproval. As she knew, mischief and modesty could go together.

3

WOMEN BEING MEN

In the nineteenth century, guessing at the gender of an unknown author became part of the pleasure of reading. The first really important such debate concerned the true identity of Currer Bell, supposed author of *Jane Eyre*, first published in 1847. Brontë was not, however, alone among women novelists in inventing an unfeminine pseudonym. When Elizabeth Gaskell began publishing her first stories, a few months before the appearance of *Jane Eyre*, she did so under the name Cotton Mather Mills. The pseudonym was wry: Cotton Mather was a late-seventeenth-century New England Puritan, notorious for his narrow righteousness (in contrast to Gaskell, whose stories, like many of her later novels, required middle-class Victorian readers to sympathize with the plight of those they might normally condemn). The name also contains a joke about the main places of industry – cotton mills – in Manchester, where Gaskell lived and where the stories were set. Three tales were published in *Howlitt's Journal*, a high-minded, politically radical journal run by William Howlitt, a friend of Gaskell. She showed them to friends and family before publication, anxiously canvassing opinions.[1] They were for limited circulation and aroused little curiosity.

Things changed with her first full-length novel, *Mary Barton*. She wanted to use a masculine pseudonym for it, even though Howlitt advised her that it would be advantageous if this and future works were 'known as the works of a lady'; 'I think they would be more popular.'[2] Gaskell was unpersuaded and asked her publisher, Edward Chapman, 'Shall you have any objection to the name "Stephen Berwick" as that of the author of "Mary Barton"?'[3] (The surname seems to have been derived from her father's birthplace.) Her request came too late; the novel was published anonymously. It seems that Gaskell wanted *Mary Barton* to be received as a book by a man: 'Stephen Berwick' is not a pseudonym that shouts its pseudonymity. In the event, there was plenty of curiosity about the authorship of this 'tale of Manchester life', especially in Manchester. The novel, featuring a central male character, Mary's father John Barton, who is driven to commit a politically inspired murder, was successful and controversial. We do not know why Gaskell belatedly wished to use a masculine pseudonym, but she may have feared for the authority of a work so sharp – to its first readers, shocking – in its depiction of the privations of working-class life.

Anonymity led to speculation. Some of the first reviewers were confident that the author was female. 'Unquestionably the book is a woman's,' wrote John Forster in *The Examiner*.[4] He cited as evidence 'the delicate points of the portraiture where women and children are in question . . . the minuteness of the domestic detail . . . certain gentle intimations of piety and pity perceptible throughout'. To discern the gender of the author was to perform a kind of literary criticism. With such a 'condition of England' novel as *Mary Barton* it meant identifying the most essential elements of its realism. This was not just a reviewer's activity. Fellow novelist Maria Edgeworth, reading *Mary Barton* shortly after its publication, also found herself guessing at a woman author. 'I opine that it is a *she*—From the great abilities, and from the power of drawing *from* the life and *to* the life so as to give the impression and strong interest of reality.'[5] Despite Gaskell fostering the rumour that the author was a Mrs Wheeler, her identity was widely known by friends and acquaintances, and only a couple of months after publication she was readily admitting authorship. When her next full-length novel, *Ruth*, was announced as 'by the author of *Mary Barton*' there was no concealment implied.

Gaskell was in her late thirties when she became a novelist, and clearly had some understanding of how authorship might be concealed or revealed. Yet she botched the chance to release what would have been the first example of a successful, ambitious and widely admired novel written by a woman under a man's name. The first really famous such example was written by a woman who was to become Gaskell's friend, and the subject of a posthumous biography by her. In October 1847, Charlotte Brontë published *Jane Eyre* under the name 'Currer Bell'. Although it would have been new to almost all her readers, it was a name that she had used before. The previous year, at her instigation, she and her sisters Emily and Anne had published their *Poems* under the names of Currer, Ellis and Acton Bell. After the deaths of both of her sisters, she was to explain the subterfuge in a 'Biographical Notice of Ellis & Acton Bell' attached to a new edition of *Wuthering Heights* in 1850. 'Averse to personal publicity, we veiled our own names under those of Currer, Ellis and Acton Bell; the ambiguous choice being dictated by a sort of conscientious scruple at assuming Christian names positively masculine, while we did not like to declare ourselves women.'[6] The explanation mixes an assertion of modesty with an admission of some more teasing motivation. On the one hand, the sisters shrink from all 'personal publicity', from being pointed out as the authors of their verses. On the other hand, they have chosen ambiguously, taking Christian names that do not declare certainly whether they are men or women. This ambiguity would become significant to many of the first readers of *Jane Eyre*, who would work away to decide the gender of its author. It was a puzzle that the author had consciously created.

The Brontë sisters were 'veiled', rather than hidden, by their pseudonyms: their initials were preserved. In her correspondence with the publishers of the *Poems*, Aylott and Jones, Charlotte's self-concealment had been slight. She had signed her letters 'C Brontë', while never explicitly including herself as one of 'the Authors' of the poems, to whom she had referred as 'the Messrs. Bell'. The publishers seem to have assumed for some time that 'C Brontë' was a man. Just before publication, Charlotte had written to put them right.

> As the proofs have hitherto always come safe to hand—under the direction of C Brontë ESQRE.—I have not thought it necessary to request you to change it, but a little mistake having occurred yesterday—I think it will be better to send them to me in future under my *real* address which is
> Miss Brontë
> Revd P Brontë's &c.[7]

(The 'mistake' was possibly the misdirection of a package to her brother, Branwell.) Yet when a reader of the poems conveyed, via the publisher, a request for the poets' signatures, Charlotte returned a note on which the three sisters had signed themselves as their pseudonyms. Her covering letter to the publishers stipulated that the note be posted in London 'in order to avoid giving any clue to residence, or identity by post-mark'.[8] When she wrote to the editor of the *Dublin University Magazine* a few months later to thank him for an encouraging review, she signed the letter 'Currer Bell' and referred to 'my brothers, Ellis and Acton'.[9] The number of reviews was greater than the number of copies sold (a year after publication, only two, according to Charlotte).[10] The largely complimentary reviewers in the *Critic* and the *Athenaeum* had both puzzled over the identity of the volume's authors, with the former presuming that the names on the title page were pseudonyms.[11] The *Dublin University Magazine* had wondered whether there really were three authors, or 'in truth but one master spirit . . . that has been pleased to project itself into three imaginary poets'.[12]

Intentionally or not, the pseudonyms seemed designed to arouse curiosity – to announce themselves as pseudonyms. It was as 'Mr Currer Bell' that Charlotte wrote to a series of publishers offering the manuscript of her first completed novel *The Professor*, though specifying that replies should be addressed to him 'Under cover to Miss Brontë Haworth Bradford Yorkshire'.[13] The novel has a male narrator and it is interesting to wonder what speculation would have been aroused if it had been published as the first work of Currer Bell, as Brontë had intended. Its narrator, Charles Crimsworth, is a young man who becomes a teacher in a girls' school in Brussels. (The same situation is reworked in Brontë's final novel, *Villette*.) *The Professor* keeps confronting its narrator with sexually alluring, scheming young women. In the school he senses sexual intrigue, explained as the tendency of a Roman Catholic culture. The girls were 'reared in utter unconsciousness of vice';

> how was it then that scarcely one of those girls having attained the age of fourteen could look a man in the face with modesty and propriety? An air of bold, impudent flirtation or a loose, silly leer was sure to answer the most ordinary glance from a masculine eye.[14]

Would this have provoked reviewers to wonder whether the author were a man or a woman, as *Jane Eyre* was to do?

The small firm of Smith, Elder & Co. rejected this apprentice work, but, on the advice of its reader, William Smith Williams, expressed an interest in any future novel, especially if it would fit into a standard three-volume format. Brontë had been working on *Jane Eyre* and, only a month later, still writing as 'Mr Currer Bell', she sent them the manuscript. In old age, George Murray Smith, the director of the firm, published his account of how

Williams had been gripped by it and had urgently asked Smith to read it himself. 'The story quickly took me captive.'[15] Putting off everything else, he read into the night until he had finished it. The next day, he wrote accepting it for publication.

> I need say nothing about the success which the book achieved, and the speculations as to whether it was written by a man or a woman. For my own part I never had much doubt on the subject of the writer's sex; but then I had the advantage over the general public of having the handwriting of the author before me. There were qualities of style, too, and turns of expression, which satisfied me that 'Currer Bell' was a woman, an opinion in which Mr Williams concurred.

Looking back, the book's success and those 'speculations' were, connectedly, uppermost in Smith's mind. Brontë's pseudonym could provoke nothing but curiosity, and especially curiosity about the sex of the author.

This curiosity was encouraged by Smith's suggestion as to the book's title page. He thought that it should include the subtitle 'An Autobiography', and Brontë happily responded that 'it would be much better' to add this.[16] This was in the same letter in which, with typical firmness, she refused to embark on any further revision of the work.

> Perhaps too the first part of 'Jane Eyre' may suit the public taste better than you anticipate—for it is true and Truth has a severe charm of its own. Had I told *all* the truth, I might have made it far more exquisitely painful—but I deemed it advisable to soften and retrench many particulars lest the narrative should rather displease than attract.

'An Autobiography' advertises Jane Eyre's earnest effort at self-explanation, the intensity with which she struggles to tell the story of her own life. Yet Brontë's letter speaks of something else too, a sense that *Jane Eyre* had an autobiographical origin and impulse, and that these might be evident to a reader who, in 1847, was allowed to know nothing of the author.

The first edition title page announced 'JANE EYRE. | An Autobiography. | EDITED BY | CURRER BELL'. Partly because of its almost immediate success – it went into a third edition within six months – and partly because of the sheer amount of book reviewing going on in the national and provincial press in the 1840s, we have a rich record of initial responses. The hunger with which Brontë herself sought reviews of *Jane Eyre* in the months after its publication is quite apparent in her letters to her publishers. At her urging Williams conscientiously sent her clippings. In her letters to him she mentions reading reviews in forty specific periodicals and newspapers, from the *Athenaeum* to the *Sheffield Iris*, the *Economist* to the *Church of England Journal.* (That other retiring, pseudonymous Victorian writer, Charles Dodgson, also asked his publisher to collect copies of all reviews of what he wrote. He kept a register of these in his diary.[17]) Brontë was more aware than anyone of how her novel was being treated by reviewers. 'I always compel myself to read the Analysis in every newspaper notice. It is a just punishment – a due though severe humiliation for faults of plan and construction.'[18] She knew that reviewers took the title page as an invitation to speculate about the sex of the author. A complimentary review in the *Examiner* talked of 'this autobiography (which though relating to a woman, we do not believe to have been written by a woman)'.[19] Another of the first reviews decided that this 'extra-ordinary book' must have been written by a man, even if it did call itself 'an autobiography':

all the serious novel writers of the day lose in comparison with Currer Bell, for we must presume the work to be his. It is no woman's writing. Although ladies have written histories, and travels, and warlike novels, to say nothing of books upon the different arts and sciences, no woman *could have* penned the 'Autobiography of Jane Eyre'. It is all that one of the other sex might invent, and much more.[20]

Brontë told Williams that this review gave her 'much pleasure'.[21]

Another review that pleased her was by G. H. Lewes in *Fraser's Magazine*. This declared, 'The writer is evidently a woman, and, unless we are deceived, new in the world of literature.'[22] Lewes, a perceptive admirer of *Jane Eyre*, interpreted the title page more subtly than others. 'It is an autobiography, – not, perhaps, in the naked facts and circumstances, but in the actual suffering and experience.' He waved away curiosity about the author – 'man or woman, young or old, be that as it may, no such book has gladdened our eyes for a long while' – yet felt strongly that it was rooted in personal experience. For Brontë herself, the most significant early response by another writer came privately, only days after publication. Thackeray had been sent an advance copy by Williams and wrote him an enthusiastic letter, which Williams passed immediately to Brontë herself.

I wish you had not sent me Jane Eyre. It interested me so much that I have lost (or won if you like) a whole day in reading it at the busiest period, with the printers I know waiting for copy. Who the author can be I can't guess – if a woman she knows her language better than most ladies do, or has had a 'classical' education ... I have been exceedingly moved & pleased by Jane Eyre. It is a woman's writing, but whose? Give my respects and thanks to the author.[23]

We can hear Thackeray wondering aloud about the sex of the author, thinking of what makes it unlikely that she is a woman, and yet deciding that she is. On the evidence of a letter that he wrote to his friend William Brookfield nine months later, there were some ingenious theories current about the masculine and feminine traits of the book. 'Old Dilke of the Athenæum vows that Procter & his wife between them wrote Jane Eyre and when I protest ignorance says "Pooh you know who wrote it. You are the deepest rogue in England &c"—I wonder whether it can be true?'[24] Speculation about the novel's authorship was a measure of its success. In her *Life of Charlotte Brontë*, Elizabeth Gaskell reckoned 'the whole reading-world of England was in a ferment to discover the unknown author'.[25] This meant discovering whether the author were male or female.

It now takes a strange effort of the imagination to think of *Jane Eyre* as a novel that might have been written by a man. It has long been appropriated by critics as a work of specifically female passion and insight. It is no accident that probably the most influential work of academic feminist criticism of the last half-century is Sandra M. Gilbert and Susan Gubar's *The Madwoman in the Attic*, whose title casts Brontë's novel as a founding myth of the suppressed female imagination. The sense that the novel must be, if not Charlotte Brontë's autobiography, then at least her spiritual autobiography, comes from the extra-ordinary directness with which her narrator addresses us. 'Reader, I married him,' the opening sentence of the book's final chapter, has become one of the most memorable sentences in all fiction. It sounds the decidedness of a woman who has learned to make her own destiny. It is characteristic of a narrator who takes us into her confidence from the first, yet with a truculence that she calls her 'plainness'. Jane is known for answering back, and her very confidences are sometimes more like retorts. The first time that she addresses the reader directly is when she is explaining her schoolgirl friendship at Lowood with the worldly, gossipy Mary Ann Wilson. 'And where, meantime, was Helen Burns?' Would not her time have been better spent with the thoughtful, faithful Helen, her first and dearest friend at the

school? 'True, reader; and I knew and felt this.'[26] Jane turns to us
as if acknowledging just criticism. But it is a kind of trick, for we
are about to be told that the consumptive Helen was ill and not
allowed to receive visitors. Jane was not, after all, so shallow as to
undervalue Helen's companionship. How could the 'reader'
have suspected it?

This is one of the ways in which the novel creates the personality of its narrator. Jane Eyre rebels against us too. She confides
in order to correct, for the truth she tells will not always satisfy
us: 'Oh romantic reader, forgive me for telling the plain truth!'
she mockingly exclaims.[27] 'Reader, though I look comfortably
accommodated, I am not very tranquil,' she says, switching to
the present tense as she recalls waiting for the coach that will
take her to the house where she is to be a governess. When she
confides, it is to put us right. Describing her 'cool' feelings for
Adèle, the small girl to whom she is governess, she bridles
against those whom she imagines convicting her of a lack of
proper affection. 'I am not writing to flatter parental egotism, to
echo cant, or prop up humbug; I am merely telling the truth.'[28]
At the novel's heart, what she tells us about her deepest feelings
is defiant as well as intimate. After her wedding to Mr Rochester
has been interrupted by the announcement that he is already
married, after she has been shown his wife raving in her con-
finement, he asks if she will ever forgive him. 'Reader! – I forgave
him at the moment, and on the spot.'[29] She must tell us that,
whatever our ideas of moral propriety, she forgives the would-be
bigamist who has destroyed all her hopes, immediately and
without reserve. Some nineteenth-century readers and reviewers
had the sense of being defied. 'I forgave him all: yet not in words,
not outwardly; only at my heart's core.' It is an heretical absolu-
tion. We are told what Rochester himself is not told. Jane the
character is silent; Jane the narrator is clear and uncompromising.
We are admitted to a special confidence, but only on her terms.

A lesser writer would have created a narrator who appealed to the reader more. Brontë's narrator does not trust that the reader will be able to understand her 'truth'. She recalls how St John Rivers persists in asking her if she will not marry him, wearing away at her resistance: 'Reader, do you know, as I do, what terror those cold people can put into the ice of their questions?'[30] She does not assume that we do. Her story is individual, not conventional. Its singularity is in the manner of its telling. This singularity made the concealment of its authorship as provoking as Jane Eyre herself. Jane recalls her dissatisfaction, as if articulating feelings that a reader might find difficult to accept. 'Who blames me? Many no doubt; and I shall be called discontented. I could not help it: the restlessness was in my nature; it agitated me to pain sometimes.'[31] This familiarity with disconcerting private feelings was evidence to some contemporaries that the author must be a woman. The reviewer in the *Christian Remembrancer* was sure of it.

> The name and sex of the writer are still a mystery. Currer Bell (which by a curious Hibernicism appears in the title-page as the name of a female autobiographer) is a mere *nom de guerre* – perhaps an anagram. However, we, for our part, cannot doubt that the book is written by a female, and, as certain provincialisms indicate, by one from the North of England. Who, indeed, but a woman could have ventured, with the smallest prospect of success, to fill three octavo volumes with the history of a woman's heart?[32]

Yet this reviewer could quite see why 'the hypothesis of a male author should have been started . . . For a book more unfeminine, both in its excellences and defects, it would be hard to find in the annals of female scholarship.'

This last judgement opens up to us some of the consequences of Brontë's self-concealment. Gaskell talks in her *Life of Charlotte*

Brontë of the novel's incidents being sifted by its first readers 'to answer, if possible, the much-vexed question of sex'.[33] It was a question about the nature of creativity. Who could ever have produced such a book? Must it be rooted in personal experiences? How might men's and women's imaginations be different? This last question was for the Victorian novel reader a common matter of practical curiosity. The success of *Jane Eyre* gave this sexing of fiction an urgent significance. For the novel's first readers, the mystery surrounding its authorship emphasized the singularity of its narrative voice. From where does the voice of Jane Eyre speak? The novel itself asks this. In its first chapter, Jane describes how, as a girl, she admonished her heartless guardian Mrs Reed for her cruelty and recalls that 'it seemed as if my tongue pronounced words without my will consenting to their utterance: something spoke out of me over which I had no control'.[34] This arresting, resentful voice has some unknown origin. Jane's dissatisfaction and rebelliousness were sometimes labelled 'masculine' in the mid-nineteenth century. One perplexed reviewer was led to guess that the work was a collaboration: 'the said Currer divides the authorship, if we are not misinformed, with a brother and sister. The works bears the marks of more than one mind and more than one sex.'[35] The novel's 'niceties of thought and emotion', as well as 'elaborate descriptions of dress, and the minutiæ of the sick-chamber', spoke of a female writer. Yet the reviewer found a 'masculine tone' prevailing, and particularly sensed 'a male mind' behind the 'representation of character, manners, and scenery' and 'scenes of passion, so hot, emphatic, and condensed in expression, and so sternly masculine in feeling'.

Such theorizing was apparently licensed by the appearance of *Wuthering Heights*, by 'Ellis Bell', and *Agnes Grey*, by 'Acton Bell', only two months after *Jane Eyre*. Some now believed that the different names announced but one author.[36] Such speculations were fuelled by Thomas Newby, the unscrupulous publisher of *Wuthering Heights* and *Agnes Grey*. He allowed prospective purchasers to suppose that Ellis Bell and Currer Bell were one and the same, advertising *Wuthering Heights* as by 'Mr Bell'.[37] Charlotte was prompted to add a prefatory note to the third edition of *Jane Eyre*, published in April 1848, explaining that 'my claim to the title of novelist rests on this one work alone'.[38] Seeking 'to rectify mistakes which may already have been made, and to prevent future errors', she denied (in the name of 'Currer Bell') 'the authorship of other works of fiction'. Soon Newby was advertising Anne Brontë's new novel *The Tenant of Wildfell Hall* as if it were by the author of *Jane Eyre*, and actually selling it to an American publisher as such. An anxious George Smith was prompted to write to his successful new author, Currer Bell, to seek reassurance that 'he' was not trading with a rival. His letter was in turn the immediate reason for Charlotte to travel to London with Anne to announce herself at the offices of Smith, Elder & Co. (Emily refused to accompany them).[39] Years later Smith recalled the arrival of the 'rather quaintly dressed little ladies, pale-faced and anxious-looking'.[40] Charlotte disclosed herself as 'Currer Bell' by pressing into his hand his own letter. 'He looked at it – then at me – again – yet again – I laughed at his queer perplexity – a recognition took place – I gave my real name.'[41]

There was another awkward consequence of Brontë's self-concealment. Encouraged by the letter from Thackeray that Williams had forwarded to her, she dedicated the second edition of *Jane Eyre* to him and praised him fulsomely in its Preface. 'I regard him as the first social regenerator of the day – as the very master of that working corps who would restore to rectitude the warped system of things.'[42] (As she wrote this, *Vanity Fair* had been appearing in monthly parts for almost a year.) She called this 'the tribute of a total stranger', but it made some readers suspicious. The widely rumoured insanity of Thackeray's wife made him look like a model for Rochester. Soon Charlotte was writing an agonized letter to Williams expressing her 'chagrin'. 'I am *very, very* sorry that my inadvertent blunder should have made his name and affairs a subject for common gossip.'[43] There were rumours that Brontë's novel had in fact been written by a former governess in the Thackeray family. 'At first it was generally said Currer was a lady, and Mayfair circumstantialized by making her the *chère amie* of Mr. Thackeray,' wrote John Gibson Lockhart, editor of the *Quarterly Review*.[44] The rumours were put into print by Elizabeth Rigby, in an article in the *Quarterly*. The novel was widely assumed, she reported, 'to have proceeded from the pen of Mr. Thackeray's governess, whom he had himself chosen as his model of Becky, and who in mingled love and revenge, personified him in return as Mr. Rochester'.[45] Such rumours circulated for at least a couple of years.

Elizabeth Rigby was 'strongly inclined to affirm' that Currer Bell was a man, her evidence being the novel's 'mistakes' about items of female knowledge. 'No woman could have said what Jane Eyre says about preparing game and dessert dishes with the same hands.'[46] 'Above all, no woman attires another in such fancy dresses as Jane's ladies assume.' Lockhart concurred: 'Your skill in "dress" settles the question of sex.'[47] Yet, in a letter to Rigby in which he tells her of 'the common rumour' that the Bells are 'brothers of the weaving order in some Lancastrian town', he still hesitates.[48] 'I think, however, some woman must have assisted in the school scenes of *Jane Eyre* which have a striking art of truthfulness to me – an igoramus, callow on such points.' This is either prejudiced or shrewd. Either he cannot believe that a man is capable of imagining the life of Lowood, an all-female school, or he grasps the harsh credibility of Brontë's depiction of the cruelly 'charitable' institution. Brontë knew nothing of Lockhart's hunches, but she did read Elizabeth Rigby's article. In August 1849 she composed a passionately sarcastic reply, 'A Word to the "Quarterly"', which she intended as the preface to her second novel, *Shirley*.[49] (Smith and Williams, flinching from its anger, refused to allow it to be included.) 'The idea by you propagated, if not by you conceived, that my book proceeded from the pen of Mr. Thackeray's governess caught my fancy singularly,' she wrote. Evidently the reviewer (Williams had told Brontë that it was a woman, but not her actual identity) knew the love of rumour amongst the inhabitants of Mayfair and 'manufactures fictions to supply their cravings'. The would-be preface goes on to mock Rigby's observations about food and dress for their prissiness, but it does so in the persona of 'an old bachelor'. Brontë could have proved the reviewer obtuse by declaring her true identity, but she did not.

This is what is so striking about Brontë's reaction to the success of her novel. Against every temptation, she maintained her disguise. She declined to confess her authorship even to her close friend Ellen Nussey, who had watched her correcting the earliest page proofs of *Jane Eyre* when Brontë was staying with her at Birstall near Dewsbury in September 1847. Almost fifty years later, Nussey recalled how she 'had seen the Proof sheets corrected and passed them to the house letter bag without glancing at the address; perceiving that confidence was not volunteered, it was not sought'.[50] Yet Nussey did not truly keep her own counsel. In April 1848 she wrote to Brontë about rumours she had heard of the true identity of Currer Bell, hinting that her friend's name was guessed at. Brontë's reply was sharp.

Write another letter and explain that last note of yours distinctly. If your allusions are to myself, which I suppose they are—understand this—I have given no one a right to gossip about me and am not to be judged by frivolous conjectures

emanating from any quarter whatever. Let me know what you
heard and from whom you heard it.[51]

Brontë had revealed her authorship to her friend Mary Taylor,
who had been sent a copy of the novel, but then she did live in
New Zealand. In contrast, Nussey was instructed in a further,
yet fiercer letter to tell anyone suggesting that 'Miss Brontë has
been "publishing",' that 'you are authorized by Miss Brontë to
say, that she repels and disowns every accusation of the kind'.[52]
'I have given *no one* a right either to affirm, or hint, in the
most distant manner, that I am "publishing"—(humbug!)
Whoever has said it—if any one has, which I doubt—is no
friend of mine. Though twenty books were ascribed to me, I
should own none.' As Juliet Barker, biographer of the Brontë
sisters, observes, the letters to Nussey are carefully phrased to
avoid a lie, even if Brontë was forcing Nussey to lie for her. 'She
never actually denies her authorship, only refuses to acknowledge it.'[53]

Elizabeth Gaskell thought that, 'in their very vehemence and
agitation of intended denial,' these letters were confirmation
enough of the truth of what Nussey had heard.[54] She supposed
that Nussey would have taken them as such. Nussey did persevere
in her hints. In June 1748 she was visiting London where, as she
recalled many years later, 'There was quite a *fureur* about the
authorship of the new novel.'[55] She 'seized upon' a copy of *Jane
Eyre* and, reading just its first half page, was, she claimed, certain
of the author. 'It was as though C. B. herself were present in every
word, her voice, and spirit thrilling through and through, till a
rapid escape was imperative for the outlet of feeling.' She wrote
to Brontë wryly asking her opinion of this 'new novel', only to
find her friend evading a confession in a pretence of unwordly
gravity: 'We do not subscribe to a circulating library at Haworth
and consequently "new novels" rarely indeed come in our way,

and consequently again we are not qualified to give opinions thereon.'[56] Quoting the correspondence with Nussey in her *Life of Charlotte Brontë*, Gaskell offered an explanation of Brontë's desire to maintain her pseudonym that has been repeated by later biographers. 'The reason why Miss Brontë was so anxious to preserve her secret, was, I am told, that she had pledged her word to her sisters that it should not be revealed through her.'[57] Charlotte was to write of her 'grand error' in admitting even to Williams that 'Ellis Bell' was in fact her sister Emily. 'I regret it bitterly now, for I find it is against every feeling and intention of "Ellis Bell".'[58] All the evidence is that Emily was especially determined that the 'Bells' remained unknown. Within three weeks of Emily's death in December 1749, Charlotte, as if released from a promise, had conceded the truth to Nussey and given her copies of all four of the novels by the Brontë sisters.[59]

Yet Charlotte's separation of herself from 'Currer Bell' went well beyond sisterly loyalty. Her second novel, *Shirley*, was completed and published after the deaths of Emily and Anne, but she insisted to Smith, Elder & Co. that she maintain her disguise, despite the firm's suggestion that she abandon it.[60] Her insistence is all the more striking as *Shirley* is peopled with characters consciously drawn from life, and especially from the area around Birstall, where she had so often stayed with Ellen Nussey. Joe Taylor, brother of Brontë's friend Mary Taylor, was told that his family was the model for the Yorkes in the novel, in which he featured as Martin Yorke, and was sent those chapters in which they appeared for his approval.[61] He duly gossiped about the true identity of 'Currer Bell'.[62] Brontë's anonymity was being eroded, yet concealment was still important to her when she visited London at the end of November 1849, a month after the publication of *Shirley*. She stayed with George Smith and seems to have expected that, as a matter of good manners, his friends would avoid any mention of her literary alter ego. She wrote home to her father that 'most people know me I think, but they are far too well-bred to shew that they know me—so that there is none of that bustle or that sense of publicity I dislike.'[63] It went further than this. She made it clear to Smith that, even though those to whom he introduced her were eager to meet the author of *Jane Eyre*, her anonymity was somehow to be preserved. At a dinner party where she first met her hero Thackeray, he angered her by contravening this rule. After dinner, smoking a cigar, he recollected a passage from *Jane Eyre* where Jane, in the garden of Thornfield, describes 'the warning fragrance' of cigar smoke which tells her of Mr Rochester's approach.

> The quotation . . . did credit to Thackeray's memory . . . but not to his memory of his agreement with me. Miss Brontë's face showed her discomposure, and in a chilly fashion she turned off the allusion . . . She cast an accusing look at me.[64]

Thackeray was present only because she was the author of *Jane Eyre*, yet this was just what he was not allowed to mention. When, on the last night of her visit, Smith gathered the literary critics of *The Times*, *Athenaeum*, *Spectator*, *Examiner* and *Atlas* to meet her over dinner, she stipulated in advance that 'she should not be specially introduced to any one'.[65] Currer Bell was not to be present.

She may have preached to Ellen Nussey about the desirability of 'profound obscurity', as opposed to 'vulgar notoriety', but obscurity was not exactly what she pursued. Juliet Barker has a puzzled footnote remarking that 'though Charlotte enjoyed anonymity when she was writing, she also craved the public recognition which allowed her to move in literary circles'.[66] It was just so. Her refusal to allow Currer Bell to be identified with Charlotte Brontë was a kind of creative principle – what allowed her to make life into fiction. We have from her London visit a

good account of the flutter caused by the steadfast anonymity
of the author of *Jane Eyre*. Brontë heard from Smith that the
formidable Harriet Martineau, whom she much admired, was
staying nearby, so she sent her a note expressing 'a very strong
wish to see you'.[67] The note was signed 'Currer Bell'. Brontë
was invited to tea at six o'clock the next day, though Martineau's hostess and cousin Lucy Martineau told her son in a letter
written after the meeting that 'the fun was, how to direct the
note, for no one has ever yet decided whether Currer Bell is a
man or a woman'.[68] The note was 'directed, quaker fashion, to
Currer Bell, alone'. Martineau had some idea that the
unknown author was female; when Brontë had sent her a copy
of *Shirley* a few weeks earlier, she had included a letter in
which Currer Bell spoke of the 'pleasure and profit she has
derived' from Martineau's writings.[69] 'She' was then crossed
out and 'he' inserted. Martineau later observed that she 'had
more reason for interest than even the deeply-interested public
in knowing who wrote "Jane Eyre;" for, when it appeared, I
was taxed with the authorship by more than one personal
friend'.[70]

Martineau claimed already to be sure that Currer Bell was a
woman: 'A certain passage in "Jane Eyre" about sewing on brass
rings cd. have been written only by a woman or an upholsterer.'[71]
Yet Lucy Martineau's description of waiting for the novelist's
arrival, however playful, makes their uncertainty vivid.

So all day long as Htt tells the story we were wondering what
sort of being this same Currer Bell wd turn out to be; whether
a tall moustached man six feet high, or an aged female, or a
girl, or—altogether a ghost, a hoax or a swindler! . . . So when
6 oclock came, I lighted plenty of candles that we might see
what manner of man or womankind it was, & we sat in wondering expectation.[72]

Harriet Martineau told how, just before the appointed time,
'there was a thundering rap: – the drawing room door was
thrown open, and in stalked a gentleman of six feet high.'[73] 'For
an instant they fancied he was Currer Bell, and indeed an Esq.'[74]
But he was only 'a philanthropist, who had an errand about a
model lodging house'.[75] He was despatched and, at five minutes
past six, Brontë – 'a *very* little sprite of a creature' – duly entered,
announced by her true name. Martineau recalled that 'we had
heard the name before, among others, in the way of
conjecture'.[76]

Martineau and her relations were sworn to secrecy about
Brontë's identity. According to a letter from Gaskell, while they
kept the secret, Thackeray did not.[77] He gossiped, supposedly
announcing to fellow members of the Garrick, 'Boys, I have been
dining with Jane Eyre.'[78] Gaskell herself had written to Currer
Bell, via 'his' publisher, earlier that month, expressing her admiration of 'his' fiction. She had probably already read *Shirley*, and
had perhaps, like Martineau, been sent a copy by its author. She
received a reply in which the author used the feminine pronoun
of herself.

> Currer Bell will avow to Mrs. Gaskell that her chief reason for
> maintaining an incognito is the fear that if she relinquished
> it, strength and courage would leave her, and she should ever
> after shrink from writing the plain truth.[79]

Even as she allowed Gaskell to glimpse her true self, she
asserted her incognito as her creative licence. Gaskell triumph-
antly told a friend that she could now be sure of the mysterious
novelist's gender. 'Currer Bell (aha! What will you give me for a
secret?) She's a she—that I will tell you—who has sent me
"Shirley".'[80] She remained hungry to know this author's identity, telling her close friend Tottie Fox to quiz a literary
acquaintance: 'Do you know Dr. Epps—I think you do—ask

him to tell you who wrote Jane Eyre and Shirley . . . Do tell me who wrote Jane Eyre.'[81]

With the publication of *Shirley* it began to be widely accepted by reviewers that Currer Bell was probably female. Yet the very discussion sometimes angered Brontë.

> I am afraid Mr. Williams told you I was sadly 'put out' by the *Daily News* . . . good resolutions . . . were tried this morning by another notice in the same style in the *Observer*. The praise of such critics mortifies me more than their blame . . . speaking for myself alone, I *do* wish these hirelings of the Press were still ignorant of my being a woman. Why can they not be content to take Currer Bell for a man?
>
> I imagined—mistakenly, it now appears—that 'Shirley' bore fewer traces of a female hand than 'Jane Eyre'; that I have misjudged disappoints me a little—though I cannot exactly see where the error lies.[82]

It is as if the discovery of 'a female hand' in her novel is a denial of her imagination. She is not timid or defensive about this, not some demure recluse flinching from public regard. There is something assertive, even aggressive, about her requirement that her authorship be de-sexed. In her letters to Smith Williams she sounds more proud than modest. She disdains reviewers whose judgements of *Jane Eyre* are shaped by their assumptions about its author's gender.

> To such critics I would say—'to you I am neither Man nor Woman—I come before you as an Author only—it is the sole standard by which you have a right to judge me—the sole ground on which I accept your judgment.'[83]

When George Henry Lewes reviewed *Shirley* for the *Edinburgh Review*, he declared it 'now scarcely a secret that Currer Bell is the pseudonym of a woman'.[84] (Lewes had just discovered

Brontë's true identity, apparently through a former school-fellow of hers.[85]) To her distress, he criticized the novel for its author's attempts to escape her femininity. It was vitiated by an 'over-masculine vigour', which 'often amounts to coarseness,—and is certainly the very antipode to "lady-like"'. Currer Bell steps 'out of her sex—without elevating herself above it'. Brontë wrote to him saying she was 'hurt' because 'after I had said earnestly that I wished critics would judge me as an *author* not as a woman, you so roughly—I even thought—so cruelly handled the question of sex.'[86] She had hoped that her pseudonym would have brought her a release from critical preconceptions.

By the end of 1849, Brontë's name and something of her history were widely known in London literary circles, and when she returned to Haworth it was to find that she was known closer to home. Her father began to tell friends of his daughter's secret and, in February 1850, Martha Brown, one of the Brontës' two servants, arrived one day 'puffing and blowing and much excited', to say that she too knew.[87] Her father had been told in Halifax, while others had heard in Bradford. The recently founded Haworth Mechanics' Institute was to order copies of the two novels. A few 'curiosity-hunters' even began finding their way to Haworth Parsonage.[88] Finally, the *Bradford Observer* announced on 28 February that 'the only daughter of the Rev P Brontë, incumbent of Haworth' was 'the authoress of *Jane Eyre* and *Shirley*, two of the most popular novels of the day, which have appeared under the name of "Currer Bell"'.[89] Yet even now she did not allow herself to become an acknowledged author. Six months later, she visited London again, staying with the Smiths, and was still trying to keep a distance from her authorial persona. This time she was invited to dine at Thackeray's house. His daughter Anne, then aged thirteen, recalled the visit in her memoirs many years later.

She enters in mittens, in silence, in seriousness; our hearts are beating with wild excitement. This then is the authoress, the unknown power whose books have set all London talking, reading, speculating; some people even say our father wrote the books—the wonderful books. To say that we little girls had been given *Jane Eyre* to read scarcely represents the facts of the case; to say that we had taken it without leave, read bits here and read bits there, been carried away by an undreamed-of and hitherto unimagined whirlwind into things, times, places, all utterly absorbing and at the same time absolutely unintelligible to us, would more accurately describe our states of mind on that summer's evening as we look at Jane Eyre— the great Jane Eyre—the tiny little lady.[90]

'The unknown power': the phrase catches what made the business of attributing the fiction seem so important. This 'tiny little lady' had been 'unknown', as readers and reviewers – 'all London' – had itched to track her down. Her 'wonderful books' were the strange progeny of some 'unknown power', some imaginative force never before encountered. In this recollection, Charlotte Brontë *is* Jane Eyre, even if Brontë never allowed it. On the way to dinner that evening, Thackeray apparently addressed her as 'Currer Bell' and was frostily admonished.

She tossed her head and said 'she believed there were books being published by a person named Currer Bell . . . but the person he was talking to was Miss Brontë—and she saw no connection between the two.'[91]

The meaning of anonymity to Brontë became clearer after her identity had become public knowledge. She continued to correspond with George Smith as 'Currer Bell', using the masculine pronoun in a correspondence that was often teasing, even flirtatious. 'The masculine *nom-de-plume* freed her from the constraints that would normally be expected in letters between a young unmarried man and woman.'[92] The pseudonym was still an escape from herself. When, in the autumn of 1850, she composed a 'Biographical Notice of Ellis and Acton Bell' to preface a new edition of her sisters' work, she declared it time to do away with 'the obscurity attending those two names'.[93] Yet, while referring to 'my two sisters', and calling them Emily and Anne, she kept herself as 'Currer Bell' and nowhere used the Brontë surname. With *Villette*, completed at the end of 1852, she planned further concealment. She told Smith Williams, 'My wish is that the book should be published without Author's name.'[94] The removal of even 'Currer Bell' from the title page would rob the publishers of their prized commercial asset, the reputation of the author of *Jane Eyre* and *Shirley*, and they persuaded her out of it. *Villette* appeared as 'by Currer Bell' in January 1853. The reviewers universally referred to the author as 'she'. Most of them politely avoided the author's real name, but some did not.[95] There was certainly no secret any more.

What Brontë had told Smith Williams in the wake of *Jane Eyre*'s success remained the case. 'Currer Bell' was 'the only name I wish to have mentioned in connection with my writings'.[96] The explanation that she then gave remained valid. 'If I were known—I should ever be conscious in writing that my book must be read by ordinary acquaintances—and that idea would fetter me intolerably.' She had to be unfettered to turn her own experiences as a teacher in Brussels into *Villette*, which, like her other novels, was peopled with characters that might have been identified from life. The handsome Dr John Bretton, with whom Lucy Snowe falls half in love, was based on George Smith, as he himself recognized. This is a novel in which the familiar is made strange – a making strange which is there in the transformation of Brussels to Villette, a place of exile and loneliness for the narrator. Brontë's removal of herself from her first novel

allowed its urgent, truculent intimacy. Now she held herself
back from a heroine and narrator who is so secretive as to keep
things from the reader, who has suffered, but will not tell us
how. At the beginning of the novel Lucy talks of enduring 'a
long time, of cold, of danger, of contention' as she grows from
childhood to womanhood.[97] What does she mean? It is all
obscure metaphor. We know only that 'there was a storm, and
that not of one hour nor one day. For many days and nights
neither sun nor stars appeared . . . In fine, the ship was lost, the
crew perished.' 'As far as I recollect, I complained to no one
about these troubles.' She hardly even complains to us. What
is extraordinary about *Villette* is all that makes it difficult to
sympathize with its narrator. Snowy Lucy stays true to her suppression of feeling – 'my natural cruel insensibility'.[98] She is
hungry for love – reviewers were sometimes shocked by the
attention to this appetite in the novel – but she is not going to
reach out for it. Her sufferings make her ill, but she is not to be
cured by some mere release of what is repressed. Suffering would
not be suffering if it could be shared. To read *Villette* is not to
know everything about Lucy Snowe. It is to share in something
stranger – a sense of the repression and evasion by which a
person makes herself known.

Brontë had made extraordinary new uses of old conventions
of self-concealment. Her pseudonym had become a sign of creative defiance. She put this squarely enough in a letter to Smith
Williams written just before the appearance of *Shirley*, as she
contemplated the spreading knowledge of her real name. 'Meantime, though I earnestly wish to preserve my incognito, I live
under no slavish fear of discovery—I am ashamed of nothing I
have written—not a line.'[99] Brontë was transforming a tradition
of feminine reticence. 'An acknowledged Novel-writer is, perhaps, one of the most difficult names to support with credit
and reputation,' a woman novelist had written early in the

nineteenth century.[100] Whatever her value for privacy, Brontë had no fears for 'credit and reputation'. Yet only with Gaskell's biography did Currer Bell become Charlotte Brontë. Compare this with the persistence of the most famous literary pseudonym of the nineteenth century: 'George Eliot'. If we still use this pseudonym of the writer who was christened Mary Anne Evans and died Mary Ann Cross, why do we not still call Charlotte Brontë 'Currer Bell'? For even after discovery, she – like George Eliot – kept resolutely to her pseudonym. Perhaps it is the problem of Eliot's 'true' name. During her adolescence she took to calling herself Marianne Evans, while known by friends and siblings as Polly or Pollian. Later she signed herself Mary Ann (without an 'e'). In 1850, at the age of thirty-one, she started referring to herself, and signing herself, Marian Evans, a new name for her new literary life in London. Five years later she was cohabiting with a married man, George Henry Lewes, and calling herself Mrs Lewes, or Marian Lewes. After Lewes's death, in the last year of her life, she reverted to Mary Ann and altered her surname by marrying John Walter Cross. At the heart of this search for identity is the audacious awkwardness of her adopting a married name to which she was not legally entitled. Eliot's publisher, John Blackwood, was anxious that her pseudonym should remain an effective disguise, fearing that bourgeois Victorian readers would desert his best-selling author if they knew of her private life. Biographers, faced with the problem of what to call her (for she was not 'George Eliot' until 1857, when she was in her late thirties), have tended to think her pseudonym her one stable identity.

Before she became 'George Eliot', she published anonymously. Her translation from the German of David Friedrich Strauss's religiously sceptical *Life of Jesus* appeared without her name in 1846. She reviewed and wrote articles for its publisher, John Chapman, owner and nominal editor of the *Westminster*

Review. For some time she namelessly edited the journal. Only once did she use a name. In 1854 Chapman published her translation of Feuerbach's *Das Wesen des Christenthums* (The Essence of Christianity) with 'Marian Evans' on its title page, the only work of hers to appear with a name other than 'George Eliot'. It was just as she and Lewes were about to begin living together as if man and wife. Knowledge of their relationship may have influenced the sarcasm of reviewer James Martineau. 'It is a sign of "progress", we presume, that the lady translator who maintained the anonymous in introducing Strauss, puts her name in the title-page of Feuerbach.'[101] She had reason to find a nom de plume.

In 1856 Lewes submitted to John Blackwood, proprietor of *Blackwood's Magazine,* the manuscript of her first story, 'The Sad Fortunes of the Rev. Amos Barton'. Lewes used the pronoun 'he' of its author, whom he described as 'a friend' with a 'shy, shrinking, ambitious nature'. Blackwood replied, 'If the author is a new writer I beg to congratulate him on being worthy of the honours of print and pay.'[102] On 1 January 1857, the first instalment of 'Amos Barton' appeared in his magazine, without any author's name attached to it. Because Lewes had referred to the author as 'my clerical friend', Blackwood had presumed that the first of what we now know as *Scenes of Clerical Life* was written by a member of the Church. 'I am glad to hear that your friend is as I supposed a Clergyman. Such a subject is best in clerical hands.'[103] Lewes later reported that those with whom he had discussed the tale 'were all sure that the author was a clergyman – a Cambridge man'. The story did have a shrewd sense of petty theological dispute in the Church of England. Although the thought amused Lewes, he disabused Blackwood of the notion that the author was a clergyman, but stipulated that the maintenance of anonymity was crucial.

At this stage, the fiction was completely anonymous. Blackwood wrote to its author, via Lewes, as 'My Dear Amos'. The author replied, with the first ever use of that now famous pseudonym. 'Whatever may be the success of my stories, I shall be resolute in preserving my incognito, having observed that a *nom de plume* secures all the advantages without the disagreeables of reputation.'[104] A pen name would establish a sense of authorship, of the special qualities of a certain imagination, without attracting any intrusive attention. She offered her 'prospective name, as a tub to throw to the whale in case of curious enquiries', signing the letter 'George Eliot'. Over twenty years later, she was to tell her husband J. W. Cross why she chose this alias. 'George was Mr. Lewes's Christian name, and Eliot was a good, mouth-filling, easily pronounced word.'[105] Perhaps it also carried memories of the most famous pseudonym of the century, before her own – George Sand, a favourite writer of hers as a young woman. Eliot was alive to the possible repercussions if her scandalous social situation were to be known by her readers. She and Lewes cohabited because his wife Agnes had left him for his friend Thornton Hunt, by whom she had had a child. Lewes could not divorce her without disgracing her. Eliot had been disowned by her brother Isaac, and under pressure from him her sisters had ceased communication with her. She knew well the hostility her choice of life could arouse.

Yet her secrecy was not just defensive. She told Blackwood,

For several reasons I am very anxious to retain my incognito for some time to come, and to an author not already famous, anonymity is the highest *prestige*. Besides, if George Eliot turns out to be a dull dog and an ineffective writer – a mere flash in the pan – I, for one, am determined to cut him on the first intimation of that disagreeable fact.[106]

Her 'incognito' was a licence to experiment upon public taste. She even used it against Blackwood, replying to some of his initial criticisms of *Scenes of Clerical Life* with a claim that was all the more authoritative for coming from an unknown source. 'My sketches both of churchmen and dissenters, with whom I am almost equally acquainted, are drawn from close observation of them in real life, and not at all from hearsay or from the descriptions of novelists.'[107] Eliot's fiction asks any reader to believe in just this acquaintance with what they read. Some of her first readers wrote to Blackwood saying that they knew the 'originals' of the characters. There was even 'a curious letter from a man who supposed he was the original Amos Barton'.[108] Eliot's was a fiction of a known world, a realism of 'ordinariness'. A masculine pseudonym was a claim to authority. When they read *Scenes of Clerical Life*, many thought that they heard the voice of a clergyman. We now hear the voice of a woman, a free-thinker, a religious sceptic. But George Eliot first won the admiration of readers who could know none of this.

Those who came to the opening of 'Amos Barton' in January 1857, when its first instalment was published anonymously, or a year later, when *Scenes of Clerical Life* appeared as 'by George Eliot', would not have had our means of knowing how to measure its tone. A narrator surveys a provincial community and its parish church, with its old-fashioned trappings of a traditional Anglicanism. 'Then inside, what dear old quaintnesses!'[109] This parochial world, of a 'neighbourhood' 'where people were extremely well acquainted with each other's affairs', is to be described with what we recognize as Eliot's tolerant irony. The tale gives us not only the 'sad fortunes' of the all-too-human clergyman Amos Barton, but also sharp sketches of other provincial clergymen. We now know they are invented by an intellectually audacious woman who wanted to extract the potentially humane content from ordinary religion. To the first readers, it was much less clear what the author's relationship to these characters might be. Many presumed that only a man of intellectual, perhaps clerical, authority could survey this world.

George Eliot reported that a friend, Agnes Owen, had unknowingly discussed the story with her and 'thought I was the father of a family – was sure I was a man who had seen a great deal of society etc.'.[110] Sometimes, as here, you can catch a fundamental delight in anonymity. Such innocent idiocies show that the narrative voice has truly been achieved. There is a letter to Smith Williams from Charlotte Brontë describing just this pleasure, as she sits with her sisters and compares them with the darkly masculine authors of their works imagined by the *North American Review*. The reviewer is one of those who has imagined that her own work must be collaborative. 'How I laugh in my sleeve when I read the solemn assertions that "Jane Eyre" was written in partnership, and that it "bears the marks of more than one mind, and one sex".'[111]

George Eliot's intimate friendship with John Chapman, once her mentor and employer, and probably her lover, was brought to an end by his fuelling rumours about her authorship of *Scenes*. Herbert Spencer told her that Chapman 'had asked him point-blank if I wrote the Clerical Scenes'.[112] Spencer was duly blamed for not having denied it. She immediately wrote an angry letter to Chapman: 'were any such rumours true', he should have realized that 'my own abstinence from any communication concerning my own writing, except to my most intimate friends, was evidence that I regarded secrecy on such subjects as a matter of importance'.[113] Three months later, Lewes told Chapman, 'Mrs Lewes ... authorizes me to state, as distinctly as language can do so, that she is not the author of "Adam Bede".'[114] Chapman revenged himself in his subsequent review of the novel in the *Westminster*, where he pretended to guess that its author was female. He quoted a passage in which Hetty Sorrel is described as being pained when Arthur Donnithorne pretends to ignore her, though she recognizes that it is a pretence. Was this touch of psychology proof of a female author?

We speak of the author as of the masculine gender, but the deliberate appreciation of feminine feelings conveyed in this question – 'What woman was ever satisfied with apparent neglect, even when she knows it is the mask of love?' – would alone make us skeptical as to whether *George Eliot* ever wrote it.[115]

In the end, Eliot revealed her identity to Blackwood, in the scene described in Chapter 1, shortly before the completion of her first full-length novel, *Adam Bede*. This was published in 1859, and was hugely successful. The identity of the author remained hidden, but aroused excited discussion. As with *Jane Eyre*, the gender of the author became a matter of much dispute. Gradually the secret was seeping out, and Eliot revealed herself to close friends who still lived in the Midlands, although Lewes advised one of them, '*Don't* say you know the authorship. Let fools and dupes continue their folly and pay for it; but don't interfere beyond the expression of your disbelief.'[116] Elizabeth Gaskell wrote jokingly to Eliot about the burden of keeping the secret.

Since I came from Manchester to London I have had the greatest compliment paid me I ever had in my life. I have been suspected of having written 'Adam Bede'. I have hitherto denied it; but I really think, that as you want to keep your real name a secret, it would be very pleasant for me to blush acquiescence. Will you give me leave?[117]

Blackwood and his partners worried about the erosion of the 'incognito', thinking that their best property was about to be discredited. *The Times* reported the speculation about the true identity of 'George Eliot'.

It was even surmised that he must be a lady, since none but a woman's hand could have painted those touching scenes of clerical life. Now, the question will be raised, can this be a young author? Is all this mature thought, finished portraiture, and crowd of characters the product of a 'prentice hand and of callow genius? If it is, the hand must have an extraordinary cunning, and the genius must be of the highest order.[118]

A few days later, an unknown clergyman called Anders wrote to *The Times* saying that *Adam Bede* was written by Joseph Liggins of Nuneaton. This was an old story. Liggins had been cited as the author of *Scenes of Clerical Life*, two years earlier. Eliot's half-sister Fanny had written to her reporting the rumour. She had been forced to reply that she had read the stories and herself recognized 'figures and traditions connected with our old neighbourhood', but that 'Blackwood informs Mr. Lewes that the author is a Mr. Eliot, a clergyman, I presume'.[119] Liggins himself produced a 'manuscript' of *Adam Bede*, which he claimed to have written ten years earlier.[120] Indeed, he complained that he had not yet been paid. Both William Blackwood and Lewes (in the name of Eliot) wrote letters to *The Times* denying his authorship. Eliot was forced to abandon her reticence – though not her pseudonym – and wrote to *The Times* to denounce Liggins. Yet only when Lewes told friends that her identity was no longer to be a secret did Liggins' claim begin to die.

By the time that *The Mill on the Floss* was published in 1860, Eliot's true identity was widely known and published. And yet this and the rest of her novels still appeared with the name 'George Eliot' on the title pages; an alias had become a kind of declaration. The author made the necessity of concealment into a virtue. 'I am very nervous about the preservation of the incognito,' she wrote to John Blackwood of *Adam Bede*.[121] 'I wish the book to be judged quite apart from its authorship.' 'Do not guess at authorship – it is a bad speculation,' she wrote to her close friend Sara Hennell. This second comment is somewhat disingenuous, for, like other anonymous authors, Eliot knew that the inquisitiveness that a disguised authorship excited was also useful. It was a curiosity that her storytelling had exploited. At first, George Eliot tried to shed the label of female authorship. In the end, she found an even better solution. Her pseudonym became her name, her disguise a kind of proclamation. Her success as a novelist overwhelmed any hostility to her lifestyle, and her nom de plume became a disguise that everybody knew about – a way of declaring the necessary fictiveness of her role as a narrator. She told the editor of the *Oxford English Dictionary*, in response to his enquiry as to what she wished to be called in citations from her work, 'I wish always to be quoted as George Eliot,' but she signed the letter, 'Yours very truly M. E. Lewes.'[122] George Eliot tells the stories, but George Eliot is invented. It is she who knows the 'Provincial' world whose epic would eventually be *Middlemarch*.

Women continued to publish novels under male (and female) pseudonyms up to the end of the nineteenth century. The examples of Brontë and Eliot provided models for turning modesty into playfulness or creative experiment. There are striking examples from the late nineteenth century, notably from Thomas Fisher Unwin's 'Pseudonym Library', of self-consciously modern fiction, much of it written by women, all of it ostentatiously pseudonymous.[123] Unwin saw that there was a market for literary fiction by new or unknown authors. Previous fiction series had reprinted novels that had already appeared in the standard three-volume format. Unwin commissioned new work to fit his unconventional format: the books, covered in cloth or paper, were an unusual (seven inches by three and a half) shape, designed, it is said, to fit a lady's reticule. 'HANDY FOR THE POCKET IN SIZE AND SHAPE', proclaimed the heading of each page advertising titles in the series. Intended for the rail travellers' market, most of the stories were no more than two hundred short pages and might be read in a couple of hours. The venture was a commercial success. The fame of the 'Pseudonym Library' was what brought Conrad to Unwin's publishing company, though he was disappointed to find that his first novel, *Almayer's Folly*, was too long for inclusion in the series.[124] He had wanted to have it published under the pseudonym 'Kamudi'.

The first volume was *Mademoiselle Ixe*, by Lanoe Falconer, the pseudonym of Mary Hawker. (It was formed by an anagram of 'alone' followed by a synonym of 'hawker'.[125]) Hawker had written stories for magazines, and was in her early forties when she wrote this short novel. It is the story of a woman with a strange name and a mysterious, cosmopolitan past, fluent in several languages and technically brilliant at the piano, who arrives in England to be the governess to the bourgeois Merrington family. It is a novel of female friendship, constructed around the growing companionship of the governess and the restless, imaginative Merrington daughter, Evelyn. The reader might be tempted to infer that the novelist was a woman. Mademoiselle Ixe speaks enigmatically of her history and, in a certain light, the lines in her face reveal 'the grim characters of suffering rather than of time'.[126] Terrible things have happened to her; naturally, 'Ixe' is not her real name. Eventually she tells the uncomprehending Evelyn of the 'monstrous tyranny' in the country from which she has fled, and her allegiance to those who would rekindle 'the sacred fire of national life'.[127] She takes a peculiar interest in a Russian count who is visiting a rich local family. When Mademoiselle Ixe sees him she turns 'deadly pale', and even though he has 'a very dark and repellent face . . . with long Eastern eyes and a protruding animal jaw', Evelyn presumes she is in love with him.[128] In fact it is hate. At a ball given by his hosts, Mademoiselle Ixe shoots the Count, whom she declares 'the enemy of my people, and of humanity too'.[129] Evelyn helps her escape. The novel ends with a letter to her from Mademoiselle

Ixe – apparently written in blood, from a Russian prison – wishing her happiness and implying that she herself will soon die. It is signed '*x*.'

The mystery attaching to the protagonist seems nicely suited to a series that positively encouraged readers to wonder about the mystery of its authors' identities. *Mademoiselle Ixe* sold some forty thousand copies and 'Lanoe Falconer' actually gave an interview with the *Novel Review*, which revealed that the novel had been attributed to 'half-a-dozen people', including one of Gladstone's daughters.[130] 'Many reviewers, because of, or in spite of, the pseudonyms, questioned the gender of the author.'[131] The Pseudonym Library seemed devised to activate such interest in attribution. According to the *Novel Review*, another of its volumes, *Some Emotions and a Moral* by John Oliver Hobbes (the pseudonym of Pearl Mary-Teresa Craigie), was 'favourably and extensively reviewed . . . and considerable interest was aroused as to the real name and sex of the author'.[132] Exciting speculation was the point. The very names devised by Unwin or his authors were often calculated to tease readers as to whether the author was a man or a woman. W. B. Yeats, writing a volume in the 'Pseudonym Library' as 'Ganconagh', was confidently identified as a woman by at least one reviewer.

A masculine pseudonym for fiction with a female focus could now be a sign of boldness rather than modesty. A celebrated example was Mary Chavelita Bright (née Dunne) who published fiction at the turn of the century under the name 'George Egerton'. She was born in Australia and had eloped with a married man, Henry Higginson, to Norway, where she had become influenced by Ibsenism. Her best-known work was *Keynotes* (1893), a collection of stories designed to illustrate the crises and ordeals of the 'new woman' – the intellectually strong-minded and independent female heroine who had begun appearing in fiction of the 1890s. These now neglected but rather brilliant vignettes were designed to be provocative. In the very first story, 'A Cross Line', we meet a restive married woman who smokes, drinks whisky, and magnetically beguiles all the men she meets. She openly tantalizes her husband, and when she 'bites his chin and shakes it like a terrier in her strong little teeth' he simply picks her up 'and carries her off to her room'.[133] She dreams of herself as a 'gauze-clad' Eastern dancer, 'with parted lips and panting, rounded breasts', swaying voluptuously to wild music, and thinks with puzzlement of women she has known who have become 'settled, patient wives'.[134] The story takes the reader into her private thoughts about women's desires, and the obtuseness of men, lapsing into the first person – 'the workings of our hearts are closed to them' – as if a female author were speaking directly.

All the stories feature emancipated but often tormented young women. In 'A Little Grey Glove', a young man is captivated by a woman who has just got divorced; in 'An Empty Frame', the protagonist is in love with a man who returns her love but will not marry her – 'I must be free and unfettered to follow that which I believe is right for me.'[135] She therefore marries another man, whom she does not love, but dreams of a more passionate life. The stories are all about women's dreams, and claim a startling intimacy with their female characters. The collection was a best-seller. Egerton's success inspired her publisher John Lane to begin his 'Keynote' series, featuring stories by leading writers, including Edith Nesbit and Thomas Hardy. The recently divorced Egerton appears to have become Lane's mistress.

Brontë and Eliot created new possibilities for women writers, and new speculations for curious readers. There is an emotionally charged illustration of this in a best-selling novel from 1898, Ellen Thorneycroft Fowler's *Concerning Isabel Carnaby*. Written at the same time as those 'New Woman' novels, it has an eponymous heroine who is renowned, and sometimes feared, for

being (as another woman puts it) 'dreadfully clever'.[136] Paul
Seaton, who is destined to fall in love with Isabel, asks in reply,
'What sort of cleverness? Does she write books?'

> 'Good gracious, no; not so bad as that!' replied Lady Esdaile,
> looking shocked. 'But she reads a good deal, and says sharp
> things, and you never know whether she is laughing at you
> or not.'

Paul and Isabel become engaged, but then separate after a foolish
argument. The next year a satirical novel appears called *Shams
and Shadows*, by one 'Angus Grey'. Flippant, mischievous and
cynical, it causes some stir with its scarcely disguised portraits of
well-known society figures. These include the heroine, who was
'the counterfeit presentment of Isabel Carnaby', shown as filled
with 'a cold and shallow selfishness'.[137] Speculation rages about
the author's identity: 'everybody was asking who Angus Grey
could be, as it was evident that he was some one well versed in
the ways of this particular set.' It settles on Paul, who has
become a literary journalist, and who does not deny that the
book is his. Though it is generally thought 'smart', his reputation suffers from the attribution, not least with his Methodist
family.

Isabel is in fact the author, and Paul is acting nobly in taking
the blame. 'I was ashamed, and felt I could not bear the disgrace
of being known as its author,' she confesses to his sister, Joanna.[138]
Even after she has been won back to Paul by this sacrifice of his
own literary standing as a notably 'moral' writer, and the two are
again betrothed, he insists that he must remain the acknowledged author of the 'horrid book'.[139] The brilliant Isabel is, as
Joanna drily puts it, 'so modern and up-to-date, that I regard her
as a sort of national institution that one ought to feel proud of—
a specimen of what the nineteenth century can produce.'[140] Yet
she must shelter behind that male pseudonym. Paul has earlier

recommended pseudonyms for the fiction writer, who will otherwise be 'handicapped' by 'circumstances and surroundings': 'If
you write under a *nom-de-plume* you are quite free.'[141] Trivialized
in his airy formula, this is just the freedom that Brontë and
Eliot had made for themselves. Fowler, a witty but amoral
writer, showed that this freedom is something from which her
thoroughly 'modern' heroine needs to be saved.

4

MEN BEING WOMEN

In 1987, the publishers Virago withdrew from publication and pulped all copies of *Down the Road, Worlds Away*, a collection of stories by Rahila Khan. Thanks to Virago's efforts, this cheaply produced paperback is now a rare book and can only be read somewhere like the British Library. It was published in the series 'Virago Upstarts', committed to showing 'the funny, difficult, and exciting lives and times of teenage girls in the 1980s'. A note on the author explained that she had been born in Coventry in 1950 and had also lived in Birmingham, Derby, Oxford, London, Peterborough and Brighton. 'In 1971 she married and now has two daughters. It was not until 1986 that she began writing.'[1] In *Down the Road, Worlds Away*, stories about the lives of young Asian women in Britain (all told in the third person) alternate with stories about a white, male working-class adolescent (told in the first person). The latter tell of a narrowed and brutalized world, with the reader being invited to sympathize with a narrator ('Boulter') who is reduced by his circumstances to habits of vandalism and petty abusiveness. The Asian stories are all about girls facing clashes of culture. In the first one, a girl angers her Muslim parents by diligently copying the Nativity scenes of her fellow pupils at primary school. In another, the same character, a few years on, is beaten by her father when he finds her with a copy of *Sons and Lovers*, given her by her English teacher. There is often this subtext: that through literature a girl might free herself from the shackles of her upbringing. The collection ends with a tale, 'Winter Wind', about an inter-racial romance (Colin and Fatima) that flares on a trip to the theatre to see *As You Like It*.

To Virago's dismay, it turned out that 'Rahila Khan' did not exist. She was the pseudonym of an Anglican vicar from Brighton named Toby Forward. The Reverend Forward was reported to be mildly perplexed, claiming that he had never expected the collection to be published.[2] The publishers spoke of being hurt rather than angry. 'It's not unknown in feminist publishing for men to pass themselves off as women,' said a Virago spokeswoman. 'But this is rather bizarre – the book was published for the Asian community and purported to represent the Asian community, and we feel particularly distressed for them.'[3] The case became a livelier matter of public controversy or amusement when, three months later, Forward published an article in the *London Review of Books* giving his side of the affair. Rahila Khan had been just one of the pseudonyms under which he liked to write, he said. 'They released me from the obligation of being what I seem to be so that I can write as I really am' (he added that this was especially important if you happened to be a clergyman).[4] He insisted that he had not aimed to mock publishers or readers; his pseudonym was but an aid to creativity. He cited Charlotte Brontë as his model. She had taken a man's name for the title page of *Jane Eyre* 'so that she could be taken seriously'. 'A woman writes as a man so that she can write about a woman. A white man writes as an Asian woman so that he can write about an Asian girl.' He sounded earnest about this, though he could not resist describing the more ridiculous aspects of his dealings (all by letter) with publishers and broadcasters. BBC Radio broadcast some of Rahila's stories, but the producer rejected those that were not about Asian teenagers. She had her ethnic slot to fill. The editor at Virago asked why the 'white' stories were in the first person and the 'Asian' stories in the third person, producing her own self-satisfying theory.

I wondered whether this represented your feelings about the place of Asian women particularly in Britain, that the sense of 'otherness' is still so great that it feels still an impossibility to write in the first person as opposed to the third.

The Women's Press, meanwhile, accepted one of Rahila Khan's stories for an anthology but asked her to rewrite it in the first person. Both publishers had to believe that the fiction was as close as possible to autobiography.

As Forward told it, he was caught up in a deception whose consequences were a surprise to him. 'I failed to pull out of the deal with Virago and now it got more and more uncomfortable.' There were requests for interviews, photographs, radio talks. Eventually, he confessed to Rahila Khan's agent who advised him to come clean with Virago. With this account, and the flurry of letters that followed, the story was picked up again by newspapers. None treated Forward's scheme as what he declared it to be: a creative strategy – a means of liberating the imagination. It was instead reported as a hoax. Reference was invariably made to a long tradition of literary hoaxes, from Macpherson's Ossian and Chatterton's Rowley, to Ern Malley, the great Australian modernist poet whose work, much admired by critics, was in fact cobbled together in nonsensical fashion by two antagonists of poetic modernism. Editors, made gullible by their preconceptions, had been fooled; 'Rahila Khan' was a satire on political correctness. Virago certainly believed that they had been hoaxed; the firm issued a public statement saying that it was 'distressed that this attempt to represent the Asian community should transpire to be a cruel hoax'. The publishers saw the book as speaking for a 'community', and therefore only credible if it were rooted in the experience of a young Asian. 'Distressed' is the usual euphemism for 'angry', and anger is frequently the response to a hoax.

A hoax is different from a literary device. 'Rahila Khan' is different from 'Currer Bell', and the many other pseudonyms of nineteenth-century novelists, if only because readers have come to have different expectations. *Jane Eyre* arrived with a sense of mystery about its authorship. Its first readers were used to speculating about the true identity of authors and took the opportunity to do so again. The first readers of *Down the Road, Worlds Away* were entirely unsuspicious, and the publisher's compliance (and biographical note on the author) made them dupes. It is hardly surprising that when Forward told the publishers of the true identity of the 'author', they were sore. They saw a satirical trick. And yet Forward's explanation of his activities is interestingly weak, exactly because it seems earnest where it could have been mocking. Rather than just making mischief, he seems to have been taking things rather seriously. The stories themselves are evidence for Forward's earnestness. There is nothing parodic about them. It is tempting to say that they are just the stories about race and class that a liberal Anglican vicar would write. Forward said that his own 'alienation' was 'too personal and painful for me to write about, but it gave me a way into the lives and minds of others who for different reasons and in different circumstances felt something of the same things'. It is not elegant, but it appears heartfelt. Even his pretensions seemed sincere. 'Rahila Khan was me,' he wrote, in some kind of echo of Gustave Flaubert's comment about his famous heroine: 'Madame Bovary, c'est moi.'

Forward claimed, for the cause of the literary imagination, that his target was a certain habit of reading. 'The unspoken assumption behind most of this was that all imaginative literature, all fiction, is autobiographical. Later I was to be accused of pretending to occupy a position I didn't hold, to speak with a voice that wasn't mine. I had thought that this was the purpose of art.' He might have argued that he was returning to the

wellspring of English fiction, where a man finds his fictional
'voice' by writing as a woman. Two of Daniel Defoe's novels,
Moll Flanders and *Roxana*, were first-person accounts in the
voices of women, and both were presented as if they were genuine memoirs, with no mark on them of Defoe's authorship.
Both are scandalous tales. *Moll Flanders* takes its lead from the
accounts of 'true' criminals popular in the early eighteenth
century. These included the tales of female criminals. *Roxana*
was in a line of so-called 'scandal narratives', often penned by
female authors (like Mrs Manley or Eliza Haywood). These
narrated the sexually shocking and politically unscrupulous
manoeuvres of courtiers, their names titillatingly 'disguised'.
Sometimes, as with *Roxana*, which is set in the Restoration, these
disguises were historical.

Anonymity is essential to the plot of *Moll Flanders*, for the
protagonist is nameless and wishes to remain so.

> My True Name is so well known in the Records, or Registers
> at *Newgate*, and in the *Old-Baily*, and there are some things
> of such Consequence still depending there, relating to my
> particular Conduct, that it is not to be expected I should set
> my Name, or the Account of my Family to this Work; per-
> haps, after my Death it may be better known, at present it
> would not be proper, no, not tho' a general Pardon should be
> issued, even without Exceptions and reserve of Persons or
> Crimes.[5]

Her 'True Name' is withheld because it endangers her. Writing of
her reluctant parting from her 'Lancashire husband', she tells us,

> I Gave him a Direction [i.e. an address] how to write to
> me, tho' still I reserv'd the grand Secret, and never broke my
> Resolution, which was not to let him ever know my true
> Name, who I was, or where to be found.

'Moll Flanders' is but a pseudonym, as indeed are the other
names (Colonel Jack, Captain Singleton) which give titles to
Defoe's fictions. This pseudonym is the work of her fellow
prisoners in Newgate, who

> gave me the Name of *Moll Flanders*: for it was no more of
> Affinity with my real Name, or with any of the Names I had
> ever gone by, than black is of Kin to white . . . nor could I
> ever learn how they came to give me the Name, or what the
> Occasion of it was.[6]

The fact that she is not 'Kin' to this name is useful to her. She
may need others to steal with, 'yet I never let them know who
I was . . . my Name was publick among them indeed; but how
to find me out they knew not'.[7] Throughout the novel, being
'known' is 'the worst thing next to being found Guilty, that
cou'd befall me'.[8]

Defoe's name was first put to the novel some forty-five years
after his death in a bowdlerized version, *The History of Laetitia
Atkins, vulgarly called Moll Flanders*, published by the bookseller
Francis Noble in 1776. The preface of this version of *Moll Flanders*
declared it to be 'Published by Mr. Daniel De Foe'. It came with
an Introduction that was 'signed': 'Islington. December 20, 1730.
Daniel Defoe'. This regretted the previous inclusion of 'many
circumstances . . . which, though they were true, upon a more
cool reflection, my judgment could not by any means approve'.[9]
Noble's invented Defoe goes on to say, 'I therefore . . . altered
many parts of it, to give it the better reading, as some little time
before had done by Roxana.' The supposed editor of the text
adds to this that Defoe was a friend of his father, who 'spoke
highly to his advantage as a moral writer . . . and wondered
much . . . to find both in his Roxana, and in his Moll Flanders,
expressions so much beneath him'. However, thanks to the
recent discovery of 'manuscripts of his alteration', we can be

given an improved version of the novel – which has been purged
by Noble or one of his collaborators of all of its sex and most of
its cynicism. 'Laetitia' (nameless no longer) dies a saintly death
at the end of the reconstituted narrative, and 'Daniel Defoe' is
made to report that in her final illness 'she was zealously fervent
in her devotions . . . constantly preparing herself for a future
state . . . frequently attended by some eminent divines', until
death came, 'to the grief and sorrow of the poor, to whom she
had been a kind benefactress'. Perhaps appropriately, Defoe's
own name had become a useful commercial property for a man
with his own fictions to sell.

Francis Noble had already been responsible for first putting
Defoe's name to *Roxana*. In 1775 he published *The History of
Mademoiselle de Beleau; or, The New Roxana*, a version much
altered from the original. Noble's Roxana is considerably less
criminal and, in lengthy additions to Defoe's text, rediscovers
the joys of being a good wife and mother. (In the original, she
ends the novel implying that she has arranged the murder of
her troublesome daughter.) This too had a title page announcing
it to be 'Published by Mr. Daniel D Foe', adding 'And from
papers found, Since his decease, It appears was greatly altered by
Himself; and From the said Papers, the Present Work is produced'.[10] In Defoe's supposed voice, the preface explains that,
since the novel's first publication, the author has been 'rallied' by
'my old friend and acquaintance Mr. Thomas Southerne' for
making 'the Lady, the Heroine of the Work, so unnatural to her
children in her disowning them'.[11] Noble's 'Defoe' defends himself saying that he has had conversations with 'the Lady herself',
'so lately as the year 1723, in which year she died', but concedes
that he had originally changed her 'true' story for the sake of the
moral. Now he has decided 'to restore the children'.[12]

Noble specialized in the publishing of novels. He was also the
proprietor, with his brother, of a circulating library, which lent

out many of those novels. He had already published editions of several of Defoe's novels without specifying their authorship, including an edition of *Moll Flanders*, published in 1741. *Moll Flanders* and *Roxana* were both successful books, going through many different editions. Now he was repackaging them. We know very little about how these particular novels were received, and how widespread was the assumption that Defoe was their author. Defoe's *Robinson Crusoe*, also anonymous, was an immediate success and did provoke interest in its authorship. We even have evidence of some initial misattribution.[13] As well as being a best-seller, and a work of startling novelty, *Robinson Crusoe* was not morally suspect like Defoe's other novels. Its narrator may have wandered from God, but he does not steal or cheat or fornicate. Ironically, the two Defoe novels that were mistaken for genuine memoirs, *A Journal of the Plague Year* and *Memoirs of a Cavalier*, both excited considerable interest in attribution.[14] But *Moll Flanders* and *Roxana* were both too 'low' to merit attribution. Defoe is often mentioned as an author in his own lifetime and shortly after, but as a controversialist or satirist (or author of *Robinson Crusoe*), never as the author of *Moll Flanders* or *Roxana*. We do not know if any reader supposed them to have female authors because they had female narrators.

Defoe's fiction is like his 'heroines': from humble origins, socially mobile, opportunistic. We have discovered its literary qualities in retrospect. Until very late in the eighteenth century, it was critically invisible, not part of literature. Much that might have seemed clumsy by older standards of literary style now seems appropriate: the narrators' checks and repetitions, their garrulity and finickiness with detail. All these are given as the effects of a character trying to order the past. Thus the phrases that especially let us hear this effort, and that punctuate the narrative: 'I should have told you . . . as I have said . . . but that by the way . . .' And thus that obsession with 'particulars', the eagerness with details, that distinguishes all Defoe's narrators. Moll and Roxana are self-made women. In novels, 'making yourself' often means making your fortune, finding a place in the world, and an ending to adventure and uncertainty. For Moll and Roxana it also means trying to make your story. Like all Defoe's adventurers, Moll Flanders looks back on a life of sinfulness and opportunism; it is a life that she must both embrace (it has made her what she is) and renounce (now she is a penitent). She tells the story in order to make sense of who she is. So when we get to her last sentence, and the resolution 'to spend the Remainder of our Years in sincere Penitence, for the wicked Lives we have lived', we are supposed to have arrived at the person who sits down to write the first sentence of the book.[15]

The other side of this opportunism is the fear that stems from the uncertainty of her origins, and her identity. This is why, while finding pseudonyms useful, she fears being named. When she is taken before a magistrate she has to face the question she most dreads: 'First he asked my Name, which I was very loath to give.'[16] Your name is the past catching up with you. When she begins to realize that she has married her own brother, and that her mother-in-law is, in fact, also her own mother, a name is what is most 'terrible': 'I began to be very uneasy, but coming to one Particular that requir'd telling her Name, I thought I should have sunk down in the place.'[17] Incest represents the ultimate loss of identity, and the ultimate risk run by those who would like to be self-made. The heroine of *Roxana* (whose proper title was *The Fortunate Mistress*) is similarly a creature of disguise, her many pseudonyms listed on the sensationalist title page of the novel's first edition. 'Roxana' is merely another one of these, a name she acquires by 'foolish Accident' when she dresses up in exotic Eastern costume for a courtly masquerade.[18] Writing as a woman, Defoe imagines a condition of shifting identity, open to opportunity yet also subject to the wishes of others.

Probably the single most influential novel of the eighteenth century (the work that made novels respectable) was another anonymous book in which a male author wrote in a female voice: Samuel Richardson's *Pamela*, published in 1740. Though its author was a successful businessman in his fifties, the novel spoke through the letters and journals of its fifteen-year-old heroine, a servant girl who has to fight for her 'virtue' against the advances of her sexually predatory master, Mr B. The novel's prefatory material in its first edition treated the story that followed as if it really did emerge from a collection of letters. The title page declared it to be 'A Narrative which has its Foundation in TRUTH and NATURE', a formulation that artfully hesitated between admitting it was fiction and pretending it was not. The book's preface was headed 'by the Editor' and recommended its instructive and improving influences with the observation that '*an* Editor *may reasonably be supposed to judge with an Impartiality which is rarely to be met with in an* Author *towards his own works*'.[19] Next came a couple of absurdly laudatory letters that Richardson had procured from acquaintances who had read the novel in manuscript; both of these were dutifully addressed to 'the Editor of *Pamela*'. The only author was supposed to be Pamela herself.

Pamela was almost immediately a huge success and it could not be long before an author already known to some would be known to all. Richardson's doctor, George Cheyne, wrote to him a month after the novel was first published in November 1740 to reassure him, 'You need not be asham'd to own it, it will do no Dishonour to either your Heart or your Head.'[20] Richardson was apprehensive, or pretending to be so. He was also exploiting the form of the novel-in-letters to present a narrative that was to seem natural, untutored, spontaneous. The writer Aaron Hill, whose daughters were in Richardson's circle, read the copy that they had been sent and found it easy enough to guess the identity of its author. 'Who is he, Dear Sir? and where, and how, has he been able to hide, hitherto, such an encircling and all-mastering Spirit?'[21] Hill later told fellow author David Mallet that Richardson had been 'very loth . . . a long time, to confess it'. Almost a year after *Pamela*'s first publication, Richardson told a friend, Mrs Mary Barber, that he had originally wanted to limit knowledge of his authorship to about six friends and that he regretted his name becoming public. 'I have suffer'd by it, as well in my own Mind, as in the Malice and Envy of others.'

Richardson's novel was successful beyond his expectations, but also controversial in ways that he cannot have foreseen. A stream of articles and sermons, parodies and mock sequels, came out in the months and years after *Pamela*'s publication. One of the many ripostes to what soon seemed the book of its age has survived that first controversy. Henry Fielding's anonymous *Shamela* was published five months after the first appearance of *Pamela*. It deliciously mocks the 'present tense manner' of Richardson's narrator, who must record things in her letters almost as they are happening.

> Mrs. *Jervis* and I are just in Bed, and the Door unlocked; if my Master should come——Odsbobs! I hear him just coming in at the Door. You see I write in the present Tense, as Parson *Williams* says. Well, he is in Bed between us, we both shamming a Sleep, he steals his Hand into my Bosom, which I, as if in my Sleep, press close to me with mine, and then pretend to awake . . .[22]

It is possible that, when he wrote it, Fielding did not know that Richardson was the author of *Pamela*.[23] Fielding knew many of the writers and journalists who would have been gossiping about the authorship of this best-seller, and, as has been pointed out in a recent scholarly compilation of responses to *Pamela*,

Richardson's identity was well enough known by the time *Shamela* appeared to be heavily hinted at in the press.[24] Fielding later became an admirer of *Clarissa* and a correspondent of Richardson's; his sister Sarah was one of Richardson's followers. While Richardson, with a parade of reluctance, owned himself the author of *Pamela*, Fielding would never admit to having written *Shamela*.

Richardson's anonymity was strangely persistent. When *Clarissa* was published – to be received with the kind of critical respect of which he had dreamt – its title page declared it to be 'published by the editor of Pamela'. Its Preface again stuck to the fiction that this was a collection of real letters, speaking for 'the editor to whom it was referred to publish the whole in such a way as he should think would be most acceptable to the public'.[25] This 'editor' remained nameless. Richardson's name was on the novel's title page, but as the book's printer rather than as its author. By all contemporary accounts Richardson was hungry for the regard of readers and critics. Though he might have been anxious to act out the modesty of a gentleman, he relished the admiration that his novels brought him. He cultivated a wide circle of mostly female 'advisers', with whom he discussed his fiction in a copious correspondence. In the cases of both Defoe and Richardson writing as women, it is not modesty or reticence that seem the best explanations of authorial disguise. It is more like creative necessity. Defoe's fabrication of memoir is his way of being true to a probable world, as well as catching the pulse of adventure and danger. Women are a special interest to this chronicler of the opportunities and risks of a commercial world because they are its most prized or most despised commodities. For Richardson, too, there is an intimate relationship between the genre in which he is writing and the experience of a young woman. His novels are the records of private feelings, the language that he supposes peculiarly feminine. Letter-writing itself

– one of the main activities of the heroines of all three of his novels – is supposed to be a feminine gift.

Richardson's virtue-loving *Pamela* influenced John Cleland's pornographic *Memoirs of a Woman of Pleasure* (1748–9), sometimes known as 'Fanny Hill'. This was similarly published as if it were the genuine autobiography of its heroine, with no indication of its true author. It is usually assumed that its anonymity was Cleland's attempt to protect himself, but in fact his authorship readily became known and the Privy Council had no problems identifying him and summoning him for indecency. We might also think of his book's anonymity as an aspect of its arousing presentation of itself as a true memoir. Some novelists went further down the road of impersonation. We now know that in the second half of the eighteenth century there were several male novelists pretending to be female, invariably under the guise of 'a lady' or 'a young lady' on the title page.[26] The possibilities of such anonymous impersonation reached well beyond fiction. There is evidence that readers and critics, aware of the increasing number of female authors publishing work from the mid-eighteenth century, were alert to the possibility that some of the new works by nameless female hands might, in fact, have male authors, albeit undistinguished ones. In 1759, writing in one of the two leading reviews of the time, Oliver Goldsmith superciliously described the recent harvest of 'Novels . . . poems, morality, essays and letters, all written by ladies'.[27] It was evident from what followed that he was referring not to the actual authorship of these works, but to the tag 'by a Lady' (or similar) on the title page.

> Yet, let not the ladies carry off all the glories of the late production ascribed to them; it is plain by the style, and a nameless somewhat in the manner, that pretty fellows, coffee-critics, and dirty shirted dunces have sometimes a share in the

achievement. We have detected so many of these imposters already, that in future we shall look on every publication that shall be ascribed to a lady as the work of one of this amphibious fraternity.

Goldsmith intends to mock the trend for more and more 'ladies' to publish their writing, yet he was himself a denizen of Grub Street and is likely to have known something of what the hacks of the time might be up to. He is thinking of men who wrote for money and might have wanted to make themselves into 'ladies' for commercial reasons. There might also have been motives of simple self-gratification. We can never know, for instance, how many male writers of the late eighteenth century published verse under female pseudonyms in magazines, where 'women's poetry' had become fashionable. Roger Lonsdale notes the example of minor poet William Upton, who boasted in 1789 that he had published verse under the name 'Louisa' and received enthusi-astic responses from male readers.[28]

When it came to novels, a reader of the time could hardly ever know, or hope to guess, the true authorship of some particular work of fiction, recently borrowed from the circulating library. James Raven cites four known examples of, admittedly obscure, novels of this period that we know to have had male authors even though they were declared to be 'by a Lady'.[29] The fact that one of these declarations was in a newspaper advertisement, where a publisher was puffing his product (Arthur Gifford's 1785 novel *Omen*), suggests that there might seem to be a commercial advantage in having a certain kind of fiction be thought of as authored by a woman. He also produces evidence that reviewers were professionally sceptical about such declarations.[30] Raven speculates that female authorship might produce greater critical leniency, but a likelier thought is that a woman writer would be supposed to know better the private worlds of courtship or familiar correspondence into which fiction liked to delve. Samuel Richardson, after all, had such a thought about his own novels.

The rapid attribution of *Pamela* to Richardson was a symptom of its literary achievement, as its author well knew. In the realm of fiction, anonymity was the rule until the end of the century; over seventy per cent of novels published between 1770 and 1800 were anonymous.[31] In the first decades of the nineteenth century, it was still common; between 1800 and 1830, almost half of new novels were anonymous.[32] The period also marks the growth of a different phenomenon, which was to become distinctive of Victorian fiction: the use of pseudonyms. The supposed authors of the novels of Defoe and Richardson were their protagonists. Truly pseudonymous authors of fiction in the nineteenth century were distinct from the characters in the novels themselves. Those who adopted pseudonyms may have sometimes wished out of timidity to remain unknown, but where they were at all successful, they made readers and critics inquisitive. They advertised mysteries. Many nineteenth-century novelists adopted pseudonyms (Cuthbert Bede, Ouida, Blanche Oram) that announced themselves as fictional.

It is hardly surprising that examples of women writers adopting masculine pseudonyms were far more frequent than the opposite. A survey of the known identities of the authors writing for Unwin's 'Pseudonym Library', discussed in the previous chapter, reveals that none of the men took a female pseudonym. Of the eleven male authors, seven took masculine pseudonyms, three wrote their names in foreign alphabets, and one used initials. Of the twenty-six female authors, thirteen took female pseudonyms, six took pseudonyms of indeterminate gender ('Lanoe Falconer'), and seven took male pseudonyms.[33] Examples of women choosing masculine pseudonyms are legion; it is much rarer to find men writing as women. One example of a novel written by a man but provoking speculation that it was by a woman was R. D. Blackmore's first novel, *Clara Vaughan* (1864). It had a female first-person narrator and was published anonymously. *The Saturday Review* took the author too to be female, detecting characteristic feminine ignorance of 'the simplest principles of physics, and of the most elementary rules or usages of the law'.[34] When Blackmore revised the novel for a new edition, published under his own name, he observed in the preface that, as well as being classified as a 'sensation novel' by 'many reviewers', it was 'even attributed by more than one to the inspiration of a popular female author'.[35] The novel is certainly sensational: its heroine and narrator tells of her daredevil exploits as she tries to trace the murderer of her father (who turns out to have been the mistaken victim of a Corsican vendetta). Perhaps given the subject-matter (the villain is a professor of anatomy whose vivisection experiments are described in disturbing detail) some reviewers presumed that the author was a man. The *Saturday Review* inferred that the author was female and launched an attack on the ignorance of 'lady novelists'. It declared with ringing confidence that 'the primary conception of the personages, the situations in which they are introduced, and the tone of speech and sentiment throughout, are unmistakeably the creation of a female mind'.[36] The reviewer in *The Athenaeum*, in contrast, while not knowing the author's identity, referred to him throughout by the masculine pronoun. ' "Clara Vaughan" is not a story that will bear criticism, but the author has shown that he possesses powers which he may use for a more satisfactory result than the present, and we hope that he will do so.'[37]

There were some odd examples of male Victorian writers who adopted female pseudonyms. The Scottish essayist John Skelton appeared in magazines under the pseudonym 'Shirley', which derived from Charlotte Brontë's novel. He published both *Nugae Criticae* and *A Campaigner at Home* under this pseudonym. His

novel *Thalatta! Or the Great Commoner* was anonymous but, as
if he were hedging his bets, had a Preface signed 'S.' Algernon
Swinburne wrote an epistolary novel, *A Year's Letters*, in 1862,
but could not publish under his own name because some of the
characters were based on members of his own family. It was
finally published in serialized form in the *Tatler* in 1877 under
the name 'Mrs Horace Manners'. It did not appear in book form
until 1904, as *Love's Cross-Currents*. In the novel the sixty-year-
old Lady Midhurst presides over the secretive adulteries of her
family. One character, Reginald Harewood, is apparently a self-
portrait by the author: he writes sonnets on the sea and dis-
courses on flagellation. An ironical preface complained that the
lady novelist had had her principles 'vitiated' by a long stay in
France. Swinburne was evidently annoyed when word got out
that he was the author.[38] William C. Russell adopted the pseudonym Eliza Rhyl Davies (as one among several) and may have
done so because he was so prolific. He was best known for his
nautical novels and biographies, which he published under his
own name. (Russell had earlier served in the British merchant
navy for eight years.) When he wished to diversify into other
fictional genres he fashioned new names and identities. The
romantic mysteries *The Mystery of Ashleigh Manor* (1874) and *A
Dark Secret* (1875) merited a female author, an escape from the
manliness of his bracing tales of the sea.

Speculation about the gender of any author who remained
truly anonymous was common amongst reviewers of Victorian
novels, and amongst readers. An 1871 review in the *Athenaeum*
of Thomas Hardy's first novel, *Desperate Remedies*, 'cannot
decide, satisfactorily to our mind, on the sex of the author'.[39]
The evidence for a female author is its 'close acquaintance . . .
with the mysteries of the female toilette'. (We might recall how
speculation about the gender of Currer Bell focused on his or
her knowledge of fabrics and styles of dresses.) On the other

hand, 'there are certain expressions to be met with in the book so remarkably coarse as to render it almost impossible that it should have come from the pen of an English lady.' The reviewer is stopped short of attributing the novel to a man by the reflection that 'all the best anonymous novels of the last twenty years . . . have been the work of female writers'.

There was one celebrated case at the end of the nineteenth century of a male author who published under a female pseudonym, and thereby inadvertently illustrated the inclination for attribution of critics and readers. William Sharp was already an established author under his own name before he began writing as a woman. Brought up in Edinburgh, he had developed a love of the Western Highlands and Islands during many boyhood visits and sailing trips with his father. This greatly influenced his future literary ventures. After failing to establish a career in law or banking, he moved to London and came into the orbit of Dante Gabriel Rossetti. His first book was an admiring study of Rossetti's work. He eventually became a successful literary journalist and art critic, as well as a biographer and poetry editor, but in the 1890s he withdrew from London literary life, travelling a good deal abroad. From 1893, when he was in his late thirties, he began writing as 'Fiona MacLeod'. Fiona Macleod was born in the Hebrides and lived on her own on Iona. She would lead a Celtic revival in Scottish literature and under her name Sharp would find temporary literary fame.

The first work he published using this pseudonym was a novel, *Pharais* (1894): the title is the Gaelic word for 'Paradise'. It is the story of Lora, who lives on the isle of Innisròn in the Outer Hebrides. Here, according to the book's preface, 'Anima Celtica still lives and breathes and hath her being.'[40] It is a primal place, whose inhabitants nurture subtle pagan beliefs and are visited by spirits and prophecies. There is much lyrical evocation of wind and water, 'the quietude of whisper-music exhaled as an odour by the sea', 'the majesty of the sea, reaching intolerably grand from endless horizons to horizons without end', and the like.[41] Lora's husband Alastair is ailing and tells her that 'the mind-dark' is coming upon him.[42] It is a fate prophesied by old Ian, the seer of the tribe, and has apparently afflicted his father and grandfather before him. Husband and wife decide to die together, along with the child that is still in Lora's womb. In the event, she gives birth and she and her child die, but Alastair lives on, mysteriously strengthened by his wife's sacrifice. As the novel ends he is gazing into 'an azure dusk', hearing from the heart of the sea 'a rumour as of muffled prophesyings, a Voice of Awe, a Voice of Dread'.[43]

Pharais was a critical if not a commercial success. There was considerable curiosity about its author, and Sharp provided evidence for his involvement by sending out some copies of the book, accompanied by a note, signed with his real name, saying how much he admired it. George Meredith received a copy in this way. The science writer and prolific novelist Grant Allen, however, received his copy accompanied by a letter signed 'Fiona MacLeod'. Allen read the book and wrote back appreciatively, asking, 'Are you Miss or Mrs. and do you live in Edinburgh?'[44] 'Questions as to the identity of the author were already "in the air",' observed his wife Elizabeth in the *Memoir* she published after Sharp's death. And by this she clearly meant that knowing readers speculated that 'Fiona MacLeod' was a pseudonym. Sharp himself took it that Allen's questions about 'Fiona MacLeod' implied just this speculation. 'If you are really going to say anything about my book,' he replied, 'I trust you will not hint playfully at any other authorship having suggested itself to you—or, indeed, at my name being a pseudonym.'[45] 'My name is really Fiona,' he added, imploring Allen not to talk of the name possibly being a disguise 'if chance should ever bring my insignificant self into any chit-chat'. Allen dutifully kept such speculation out of his enthusiastic review of the novel in the *Westminster Review*. Yet he also wrote to Sharp to say that he read *Pharais* 'with some doubt as to whether it was not your own production'.[46] Others, he said, thought likewise. Allen detected 'great likeness of style' between Sharp and Fiona MacLeod, yet also sensed in the latter a genuine 'feminine touch'. Already under pressure, Sharp declared that Fiona MacLeod was his cousin. Allen said archly that he would not be satisfied until Sharp showed him 'the "beautiful lassie" in person'.

Two more novels, *The Mountain Lovers* and *The Sin Eater*, appeared in the next year. In 1897 there was a volume of MacLeod's poems, *From the Hills of Dream: Mountain Songs and Island Runes*, which included the 'songs' that Sharp had composed for MacLeod's 1896 volume of stories, *The Washer at the Ford*. The 'hills of dream' of the title poem are a place in the imagination, where the inspired female bard is closer to the Celtic spirits that haunt her poems ('There is a land of Dream; / I have trodden its golden ways').[47] They are also real: the mountains and islands of the west of Scotland, whose landscapes are lyrically celebrated. (Under his own name, Sharp was simultaneously working on an edition of the poems of Ossian, 'translated' by James Macpherson in the mid-eighteenth century: a fake, we might say, deceived by another fake.) The poems mix ecstatic description and verse tales, the latter appearing to have some folk origin. Spirits of the dead speak to the poet.

> I have heard the sea-wind sighing
> Where the dune-grasses grow,
> The sighing of the dying
> Where the salt tides flow.[48]

There is nothing specifically female about most of the poems, but the volume ends with a section of 'Lyric Runes' that does purport to give us the chants and laments of Celtic women.

O most bitter for the heart of woman
To have loved and been beloved with passion,
To have known the height and depth, the vision
Of triple-flaming love—and in the heart-self
Sung a song of deathless love, immortal,
Sunrise-haired, and starry-eyed, and wondrous.[49]

At the back of the book were three pages of highlights from reviews that had lauded the achievements of 'Miss MacLeod'. Critical sentiment was epitomized by the notice in the *Pall Mall Gazette*, which clearly knew the true voice of a Celtic spirit when it spoke.

A Celt of the Celts, Miss Macleod loves this people, who have the gift of charm—loves them, their country, and their legends, knows every curve and spiral of their nature as she knows the aspects of the hills, the pull of the currents, and the voice of the storm. The elemental passions of an elemental race are the themes of her stories.

Fiona MacLeod was becoming a fully fledged literary figure. In a rush there followed more poems, some essays and even a couple of plays. Through all these, as Macleod's foreword to a collection of her tales put it, 'goes the wind of the Gaelic spirit, which everywhere desires infinitude, but in the penury of things as they are turns upon itself to the dim enchantment of dreams'.[50] All this time Sharp also published as before under his own name and carefully kept the secret of his dual identity. A small number of friends were told and were sworn to secrecy. Yet the evidence is that acquaintances and fellow writers worked out who the true author was. One keen reader of MacLeod who knew the Sharps wrote to say that 'he was finally convinced from internal evidence that William Sharp was the author of these books under discussion'.[51] But some readers at least were fooled.

One enthusiast, according to Elizabeth Sharp, wrote proposing marriage to Fiona MacLeod. 'Similarities of taste, details of position, profession, etc., were carefully given.' Sharp had created an author who spoke for the fading spirit of Celtic culture, divorced from his own experience as an educated, cosmopolitan, modern man.

By becoming a woman, he also proved 'the theory then in vogue among some men and women of his artistic generation that the prophetic artist was hermaphroditic by nature'.[52] When he invented an entry for her in the 1900 *Who's Who* he believed that he was giving conventionalized form to a real presence. In her memoir his widow explained that she was setting out to explain and vindicate 'the dual literary expression of himself'.[53] In 1902 he wrote in a letter to a friend of 'the overwhelmingly felt mystery of a dual life, and a reminiscent life, and a woman's life and nature' within him.[54] Clearly this invented personage took him over. Elizabeth Sharp also believed that 'Fiona MacLeod' was an aspect of her husband's personality, as did those friends who were in the know. Patrick Geddes, who was one of these, wrote to Elizabeth Sharp saying that 'W. S. in his deepest moods became F. M., a sort of dual personality in short, not a mere nom-de-guerre'.[55] The possession of his imagination was, by all accounts, traumatic as well as enthusing. Sharp's health was always fragile, and periods of inspiration in the guise of Fiona MacLeod tended to culminate in nervous collapse.

'The production of the Fiona Macleod work was accomplished at a heavy cost to the author as that side of his nature deepened and became dominant,' recalled his wife.[56] The stress might have been increased by the continuing speculation about the identity of Fiona MacLeod. This was but the natural consequence of the interest aroused by Sharp's Celtic dreams amongst a readership used to pseudonyms and habituated to the game of attribution. Sharp was indignant about these inevitable responses and began publicly denying authorship. In 1896 *The Highland News* published an article headed 'Mystery! Mystery! All in a Celtic Haze', in which it was decided that 'Miss Fiona Macleod does not exist'. No one has seen her. No one knows her in Iona (a 'literary detective' has enquired).[57] As 'Mr. William Sharp has declared himself to be Miss Fiona Macleod's uncle', and is himself interested in 'Celtic things', the 'natural inference' must be that 'he has written the books'. The author was rather encouraged in the thought by the fact that Sharp had written a letter to the Glasgow *Evening News*, which had also doubted the existence of this lyrical new writer, explicitly declaring 'Miss Fiona Macleod is not Mr. William Sharp'. Yet everywhere – and in print – the two names were being associated.

W. B. Yeats, who was already an acquaintance of Sharp's, became another of Fiona MacLeod's admirers. He discovered in her inspired rendition of Hebridean life and death something akin to what he discovered amongst the people and legends of Ireland. For, as he put it, 'She felt about the world, and the creatures of its winds and waters, emotions that were of one kind with the emotions of these grave peasants, the most purely Celtic peasants in Ireland.' 'Like all who have Celtic minds', he added, she had 'in her hands the keys of those gates of the primeval world, which shut behind more successful races, when they plunged into material progress'.[58] Yet eventually Yeats took to putting 'Fiona MacLeod' in inverted commas in his letters to Sharp and it is likely that by 1897 Sharp had had to confess his authorship to Yeats.[59]

Publicly he resolutely kept the secret of her identity. When an anonymous article in the *Daily Chronicle* in 1899 claimed that Sharp and MacLeod were one and the same, Sharp wrote to deny it.[60] In 1902 he was put forward for a civil list pension but, despite a perilous financial situation, refused to have the application pursued because he would have had to admit to his invention of Fiona MacLeod.[61] ('Her' oeuvre rather than 'his' made him a deserving case.) He died in 1905, leaving a letter that disclosed his identity. As well as admitting that he was 'Fiona Macleod', he acknowledged that some might feel that he had 'deceived' them. 'But, in an intimate sense this is not so . . . Only, it is a mystery. I cannot explain.'[62] He was unprepared to admit that the critics and readers of his age were able to detect a common authorial ruse. By 1905, perhaps only a writer with such strange belief in his own creative impulses could live out his self-concealment so completely.

5

DANGER

In the last week of February 1663, the London printer John Twyn awaited execution in Newgate Prison. Convicted of treason, he faced a terrible end: he was to be hanged, drawn and quartered, made to die in prolonged agony as a terrifying lesson to onlookers. His offence was to have printed an anonymous pamphlet, *A Treatise of the Execution of Justice*, which described the monarch as accountable to his subjects and justified the people's right of rebellion. Only three years after the Restoration of Charles II, with the memory of the execution of his father Charles I still sharp, this was extremely dangerous ground. According to the tract's full title, read out in court, it showed that 'if the Magistrates pervert Judgement, the People are bound by the Law of God to execute Judgement without them and upon them'.[1] There was no suggestion that Twyn had written it, only that he had turned it from manuscript to print. In his condemned cell he was visited by the Ordinary of Newgate – the prison's chaplain. According to an officially licensed account, the Ordinary spent 'much time and pains . . . pressing him to a *confession* both of his *offence*, and of the *Author* of that Treasonable Piece, for which he was to Die. His Answer was, That *it was not his Principle to betray the Author*.'[2] The Ordinary told him that the disclosure might save his life, implying that if the State were able to find and punish the author, the printer might yet be allowed to live. Twyn replied 'that he neither could do it, nor did believe himself obliged to it if he could; for better (sayes he) *one* suffer, than *many*'.[3]

It is unclear whether Twyn himself knew the author's identity or not, whether he was unwilling or simply unable to seek escape through attribution. Having refused Anglican communion – a sign that he was a Protestant dissenter, and more likely to be anti-monarchist – he went to his death. In the cautionary manner of the times, his head was placed on a spike over Ludgate and his quarters on other city gates. Even on the scaffold, Twyn had protested, as he had maintained throughout his trial, that he had not been aware of the substance of what he had printed. One of the main issues during that trial had been whether or not Twyn had read the work that he was printing. The night-time raid on his premises in Cloth Fair, near Smithfield, was led in person by the Surveyor of the Press, Sir Roger L'Estrange, the man in charge of regulating publishing in England. He had testified that Twyn had admitted correcting the printed sheets and that, when asked what he thought of the contents, had said, '*Methoughts it was mettlesome stuff, the man was a hot fiery man that wrote it*, but he knew no hurt in it.'[4] Dickenson, one of L'Estrange's constables, had testified that he had said to Twyn, 'I wonder you would Print such a thing as this, you could not choose but know it was very dangerous to do any such thing.'[5] Twyn had apparently replied, '*I thought he was a good smart angry fellow, it was mettlesome stuff.*' Joseph Walker, Twyn's apprentice, had been pressed to say not only that Twyn had been present, superintending the impression of the *Treatise*, but that he had personally corrected sheets as they were printed. Lord Chief Justice Hyde, presiding at the trial, had extracted the agreement that the corrections had been made in handwriting much like Tywn's, and that no other person had been present to make these corrections.

All this was to show that Twyn was an active promoter of sedition rather than a mere functionary of the press. There seems little doubt that he did sympathize with the tract he was producing.[6] With the author concealed, the state made him responsible. Its agents would dearly have liked to discover the author. L'Estrange had questioned Twyn closely about the origins of the 'copy' – the manuscript from which the pamphlet was printed.

> I asked him where he had the *copy*? He told me *he knew not; it was brought to him by an unknown hand*; I told him he must give an account of it; he told me at last *he had it from* Calverts *Maid*: I asked him where the copy was, he told me *he could not tell.*[7]

Calvert seems to be the London bookseller Giles Calvert, whose business at the sign of the Spread Eagle in St Paul's Churchyard was later run by his wife, Elizabeth. Notable as a publisher of Quaker texts, under Cromwell he was appointed official printer to the Council of State, an indication of some political affinity with the republican regime.[8] Both Calverts disappear from imprints in 1663. Giles Calvert might have been in hiding, and seems to have died within the next year. Elizabeth Calvert was arrested soon after Twyn and appears to have been imprisoned for a while, though in 1665 she was again at large and her name was appearing on imprints, mostly of devotional texts. Identifying Calvert did not help the authorities to the author. L'Estrange had told Twyn, 'If you will be so ingenuous to produce the Copy, and discover the Author you may find mercy for your self.' A servant had then produced part of the manuscript. The rest of it, according to Twyn, had been delivered 'to Mistriss *Calverts* maid, at the Rose in *Smithfield*'.[9]

At his trial, Twyn had denied knowing the handwriting on the fragment of the manuscript that was recovered. Hyde had insisted, to no avail, that exposing the author was the printer's one chance of mercy. 'The best you can now do toward amends for this Wickednesse you have done, is by discovering the

Authour of this Villainous Book; If not, you must not expect, and indeed God forbid that there should be any mercy towards you.'[10] 'I never knew the Author of it, nor who it was, nor whence it came, but as I told you.' Three days later, an associate of Twyn's, the bookseller Thomas Brewster, was tried, alongside a printer and a bookbinder, for publishing the supposed dying speeches of the men executed for condemning Charles I to death. Brewster defended himself by saying, 'I did it in my Trade, we do not use to read what we put to Print or Sell ... The Bookseller only minds the getting of a penny.'[11] In reply, Hyde expressed clearly the principle underlying the verdict on Twyn. Passing sentence, he declared that a printer or a publisher is responsible for what a book contains. 'He must not say *He knew not what was in it*; that is no Answer in Law.'[12] Yet clearly Twyn was made to suffer in an author's stead. His was an extreme example of what occurred commonly before the nineteenth century: where anonymity was a necessary way of hiding from danger, that danger passed to others involved in the production of the offending work. The search for an author was sometimes undertaken by the state itself. When a provoking anonymous publication could not be attributed, it was often easiest to identify and punish the printer.

For the first three centuries or more of printing, danger lay mostly in matters of politics and religion. Twyn was not the first printer to be executed for the output of his press. In 1584, William Carter had been convicted of treason and hanged, drawn and quartered for printing a London edition of Gregory Martin's *A Treatise of Schisme* (1578), a work of Catholic polemic that argued against the practice of outward conformity with the Church of England.[13] It was not anonymous, but Martin had left England and was safely ensconced in the English College in Douai. After Twyn two more printers were put to death for what they printed, and in both cases the offending works were

anonymous. In 1693 William Anderton was tried for high treason for printing and publishing two Jacobite pamphlets, *Remarks
upon the present confederacy and late revolution in England* and
A French Conquest, neither desirable nor practicable. Anderton
had produced these works, which declared King William an
illegitimate ruler and advocated the return of James II, on a
secret press and was clearly aware that risk was involved. Despite
insistent questioning, he refused to name the author or authors.[14]
He was sentenced to death and hanged at Tyburn on 12 June
1693. In 1720 the eighteen-year-old printer's apprentice John
Matthews was executed for printing an anonymous pro-Jacobite
pamphlet, *Vox Populi Vox Dei*, which supported the claim to the
throne of James II's son, the so-called Pretender. This was the
only case during the eighteenth century when a publication
brought a conviction for treason. Matthews was the last printer
in England to die for what came off his press.

From the sixteenth to the eighteenth centuries, printers suffered in other ways in the place of unnamed authors. With the
physical evidence upon them – the printed sheets, the type, the
secret press – they were often easier to detect than authors. For
more than two centuries, printers were fined, imprisoned or put
in the pillory for printing supposedly seditious works whose
authors remained concealed. In any survey of the dangers that
have sometimes made authors anonymous, their printers become
part of the story. Different things have made publication dangerous at different times. In 1538 the first licensing law was
introduced, requiring all books to be approved by the Privy
Council or another royal nominee. Proclamations issued and
Statutes passed during the reign of Henry VIII were aimed at
controlling religious doctrine. There was no interest in publications that 'meddle not with interpretations of Scripture'.[15]
Scripture itself was contentious. William Tyndale's translation of
the New Testament, the first English version ever published, was

printed in the German city of Worms in 1525 or 1526. Of the
thousands that were produced, only two copies survive. Both
lack a title page, but we know from comments that Tyndale
made elsewhere that he did not put his name to the book.[16]
Some two years later he thought better of his self-concealment,
declaring in a signed preface to a later work,

> The cause why I set my name before this little treatise and
> have not rather done it in the new testament is that then I
> followed the counsel of Christ which exhorteth men Matt. vi.
> to do their good deeds secretly and to be content with the
> conscience of well doing, and that God seeth us, and patiently
> to abide the reward of the last day, which Christ hath pur-
> chased for us and now would I fain have done like wise but
> am compelled otherwise to do.[17]

Tyndale now declared himself. It was also a matter of pride:
he wished to dissociate himself from his assistant on the New
Testament translation, William Roye. So when he published a
translation of the first five books of the Old Testament a year
later, its prologue was headed 'W. T. The Reader'. His notoriety
placed Tyndale at great risk. He was pursued by Cardinal Wolsey's
agents, eventually arrested in Antwerp and executed in Vilvorde,
north of Brussels, in October 1536.

In the long history of attempts by rulers to control what was
published, anonymity was frequently seen as a special threat and
sometimes outlawed. In 1546 Henry VIII issued a proclamation
requiring any printer to set out on every copy of a work his own
name and that of the author, as well as the date of printing.
Anyone disobeying would be liable to 'imprisonment and punishment of his body'.[18] Under Edward VI, after a period of per-
missiveness, stern new measures to control printed material
were enforced. All works were to be licensed before publication
by the King or a committee of his privy councillors. The measure

was the idea of John Dudley, Duke of Northumberland, a zealous Protestant who wished to do away with merely diverting
reading as well to suppress works with Roman Catholic sympathies.[19] With Mary's accession, Parliament extended the treason laws to cover printed material. A series of prohibitions and
proclamations were then directed against any Protestant 'books,
writings and works'. The punishment of the loss of the right
hand for slanders against the crown was introduced in 1555.[20]
In 1557 the Stationers' Company received its charter of incor-
poration and took up its role as the agency of state control.
Only its members, or those holding a special patent, could print
any work.

Under Elizabeth, an avowedly comprehensive licensing system
was established. From 1559, no book might be published without having first been approved by state censors. In reality, the
regulations were inconsistently obeyed or enforced.[21] The highest priority was given to suppressing Catholic texts, most of
them imported; next were the controversial works of radical
Protestants. A series of statutes passed through Parliament in
Elizabeth's reign forbidding almost anything written against the
monarch. Authors were not always within reach, even when
identifiable. The works most actively suppressed were Catholic
texts, whose authors, if living, were often in exile. In their stead,
the state pursued distributors and printers.

When the author could be found, the printer might escape
punishment, as in a notorious early case of a controversial
anonymous work. In 1579 John Stubbs (or Stubbe) had his
right hand cut off for writing *The Discoverie of a Gaping Gulf
Whereinto England is like to be swallowed by another French marriage*, a work opposing the proposed betrothal of Elizabeth I
to Francis, Duke of Alençon and Anjou. The pamphlet had
infuriated the Queen, who had issued a proclamation against it,
'being lately informed of a lewde seditious booke, of late rashly

compiled and secretly printed . . . to imprint a present feare in
the zealous sort, of the alteration of Christian Religion, by her
Majesties marriage'. It is 'a trumpe of sedition, secretly sownd-
ing in every subjects eare'.[22] There was a successful search for
both author and printer, though we do not know how they were
found. Stubbs seems to have made no effort to deny his authorship. According to William Camden's *Annales* (1625), when
Stubbs came to have his hand cut off he displayed his loyalty by
removing his hat with his other hand, crying 'God save the
Queen.'[23] He then spent a year and a half in prison. The book's
distributor, William Page, also lost his right hand, but its printer,
Hugh Singleton, though condemned by the court to the same
punishment, kept his hand 'for some undiscovered reason'.[24]

When a work antagonized the authorities, someone had to be
made responsible. John Field and Thomas Wilcox were the
scribes for the Puritan *Admonition to the Parliament* (1572), an
anonymous pamphlet that attacked the Church of England for
its system of bishops and archbishops and for its preservation of
vestiges of Roman Catholicism. They were sentenced to a year's
imprisonment. The pamphlet was secretly reprinted with additions by other members of their group, to be followed by further works in its defence. There was a royal proclamation against
Puritan publications the next year, but the future Archbishop of
Canterbury John Whitgift reported that pamphlets were 'in
every man's hand and mouth'.[25] The reign of Elizabeth saw the
first age of pamphlet controversy; few controversial publications
were not related to the cause or influence of Puritanism. Though
concerned with Christian doctrine, they opened the possibilities
– for mockery, mischief and anonymous provocation – that
more literary satirists would pursue in the seventeenth and
eighteenth centuries. An anecdote of the times nicely represents
the mix of political and literary considerations involved in the
business of discovering authors. Queen Elizabeth apparently

told Sir Francis Bacon that she would have the person whose name appeared on the title page of a treasonable publication 'racked, to produce his author'. Bacon replied, 'Nay, madame, he is a doctor: never rack his person, rack his style; let him have pen, ink, and paper and help of books, and be enjoined to continue his story, and I will undertake, by collating his styles, to judge whether he were the author.'[26] The attributor of texts needed to be a good reader.

Torture, as recommended by the Queen, was to play its part in the efforts of the authorities to solve the most notorious case of anonymity during Elizabeth's reign. This was the taunting pseudonymity of the so-called Martin Marprelate tracts, seven pamphlets that appeared at intervals between October 1588 and September 1589. They are the first important example of anonymous works where the author hides from danger, but also uses anonymity creatively. Martin Marprelate ('bad priest') was the fictional writer of these mocking Puritan descriptions of the corruption of the Church of England. Unlike other Puritan publications of the period, they risked direct attacks on named individuals, senior members of the Anglican hierarchy. They openly broke the law of libel, which forbad any one to 'tele any false Newes lyes or other such lyke false things of Prelats'.[27] Indeed, they ridiculed the very existence of bishops and archbishops. One of their main targets was John Whitgift, a noted foe to Puritanism, who had become Archbishop of Canterbury in 1583. Whitgift had set out to enforce obedience to monarch and established church. In particular, he had required members of the clergy to endorse the Book of Common Prayer in every aspect, and to use it in all religious services. To restrain Puritan influence he had obtained a decree from the Star Chamber forbidding any publication not authorized by himself or the Bishop of London. This allowed him to control the Stationers' Company and decide the number of printing presses permitted.

He revived a law decreeing the severest penalties for seditious or libellous books and appointed twelve persons to be responsible for licensing works for printing. The Marprelate pamphlets were responses to this as well as to his theological stringency. Their very existence, daring Whitgift to discover their origins, mocked his efforts at the control of opinion. Their anonymity was designed to protect their author or authors; it also permitted their satirical use of parody and impersonation.

The first tract, published in October 1588, is usually called *The Epistle* and presents itself as an introduction to the forthcoming epitome of an anti-Puritan tome by John Bridges, Dean of Salisbury. Bridges was a diligent, prolix advocate of Anglican orthodoxy, and *The Epistle* regrets that, to do justice to his plodding prose, it too must be 'sometimes tediously duncical and absurd'.[28] Soon it is veering into cheerful name-calling, denouncing bishops as 'pettie popes / and pettie Antichrists', while the Archbishop of Canterbury himself is 'the 'Pope of Lambeth' and is elsewhere variously dubbed Canterbury Caiaphas, His Gracelessness, your Canterburiness, His Grease, John of Kankerbury and simply John of Cant.[29] It is spiced with anecdotes about the private vices of particular bishops. John Aylmer, Bishop of London, is a petty pilferer, who receives stolen cloth for his cushion covers.[30] He fails to pay his servants or his grocer and likes to play bowls on the Sabbath.[31] 'I warrant you Martin will be found no lyar / he bringeth in nothing without testimonie.'[32]

Whitgift is a closet Catholic, cardinal in waiting, who allows recusant printers to ply their nefarious trade while the Puritan printer Robert Waldegrave 'dares not shew his face for the bloodthirstie desire you have for his life'.[33] As it happens, Waldegrave, who had already suffered imprisonment for printing Puritan tracts, and had had his press destroyed by the authorities, was the printer of *The Epistle*, and of the next three Marprelate tracts.

His press was moved from one sympathizer's house to another to avoid detection: from Kingston-on-Thames to Northampton-shire to Coventry. A proclamation was issued against 'sundry schismatical and seditious bookes, diffamatorie Libels and other fantastical writings', which had been 'secretly published and dispersed'.[34] Official efforts to find who was behind Marprelate were fevered, and duly became the subject matter of the second Marprelate tract, *The Epitome*. This begins by speaking in the voice of a 'poor gentleman' who wonders, in its opening para-graph, why 'my cleagie masters' put themselves to the trouble of 'posting over citie and countrie for poor Martin'.[35] The taunts return at the opening of the fourth tract, *Hay any worke for Cooper* (the title, a street cry of the time, is a mocking reference to Bishop Cooper of Winchester, ridiculed for his self-importance). 'I thought you to bee verye kind when you sent your Purcivaunts about the countrie to looke for me.'[36] Martin regrets that he will not tell them where he is, 'because I love not the ayre of the Clinke or Gatehouse in this colde time of Winter'. He goes on to glory in the heat of the controversy, remarking that the various ripostes to him have made more and more people aware of the arguments.

There was something heady for the satire's author or authors about its very danger, and you can hear this in its anonymous voice. By the time of the final pamphlet, *The protestatyon of Martin Marprelate*, Martin refers to the secret production of the Marprelate texts with something like bravado. He gives Whitgift a speech to his 'pursuivants' (his agents pursuing the producers of Marprelate's works) in which he asks,

Have you diligently soght mee out Walde-grave the Printer, Newman the Cobler, Sharpe the book binder of Northampton, and the seditious Welch man Penry, who you shall see will proove the Author of all these libelles.[37]

Soon it becomes a frenzied rant about trying to track down the
producers of these pamphlets, in which he advises his agents 'to
have a watch at al common innes, to see what carriage of paper,
and other stuffe, either goes from, or commes to London'. 'Ande
I thinke I shall grow starke madde with you, unlesse you bring
him.' The tracelessness of Martin is maddening evidence of
the prevalence of Puritanism in the country. A royal proclamation ordering the destruction of all Marprelate's works was
confirmation of their efficacy.

The pursuivants had had some success. After the fourth tract
was printed, John Hodgkins took over as printer from Waldegrave. The press was moved again. While printing a Marprelate
tract called *More work for the Cooper* in the summer of 1589,
Hodgkins and two assistants were arrested near Manchester and
the press, type and manuscript seized. Hodgkin was examined
under torture. His two assistants were also tortured. The three of
them had been taken to the Tower, where Hodgkin was interro-
gated and racked over some six weeks. It appears that the Queen
herself encouraged the interrogators in their brutal efforts.[38] He
admitted to being the printer, but repeatedly claimed not to
know the author. We do not know if he was eventually executed
or freed. After helping to produce the final tract, *The protestatyon*, Waldegrave fled to Scotland with one of those suspected
of being the author, John Penry. Others involved in harbouring
the press were betrayed by the bookbinder Henry Sharpe. The
Bishop of Rochester was charged with interrogating them and,
with others, using 'their best and uttermost endeavours to finde
the author of the said libells'.[39]

More than two years later, Penry returned to England. In May
1593 he was hanged for treason, his part in the Marprelate controversy perhaps the real reason. In prison, shortly before his
execution, he declared that the accusation that he had written
any of the Marprelate material was false.[40] In a letter to Lord

Burghley Penry said that he disliked Marprelate's jesting and raillery. Many Puritan preachers did indeed object to the tracts' scandalous humour.[41] Another prime suspect as the author, John Udall, a veteran of pamphlet attacks on the Anglican hierarchy, was arrested and later died in prison. In 1590 their associate Job Throckmorton had been charged with participating in the printing of the tracts, and found guilty. Throckmorton was an MP outspoken in his Puritanism. At his trial he swore 'he was not Martin and knew not Martin'.[42] For reasons that remain unclear, he survived conviction and was eventually released. In 1595 Matthew Sutcliffe published an indictment of Throckmorton as Martin Marprelate, comparing the 'phrase and manner of writing' in Throckmorton's own letters with the style of the tracts.[43] Marprelate, meanwhile, had disappeared, though his satires had provoked responses from many writers, including Thomas Nashe and Gabriel Harvey. Modern scholarship has continued the work of Whitgift's pursuivants, and academics have minutely detailed their hunt for the author, or authors.[44] Their suspects are the same as Whitgift's. The Marprelate tracts showed how prose satirists could exploit a self-protective anonymity to let loose something more complex than polemic: mockery, parody, impersonation.

The last, politically uncertain years of Elizabeth's reign saw sterner measures than ever against dangerous publications. In 1599 there was a ban on the publication of all satires (see Chapter 7). In 1601 a royal proclamation offered the huge sum of a hundred pounds to anyone offering information about the authorship of 'libels . . . tending to the slander of our royal person and state'.[45] The same year a lawyer's clerk was hanged in Smithfield after being identified as author of a published 'libel'. In the seventeenth century courts began to use the law of seditious libel, instead of that of treason, to chasten authors and publishers. The Court of Star Chamber developed with a special role in prosecuting political offenders. In 1630 the Court tried

Alexander Leighton, who had been informed against as author
of the anonymous pamphlet *An Appeal to the Parliament; or
Sion's Plea against the Prelacie* (1628). According to his prosecu-
tors, Leighton's book declared that 'the maintaining and estab-
lishing of bishops within this realm is a main and master sin',
that the King had been 'corrupted' by leading members of the
Church and that some Anglican ceremonies were spurious.[46]
Either Leighton was in no position to deny authorship, or
chose not to. 'The defendant in his Answer confessed the writing of the Book, but with no such ill intention, as by the said
information is suggested.' He was sentenced to be pilloried,
whipped, his ears cut off, his nose slit and his face branded. In
addition he would be imprisoned 'during life, unless his majesty shall be graciously pleased to inlarge him'.[47] In the same
year, the Bishop of London, to whom the Stationers' Company
was directly responsible, ordered that the printer of any book
must print his name on it. During the seventeenth century,
there were short periods when an author was also legally
required to declare himself on the title page. In particular, a
Star Chamber Decree of 1637 required the author's name to be
printed on any book or pamphlet. In 1641, however, Parliament
abolished both the Star Chamber and the Stationers' Company's
monopoly on printing. A 'flood of anonymous publication'
followed this new and short-lived liberation of printers and
authors.[48]

Parliament responded in 1642 with an edict requiring the
master and wardens of the Stationers' Company to make sure
that printers did not print anything 'without the Name and
Consent of the Author'. If a printer did not identify an author,
he would be treated as if he were the author. This was a temporary measure. It was followed in 1643 by a new licensing law and
in 1647 a further Act 'for the better Regulating of Printing'. This
required that any publication should have 'the name of the

Author, Printer and Licenser thereunto prefixed'.[49] The stipulation was repeated in Acts of 1649 and 1653. The Journals of the
Houses of Parliament for this period show printers and booksellers constantly being questioned about the authorship of controversial anonymous texts. The parliamentary Committee for
Printing, charged with the suppression of unlicensed printing,
was in the business of seeking out and punishing unnamed
authors.[50] The 1643 'Ordinance for the Regulation of Printing'
provoked Milton's *Areopagitica* (1644), his impassioned argument, as his subtitle put it, 'For the Liberty of Unlicenc'd
Printing'. (Ironically, Milton would himself become a licenser
under the Commonwealth.) Yet the very freedom that Milton
advocated required that 'no book be Printed, unless the Printers
and Authors name, or at least the Printers be registered'.[51] By
Milton's logic, those who published should be willing to take
responsibility. Truly anonymous publications, 'if they be found
mischievous and libellous', might properly be burned.

The first statute passed by Parliament after the Restoration
of Charles II in 1660 was a Treason Act which included 'all
printing, writing, preaching, or malicious and advised speaking
calculated to compass or devise the death, destruction, injury, or
restraint of the sovereign, or to deprive him of his style, honor,
or kingly name'.[52] The Printing Act of 1662 prohibited publications 'contrary to the principles of the Christian faith or to
the doctrine of government or governors in Church or State'.
However, it included no stipulation that an author's name be
prefixed to any publication.[53] In the early years of Charles II's
reign, John Twyn was not the only man put to death for anonymous, politically subversive publications. In Scotland, where the
imposition of penalties was probably stricter than in England,
two carpenters, James Guthrie and Archibald Johnston, were
executed in 1661 and 1663 for their part in the anonymous
Causes of God's Wrath. This declared that the cause of the

Covenanters had been defeated by an 'ungodly King'.[54] Guthrie and Johnston were found guilty of being its co-authors, the court deciding the question of attribution before it pronounced punishment.

Charles II's reign also saw a new use of anonymity to publish audacious sentiments. Verse satires proliferated, usually circulated in manuscript for the amusement of a coterie readership. Some were written in opposition to the King's ministers, and even to his policies. Very few such poems were actually printed before 1688. The few that were came from unlicensed presses. Often frequently copied, most remained in manuscript, in which form their authors were protected by apparent anonymity. Most clandestine satire of the Restoration, however, was personal rather than political. The distinctive genre of court culture was the lampoon: a satire directed at a particular person. Necessarily insulting, lampoons were invariably anonymous. 'Personal insult in seventeenth-century England was liable to provoke retaliatory violence, administered through the duel for social equals or the beating for inferiors.'[55]

The life of a satirist could certainly be dangerous in Restoration London. One evening in 1679, John Dryden, the leading writer of the age, was badly beaten because of an anonymous poem that was attributed to him.

> Last night Mr. *Dryden*, the famous *Dramatic* Poet, going from a Coffee-house in *Covent-Garden*, was set upon by three Persons unknown to him and so rudely by them handled, that it is said, his Life is in no small danger.[56]

Several accounts of the time concur that the assault was provoked by Dryden's supposed authorship of *An Essay upon Satire*, a poem recently circulated in manuscript that had attacked a whole gallery of courtiers, including the Duchess of Portsmouth, one of Charles II's mistresses.[57] So many individuals had been

scornfully treated in the poem that we can only guess (as contemporaries did) who recruited the assailants. Yet they were
motivated by a misattribution. It became clear two or three decades later that the true author was not Dryden but one of his
patrons, John Sheffield, third Earl of Mulgrave. The prevailing
anonymity of lampoons encouraged readers (and rival writers)
to 'discover' the authorship of authorless works. There were
other cases where discovery threatened violence. According to
one contemporary account, the playwright Thomas Otway challenged Elkanah Settle to a duel over the character of him in *A
Session of the Poets*. Settle apparently wrote an apology in which
he admitted to his authorship, which he had previously denied
strongly. '*I confess I Writ the* Session of the Poets, *and am very
sorry fo't and am the Son of a Whore* for doing it.'[58]

When satire veered to politics, and broached the King's right
to rule, its attribution could become a matter of life or death. In
July 1681, Stephen College, a vehement anti-Catholic and writer
of political ballads, was charged with being the author of an
anonymous broadside called *A Raree Show*. This mockingly
described Charles II's supposedly contemptuous treatment of
Parliament and his determination to deliver the country to
Catholicism. On 11 June the printer Francis Smith was tried
before Judge Jeffreys for 'printing and publishing a scandalous
libel called *The Raree Show*'.[59] Smith was fined the huge sum of
£500 and made to stand in the pillory. The printer would, however, escape with his life: the state felt that it had its author. At
his trial in August 1681 College was accused of singing the
ballad and distributing it, as well as writing it.[60] He denied
authorship. Found guilty, he was hanged, drawn and quartered
on 31 August.

Controversial writers who ventured into the realms of politics
and religion risked being pursued by the state, usually in the
person of Sir Roger l'Estrange and his 'searchers'. They tried

hard to find the author and the printer of the *Second Advice to a Painter* and *Third Advice to a Painter*, now widely believed to be by Andrew Marvell. These scathing attacks on those responsible for disastrous naval actions against the Dutch were both published in 1667, though in circulation in manuscript a year earlier. Their titles mocked Edmund Waller's windy *Instructions to a Painter* (1665), a verse panegyric to the Duke of York, celebrating his naval victory over the Dutch off Lowestoft. Modelled upon a poem by Giovanni Francesco Busenello celebrating a Venetian naval victory over the Turks, which had been translated into English in 1658, Waller's poem imagines instructing a painter how to depict the battle and the victorious admiral of the English fleet. *The Second Advice to a Painter* is a satirical rejoinder, covering the entire disastrous campaign against the Dutch. Most of the English commanders are corrupt, obese or seasick. It dwells on the Duke of York's failure to pursue the defeated Dutch fleet, which became the topic of a parliamentary inquiry. In the poem, he retires for a sleep just as the Dutch are at the point of defeat.

> But first he orders all besides to watch,
> That they the foe (whilst he a nap) might catch.[61]

Pepys noted receiving a copy of the poem, 'abusing the Duke of York, and Lord Sandwich, Penn and everybody and the King himself' (14 December 1666).[62] He also obtained a copy of the *Third Advice*, confessing himself 'mightily pleased with it'.[63] This sequel dealt with a further failed naval action, the Four Days' Battle of June 1666, again blaming English commanders. With its jokes about Prince Rupert's venereal disease and the Duke of Albermarle's 'monkey Duchess', it is hardly surprising that its author chose to remain well hidden. There is still some doubt about Marvell's hand in these satires and the standard Oxford University Press edition of Marvell's poems still chooses to exclude them. Recent scholarly scrutiny has tended to confirm what several of Marvell's contemporaries asserted (without the advantage of the stylometric tests trusted by some academics).[64] John Aubrey straightforwardly attributes 'the verses called *The Advice to the Painter*' to Marvell. In his entry on Denham in *Athenae Oxonienses*, Anthony Wood says 'they were thought by many to have been written by Andr. Marvell, esq. The printer that printed them, being discover'd, stood in the pillory for the same.'[65] More significantly, the two *Advices* were both included in a manuscript volume of Marvell's poems owned by his nephew William Popple.[66]

Marvell was a man of great circumspection, whose private life remains veiled from modern biographers. Only by habits of caution and secrecy did he survive from being a successful politician during Cromwell's rule to being a successful politician in the reign of Charles II. Yet he had strong religious and political convictions, and was drawn to dangerous publications. In 1672 he published his prose polemic *The Rehearsal Transpros'd* anonymously and with a mock imprint. Printed secretly and without licence, its authorship was widely recognized: amongst the replies that it immediately provoked are heavy hints about the author's '*Marvelousness*' and his work being 'a *marvel*'.[67] It was directed against Samuel Parker, an Anglican clergyman virulently opposed to toleration for Nonconformists. Charles II had issued a Declaration of Indulgence for Catholics and Dissenters, making the topic a pressing one. Sir Roger L'Estrange was told by the Earl of Anglesey that 'the King says he will not have it suppressed; for Parker has done him wrong, and this man has done him right'.[68] In the end, L'Estrange licensed a second edition, with a few changes introduced by himself. *The Second Part* was published in 1673, without difficulty and with Marvell's name on the title page. This declared Marvell's continuation to have been 'Occasioned by Two Letters', one of which was '*left for me at a Friends House, Dated* Nov. 3. 1673. *Subscribed* J.G. *and concluding with these words*; If thou darest to Print or Publish any Lie or Libel against Doctor *Parker*, by the Eternal God I will cut thy Throat.' Clearly some of Marvell's enemies had no doubt about the attribution of the earlier work.

In 1676 Marvell published *Mr Smirke: Or, The Divine in Mode* and his *Short Historical Essay touching General Councils, Creeds, and Imposition in Religion*, declared on its title page to be 'by Andreas Rivetus, Junior'. The authorship of this polemic in favour of religious toleration was again recognized, but though the printer was imprisoned for printing it without licence and admitted he had the papers from Marvell, the author escaped without sanction.[69] In a letter to his friend Sir Edward Harley, he revelled in the consternation caused by his pamphlets, but punctiliously maintained his anonymity. 'The book said to be Marvels makes what shift it can in the world but the Author walks negligently up & down as unconcerned.'[70] He left the letter unsigned, as if fearing its interception. Yet Marvell's authorship was widely known.[71] In 1677 he published anonymously *An Account of the Growth of Popery and Arbitrary Government in England*. Examining in detail the political events of the previous two years, it argued that there was 'a design ... carried on, to change the Lawfull Government of *England* into an Absolute Tyranny, and to convert the established Protestant Religion into down-right Popery'.[72] Marvell took care to cast Charles II as himself a victim of these machinations, and to avoid suggesting that the King's heir, his Roman Catholic brother James, was a would-be tyrant. He also repudiated the Commonwealth of Oliver Cromwell, which he had himself served. 'And as none will deny, that, to alter our *Monarchy* into a *Commonwealth* were *Treason*, so by the same Fundamental Rule, the Crime is no lesse to make that *Monarchy Absolute*.'[73] In his last surviving letter, to his nephew William Popple, Marvell wrote, with characteristic canniness,

There came out, about Christmass last, here a large Book concerning *the Growth of Popery and Arbitrary Government.* There have been great Rewards offered in private, and considerable in the Gazette, to any one who could inform of the Author or Printer, but not yet discovered. Three or four printed Books since have described, as near as it was proper to go, the Man being a member of Parliament, Mr. *Marvell* to have been the Author; but if he had, surely he should not have escaped being questioned in Parliament, or some other Place.[74]

The *London Gazette* for 21–25 March 1678 had carried an advertisement offering £50 to anyone informing on 'the Printer, or the Publisher' of *An Account of the Growth of Popery*, and £100 for the name of 'the Hander of it to the Press'.[75] If 'the Discoverer' be a printer, and 'in case of tracing the Proof up to the Author', he is offered the extra incentive of being allowed to set up his own printing house. (The Licensing Act banned printers from setting up new presses.)

Marvell died in August 1678, having successfully dodged identification until the end. Sir Roger l'Estrange identified him as the author shortly afterwards. L'Estrange himself wrote an anonymous rejoinder, *An Account of the Growth of Knavery* (1678), published a couple of months before Marvell's death. Here he declined to identify the author, but made it clear to the knowing that he could do.

The Man, I confess, is a great Master of Words . . . You would have me guess at the Author; and you might as well bid me tell you the right Father of a Child by a common Strumpet: But I think I may call him *Legion*, for they are MANY; and there's a *Club* to his *Pen*, as well as to his *Pocket.*[76]

He nudgingly calls him 'a *Merry-Andrew*' and, after various hints about the author's affiliations, he gave the broadest hint of all as to his identity. 'By his Vein of improving the Invective Humour, it looks in some places as if he were *Transprosing* the *First Painter*.'[77] This allusion to earlier works by Marvell is l'Estrange's way of showing his inside knowledge.

The danger of publication was not just a matter of fact; it also existed in the imaginations of writers. Other authors who lived through the same dangerous times as Marvell developed more anxious habits of secrecy. One of these was John Locke, who shared Marvell's beliefs in the importance of toleration and liberty and the threat of monarchical tyranny. Arguing from these beliefs, he showed himself both more audacious and more cautious than Marvell. Audaciously he pressed his arguments to conclusions that undermined monarchical authority and Christian orthodoxy. His caution lay in his use of anonymity. Locke's major works were all published after the so-called Glorious Revolution of 1688, which saw the Roman Catholic James II driven from power and William and Mary established as Protestant rulers. Locke's *Essay concerning Human Understanding* was published in 1689, as a grand folio volume with his name announced fearlessly on the title page and an engraved portrait as a frontispiece.[78] He proudly distributed copies to friends. Framed as a philosophical companion to the great discoveries of Locke's scientific contemporaries, 'master builders' like Boyle and Newton, it described how knowledge derives from experience. It quickly made him famous. Politically in sympathy with the new regime, he found himself patronized by great men and rewarded with public positions. He was renowned, through Europe as well as in his own country.

The other major works he published in his years of fame appeared without his name on their title pages, and he went to great and fearful lengths to preserve their anonymity. In the same year as *An Essay concerning Human Understanding*, he also published his *Two Treatises of Government*, which would become one of the most influential works of political philosophy in the English language. It presented itself as a book for its times, an intellectual justification of the deposing of James II. The Preface said the work was published '*to establish the Throne of our Great Restorer, Our present King* William; *to make good his Title, in the Consent of the People*' and '*to justifie to the World, the People of* England', who had saved themselves from '*Slavery and Ruine*'.[79] It braved controversy by arguing that rulers governed only by consent of their people, and that this consent could properly be withdrawn if a ruler abused his power and betrayed the people's trust. A monarch's authority was not God-given but a human convention. A king had a duty to protect the rights of his subjects; if he failed in this duty, they had a right to resist his power and ultimately to rebel against him. The writer of this work reached such conclusions reasonably and unfearfully, yet he would not say who he was.

Locke was almost obsessive in his attempts to preserve the anonymity of the *Two Treatises*. 'He destroyed all his workings for the book and erased from his papers every recognizable reference to its existence, its composition, its publication, printing and reprinting.'[80] Like others whom we encounter in this book, his discussions with both printer and publisher were carried out via a third party, his friend Edward Clarke, who had strict instructions never to mention Locke's name.[81] In the 1690s, he was widely talked of as its author, but though he confessed the fact to a few friends, he swore them to secrecy. When he recommended his book to a relative just a year before his death, he mentioned it as if it were by another man.[82] He was furious with his lifelong friend and sometime collaborator James Tyrrell when he believed that Tyrrell had leaked the secret. In their correspondence, Tyrrell at first maintained the pretence, even as he nudged his friend for confirmation of his authorship. Soon after the publication of the *Two Treatises* he wrote to Locke reporting that 'some people doe me the favour to make me the authour of it'.[83] Could Locke 'aske your Friend Mr. Churchill who prints it who is the Authour of it if it be not a secret; and let me know it'. Before long he was asking Locke what he should say to those he met in Oxford who made Locke the author of the *Two Treatises* and the *Letter concerning Toleration*, another of Locke's anonymous works.[84] We do not have Locke's response. Two years later Tyrrell was presuming Locke's author-ship of the *Two Treatises* when writing that he did not resent his friend producing a refutation of Filmer that trumped his own earlier *Patriarcha non Monarcha*.[85] In the same month, William Molyneux told Locke that, admiring his *Essay*, he had asked 'some of My Learned Friends' what else the great philosopher had written.[86]

> I was recommended by some to *Two Discourses Concerning Government*, and a Little *Treatise Concerning Toleration*. there is neither of them Carrys your Name. and I wil not venture to ask, whether they are yours or Not. This only I think, No Name need be ashamed of Either.

In his reply, Locke simply declined to say anything about the matter.

Locke had lived through three sudden changes of regime and could not know that James II and his descendants would not return. Only William's military successes of the 1690s staved off this possibility. A justification of the so-called Glorious Revolu-tion might, under some future dispensation, become a work from which he would need to distance himself. But it was more than this. The sense of danger that attached to his studiedly rational arguments had been with him since the hazardous years of the late 1670s and early 1680s. His employer had been the Earl of Shaftesbury, the leading Whig politician and the organizer of parliamentary attempts to have Charles II's brother

James excluded from the throne. Locke had been a known associate of men like the Earl of Essex, imprisoned in the Tower for plotting against the monarchy, and Algernon Sidney, executed for his part in the Rye House Plot. Locke had been watched by government spies. We now know that much of the *Two Treatises* was written between 1679 and 1681 and was not a safely retrospective vindication of a revolution that had happened, but an intellectual justification for one that might happen. In the years in which it was composed it was a very dangerous work. It is likely that Locke kept the manuscript amongst his papers disguised as *De Morbo Gallico*, ostensibly a medical study of venereal disease.[87]

It had to be carefully concealed because in 1683 Locke followed his patron Shaftesbury into exile in Holland, leaving most of his papers in the care of friends. When, after James II's flight to France, he returned to England, his feeling for the dangers of his ideas was ingrained. The other major work published in the year of his return was his *Letter concerning Toleration*, which was first published in Holland in 1689 in Latin. This had announced on its title page that it was written by '*P. A. P. O. I. L. A.*'. Only after Locke's death was this revealed by a friend to stand for 'Pacis Amico Persucutionis Osore Ioanne Lockio Anglo' ('By a friend of peace and enemy of persecution, J. L. Englishman').[88] In Holland the work was widely misattributed. When William Popple's English translation was published it was, naturally, anonymous. When a friend wrote to Locke from Amsterdam suggesting that he was the author, Locke wrote in consternation to Philip van Limborch, the man to whom the work had originally been addressed.[89] Locke was beside himself. Limborch must have betrayed the secret. Even though he was widely known in England to have written the book, Locke angrily and anxiously insisted that Limborch do everything possible to conceal his authorship. A leading Locke scholar has accurately described

Locke's reactions to the loss of his anonymity as 'more than a little hysterical'.[90]

The *Letter concerning Toleration* argued that it was wrong for the state to meddle in matters of religious belief. 'The care of souls cannot belong to the civil magistrate.'[91] It is unreasonably presumptuous for one Christian to believe that he or she has a better idea of God's will than another.

> The toleration of those that differ from others in matters of religion, is so agreeable to the Gospel of Jesus Christ, and to the genuine reason of mankind, that it seems monstrous for men to be so blind, as not to perceive the necessity and advantage of it, in so clear a light.[92]

Even in Popple's translation, the tone of Locke's open reasonableness seems unmistakable (though a modern reader might flinch from his justifications for denying toleration to Roman Catholics, Muslims or atheists). Yet Locke anxiously kept his distance from his own candid arguments. It was the same when he published his last major work, *The Reasonableness of Christianity as delivered in the Scriptures*, anonymously in 1695. It argued that most doctrinal 'niceties' were human inventions, unconnected to the simpler truths that God had 'delivered in the Scriptures'. 'Where the hand is used to the Plough, and the Spade, the head is seldom elevated to sublime Notions, or exercised in mysterious reasonings.'[93] A merciful God had communicated religious truths 'that the labouring and illiterate Man may comprehend'.[94] Such arguments were likely to exasperate members of many religious groups. The book aroused controversy and sparked hostile replies, as well as two anonymous vindications.

Locke wrote to his Dutch friend Van Limborch about the book, ending with the warning, 'All this must be for your private ear, for I want my having treated this subject to be communicated to you alone.'[95] 'He refused to admit in writing his authorship of the *Reasonableness*, even when he discussed the book in letters to his closest friends.[96] As with other books, he did not even catalogue it under his own name in his own library. Yet his authorship was guessed at by his major antagonists, as well as his friends.[97] Fear of prosecution for heresy would not have been entirely irrational. In 1697 the work was reported to magistrates by the Grand Jury of Middlesex as contributing to atheism.[98] Locke was probably also trying to keep the *Essay Concerning Human Understanding* free of the taint of his religious and political beliefs. Locke was capable of making a virtue of his philosopher's self-concealment. In 1660 when he intended to publish anonymously a work that became known as *Two Tracts on Government*, he explained in its preface that 'by concealing my name' he would leave the reader 'concerned for nothing but the arguments themselves'.[99] His former pupil, the third Earl of Shaftesbury, would publish his own philosophical writings anonymously not out of any attempt at concealment, but with the lordly modesty of a writer dedicated to letting Reason win its own way. Yet everything in Locke's behaviour seems fearful. His only recorded acknowledgement of his authorship of all these anonymous works came in a codicil to his will, signed no more than a fortnight before he died.[100] Here he mentions that the Keeper of the Bodleian Library has asked him for copies of 'treatises whereof I was the Author which had been published without my name to them'. Now he lists these anonymous works, flattered by the honour of having them go under his name 'among the works of the learned in that August repository'. He was proud of the writings from which he so carefully detached his name, the rational arguments by which men and women might be guided, yet experience had taught him to own those arguments only to posterity.

Locke himself played an important part in the abandonment of state censorship of published material. He advised members

of the House of Commons committee examining the renewal of
the Licensing Act, arguing against state regulation and for what
we would call the freedom of the press.

> I know not why a man should not have liberty to print what-
> ever he would speak; and to be answerable for the one just as
> he is for the other.[101]

He was on the winning side. The Licensing Act lapsed in 1695
and was not renewed. Now we can see the irony of his lucid
arguments against 'gagging' writers, given that he so busily
avoided being answerable for much that he had published. The
age after licensing promised new liberty for authors, but the
fears of writers did not evaporate. The law of seditious libel
continued to be used to prosecute writers who reflected on the
government in any way that it disliked. The fear of prosecution
shaped the career of one of the major authors of the early eighteenth century, Daniel Defoe. Defoe went into hiding shortly
after the publication of *The Shortest Way with the Dissenters* in
1702. It attacked High Church intolerance of religious dissent by
parodying it. Anonymity was a necessary part of the pamphlet's
satirical design: the piece purported to have been written by
some unnamed supporter of the High Church cause, a bigot
foaming at the mouth as he listed the extreme penalties that
should be inflicted on dissenters (of whom Defoe was himself
one).

> 'Tis Cruelty to kill a Snake or a Toad in cold Blood, but the
> Poyson of their Nature makes it a Charity to our Neighbours,
> to destroy those Creatures, not for any personal Injury
> receiv'd, but for prevention; not for the Evil they have done,
> but for the Evil they may do.[102]

Even here, the author was making mischief as well as playing
safe. A High Church antagonist advised him in a pamphlet to

remain hidden rather than suffer the 'brutal punishment' that he deserved.[103] His authorship was announced in a London journal by a former ally, John Tutchin, and a week later the *London Gazette* announced that there would be a reward of fifty pounds for information leading to the apprehension of 'Daniel de Fooe', author of a 'Scandalous and Seditious' pamphlet.[104] In the next issue the journal gave a description. 'He is a middle Sized Spare Man about 40 years old, of a brown Complexion, and dark brown coloured Hair wears a Wig, a hooked Nose, a sharp Chin, grey Eyes, and a large Mould near his Mouth.' While Defoe was in hiding, the printer, George Croome, was arrested and the House of Commons resolved that, the pamplet 'tending to promote Sedition', all copies 'be burnt by the hands of the common Hangman'. Edward Bellamy, a noted Whig agitator, was also arrested and admitted taking Defoe's manuscript to the printer. Croome and Bellamy implicated Defoe and agreed to testify against him.[105] An informer told the authorities that Defoe was hiding in the house of a French weaver in Spitalfields.[106] He was arrested and sent to Newgate.

Defoe was eventually charged with libel. He admitted authorship and pleaded guilty. After being made to stand in the pillory he was returned to Newgate from where he was rescued by the powerful politician Robert Harley, who put him to work as a propagandist. Defoe was free to publish without first seeking the permission of a licenser, but always ran the risk of being charged with seditious libel. On another occasion, he was arrested for libel at the behest of political rivals. They relied on the evidence of print-shop workers, who claimed to have seen the manuscripts of offending pamphlets in what they knew to be Defoe's handwriting – or rather, as his most authoritative biographer puts it, 'handwritings, since they claimed that they could recognize the variety of disguised scripts that he used'.[107] It is a nice irony that in his 1704 *Essay on the Regulation of the Press* Defoe should argue that anonymity be made illegal. Probably no other great writer made such extensive use of anonymity and pseudonymity during the course of a career. Defoe wanted to argue down any reintroduction of pre-publication licensing and believed that anonymity gave the state the excuse it needed to vest authority in someone like Sir Roger l'Estrange. 'All the Excuse that ever I could meet with for a Licenser, was built upon the Difficulty of discovering the true Author of a Book.'[108] If someone were named on the title page as responsible for the publication, punishment for any offence would always be possible. Defoe proposed a law that would 'oblige the Printer or Bookseller to place the Author's Name in the Title, or himself'.[109]

As well as intimidation by agents of the State, there was the threat of privately administered violence. Defoe received threats of murder. John Tutchin was beaten up by political opponents and died of his injuries in 1707.[110] After the publication of *The Dunciad*, the mock epic in which he satirized the hacks and dunces of his age, Alexander Pope clearly received threats of violence. Our best evidence is the admiring account of his response recorded after his death by his half-sister Magdalen.

> My brother does not seem to know what fear is. When some of the people that he had put into his Dunciad, were so much enraged against him, and threatened him so highly: he loved to walk out alone, and particularly went often to Mr Fortescue's at Richmond. Only he would take Bounce [his Great Dane] with him; and for some time carried pistols in his pocket.[111]

The son of the critic John Dennis, one of Pope's chief butts in *The Dunciad*, is said to have arrived one night at the house of Lord Bathurst, where Pope was staying, and sent in a message saying that he was waiting outside with his sword.[112] Bathurst apparently persuaded him to retire peacefully.

Pope used anonymity to provoke, but his friend Jonathan Swift did sometimes wish to protect himself, if not from the guesses of readers, then at least from prosecution. In 1714, with the childless Queen Anne ailing, he produced *The Publick Spirit of the Whigs*, an acid reply to Richard Steele's pamphlet in favour of the Hanoverian succession, *The Crisis*. Swift vindicated Queen Anne's ministers, but offended Scottish members of the House of Lords by speaking disdainfully of their motives for the Union of England and Scotland in 1707. Both its publisher, John Morphew, and its printer, John Barber, were taken into custody. They and their servants were questioned as to the identity of the author. An address from the House of Lords to the Queen asked her to issue a proclamation offering a reward for the discovery of this author. She consented, offering three hundred pounds and 'Her Majesty's Gracious Pardon to such Person as shall make such Discovery'.[113] Swift was not exactly hidden. A contemporary observed, 'The Whigs guesses it to be Dr. Swift's.'[114] No one came forward, and neither publisher nor printer betrayed the author. Swift proudly recorded the episode in his verse fragment 'The Author upon Himself', written in 1714 though not published until 1735.

> Now, through the realm a proclamation spread,
> To fix a price on his devoted head.
> While innocent, he scorns ignoble flight;
> His watchful friends preserve him by a sleight.[115]

He escapes thanks to the loyalty of his important friends. He was indeed protected by his patrons in the Ministry, for the pamphlet had been written on their behalf. A prosecution of Barber was begun for show but soon abandoned.

Being Swift's printer could be genuinely risky. Edward Waters, the Dublin printer of his anonymous *Proposal for Irish Manu-facture* (1720), which argued that the Irish should rebel against English colonialism by refusing to buy English goods, was arrested.[116] Although a jury found him not guilty of having printed a 'false, scandalous, and seditious' pamphlet, the Chief Justice of the King's Bench made them reconsider their verdict. Waters remained imprisoned. Swift embarked on a campaign of lobbying great men on his printer's behalf.[117] It took more than a year before Waters was released. Swift's greatest triumph as a writer on public affairs cost another printer dear. Swift's *The Drapier's Letters* (1724) opposed the granting of a patent to an English manufacturer, William Wood, for the provision of a new copper coinage for Ireland. It seemed a corrupt scheme (Wood had paid handsomely to obtain the patent) calculated to debase the currency: Wood would have every incentive to reduce the amount of copper in his coins in order to increase his profits. There would be no regulation of the supply or the quality of this currency. The Irish parliament had not been consulted; Ireland was being treated as a mere source of gain for the English adven-turer. Swift began his campaign with a letter addressed 'To the Shopkeepers' Tradesmen, Farmers and Common People of Ire-land' and written in the person of M. B., a Dublin draper. It encouraged the Irish to boycott the new coins: 'My *Friends*, stand to it One and All, refuse this *Filthy Trash*.'[118] It was calcu-lated to be provoking, referring amongst other things to Wood's bribing of 'GREAT MEN' and their recruitment of the King him-self on behalf of the project. The anonymous pamphlet declared itself to be 'Printed by J. Harding'. John Harding's name appeared on a series of the Drapier's pamphlets, and he would suffer for it.

   The campaign was popular. Leading public figures in Dublin, including Swift's own superior, Archbishop King, were openly hostile to the recoinage scheme. Swift's own involvement was hardly a secret. At just this time Walpole appointed Lord Carteret, an acquaintance of Swift's, as Lord Lieutenant of Ireland and Swift sent him a letter of welcome which referred archly to his own polemical pamphlet. He wrote to Carteret as 'one who has always loved and esteemed you' to describe the 'apprehensions' of 'many of the principle [sic] persons in this kingdom' about Wood's patent. You can hear in his reference to his own provoking pamphlet the curious, self-protective convention by which a merely official anonymity was maintained.

> I have made bold to send you enclosed two small tracts on this subject; one written (as it is supposed) by the Earl of Abercorn; the other is entitled to a Weaver, and suited to the vulgar, but thought to be the work of a better hand.[119]

When a British parliamentary inquiry cleared the scheme, Swift wrote a second *Drapier's Letter*, and then a third. Public anger was roused. In a procession through the streets of Dublin Wood's effigy was burned. On the day that Carteret arrived to take up his post, a fourth *Drapier's Letter* was published. Carteret ordered that the printer should be prosecuted and that a reward of three hundred pounds be offered for the identification of the author. It appears the members of the ruling Privy Council knew well who this author was. Thomas Tickell, Carteret's secretary, certainly identified Swift in his correspondence.[120] But no informer came forward.

Archbishop King told Carteret that the author was considering declaring himself in order to stand trial.[121] Carteret wrote to Lord Newcastle, one of George I's ministers, that such a declaration would indeed bring the author's arrest. ''Tis the general opinion here that Doctor Swift is the author of the pamphlet, and yet nobody thinks it can be proved upon him, though many believe he will be spirited up to own it.'[122] William Nicolson, Bishop of Derry, also wrote of the efforts to identify an author whose identity he well knew.

'Tis expected that in the course of their enquiries, they'll discover the true author of the *Drapier's Letters*. I do very much question whether such a discovery will be of any sort of use in our present circumstances. That writer is, at present, in great repute, the darling of the populace, his image and superscription on a great many signposts in this city and other great towns.[123]

When the Grand Jury refused to condemn the fourth *Drapier's Letter*, it was discharged and a new jury summoned. Swift may well have been in court for this proceeding, intimate with the controversy even as his anonymity removed him from it.[124] His subsequent fifth *Drapier's Letter* even playfully contains a self-reference, M. B. Drapier mentioning 'the Advice given me by a certain *Dean*', who counsels him about the dangers of his campaign.[125] Swift and Carteret (who had privately already recommended that Wood's patent be cancelled) were soon to meet, with apparent cordiality. Swift entertained Carteret's wife at a picnic.[126] The private man and the anonymous author were distinct.

John Harding had been arrested, along with his wife, but claimed that he did not know the identity of the Drapier. The *Letters* had come to him from an unknown hand. He was charged with publishing a seditious pamphlet. In defence of Harding, Swift published his anonymous *Seasonable Advice to the Grand Jury*. Meanwhile, on Carteret's advice, the Government in London decided to cancel Wood's patent. Swift, now 'The Hibernian Patriot', was triumphant. Yet Harding, the printer, died in prison shortly before this was announced, a victim, we might think, of the satirist's anonymity. Mrs Harding printed the anonymous poem 'On Wisdom's Defeat in a Learned Debate', mocking the readiness of Irish bishops to kowtow to the Ministry in London. Carteret offered a hundred pounds as reward for identification of its author, though again he remained hidden. It is likely to have been Swift.[127]

The Drapier's Letters finally appeared with Swift's name upon them in Faulkner's edition of his *Works* in 1735. Swift made the victory part of a personal mythology. Years later, probably in 1731, he referred to the effort to find the author of *The Drapier's Letters* in his 'Verses on the Death of Dr Swift'. The poem imagines what a fair judge, 'One quite indifferent in the cause', might say of him after his death. This persona speaks of his fearlessness in the face of what sounds like real danger.

> Fair LIBERTY was all his cry;
> For her he stood prepared to die;
> For her he boldly stood alone;
> For her he oft exposed his own.[128]

The failure of the authorities to get past the official anonymity of either *The Publick Spirit of the Whigs* or *The Drapier's Letters* is a sign of his integrity and status.

> Two kingdoms, just as factions led,
> Had set a price upon his head;
> But, not a traitor could be found,
> To sell him for six hundred pound.[129]

The 'six hundred pound' is the sum of the two rewards that were offered. This feels much like boasting, and when the verses were eventually published, Swift's friends, anxious about the appearance of vanity, had a section of the poem including this lines excised.[130]

Swift liked to look back at the dangers he had successfully passed for the sake of 'Liberty', but he worried about less glamorous risks too, like the possibility of jeopardizing his career. When he published his *A Tale of a Tub* in 1704, he knew that his satire on religious hypocrisy could impede his advancement in

the church. He omitted not only his own name but also that of
the printer, Benjamin Tooke, who was commonly associated
with him. Yet he was prouder of this work than of anything else
he wrote. So while removing evidence of his authorship, he
allowed it to be known. To his confidante Esther Johnson (Stella)
he referred to the work as 'the *you know what*'.[131] But then he
added, 'Gad, if it had not been for that, I should never have been
able to get the access I have had.' He wrote this from London,
where he was enjoying the company of great men because they
knew he was the author of the most ingenious book of the
season. In letters to friends he continued to avoid admitting to
his authorship. Swift behaved as if those on whom he depended
for advancement would be able to admire his heterodox writings
– or ignore them – provided he did not actually own up to them.

The new freedom to print made published material more and
more difficult to control, or even monitor. It allowed a burgeon-
ing of periodical writing, almost all of it anonymous, Political
journalism presented the authorities with special problems. In a
test case in 1704 John Tutchin was tried for seditious libel after
his journal the *Observator* accused leading politicians of being
bribed by the French. He was found guilty of publishing the
offending material, but not of writing it. In the end, the case
against him was dropped.[132] Publishers and printers of anti-
government journals were intermittently harried. In 1728 those
who printed *Mist's Weekly Journal* were sentenced to the pillory.[133] In 1738 the printer Richard Franklin was fined and
imprisoned for producing the *Craftsman*.[134] In 1769 Henry
Woodfall, publisher of the *Public Advertiser*, was unsuccessfully
tried for seditious libel after printing an article by 'Junius' that
directly attacked King George III. As it was reprinted in other
periodicals it became impossible for the Government to prosecute every printer and publisher. Junius, meanwhile remained
unidentified.

Anonymous writers for periodicals were usually beyond pursuit. A rare exception is an author who was vulnerable because he was also the proprietor of the journal in which he wrote. In 1758 the irascible Tobias Smollett reviewed in his monthly journal, the *Critical Review*, a pamphlet by Admiral Charles Knowles vindicating his involvement in an unsuccessful naval expedition against the French port of Rochefort. Smollett had had his own bitter experience of naval incompetence when, as a ship's doctor, he took part in the disastrous 1741 attack on Cartagena in the West Indies. His review seethed at 'a dirty expedition, which has stunk so abominably in the nostrils of the nation' and suggested that the admiral was adept only at disengaging himself from any danger. Knowles was, amongst other things, 'an ignorant, assuming, officious, fribbling pretender; conceited as a peacock, obstinate as a mule, and mischievous as a monkey'.[135] Smollett was tried for libel. Originally, the printer (whose name was announced on the review) was to have been prosecuted, but Knowles agreed to drop this prosecution if the reviewer's identity was revealed. Smollett duly admitted in court that he was the author. He was fined a hundred pounds and sentenced to three months in the King's Bench Prison.

Knowles took Smollett to the courts, but other authors were threatened with less official revenge. James Boswell narrowly avoided being challenged to a duel by the son of a judge whom he attacked in an anonymous letter in the *London Chronicle*.[136] Half an century later in 1822, his son, Alexander Boswell, was killed in a duel over anonymous articles. He had been challenged by James Stuart, who had discovered that Boswell was the author of unsigned attacks on him published in the *Glasgow Sentinel*.[137] The wound was made worse by the fact that the two men were related and had been friends. Ironically, Alexander Boswell had helped abolish Scottish statutes making duelling illegal.[138] He and Stuart duelled with pistols, and Boswell was killed. After fleeing abroad, Stuart returned to be tried and was acquitted.

At a time when duelling was not uncommon, the man who hid behind his anonymity was shamefully avoiding a challenge. John Wilkes, the leading political agitator of the 1760s and 1770s, was challenged to a duel more than once because of his writings. In his journal the *North Briton* he anonymously attacked the MP Samuel Martin as an egregious 'tool of Ministerial persecution', and 'the most treacherous, base, selfish, mean, abject, low-lived, and dirty fellow that ever wriggled himself into a secretary-ship'.[139] In a speech in the House of Commons Martin complained of being 'stabbed in the dark', prompting Wilkes to retort in a letter, 'I believe you were not so much in *the dark* as you affected and chose to be.' It was hardly a secret who conducted the *North Briton*, and Wilkes was not going to allow his foe to take refuge in affected ignorance.

> To cut off every pretence of this kind, as to the author, I whisper in your ear, that every passage of the 'North Briton' in which you have been named, or alluded to, was written by your humble servant,
> John Wilkes.[140]

Martin duly challenged Wilkes to a duel in Hyde Park. Martin emerged unscathed, but Wilkes was wounded in the stomach and, for a while, was thought close to death. The affair was a public event, a report appearing in *St. James's Chronicle* for 17 November 1763.

The dangers that could press an author to use anonymity were becoming more personal. There was a brief re-flowering of state control in the 1790s, when Pitt's government feared a British imitation of the French Revolution. In 1799, one of its measures to control printing and publishing was a law obliging every printer to place his imprint on the first and last pages of any book, and to keep a register of his customers. Authors must be traceable. Yet the convention whereby an author, like Marvell or Swift in the past, could remain officially anonymous even if widely known seems to have remained. An example is Byron's *Don Juan*, whose first two cantos appeared anonymously in 1819. Friends who saw the first canto of *Don Juan* advised Byron against publishing it. Its tolerant amusement at sexual passions seemed libertine, its scarcely disguised mockery of Lady Byron in the person of Donna Inez scandalous. At first the poet was willing to print only fifty copies for private distribution.[141] As he was completing the second canto, he changed his mind. 'After mature consideration I have determined to have Don Juan published (*anonymously*).'[142] He seemed insouciant about any offence he might cause. There were to be no 'curtailments' of the text that he had dispatched from Italy, he warned his worried publisher John Murray. 'The poem will please if it is lively—if it is stupid it will fail—but I will have none of your damned cutting & slashing.'[143] Yet he insisted on the anonymity.

Murray was in favour of anonymity, prompting a lordly scruple on Byron's part. If the work was not to declare his name, then the scathing mock dedication to Southey should be omitted. 'I won't attack the dog so fiercely without putting my name—that is reviewer's work.'[144] The first two cantos were published in July 1819, without either Byron's name or Murray's. No reviewer seems to have been in any doubt as to his identity. Soon after publication Byron even gave Murray permission to drop the pretence in conversation: '*Own that I am the author. I will never shrink.*'[145] When he was arranging, almost a year later, for the publication of volumes III and IV of *Don Juan*, Byron thought of the work's official anonymity as a defence against a particular danger. He explained to his friend John Cam Hobhouse, his agent in negotiations with publishers,

—You must premise that the third & fourth Cantos of Don J
must be published anonymously & this merely because in the
present state of Cant and hypocrisy in England—any freedom
of expression on Creeds or manners—would prevent the
author from asserting the guardianship of his own children—
this I know—for on this ground the Chancellor decided on
Shelley's case—and would be but too happy to do likewise by
any other person obnoxious to the present rulers.[146]

Ribbing Murray for not putting his name to the poem, he
described the reasons for his own anonymity as 'family ones
entirely'.[147] He withheld his name from a poem that was so
much in his voice because he was engaged in a custody battle
with his estranged wife over their daughter, Ada. He was afraid
that it would count against him in any court judgement on his
parental rights. The reference to Shelley is telling: Shelley's athe-
istic writings had been held against him when a court had
denied him parental rights after his separation from his first wife
Harriet. Byron seems to have believed that if he did not publicly
own up to the satire, it could not legally be invoked in court.

In the early nineteenth century there was one arena in particular where anonymity sheltered authors from the consequences of
what they wrote: reviewing. Literary duels were fought out in the
reviews, where all contributions were anonymous. Sometimes
the duels became real. In 1806 an anonymous critical review
of his *Odes and Epistles* in the *Edinburgh Review* goaded Tom
Moore to challenge editor Francis Jeffrey to a duel, a challenge
that Jeffrey accepted. A friend had reported to Moore that Jeffrey
had implied his authorship of the offending article in a dinner-
party conversation.[148] The men met at Chalk Farm with their
seconds, but the constabulary, forewarned, arrived to prevent the
combat. Byron would laugh at 'JEFFREY's harmless pistol' in his
satirical poem *English Bards and Scotch Reviewers* and Moore

and Jeffrey would later become friends.[149] Byron had himself been tempted to strip away a hostile reviewer's anonymity via a challenge to a duel. His youthful volume of poems *Hours of Idleness* had been mocked in *The Satirist*, which also reprinted negative extracts from other reviews. Byron wrote to its editor, Hewson Clarke, declaring that 'Report universally attributes to your pen' the mockery in question.[150] He required either '(if you are not the author) an immediate & unequivocal disavowal', or 'an explanation'. The formula implied that Clarke would either have to apologize or fight a duel. It is likely that the letter was not sent, Byron revenging himself by adding Clarke to his gallery of dunces in *English Bards and Scotch Reviewers*.

In his Postscript to the second edition of *English Bards*, Byron said that, though the first edition had been published anonymously, he had been in London 'in daily expectation of sundry cartels [i.e. written challenges]; but, alas! "the age of chivalry is over"'.[151] The quotation from his ideological foe Edmund Burke makes more facetious the satirist's talk of duelling over his mockery. Yet in Byron's age some literary duels over anonymous articles were fatal. In 1821 John Christie killed John Scott, editor of the *London Magazine*, in a duel at Chalk Farm. Scott had complained about personal attacks in *Blackwood's* and attributed them to Lockhart. He retaliated with a sequence of three anonymous articles attacking *Blackwood's*, in the third of which he accused Lockhart of concealing his involvement in the magazine. Breaching his antagonist's anonymity he printed Lockhart's name in bold capitals. Lockhart travelled to London and demanded through Christie, a friend who was also a barrister, that Scott acknowledge his authorship of the articles and apologise for them. Lockhart returned to Edinburgh and Christie became involved in a bad-tempered correspondence with Scott. Scott demanded an apology and, when Christie refused, challenged him to a duel. The two men fought with pistols by moonlight. Their first shots were harmless, but when they fired again Scott was fatally wounded. He died a fortnight later. Christie and the two seconds were tried for murder at the Old Bailey and were acquitted after a notably sympathetic summing up by Chief Justice Abbott.

Reviewing could be dangerous. The robust William Blackwood, proprietor of *Blackwood's Magazine,* paid large sums in damages for the libels he published.[152] He also appears to have been horsewhipped in his Edinburgh shop at least twice by aggrieved victims of his mocking authors' unsigned attacks.[153] In 1836 there was a much publicized case of a physical assault by an aggrieved author. A mocking review of *Berkeley Castle* by the fashionable novelist Grantley Berkeley appeared in *Fraser's Magazine. Fraser's* had taken over from *Blackwood's* as the most combative and provoking periodical of its day. The review was written by its editor, William Maginn, but was unsigned. It infuriated the self-consciously aristocratic Berkeley by ridiculing his family's pretensions and, in particular, by asserting that his father had lived with his mother as his mistress for a long time before they ever married. Berkeley arrived at the office of James Fraser, proprietor of *Fraser's.* Fraser (according to Berkeley) refused to divulge the reviewer's name, so Berkeley, while his brother Craven watched the door shouting him on, beat him severely with his riding crop. Fraser was badly injured and never fully recovered. It is thought that the beating hastened his death, five years later.

Hearing of the attack, Maginn owned himself the author of the review. Reviewer and reviewed then fought a duel, in a field near the Edgware Road. Neither was badly hurt. The affair was widely publicized, not least in *Fraser's,* which printed a lengthy transcript from the trial, after which Berkeley was ordered to pay damages of a hundred pounds. In the trial, the question of whether Berkeley had asked for the name of the anonymous reviewer was central. Fraser's counsel claimed that Berkeley had made no such enquiry. The judge, Lord Abinger, advised the jury that, if Fraser had refused to divulge the author's name, he should expect to be treated as if he were the author himself, but that, equally, 'the first step a gentleman would take, before he aimed his vengeance at the bookseller, would be to endeavour to obtain the name of the author'.[154] He judged that there was no evidence that Berkeley had made this endeavour.[155]

It is an extreme case, but, in many less bloody ways, anonymous reviewing became a means of attacking enemies, and hiding from them. Yet the reviewer's anonymity did not only allow for the venting of animosity. As we will see next, it permitted the repaying of favours, and every variety of literary puffing.

6

REVIEWING

Only in two significant places does anonymous reviewing continue in Britain. One is in *The Economist*, which includes only a few book reviews, but where anonymity is an element in its authority, signalling that it is it undistracted by passing trends and personalities. The other is in *Private Eye*, whose book reviews (anonymous since May 1986) specialize in making the case against writers elsewhere garlanded with praise by fellow writers – and, it is implied, cronies. *Private Eye*'s literary pages scorn the complicity between authors and reviewers that sometimes seems to be the rule elsewhere. But until recently anonymity was the policy in Britain's most august literary review, the *Times Literary Supplement*. Readers and writers were reminded of this in 1999 with the announcement of the *TLS* Centenary Archive. This promised to make available all back numbers in an electronically searchable form along with contributors' names (the vast majority of which are recorded in marked copies of original issues and editorial diaries owned by *The Times*). The prospectus by the editors, Jeremy Treglown and Deborah McVea, promised 'a store of discoveries'.[1] Scholars would be delighted to be able to identify previously unknown articles by the likes of Galsworthy and Gissing, Aldous Huxley and Edith Wharton. Research into 'the workings of the hitherto anonymous literary establishment' would be greatly facilitated.

Members of that 'establishment' who had once reviewed anonymously for the *TLS* were not all delighted. In the letters column of the rival *London Review of Books*, John Sturrock, for many years deputy editor of the *TLS*, expressed his dismay at having his own past contributions identified. He wondered how many other past contributors 'feel as I do that pieces of work contracted for on the understanding that their authorship would not be revealed should remain anonymous'.[2] Treglown and McVea replied that they would respect the wishes of any contributor who wanted to remain unidentified, and that announcements of the index had always made this clear. Sturrock retorted that these had been insufficiently publicized and that an 'ethical issue' had been treated casually: 'Anonymity was a principle, not an editorial aberration awaiting normalisation by a more enlightened generation coming after.'[3] In the next issue a former *TLS* reviewer signing him- or herself 'Your Correspondent' joined Sturrock's complaints, rehearsing 'some old, sound reasons' why anonymity in reviewing might be a good thing. It allowed a reviewer to be 'honest and uninhibited about the work of friends or the famous'.[4] 'I liked to think that anonymity provided the chance of being generous without lending my name to self-seeking flattery or lenience.' Readers could judge reviews on their merits 'rather than by the notoriety or obscurity of revealed names'.

These are, in fact, old arguments. The reviewing of books was long the area where debates about anonymity were both most bitter and most high-minded. This has been the case since systematic reviewing began with the *Monthly Review*, founded in 1749, and its later rival the *Critical Review*, founded in 1756. All articles in both publications were anonymous. In its early years, speculation about their authorship was rare. Partly this is because the reviews were not yet truly influential; partly it is because many of the reviewers were unidentifiable: provincial clergymen or obscure literary enthusiasts. A gentlemanly convention of anonymity for reviewers was often treated with peculiar respect.[5] Laurence Sterne, the best-selling author of one of the first major novels of the age of reviews, *Tristram Shandy*, was combative about his reception by the reviews, yet never named any of his reviewers, even though he must have known who they were. While attribution of most articles in the *Critical* is still uncertain, a complete run of the *Monthly*, annotated by its editor Ralph Griffiths with the initials of contributors, allows us to know much about its composition. What is striking is how few men wrote much of the copy. At certain times in the late eighteenth century one particular reviewer might be producing half or more of the reviews of all published novels.[6] The fact that reviewers might be obscure could itself attract opprobrium. Hurling insults at the *Monthly Review*, the rival to his own *Critical Review*, Tobias Smollett declared in his 1755 manifesto for the *Critical* that its rival's critics were 'obscure Hackney Writers, accidentally enlisted in the Service of an undistinguishing bookseller'.[7] The *Critical* purported (like several other periodicals of the age) to be produced by a 'Society of Gentlemen'. While the *Critical* and the *Monthly*, the two most powerful reviews, were sometimes sour rivals, anonymity allowed an adept hack like Oliver Goldsmith simultaneously to write for both.[8] The frequent acrimony of the *Critical* itself excited curiosity about its editorship, and rumours of Smollett's involvement did circulate.[9]

There is early evidence of anonymity allowing writers to arrange the promotion of their work. Before reviewing had become a regular fact of periodical life, the novelist Samuel Richardson was helping ensure the success of his first novel *Pamela* by calling in what was owed him by William Webster, editor of the *Weekly Miscellany*. Richardson had forgiven Webster a debt of ninety pounds. Webster duly inserted in his journal a long ecstatic 'letter' to 'the Editor of *Pamela*', on the eve of the novel's publication, celebrating its 'Spirit of Truth', its arousal of 'Concern and Emotion' and its exemplary '*Instruction* and *Morality*'.[10] This anonymous letter was duly reprinted as a preface to the first edition of *Pamela*. The *Weekly Miscellany* added further advertisement and praise in subsequent issues; no one was to know of Richardson's leverage upon the periodical's editor until academic biographers discovered it a couple of centuries later.

As reviews became more important, anonymity allowed canny writers to arrange the charitable reception of their books. Smollett almost certainly wrote the complimentary review of his own *The Complete History of England* (1757–8) that appeared in the *Critical Review*.[11] Well-informed readers would have known of the author's involvement in the *Critical* and perhaps been forearmed. In other instances, review readers could not have known what was going on. In 1763 James Boswell published his *Letters between the Hon. Andrew Erskine and James Boswell*, a dry run for his later autobiographical writing and the first of his works to bear his name. It presented to the public his often facetious correspondence with his friend Andrew Erskine, only slightly doctored. Many who knew Boswell were appalled that such private communications, full of references to their acquaintances, should be, as his own father put it, 'perused by all and sundry'.[12] Reviews were mixed, but the *London Chronicle* of 27 April 1763 recommended it as 'a book of true genius, from the authors of which we may expect many future agreeable productions'. Unknown to readers, the review was written by Boswell himself. In the same year, Oliver Goldsmith reviewed favourably for both the *Monthly* and the *Critical* Richard Brooke's *New and Accurate System of Natural History*, the introduction and prefaces to which he had written himself.[13] Henry Fuseli appears to have reviewed his own *Remarks on Rousseau* (1767) in the *Critical*.[14] He later reviewed his own translation of his own brother's *Archives of Etymology* (1795).

An expert at procuring friendly reviews was Charles Burney, father of the novelist Fanny Burney, who worked for the *Critical Review* in the 1770s and 1780s. Roger Lonsdale's biography of the musicologist vividly depicts the shifts that anonymous reviewing made possible. In 1771 Burney published his *Italian Tour* and nudged a friend who reviewed regularly for the *Monthly Review*, William Bewley, into asking its editor, Ralph Griffiths, if he could review it. Bewley felt some 'casuistical niceties, or scrupulosities, quite habitual to me in the exercise of my new profession', but finally agreed.[15] He told Griffiths that he was Burney's friend, but still received the commission. The eventual review not only praised the *Tour* but recommended Burney's forthcoming *History of Music*. Meanwhile, the author had arranged that close family friend Samuel Crisp should review the book anonymously in the other leading review, the *Critical*. This too commended the forthcoming work as well as the one reviewed. In Burney's remaining correspondence, his embarrassed daughter Fanny deleted under thick black ink her father's reference to the article in a letter to Crisp. Scholarly detective work has, however, uncovered it, making clear that Crisp actually showed Burney a draft of the review in manuscript.[16] Two years later he published his *German Tour* and again made sure that Bewley reviewed it in the *Monthly*. 'I wish—as Reviewer only, by the bye—I had not known you,' wrote the troubled reviewer.[17] His review was restrained in its praise, but urged readers to buy the *History of Music* as soon as it appeared. And again Burney seems to have made sure that Crisp reviewed the work in the *Critical* (in a series of three articles).

In 1776 the first volume of Burney's magnum opus was published. Again Bewley provided, at Burney's prompting, complimentary coverage in the *Monthly*. The *Critical* reviewed Burney's *History* in fulsome terms over five articles between February and June 1776. The reviewer's identity is not known for certain, though Lonsdale speculates that it was Crisp or even Burney's daughter Susanna.[18] The second volume of Burney's (now highly regarded) work did not appear until 1782, when it was yet again honoured anonymously by Bewley in the *Monthly* and by what Lonsdale calls a 'friendly hand' in the *Critical* (in four articles). When Burney published his *Account of the Commemoration* he sent a copy to his friend Thomas Twining, asking that he provide a review. Twining was happy to do so, suggesting the *Monthly*, and even asking Burney for 'any particular wishes as to anything that I *shou'd*, or shou'd *not*, say'.[19] In a letter to the author, he explained that he would be including in the review '*some* little objection, or petty criticism, or minikin diff. of opinion . . . if only for a *blind*, that the reviewer may not seem troppo amico'. Twining sent his review to Burney – a 'dish of praise', as he accurately called it. Burney arranged for it to be inserted into the *Critical*, while in the *Monthly* he was being reviewed by another friend, George Colman. When, three years later, the last volume of the *History of Music* was published, Twining was again on hand with a celebratory review, this time for the *Monthly*.[20]

By the time that the young Coleridge was writing in the first number of his short-lived periodical *The Watchman* in 1796, the anonymity of reviewers could be seen as ensuring their corruption. 'I never purchased a book entirely on the credit of the reviews, in which I did not find myself disappointed.'[21] For 'it is hardly possible for an author, whose literary acquaintance is even moderately large, to publish a work which shall not be flattered in some one of the reviews by a personal friend, or calumniated by an enemy.' 'Far from the haunts of literary men, and personally acquainted with very few of them', his own reviews, he promised, could be trusted. Years later, his *Biographia Literaria* resounded with complaints about 'the dirty passions and impudence, of anonymous criticism'.[22] The convention of anonymity removed reviewers from debate. 'They are then no longer to be questioned without exposing the complainant to ridicule, because, forsooth, they are *anonymous* critics, and authorised as "synodical individuals" to speak of themselves plurali majesta-tico!'[23] The Latin phrase means 'with the royal plural', a sarcastic reference to the 'we' that was now established as the reviewer's impersonal pronoun. Coleridge felt he had 'run the critical gauntlet' of the reviewers for two decades, but he had himself used anonymity to skewer a rival in a review.[24] The *Biographia* reproduced his lengthy critique of Charles Maturin's play *Ber-tram*, which had itself first appeared anonymously. Coleridge's hostility to *Bertram* had been fired by its selection to be pro-duced at Drury Lane shortly after his own *Zapolya* had been rejected. However, no one who read the series of scathing reviews of Maturin's popular play that appeared as anonymous 'letters' to *The Courier* in 1816 would have known that they were penned by a disappointed rival.[25]

In the *Biographia* Coleridge protested that, having lived mostly 'either abroad or in retirement', his 'acquaintance with literary men' was 'limited and distant'.[26] Anonymity concealed the net-work of alliances, hidden from him, that prescribed ruling tastes. In a lengthy footnote (suppressed by his embarrassed son in posthumous editions) Coleridge described how dismissive refer-ences to himself, Wordsworth, Southey and Joanna Baillie in an *Edinburgh Review* article originated in personal grudges on the part of the reviewer, Francis Jeffrey. Baillie had snubbed Jeffrey socially, Southey had 'written against him', Wordsworth 'had talked contemptuously of him'.[27] Coleridge had heard that Jeffrey had admitted that his own name had been included in the tirade 'merely because the names of Southey and Wordsworth and Coleridge always went together'. Coleridge claimed that he knew many such 'anecdotes' concerning 'the characters, qualifica-tions, and motives of our anonymous critics, whose decisions are oracles for our reading public'. He grumbled in a later part of *Biographia* that Francis Jeffrey had spoken privately to him of his liking for *Lyrical Ballads*, even while justifying his antagonistic treatment of the work in the *Edinburgh*. Because 'a Review, in order to be a saleable article, must be *personal, sharp,* and *pointed,*' anonymous reviewers act as 'rogues'.[28] 'With the pen out of their hand they are *honorable men.*'

Those who write reviews are pursuing unacknowledged antagonisms or counterfeiting animosity that, in private, they admit to be a '*game*'. In 1809 Richard Cumberland's *London Review* briefly challenged this game, attaching to each of its reviews the name of the reviewer. In an Introductory Address, Cumberland declared that the impartial critic 'has no more need to hide his name than the tradesman has, who records himself over his shop-door'.[29] The *London Review* perished after only four issues. In the early nineteenth century, when quarterly periodicals thought themselves august publications, anonymity made the reviewer speak for the publication. The editors of the great quarterly reviews like the *Edinburgh, Quarterly* and *Westminster* felt free to revise reviews themselves, without consulting their authors. The journal gave the review its standing. Henry Cockburn, friend and biographer of Francis Jeffrey, editor of the *Edinburgh Review,* made a record of contributors to the journal; he noted that while most of these reviewers were happy to confirm their authorship (pleased to be recognized), Jeffrey and his successor, Macvey Napier, were reluctant to divulge such information.[30] The review's authority relied on its appearance of impersonality.

Jeffrey's identity as editor was known, as were the names of some of his main contributors. There was some sense of how much of the copy was produced by a few individuals. Hazlitt, for instance, in *The Spirit of the Age* (1825), reported that Jeffrey 'is the editor of the *Edinburgh Review,* and is understood to have contributed nearly a fourth part of the articles from its commencement'.[31] The *Wellesley Index to Victorian Periodicals,* published in the 1960s, first brought together all the evidence for the attribution of articles in nineteenth-century reviews. For the most part, it was composed from the publishers' indexes of contributors and payments made to them. We now know that, in its first two decades, almost half the *Edinburgh Review* was written by just three men: Sydney Smith, Henry Brougham and Jeffrey himself. Frequently, invisibly, the same issue would contain several reviews by the same man.

Authors would often believe they knew the identity of a reviewer in this periodical, and would often be wrong. Byron attacked Francis Jeffrey in *English Bards and Scotch Reviewers* because he thought him responsible for a disparaging review of his first collection of verse, *Hours of Idleness*, in the *Edinburgh Review*. The reviewer had in fact been Henry Brougham. After the *Edinburgh* praised *Childe Harold*, Byron wrote to Jeffrey apologizing for attacking him and received a reply hinting that he had misattributed the review: 'Perhaps I may at some future time disclose some particulars in our Reviewing history which may convince you that your resentment has hitherto been misdirected.'[32] Jeffrey's circumlocutory phrasing makes the point that actually revealing the authorship of a review would be a failure of editorial duty. Yet for many authors, anonymous reviewing excited energetic suspicion. It was natural to come to conclusions based on suppositions about personal grudge or ideological hostility. Coleridge was convinced that a mocking 1816 review of his poem 'Christabel' in the *Edinburgh Review* was written by his former admirer, now grown critic, Hazlitt (an attribution followed by many critics and biographers). In fact, it was by poetic rival Tom Moore.[33]

When Shelley wrote 'Lines to a Critic' in 1819 or 1820 he was probably addressing Robert Southey, whom he had identified as the author of a dismissive review of his poem *The Revolt of Islam* in the *Quarterly* in April 1819. Shelley, according to the reviewer, is 'imperfectly educated, irregular in his application, and shamefully dissolute in his conduct', 'a very vain man', 'too ignorant, too inexperienced, and too vicious to undertake the task of reforming any world, but the little world within his breast'.[34] Shelley read this in the reading room of Delesert's English Library in Florence. Having left Britain almost two years earlier, he was perhaps not in a good position to guess at its authorship. Hints of intimate biographical knowledge convinced Shelley that Southey, whom he had known a few years earlier, was the author. In June 1820 he wrote to ask him if he were indeed responsible: 'Some friends of mine persist in affirming that you are the author.'[35] Southey replied to deny it, but poured scorn on Shelley's beliefs and implicitly his sexual morals. A brief, heated correspondence ensued. Shelley remained convinced that Southey was the author of the offending review. In fact, it was John Taylor Coleridge, who had been at school with Shelley.

Particularly offensive reviews naturally provoked authors to try to discover the identity of the reviewer. A now notorious example is the review in *Blackwood's Magazine* by 'Z' of Keats's *Endymion* (1818). Keats's volume received several disparaging reviews, and it was J. W. Croker's anonymous critique in the *Quarterly Review* that, according to Shelley's Preface to *Adonais*, produced the ruptured blood vessel that eventually killed the poet. The *Blackwood's* review was the fourth of a series on 'The Cockney School of Poetry' that had already provoked Leigh Hunt, its main target, to challenge the reviewer to reveal himself and Hazlitt to sue for damages. Hazlitt had been told by his publishers that they were no longer willing to purchase his volume on *Comic Writers* for two hundred pounds because the belittling treatment of him in *Blackwood's* had lessened the value of his work.[36] Hazlitt wrote to Blackwood requiring the name of the anonymous author and, when Blackwood refused, began an action for damages. After a flurry of pamphlets and articles, Hazlitt agreed to settle privately. Keats spoke of requiring satisfaction from (in other words, fighting a duel with) the *Blackwood's* literary assassin, but his identity remained unknown. The review was probably written by John Gibson Lockhart and John Wilson. Coleridge considered suing *Blackwood's* for its review of *Biographia Literaria* in October 1817. In its early years, *Blackwood's* was dedicated to mischief and anonymity was its precondition. The attack on Keats and the 'calm, settled, imperturbable drivelling idiocy' of his poems is gleeful.[37]

Blackwood was, in effect, its editor-in-chief, but he was not named as such. When Walter Scott complained to him about the notorious October 1817 issue of the magazine, which mocked the Whig literati of Edinburgh, Blackwood typically replied, 'The Editor took his own way, and I cannot interfere with him.'[38] He commonly (and deceitfully) wrote to those who complained about the reviews as if he had no advance knowledge of them. In his periodical, the disguising of the identity of its writers became a game in which the clubbishness of his initial contributors was mischievously acted out. Some pseudonyms became well known, particularly those of John Wilson ('Christopher North') and James Hogg ('The Ettrick Shepherd'). In the now impenetrably specific 'Noctes Ambrosianae' they would talk boisterously in Ambrose's Tavern with other fictionalized characters from Blackwood's circle: 'Timothy Tickler', 'The Opium Eater' and 'Ebony' (the last being Blackwood's own transparent disguise). For the sake of stirring argument, contributors to *Blackwood's* became adept at producing contradictory views of the same author or work. John Wilson wrote an anonymous letter for the magazine in October 1817 energetically defending Wordsworth from anonymous criticism in the issue of June 1817 – which he had himself written, and was to resume in the very next issue, of November 1817.

Misattribution became an inevitable response of victims. The writer and editor John Scott complained to a publisher about being taken as the author of the articles on Leigh Hunt in

Blackwood's: 'Some one had said (I was told) that *I* had written the scandalous articles on Mr. Hunt! Articles which I read with disgust and abhorrence.'[39] As we have seen in the previous chapter, attribution was a mortal business for Scott. Elsewhere, William Gifford became known as the editor of the *Quarterly Review* and was assailed by those who suffered from his reviewers. Hazlitt's essay on Gifford in *The Spirit of the Age* passes on speculations about the various contributors to the *Quarterly* while treating the editor as personally responsible for the content of each. Yet cosiness was possible too. In the Introduction to *Chronicles of the Canongate* (1827), when Walter Scott acknowledged in print his authorship of the Waverley novels, he mentioned without apparent embarrassment that his friend William Erskine had reviewed 'Tales of my Landlord' in the *Quarterly Review* 'with far too much partiality'.[40] He even explained that 'other illustrations of the Novels' in this review were supplied by Scott himself. Here reviewing is naturally a kindness done between friends, a gentlemanly favour. The twist is that the manuscript of this review has survived and is mostly in Scott's own hand,[41] though with additions by Erskine and by William Gifford, the editor of the *Quarterly*. Erskine may have helped, but the article was an auto-review, the sceptical self-valuation that I discussed in Chapter 1. 'Provided the author can but contrive to "surprize and elevate", he appears to think that he has done his duty to the public.'[42] This is perhaps a flattering complaint. Yet there is no way that the average reader of the *Quarterly* might guess the playful purposes of the review. It is a rather brilliant exercise in self-promotion by pseudo-criticism. Scott is testing his fiction against inappropriate standards, mocking the ways in which his fiction was criticized. Yet the humour is too deeply buried to be enjoyed by any but a very few.

Supposedly, it was the periodical rather than the writer of a particular article that had the personality. An example of how anonymity might ease the making of this collective personality, whilst tickling readers' curiosity, is the self-projection of *Fraser's Magazine*. In 1835 it not only included an article on 'The Fraserians', describing an animated dinner party involving many of its supposed contributors, but also printed a drawing of the company by Daniel Maclise.[43] Here was the spirited, bibulous, irreverent circle into which the magazine's purchaser could enter. Its articles might be anonymous, but every reader was invited into the company of those who wrote them. Yet these 'Fraserians' were not quite the men who wrote *Fraser's Magazine*. Many of the writers pictured (including Southey and Thackeray) had at the time written nothing for *Fraser's*, while at least one (Coleridge) was actually dead. On the other hand, some of the magazine's most prolific contributors, being unknown literary hacks, were simply not present in the group portrait.[44] A year later, *Fraser's* turned the same trick with a group portrait of its supposed female contributors, 'Regina's Maids of Honour'.[45] Most of the notable women writers depicted were not actually contributors to the magazine. While apparently breaking through the conventional anonymity of the literary periodical, *Fraser's* was projecting a fiction about the origins of its articles.

The trick was characteristic of *Fraser's*, which relished critical mischief. To the more high-minded, anonymity in reviewing prevented what one defender of the practice called 'the establishment of a critical oligarchy'.[46] Instead, articles had to make their way on their intrinsic strengths. When the young Thomas Carlyle was living in an isolated Scottish farm in 1830, devouring the periodicals that were sent to him through the post, he wrote to his brother John in London to catch at his metropolitan knowledge. He had been reading the newly published *Fraser's Magazine* and was oddly impressed: 'Tell me if you can who manages it, who writes in it; how it works and has its being.'[47] As an aspiring writer, Carlyle needed to know more than the average reader, and especially what individuals were behind its unsigned articles. 'Who cannot, at a moment's notice, find out the author of an article in the *Edinburgh*, or the *Quarterly*, or *Blackwood*, or *Fraser*, or the *Times*, or the *Standard*, or the *John Bull*, or the *Examiner*?' asked William Maginn, editor of *Fraser's*.[48] The question was disingenuous. It might be the case that for such an insider as Maginn, knowing 'fifty names' that provided most published reviews, 'there is really no such thing as an anonymous writer,' but for his readers things were different.

In the same year in which Carlyle wrote his letter, a long and respectful review of William Godwin's new novel *Cloudesley* appeared in *Blackwood's*, one of the very magazines that he was reading. It could scarcely have praised more highly the work of an author who had long been neglected and now scraped a living from various kinds of literary hackwork. 'Of all modern writers, Mr Godwin has arrived most sedulously, and most successfully, at the highest species of perfection his department of art affords.'[49] The reviewer recalls his earlier novels; in reading each one, 'Our hearts swell responsive to every emotion he delineates.' *Cloudsley* is a fresh example of Godwin's powers. 'The composer rapts us from ourselves, filling our bosoms with new and extraordinary emotions, while we sit soul-enchained by the wonders of his art.' The reviewer notes that the novel records the 'truths and sentiments' learned by 'one who has lived so long, and, synonymous with this expression, suffered so much'. Godwin's faith in human nature and improvement is mentioned, every page of his book 'containing some lesson to teach us confidence, love, and hope'. But most of all the review is an awed testimony to the novelist's powers of narration and characterization.

The interest is imperative, but unconstrained; nature dwells paramount in every part. As it proceeds, it becomes

high-wrought, without being harrowing. To the end, the tragedy is tempered by the softest spirit of humanity; it touches
the verge of terror, only to bring us more soothingly back to
milder feelings.

Godwin, who had never got used to losing the fame and status
that he had enjoyed in the 1790s, must have been highly gratified.
   What most readers of *Blackwood's* would not have known was
that the review was written by Godwin's own daughter, Mary
Shelley. William Blackwood wrote to Mary Shelley to thank her
for the article. He enclosed a copy of it printed 'without omission or alteration, though a fastidious person may perhaps consider some expressions as rather a little partial'.[50] His comment
borders on admonishment. Clearly he did not believe that it was
wrong for her anonymously to review her own father's work, but
he did imagine that she might better overcome her partiality. Or
disguise it. The daughter's review of a father's book would have
been impossible without anonymity, but more common were
more subtle cases of partiality. When *Pauline*, his first published
poem, appeared anonymously in 1833, the twenty-one-year-old
Robert Browning swiftly wrote to William Johnson Fox, a friend
of friends who was the proprietor of the *Monthly Repository*.
With a mixture of flattery and humility, Browning duly prodded
Fox into producing the required review.[51] The later advent of
signed reviews would not prevent such manoeuvres, but would
certainly make them more difficult.
   The anonymity of reviewers troubled some writers. It sometimes seemed to stand for an essential fraudulence at the heart of
literary culture. In the 1830s the loudest enemy of anonymity was
Edward Bulwer (later Bulwer Lytton), who mounted his attack
in his anatomy of the state of the nation, *England and the English*
(1833). Bulwer, a fashionable novelist and journalist, angrily
rejected the idea that anonymity allowed reviewers impartiality.

The reality was that 'the very partiality and *respect* to *persons*, which the custom of the anonymous was to prevent, the anonymous especially shields and ensures'.[52] Various 'private feelings . . . colour the tone of the great mass of reviews.' His own considerable experience as an author taught him that this was because the reviewer's obscurity was usually only partial.

> This veil, so complete to the world, is no veil to the bookwriting friends of the person who uses it. *They* know the hand which deals the blow, or lends the help; and the critic willingly does a kind thing by his friend, because it is never known that in so doing he has done an unjust one by the public.[53]

Anonymous reviewing divided readers into the knowing and the unknowing. 'Were a sudden revelation of the mysteries of the craft now to be made, what—oh what would be the rage, the astonishment, of the public!'[54] If only readers realized, 'Nearly all criticism at this day is the public effect of private acquaintance.'[55]

Anonymous reviewing had become a matter for debate. A proponent of anonymity, answering Bulwer in the *New Monthly*, thought that 'criticism, by unveiling its mysteries, would sacrifice its power over others, and would itself degenerate into feebleness'.[56] The benighted reading public needed the illusion of impersonality, without which 'all the jealousies and enmities, the partialities and sycophancies' of the world of letters would become visible. Do away with the 'mysteries' and 'the literary profession would become odious and contemptible'. Some took Bulwer's side. In a signed article in *Fraser's Magazine* in 1835, John Galt deplored the 'gross libels' permitted by anonymity in reviewing and argued that authors should be required by law to reveal their identities on 'every work, small or great, in which others are concerned'.[57] During the 1830s, Thackeray was toiling at much anonymous literary journalism and often wrote for *Fraser's*. He turned to his Grub Street memories when he wrote his deeply autobiographical novel *Pendennis* (1848–50). Through the involvement of his hero, 'Pen', with the fictional *Pall Mall Gazette* he gives us a cameo of the life of a periodical a decade or more earlier and a satirical sketch of how anonymity worked.

Pen's uncle finds out at his London club that his nephew is responsible for a review making 'bitter fun' of a foolish, modish travel book by the Countess of Muffborough. He is complimented by a couple of her amused foes, the fellow critic Wenham and Lord Falconet, 'who had had the news from Percy Popjoy'.[58] The 'news' here is the fact that Pen is the author of the mocking article (the ridiculous would-be poet Popjoy, Lord Falconet's son, knows because he is one of Pen's circle). Major Pendennis is duly impressed and passes the attribution on proudly to important acquaintances. News of the reviewer's identity is the currency of a small part of the review's readership. Meanwhile, the *Pall Mall Gazette* more generally relies on the misinformed attribution of its articles by the wider public:

> Great names were cited amongst the contributors to its columns. Was there any foundation for these rumours? We are not at liberty to say whether they were well or ill founded.[59]

Thackeray parodies the bogus discretion with which editors excited the curiosity of the readers of periodicals. He lets us know that the 'columns' are being manufactured by two hacks. An article on foreign policy 'which was generally attributed to a noble lord' was 'in reality composed by Captain Shandon in the parlour of the "Bear and Staff" public house near Whitehall Stairs'. Some papers on high finance 'which were universally supposed to be written by a great statesman of the House of Commons' are actually fabricated by Pen's friend George Warrington.

The main reason to be suspicious of anonymous reviewing

was the puffing that it permitted and obscured. In her sketch of 'a heyday of puffing', Laurel Brake quotes from a letter from Thomas Hood, editor of Henry Colburn's *New Monthly Magazine*, to a prospective reviewer in 1843. 'I write in haste a few lines to put you on your guard, by telling you of the arrangements for reviewing in the Magazine.' Hood arranges, he says, all reviews except those of books published by Colburn himself. 'They are *done* by the persons of the establishment—Patmore, Williams or Shoberl. If you see the Mag. you will know what wretched things these reviews are.'[60] Hood was 'ashamed' of them – 'or should be were it not pretty well known that I have no hand in them'. Several publishers of books were, like Colburn and Blackwood before him, also the proprietors of periodicals that reviewed books. Elsewhere, daily and provincial papers, without literary staff, often took 'paid paragraphs' from the publishers of books. Professional writers knew all about this, but anonymity made the sources of these puffs invisible to the majority of ordinary readers.

As a refined hack living off what he called 'odious magazine-work' in the ten years before *Vanity Fair*, Thackeray used his contacts to try to ensure a good reception for the fiction that might purchase him an easier living. In July 1840 he was sending a copy of *The Paris Sketch Book* to John Forster and hoping for 'a good notice from you'.[61] His note accompanying the copy he sent to James Wilson, editor of the *Anti-Corn Law Circular*, on the same day was entirely candid. 'I do solemnly and pathetically adjure you to give poor Titmarsh a puff, for surely no man ever wanted one more than he.'[62] Forster duly (and anonymously) reviewed the book in the *Examiner*, without giving any indication as to the identity of its author. Forster, Thackeray thought, 'has tried to praise Titmarsh', even while not really caring for the book.[63] Henry Chorley, a friend of Thackeray's friend Bryan Waller Procter, reviewed the book anonymously in the *Athenaeum*. He knew

Thackeray's identity and sent him an advance copy of the review.[64] Thanks to his literary contacts, Thackeray knew his identity and wrote to him in gratitude. 'Name anything you wish as proof of my gratitude . . . Never was such a good-natured puff.'[65]

He asked Jane Carlyle to use her influence with Edward Sterling to procure a favourable review for his recently published *Comic Tales*. 'You can incite Sterling to get me a great puff of the reprint of YPlush in the Times.' His wife's sickness had left him in pressing need of money. Perhaps she could also use her influence with John Forster? 'Do not if you please now imagine that I want anything out of any body's pocket: but puffs puffs are what I desire.' A couple of years later he sent a pre-publication copy of his *Irish Sketch Book* to his great friend Percival Leigh asking him for the 'modest service' of a swift review in *Fraser's Magazine*.[66] 'Not a puff you understand, hit as hard as you like but in a good natured way.' Thackeray clearly felt some awkwardness about recruiting a reviewer whose loyalty was concealed from most readers by anonymity. We can see him being tempted to fix a review for *Vanity Fair* and then stepping back from doing so. He wrote to his friend William Aytoun seeking a favourable notice ('a push') for the new novel in *Blackwood's*. He then retracted the request. 'Puffs are good and the testimony of good men; but I don't think these will make a success for a man and he ought to stand as the public chooses to put him.'[67] The end of Thackeray's appeals for puffs, we might notice, came with the end of his anonymity.

The mutual back-scratching did not go without saying. Tennyson may not have actively endeavoured to procure a good reception for his reputation-making *Poems* of 1842, but genteel Victorian readers would not have been able to see the allegiances between himself and the particular reviewers in influential periodicals. Four of the reviewers – in the *Edinburgh Review*, the

Quarterly, the *Christian Remembrancer* and the *Westminster* –
were former fellow members of Cambridge University's Apostles
(itself a secret society).[68] We know that at least one of these, John
Sterling, had private reservations about the volume, which he
kept out of his review. Another, James Spedding, author of the
review in the *Edinburgh*, was a very close friend of Tennyson.
Spedding's praise came to seem close to the truth of Tennyson's
talent.

> The human soul, in its infinite variety of moods and trials, is
> his favourite haunt; nor can he dwell long upon any subject,
> however apparently remote from the scenes and objects of
> modern sympathy, without touching some string which brings
> it within the range of our common life.[69]

Yet the review-reading public was being tricked into believing this
an impartial verdict.

In the mid-nineteenth century, though the vast majority of
articles were still anonymous, there were principled moves
against the practice.[70] When John Stuart Mill took over the *Westminster Review* in the late 1830s, he introduced signatures for
reviews, if only in the form of initials or pictograms. The convention had been used sometimes in eighteenth-century periodicals. A writer's contributions were thus made singular – his
property rather than the journal's. A regular reader could recognize a regular reviewer, without actually knowing his or her
identity. However, strict imposition of this policy ceased when
Mill relinquished editorial control in 1840. Other journals came
to have comparable 'rules'. In 1856 George Eliot explained what
had become the convention in *Fraser's Magazine* to Sara Hennell.
'The rule in Frazer [sic] is to put your initials to your articles
unless there is a reason to the contrary.'[71] Yet evidently even this
did not amount to a clear declaration. Eliot added that a review
by G. H. Lewes in *Fraser's* had prompted a letter from an

admirer who 'didn't seem to have a suspicion that G. H. L. was
G. H. Lewes!' Eliot was amused because the correspondent was
George Combe, who had earlier clashed with Lewes and called
him a 'shallow, flippant man'. 'However, we should all of us pass
very different judgements now and then, if the thing to be
judged were anonymous.'

Those who lived by anonymous reviewing found themselves
fending off wrong guesses. There is much of this in Eliot's letters,
often on behalf of Lewes. Sometimes she is delighted by readers'
errors, sometimes irritated. Even those close to her made mistakes about his output of reviews. Underlining her words, she
sternly told Charles Bray the previous year, '*Mr. Lewes* has <u>never
written a line about Mr. Silk Buckingham</u> in the Leader.'[72] Bray
had supposed that Lewes might have written a satirical review of
Buckingham's *Autobiography*. 'This is another admonition not
to be too hasty in judgement,' wrote Eliot. A few months later
she was telling Sara Hennell, 'If you should happen to hear any
one imputing articles in the Leader to Mr. Lewes, be so good as
to say that he only writes the summary and *occasional* reviews.'[73]
A year later, writing to Hennell, she is positively cross that a dismissive account of the sentimental poems of Caroline Phillipson
in the *Westminster Review* had been attributed by the author to
Lewes in a satirical pamphlet. 'I was annoyed at her attributing
the criticism to Mr. Lewes and wished to deny for the Westminster reading public in general that he has anything to do with the
Contemporary Literature.'[74] In fact, she had written the offending
notice herself.

Read Eliot's correspondence from her time with the *Westminster Review* and you keep glimpsing the influence of anonymity
in reviewing. With close friends she is often playful about the
attribution of reviews by her and her 'husband'. 'Since you have
found out the "Cumming," I write by today's post just to say, that
it is mine,' she tells her former mentor Charles Bray, a Coventry

ribbon-maker. He has guessed at her authorship of a deeply antagonistic article on the evangelical writings of Dr John Cumming.[75] She goes on 'to beg that you will not mention it as such to any one likely to transmit the information to London, as we are keeping the authorship a secret'. It is now often thought that Eliot's sarcastic, indignant assault on the teachings of this notable Calvinist writer gains some of its force from the writer's engagement with beliefs that she had been taught in her youth. She originally wanted, however, to separate the argument from herself. 'The article appears to have produced a strong impression, and that impression would be a little counteracted if the author were known to be a *woman*,' she told Bray.

In controversial cases like this anonymity could set her at liberty. Eliot's confession of authorship had been made in response to Bray's urgent inquisitiveness.

> Mrs John Cash read aloud to us the article on the 'Cumming' in the Westminster – We all said it must be yours, or we wd never guess again – No-one else *could* do it, altho' I shd be pleased to think that we had another person who could do it. *Tell us.*[76]

Bray and his free-thinking friends relished the assault on evangelical self-regard and irrationality. What is most telling is Bray's expression of their confidence that the author must be his former protegée. 'We all said it must be yours, or we wd never guess again.' A highly unlikely eventuality. The very comment indicates how inescapable 'guessing' was for the adept review reader. Speculating about the authorship of provocative reviews was the habitual activity of those in the know. The attempts at author-spotting of Bray and his friends show that even those who found themselves geographically remote from the intellectual life of the metropolis could, by attributing reviews, become insiders. The *Westminster Review* was produced by a circle of liberal intellectuals. To be able to 'discover' some of its writers was, in imagination at least, to belong to that circle. Guessing at authorship was often a way of claiming kinship.

The last review article that George Eliot wrote before she began *Scenes of Clerical Life* was 'Silly Novels by Lady Novelists', published in October 1856 in the journal that she had (anonymously) edited from 1851 to 1854, the *Westminster Review*. This piece discussed five recent novels by women (though two were anonymous and were assumed by the reviewer to have female authors). It is a tour de force of mockery by quotation, in which the works described are satirized for their curious mixtures of intellectual pretension and stylistic ineptitude. It has seemed unsisterly to some, but its final, earnest argument is that women should have higher literary ambitions. Regretting 'the fatal seduction of novel-writing to incompetent women', it professes great hopes for 'the share women may ultimately take in literature'.[77] It is written in the disembodied first-person plural that was conventional in Victorian reviewing. 'We had imagined that destitute women turned novelists, as they turned governesses, because they had no other "lady-like" means of getting their bread . . . But no! This theory of ours, like many other pretty theories, has had to give way before observation.' It must once have been easy to hear in the reviewer's disdain for 'lady novelists' an educated masculine condescension. Imagine reading sentences like the following under the assumption that the writer is male. 'There seems to be a notion abroad among women, rather akin to the superstition that the speech and actions of idiots are inspired, that the human being most entirely exhausted of common sense is the fittest vehicle of revelation.'[78] Marian Evans was conscious of her readers' expectations and played up to them. When the review says that 'the severer critics are fulfilling a chivalrous duty in depriving the mere fact of feminine authorship of any false prestige', it implies that this duly severe reviewer is indeed a man, laughingly excusing himself of impolite treatment of a 'lady'.

In response to curiosity about the authorship of reviews, some who practised anonymity made it a code of honour and even an obsession. Charles Wentworth Dilke, editor of the influential *Athenaeum* magazine, never signed anything he wrote and scrupulously guarded against the names of his reviewers ever escaping the office. He would severely admonish any staff member who confided the name of a reviewer to anyone outside the magazine.[79] Dilke fought a long, determined campaign against puffery. For him, anonymity in reviewing, sternly maintained, was a guarantee of integrity, not just a formal convention. Anonymity became a kind of critical value; all critics should aim to transcend personality. Dilke felt this so strongly that he himself became reclusive so as to avoid compromising literary acquaintanceships.[80]

For jobbing reviewers, there was a more practical consideration. Anonymity cloaked from the majority of readers the fact that particular reviewers wrote for rival reviews. It enabled George Eliot, for instance, to 'double dip', reviewing in the mid-1850s for the *Leader* books about which she would also write notices in the *Westminster*.[81] If it had not been for anonymity, apparently rivalrous publications would have been shown to rely on many of the same writers. When Francis Espinasse, writing in the *Critic* under the pseodonym 'Herodotus Smith', exposed to the public the editors and reviewers of several leading journals, he identified in articles in *Blackwood's Magazine* 'the sparkles of an unmistakeable and unique vivacity'.[82] 'The reader has already guessed the name, and . . . murmurs fondly: "Once more the omnipresent LEWES!".' Lewes's reviewing style might have a 'unique vivacity', but it seemed to be everywhere. In fact, in forty years Lewes wrote more than five hundred periodical articles, the great majority anonymous. And only modern scholarship has revealed the previously concealed productivity of a man like William Maginn, who was not just editing but writing a large fraction of *Fraser's Magazine*, while simultaneously editing and writing for the *Standard*, as well as regularly providing articles for several other papers.[83]

Equally, we now know of some of those invisible arrangements that versatile literary journalists could make with those whom they liked or admired. When Sara Hennell was about to publish her book *Christianity and Infidelity* (1857), her friend George Eliot asked her, 'Should you like *me* to review it for the Leader or Mr. Lewes?'[84] Eliot had given up reviewing to concentrate on her fiction, 'But your book is exceptional, and I should like to do what you wish.' Eliot had already helped Hennell revise her book. In the event, Lewes wrote the anonymous review (*The Leader*, 28 February 1857). He was used to this sort of thing. Reviewing under the pseudonym of 'Vivian' for the liberal weekly *The Leader*, he loyally puffed the work of his friend Richard Henry Horne, whom Lewes thought unfairly neglected by critics and readers. In March 1856 he reviewed *Principles of Psychology* by his old friend Herbert Spencer. Eliot might be thought to have taken loyalty to an extreme when she anonymously reviewed Lewes's own *Life and Works of Goethe* (1855) in *The Leader*. Her judgement was peculiarly compromised as she had actually helped him compose it. Reading the review now, one can sense Eliot's reticence about praising the book, which is recommended more by talk of the interest of Goethe than of the achievements of Lewes. Yet there is praise: of Lewes's 'honest' ability to make a mass of material coherent, of his capacity to give 'vividness and reality' to his account of Goethe's life as a young man.[85] There is no hint that the reviewer is acquainted with the author.

Metropolitan writers were frequently able to identify anonymous reviewers when they wished to do so. Anthony Trollope recalled how, when a laudatory, anonymous review of his fiction appeared in *The Times* in 1859, he used his contacts to find out its author, E. S. Dallas, in order to thank him. 'I told him that he had done me a greater service than can often be done by one man to another, but that I was under no obligation to him.'[86] An opponent of anonymity, Trollope emphasized that he would be part of no hidden system of favour and flattery. He disapprovingly told the story of how Dickens gave a certain critic (Dallas again, though Trollope does not name him) the bound manuscript of *Our Mutual Friend* 'as an acknowledgement for a laudatory review in one of the leading journals of the day'.[87] Dallas proudly showed it to Trollope, asking 'whether I did not regard such a token as a sign of grace both in the giver and in the receiver'. When Trollope expressed his disquiet at the transaction, his scruples were 'repudiated with scorn, and I was told that I was straight-laced, visionary and impracticable!'

Sometimes the reasons for a reviewer's partiality remained hidden until academic research discovered them. In 1857 Dickens was driven to reply in *Household Words* to a fierce, unsigned attack on *Little Dorrit* in the *Edinburgh Review*. The reviewer conceded that Dickens 'has described modern English low life with infinite humour and fidelity', but denounced his treatment of 'the institutions of the country, the laws, the administration, in a word the government under which we live'.[88] In particular the reviewer objected to the depiction of the 'Circumlocution Office', which stands for the British Civil Service. One of its leading representatives is Barnacle Tite, a fictionalized version of the high-ranking civil servant Sir James Stephen; the reviewer (unknown to Dickens) was his son, James Fitzjames Stephen. Dickens saw the reviewer's 'zeal for the Circumlocution Office', as he put it, but not exactly his motivation.[89]

Dickens himself played an important role in the increasing frequency of 'signed' contributions to journals. In his own weeklies, *Household Words* and *All the Year Round*, his fiction was sold under his name, and soon his other contributions were also being signed. By the 1860s it was usual for popular novelists to attach their names to the fiction they serialized in periodicals. This became one of the most important ways in which many periodicals were marketed. In the 1860s, several serious journals began publishing signed reviews as a matter of policy and the argument over anonymous reviewing acquired a new momentum. The *Fortnightly Review*, founded in 1865, solemnly announced that its articles would all have 'the gravity of an avowed responsibility'. 'Each contributor, in giving his name, will not only give an earnest of his sincerity, but will claim the privilege of perfect freedom of opinion, unbiased by the opinions of the Editor or of fellow contributors.'[90] One of the founders of the *Fortnightly* was Trollope. Looking back ruefully in his *Autobiography*, Trollope recalled that its two founding principles were 'freedom of speech' (that it should have no particular ideological affiliation) and 'personal responsibility' (everything would be signed).[91] An early issue contained a substantial article by Trollope, arguing that the anonymous writer in periodicals 'will not be on his mettle, and will dare to be slovenly, inconsequential, and unjust', and that the critic, in particular, has a public duty to declare his name (though conceding that a woman writer has good reason modestly to conceal herself).[92] The *Fortnightly's* first editor was Lewes. George Eliot's first ever signed review (as 'GE') appeared in the *Fortnightly* in 1865.[93] Others followed the lead, with journals like the *Contemporary Review* and the *Nineteenth Century* selling themselves on the names of their contributors. Some individuals became known for refusing on principle to review anonymously. On the other hand, the defences of anonymity at this time often spoke in terms of high literary idealism. 'The anonymous author', the experienced *Spectator* reviewer Alexander Ross wrote in 1869, 'is at liberty to refer continually to an ideal standard — to what is strictly impersonal.'[94]

Most reviewing remained anonymous. Thomas Hardy's novel *A Pair of Blue Eyes* (1873) dramatizes the distance between the literati who think they know the arbiters of literary achievement, and the reading public who know nothing. In Hardy's novel, the distance is geographical. Elfride Swancourt is an intelligent young woman with ambitions to be a novelist who lives at 'the sea-swept outskirts of Lower Wessex' (Hardy's version of Cornwall) and reads highbrow periodicals.[95] She has never heard of her suitor-to-be Henry Knight, even though he is an influential literary journalist. Her lover Stephen, who admires Knight's writing, explains why. 'Because his personality, and that of several others like him, is absorbed into a huge WE, namely, the impalpable entity called THE PRESENT – a social and literary Review.'[96] Elfride is impressed, for she reads this review. 'We have it sent to us irregularly. I want papa to be a subscriber, but he's so conservative.' Later her novel, an Arthurian romance, is reviewed in *The Present*. The anonymous reviewer immediately discerns that, although it has been published as by 'Ernest Field', it is certainly by 'some young lady'.[97] The review is mostly satirical, while discerning some surprising signs of talent. Elfride does not know the identity of the critic, yet 'a stranger with neither name nor shape, age nor appearance, but a mighty voice, is naturally rather an interesting novelty to a lady he chooses to address.'[98] She replies to the reviewer, justifying herself and signing the letter with her initials. 'The less you are known the more you are thought of,' she observes. The reviewer, of course, is Knight, who easily penetrates the secret of her identity and is, in effect, introduced to her by this odd literary exchange.[99] Inevitably, he displaces Stephen in her affections.

A year later, in *The Way We Live Now* (1874–5), Trollope

satirized the manoeuvres of those 'in the know'. The novel opens with the impecunious Lady Carbury writing to the editors of three periodicals in an attempt to arrange sympathetic reviews of her pseudo-historical book *Criminal Queens*, soon to be published. She wins over Mr Broune of the 'Morning Breakfast Table' (probably based on the *Daily Telegraph*) by assiduous flirtation, but Mr Booker of the more academic 'Literary Chronicle' is contemptuous of her book. Lady Carbury is careful to let him know that, by arrangement with the enamoured Mr Broune, she is to review his own latest book for the 'Morning Breakfast Table'. Mr Booker has little choice:

> he was quite alive to the fact that a favourable notice in the 'Breakfast Table' of his very thoughtful work, called the 'New Tale of a Tub,' would serve him, even though written by the hand of a female literary charlatan, and he would have no compunction as to repaying the service by fulsome praise in the 'Literary Chronicle'.[100]

None of this, naturally, would be so easily managed without anonymity.

Lady Carbury dedicates herself to winning over the reviewers. 'She had no ambition to write a good book, but was painfully anxious to write a book that the critics should say was good.'[101] The anonymity of reviewers makes her enterprise possible. Despite Trollope's own assault on anonymous reviewing in the 1860s, it was still the rule. The novelist tells us that Mr Booker was 'an honest man' who 'had set his face persistently against many literary malpractices', but was helpless to resist:

> circumstanced as he was he could not oppose himself altogether to the usages of the time. 'Bad; of course it is bad,' he said to a young friend who was working with him on his periodical. 'Who doubts that? How many very bad things are

there that we do! But if we were to attempt to reform all our bad ways at once, we should never do any good thing. I am not strong enough to put the world straight, and I doubt if you are.'[102]

The puffing and the corruption of judgement are 'bad', but the truly bad 'usages of the times' are the effects of anonymity. Trollope suggests that it is *the* guilty secret of the literary world. For good measure, he shows how futile is Lady Carbury's third letter of ingratiation, to Mr Ferdinand Alf of the 'Evening Pulpit'. This paper makes its name and pleases its readers by always finding fault, so despite 'the dear friendship between her self and Mr. Alf', 'One of Mr. Alf's most sharp-nailed subordinates had been set upon her book, and had pulled it to pieces with almost rabid malignity.'[103] This anonymous reviewer researches her many errors. 'He must have been a man of vast and varied erudition, and his name was Jones.' Beneath his anonymity, Mr Alf's hack can affect any degree of superiority. 'The world knew him not, but his erudition was always there at the command of Mr. Alf,—and his cruelty.'

By the 1880s, previously obdurate journals had begun to use signatures for reviews, though some weeklies kept to anonymous reviewing: the *Spectator* and *Athenaeum* stayed anonymous to the end of the century, while the *Saturday Review* only began regularly attributing reviews in the 1890s. Most contributions to the *Edinburgh Review* remained anonymous until 1912. Writing in the 1880s, Trollope was pleased that 'signatures to articles in other periodicals have been much more common since *The Fortnightly* was commenced'.[104] Yet he also reflected that 'an ordinary reader would not care to have his books recommended to him by Jones; but the recommendation of the great unknown comes to him with all the weight of the *Times*, the *Spectator*, or the *Saturday*'.[105] When Tighe Hopkins surveyed the debate about anonymity in the *New Review* in 1889, he could draw a clear distinction between the weekly and monthly reviews, which were learning the benefits of signature, and 'the newspaper Press', which maintained the 'immemorial usage' of anonymity.[106] He felt confident that signed reviews in monthly periodicals had shown that 'the employment of the signature secures to the writer all the freedom of expression that just criticism requires'.[107] 'The new system is making way, and much more rapid way at present than it has made at any previous time.'[108] In the same year Edmund Gosse looked back with some incredulity on the past dominance of the convention of anonymous reviewing. 'A more *naïve* generation was overawed by the nameless authority that moved behind a review.'[109] Before the end of the century signed reviews were becoming common in London daily newspapers.

In George Gissing's unenchanted account of the life of writing in late Victorian London, *New Grub Street* (1891), the widowed Amy Reardon, who is being courted by the literary journalist Jasper Milvain, shows that she is taking an interest in him by claiming that she does not miss many of his articles. 'Sometimes I believe I have detected you when there was no signature.'[110] Now she really is learning to belong to his world. A clever reviewer might hope to be recognized by the informed reader. Aspiring writers hoped to be allowed to sign an article in a daily: to have a name was to be somebody. There is another nice illustration in *New Grub Street*. The grim Alfred Yule, who makes a poor living as a literary journalist, realizes that his daughter and co-labourer Marian has literary gifts that have been denied to him. Her articles, published anonymously, have a 'grace' that his entirely lack. 'It began to be a question with him whether it would not be advantageous to let the girl sign these compositions.'[111] If her published work had her name, that name might begin to increase the market value of her writing. 'A matter of business, to be sure.'

Yet enough reviewing was anonymous to make the old tricks playable in new ways. Amongst lesser-known writers self-reviewing was still possible. Leslie Marchand notes Henry Reeve's review in the *Athenaeum* praising his own translation of Guizot's *Washington*.[112] The same periodical saw something close to self-reviewing in the anonymous article written jointly by Leonard and Virginia Woolf about two of the first publications by their own Hogarth Press, T. S. Eliot's *Poems* and John Middleton Murray's *The Critic in Judgement*. What is more, Murray was the (nameless) editor of the *Athenaeum*. On Eliot, the review affects a certain bewilderment. 'Mr Eliot is certainly damned by his newness and strangeness.'[113] Yet it manages to imply that the reviewer's uncertainty is a consequence of the poet's achievement, and that the review cannot help praising him: 'The poetry of the dead is in his bones and at the tips of his fingers,' and the like.

Jeremy Treglown, co-editor of the *TLS* electronic archive, has happened upon instances of disguised self-praise in early issues of the *TLS*.[114] Stanley Morison, editor of the *TLS* from 1945 to 1947, was to claim, without apparent irony, that the self-review was the ideal.

> The best reviewer of the book is the author. I asked an author the other day whether he could suggest anybody who would review his book, – thus giving him the chance to do it himself. Unfortunately he was such an English gentleman that he did not even like such a question being put to him. So of course I had all the trouble of finding an alternative.[115]

The anonymity of *TLS* reviews might have allowed coteries more easily to gather influence, but it could also allow reviewers to pretend to a status as outsider. So, for instance, Ezra Pound was reviewing for the *TLS* during the First World War, even as he was complaining that he was ostracized by London editors.

The *TLS*'s first influential editor, Bruce Richmond, made an ethic of self-effacement. He was to edit the *TLS* for thirty-five years, believing in the ideal of a kind of tonal unanimity: the voice of authority. Virginia Woolf, whose career as a reviewer was closely tied to the development of the *TLS* and the patronage of Richmond, was one of many who adapted her style to meet his ideal. Her biographer Hermione Lee notes that in her early reviews, 'She assumed an impersonal, authoritative tone . . . to the point of sounding sometimes absurdly formal.'[116] It was standard practice for sub-editors to remove the first-person pronoun from articles submitted by contributors who had not understood what a later editor Alan Pryce-Jones called 'our scheme of anonymity'.[117] But she was writing namelessly. 'Read your Guardian carefully and see if you find anything about Henry James; the first words, like a coin with a head on it, will tell you who wrote it,' she wrote to Violet Dickinson.[118] Presumably the readers of the review (of *The Golden Bowl*) would not have known that the author was an old friend of the reviewer's family. Nor would readers of the *Lit Supp* have known that the reviewer who in 1907 found Henry James's travel book *The American Scene* 'crowded, sensitive, intricate . . . probably the most remarkable book of impressions of travel which we possess' was his friend and devotee Percy Lubbock.

The dispassionate self-image of the *TLS* belied networks of allegiance and intimacy. Woolf reviewed the work of various friends and relatives: Forster, Roger Fry, Vanessa Bell. In October 1924 she wrote to her old friend Molly MacCarthy admitting playfully that she had reviewed her autobiographical *A Nineteenth Century Childhood* in the *TLS*.[119] However, the tricks of intimacy did sometimes trouble her. In her diary she recorded receiving a review copy of a new book by Molly MacCarthy's husband Desmond, 'sent, I'm sorry to say, by request of the author'.[120] He wanted her to be its reviewer, and she clearly did

not like being asked for the favour. Yet she did ask *TLS* editor
Bruce Richmond if she might review MacCarthy's book, as well
as Lytton Strachey's *Eminent Victorians*. Strachey had asked her
a month earlier to review his book. 'I agreed without thinking,'
Woolf wrote in her diary.[121] 'On second thoughts I don't much
want to write under surveillance, or to ask B[ruce]. R[ichmond].
for what he must know to be the book of a friend.' Her subsequent diary entry gives a strange sense of what might be called
the ethics of anonymous reviewing.

> Richmond, when I asked for D.'s and Lytton's books said
> 'Certainly—if you can keep it secret.' I couldn't promise to do
> this, & therefore wrote to tell him not to send them. And now
> I must inform Desmond & Lytton. They won't suffer really I
> believe, but they will be anxious instead of safe, & I'm in two
> minds as to whether I'm glad or sorry. I think I could have said
> some very clever things, & a few true things, but undoubtedly
> one can't avoid a certain uneasiness in writing formally of
> people one knows so well.

Richmond was requiring some real vow of silence, as if the convention of anonymity were a trust to be kept beyond the pages of
his journal – even in the drawing rooms of Bloomsbury. Woolf
was not prepared to keep her authorship a secret from her own
circle, which included the two authors themselves, and therefore
declined writing the review. She was, we might note, quite content that a metropolitan literary circle should know of the article's authorship while the bulk of readers of the *TLS* would
remain entirely oblivious to the intimacy between reviewer and
reviewed.

Under Richmond the *Lit Supp*, as it was usually known, did
sometimes find it necessary to signal some kind of intimacy
between reviewer and reviewee. When the author of a book had
some close association with the paper or with *The Times*, it was

normal to name the reviewer. Guarding against possible accusations of nepotism was obviously thought necessary. For literary
men and women, the authorship of a review was often discoverable (and therefore worth lively curiosity); for a larger public, the
anonymity was invariably real. His eyes raised above the business of favours and enmities, T. S. Eliot, who wrote what were to
be influential early essays for the *TLS*, celebrated 'the discipline
of anonymity'. 'I am firmly convinced that every young literary
critic should learn to write for some periodical in which his contributions will be anonymous . . . I learn to moderate my dislikes
and crotchets, to write in a temperate and impartial way.'[122] In a
letter of 2 October 1919, he told his mother that being asked to
write a 'Leading Article' in the *TLS* was 'the highest honour
possible in the critical world of literature'.[123]

Many still took this stance. Stephen Spender's first contribution to the *TLS* was a signed article in October 1938 calling for
more anonymous reviewing. (By the 1940s, a quarter of the
articles in the *TLS* were signed.) In 1958, when a debate about
anonymity in the *TLS* broke to the surface, Eliot wrote to the
journal saying that a 'young reviewer' needs access to a 'prominent review' which publishes its articles anonymously.[124] The
argument about anonymity had been triggered by an article by
F. W. Bateson in *Essays in Criticism* arguing forcefully that 'the
worth of an opinion varies with the degree of respect we have for
the holder'. Pryce-Jones replied with an (anonymous) *TLS* editorial on the virtues of anonymity, which in its turn provoked
a copious correspondence. The debate was still rumbling in
January 1961, when T. S. Eliot wrote an article for Bruce Richmond's ninetieth birthday in which he talked of the benign
effects of the discipline of anonymity.[125]

The importance of anonymity to the meaning of a review
could still be measured in the oddness of some of its effects. In
1962 the *TLS* printed a letter from M. C. Bradbrook on a piece

about Blake which, she complained, had slighted Kathleen Raine
– who had in fact been the author of the review.[126] In May 1967
an anonymous article in the *TLS* attacked a scientific publisher
for its supposedly excessive charges for abstracts of articles from
Russian scientific journals. The publisher, Eugene Gros, sued for
libel, and in the course of the case it was found that the author of
the piece, Serweryn Chomet, was a former employee of the company he attacked. The judge found for the publisher, deciding
that the article had been motivated by malice. Yet the issue was
no longer being debated in the journal's pages. Bateson returned
to the attack in *Essays in Criticism* in April 1971. More powerfully,
the American historian J. B. Kelly published a detailed attack
on the *TLS*'s coverage of books on the Middle East in 1973,
claiming that anonymity had allowed anti-Zionist propaganda
and inexpert commentary. The following year, on 7 June 1974,
editor John Gross announced the phased ending of anonymity.

7

MOCKERY AND DEVILRY

In 1601, late in Elizabeth I's reign, there appeared a pamphlet entitled *The Whipping of the Satyre* and signed 'W. I.', which condemned the ill spirit of some of the writers of the age. Its speaker describes in stanzaic verse how he comes as a pilgrim to an earthly paradise, a 'blessed Land' of eternal Spring whose inhabitants sit by 'Azure brookes' in fragrant 'bowres of shady wandring vines', clapping their hands and 'Singing *Eliza*'.[1] All is well in this happy Elizabethan country, yet three madly malcontented characters, 'the Satyrist, Epigrammatist, and Humorist', snarl and complain, 'peevishly displeasing all that heares'.[2] These three are the authors of satires, compositions achieved only by perverse self-torment. 'O, ye were as busie as a Bee, and as angry as a Wasp, the heate of your colour euaporated her imagination, and the liberality of your tongue maintained most absolute lyes for the atchieuing of the whetstone,' W. I. tells one of the authors.[3] The baleful satirists deserve punishment for their poisoned inventions.

> Was not one hang'd of late for libeling?
> Yes questionlesse. And you deserve the same.[4]

(The 'one hang'd of late' was the unfortunate lawyer's clerk mentioned in Chapter 5.)

We now know that the three sour characters were, respectively, John Marston, Everard Guilpin and Ben Jonson, though it is not certain that W. I. knew their true identities. Marston and Guilpin had both contributed anonymously to a flurry of verse

satires published in the 1590s. In his hostility to the genre W. I.
had the authorities on his side. In 1599 the Archbishop of
Canterbury John Whitgift (the same man who had been the target of the Marprelate pamphlets, a decade earlier) and the Bishop
of London Richard Bancroft (active in the pursuit of the Marprelate printers) had issued an order to the Stationers' Company
banning the printing of satires. 'Satyres tearmed Halls Satyres,
viz' Virgidemiarum, or his tootheles or bitinge Satyres' were
named first on a list of those to be collected and burned.[5] The
other books included 'Pigmalion with certaine other Satyres',
'The scourge of villanye', 'The Shadowe of truthe in Epigrams
and Satyres' and 'Snarlinge Satyres'. The authors of these were
not named. They were duly 'called in' and burned on 4 June
1599. (Hall's satires were eventually reprieved from destruction,
perhaps in order to be examined further.) It is clear that the two
bishops were acting with the approval of the Queen's Privy
Council, and specifically of Secretary of State Robert Cecil.[6]

A vogue for formal verse satires had been excited by Joseph
Hall's collection *Virgidemiae* (the title means 'a harvest of
rods'), which had appeared anonymously in 1597, with a second
part, to which Hall set his initials, in 1598. A Latin epigram by
Charles Fitzgeoffrey suggests that it excited speculation about
its authorship.[7] *Virgidemiae* mocked the followers of the age's
literary fashions: tragedians, romancers and the 'loue-sicke
Poet'.

> Then poures he forth in patched *Sonettings*
> His loue, his lust, and loathsome flatterings.[8]

The satirist was to be distinguished from the favour-seekers of
the day.

> Nor can I crouch, and writhe my fauning tayle
> To some great Patron, for my best availe.[9]

It was followed in 1598 by John Marston's *The Metamorphosis of Pigmalions Image and Certaine Satyres*, its prefatory verses signed 'W. K.' The four verse satires that Marston included may have been written to 'vexe the guilty of our time', but the targets are general: a young man trained in 'all the points of courtship' who writes 'dainty rimes' to his mistress; a 'meale-mouth'd' Puritan who rails against the times but is really a usurer, hungry for worldly profit; a 'dapper' young man who prides himself on his exquisite dress.[10] The only personal abuse comes in the verses labeled 'Reactio' which are directed at Hall and which include lines quoted or parodied from *Virgidemiae*.[11] The exact reasons for the antagonism are now obscure; Marston lambasts his fellow satirist, whom he never actually names, for his bitterness and misanthropy.

A second collection by Marston, *The Scourge of Villanie*, was published in 1598 under the pseudonym 'W. Kinsayder'. Here the poet speaks as the indignant malcontent, tormented by the follies and vices of the age. 'My soule is vext, what power will'th desist? / Or dares to stop a sharpe fanged Satyrist?'[12] The same year saw another of the collections named in the bishops' ban, Everard Guilpin's *Skialetheia. Or, A Shadow of Truth, in certaine Epigrams and Satyres*, published anonymously. It justifies satire, like Hall, by dismissing less astringent poetic genres of the day.

> Hence with these fiddlers, whose oyle-buttred lines,
> Are Panders unto lusts, and food to sinnes,
> Their whimpering Sonnets, puling Elegies
> Slaunder the Muses; make the world despise,
> Admired poesie, marre *Resolutions* ruffe,
> And melt true valour with lewd ballad stuffe.[13]

Satire is a generic malcontent, set upon scourging, biting, and snarling. It flourishes in a special domain. In his satires Guilpin says that he is surrounded by 'other wits which make court to bright fame'.[14] Hall, Marston and Guilpin were all students at the Inns of Court. Educated and ambitious young men, they had come to London to study law but also to look for advancement at court. To some extent, they wrote for (or against) each other. Another of their number was John Donne, who wrote (but did not publish) a series of verse satires between 1592 and 1594. These circulated in manuscript, though Donne was far too cautious to let them be printed. 'To my satyrs there belongs some fear,' he conceded some years later, when he was busily trying to win a career as a courtier.[15] Guilpin was a familiar of Donne's, the addressee of his verse epistle 'To Mr. E. G.' The fifth satire in *Skialetheia* closely imitates Donne's first satire, where the speaker, 'coffin'd' in his chamber in Lincoln's Inn, finds himself drawn to the London street where the characters of satire throng.[16] 'I shut my chamber door, and come, lets goe.' The scenario is modelled on Juvenal's First Satire, where the streets of Rome display to the poet the grossest specimens of vice and absurdity.

> Look: here comes a brand-new litter,
> Crammed with its corpulent owner, some chiselling advocate.
> Who's next? An informer. He turned in his noble patron . . .
> Don't you want to cram whole notebooks with scribbled
> 　　　invective
> When you stand at the corner and see some forger carried past
> On the necks of six porters . . .?[17]

In Guilpin's version, the poet simply walks into the crowded London street and describes the types that he sees. 'The Cittie is the mappe of vanities.'[18] At its end, as if exhausted by London's mockable variety of character types, he returns to the Inns of Court.

> Henceforth, I'le keep my studie, and eschew
> The scandal of my thoughts, my follies view.[19]

Behind these satires is a network of acquaintance. Guilpin was a friend of Marston and shared his antipathy to Hall. Anonymity helped keep their inventions within the circumference of their acquaintance, even as they were made public. Friends and rivals certainly knew enough to insert the missing authors' names. The business of attribution was important because these writers were scoring off each other, and needed to know where their revenges should be directed. The display of poetic wit was an advertisement of a young man's abilities, yet satire required private manuscript circulation or anonymity. The milieu of the Inns of Court licensed these young men to speak in mockery of their frustrated ambitions; anonymity permitted them to satirize the very patronage culture in which they plotted to advance themselves. *Skialetheia* sets out with portraits of the false friends and false-promising patrons whom the satirist knows too well from his little world.

> Make sute to *Fabius* for his fauour, he
> Will straight protest of his loues treasurie:
> Beleeu'st thou him, then weare a motly coate,
> He'le be the first man which shall cut thy throat.[20]

Guilpin's satires are full of the times – one describes the cosmetic obsessions of Elizabethan ladies, another gives us the character of a friend who has become a ridiculous young gentleman of fashion – yet they also give us the classically approved types of folly.

Though no public persons were obviously attacked, the malcontented satire mocking the age offended by its very misanthropy. In 1599 came another example to irk the authorities, Thomas Middleton's *Micro-cynicon*, its prefatory verses, 'His defiance to Envy', signed 'T. M. Gent.' Middleton had not yet made his name as a playwright and it is not clear whether the initials amounted to a disguise or a declaration. 'It is good to set a name to the booke: For a booke without name may be called a libell,'[21] declared a contemporary. Yet the author's removal from his satire did have a creative rationale. In *The Arte of English Poesie* (1589), George Puttenham gave a richly imagined (if false) explanation of the original naming of 'satire':

> the first and most bitter invective against vice and vicious men, was the *Satyre*: which to th'intent their bitternesse should breede none ill will, either to the Poets, or to the recitours, (which could not have bene chosen if they had bene openly knowen) and besides to make their admonitions and reproofs seeme graver and of more efficacie, they made wise as if the gods of the woods, whom they called *Satyres* or *Silvanes*, should appeare and recite those verses of rebuke, whereas in deede they were but disguised persons under the shape of *Satyres* as who would say, these terrene and base gods being conversant with mans affaires, and spiers out of all their secret faults: had some great care over man, & desired by good admonitions to reforme the evill of their life, and to bring the bad to amendment by those kinde of preachings, whereupon the Poets inventours of the devise were called *Satyristes*.[22]

The satirist, tricked out in inhuman disguise, performs a role that must be separated from his personality. His voice commands attention because it represents no particular interest or animosity.

Marston seems to have one effect of the ban on satire in mind in a knowing analogy in his 1605 play *The Dutch Courtesan*. Here the anti-Puritanical, free-speaking Crispinella argues that 'in nature those actions that are most prohibited are most desired', just as 'in the fashion of time, those books that are called in, are most in sale and request'.[23] The Elizabethan satirists took few thorough measures to hide themselves, and treated anonymity as a conventional licence. Sometimes the satirist even had the diabolical purpose of exciting curiosity. 'Autorem quaeris? Frustra,' begins John Donne's anti-Jesuit satire *Ignatius His Conclave* (1611); or, as he translated it for an edition in English, 'Doest thou seeke after the Author? It is in vaine.'[24] Here is a literally devilish satire – a work whose anonymity allows the author to take us to hell, where we hear a competition between its denizens over who has caused most mischief to humanity.

It is likely that Donne, so cautious about his verse satires, wrote his mocking account at the behest of James I himself. According to Walton's *Life of Dr. John Donne*, the King had asked Donne to contribute to a fierce debate that he was waging with Rome over the Oaths of Supremacy and Allegiance, by which James's subjects acknowledged him as head of the Church. James had himself written two short books defending his own clemency and attacking the Pope. In 1610 Donne had produced his *Pseudo-Martyr*, earnestly arguing that Roman Catholic 'recusants' who refused to take the Oath of Allegiance and risked execution were not potential martyrs but suicidal sinners. Donne, having once been a Roman Catholic himself, might have been thought well equipped to speak to James's wavering Catholic subjects. The title page proclaimed its author's name. Shortly afterwards there appeared the devilish (and far more entertaining) twin to this work: *Ignatius His Conclave*. It was directed against the state's enemies. The text's modern editor thinks it likely, from its quotations and allusions, that someone in power must have supplied Donne with the rare and expensive books of controversy that he needed to point his satire. It has a 'quasi-official character'.[25] There is more evidence to suggest that Donne's authorship was no true secret. On the title page of his copy of the first (Latin) edition, now in the Library of Christ Church, Oxford, Robert Burton wrote 'John Donne 1610'.

The doctrinal polemic of *Pseudo-Martyr* bore its author's name, but anonymity allows *Ignatius His Conclave* to play at mockery. The author has a diabolical vision. 'In the twinkling of an eye, I saw all the roomes in Hell open to my sight.'[26] In the

most secret and inward part of Hell, he finds Lucifer's most
select company, those who 'had so attempted any innovation in
this life, that they gave an affront to all antiquitie, and induced
doubts, and anxieties, and scruples, and after, a libertie of beleev-
ing what they would'. Various candidates plead their cases to
be admitted to Lucifer's prized inner sanctum. Ignatius's most
impressive rival is Machiavelli, who claims credit for having
taught 'those wayes, by which thorough *perfidiousness* and *dis-
sembling of Religion*, a man might possesse, and usurpe upon the
liberty of free *Commonwealths*'.[27] Even Ignatius has to acknowledge that he is a worthy competitor: after all, 'the *Clergie of Rome*
tumbled down to *Hell* daily, easily, voluntarily, and by troupes,
because they were accustomed to sin against their conscience'; the
laity, however, were less natural sinners, and needed Machiavelli
to awaken them to 'greater, and more bloody undertakings'.[28]
Ignatius is stirred by this challenger to detail the damnable influences of the Jesuits over the centuries and embarks on a long
speech boasting of all the evil for which Jesuits are responsible.
Machiavelli teaches men cynicism and ruthlessness, but Ignatius
and his followers have taught truly ingenious sins and perver-
sions. He lists some of the more exotic supposed sins of popes
and cardinals: for example, 'Pope *Paulus Venetus*, which used to
paint himselfe, & desired to seeme a woman, was called the
Goddesse Cibele (which was not without mysterie, since, prostitute boyes are sacred to that Goddess).'[29] And he vaunts the
efforts of Jesuits to subvert monarchies, bribing courtiers away
from their monarchs and engineering 'King-killings'. The satire
ends with Hell in uproar after Ignatius attempts to take the seat
in Satan's inner sanctum, which is possessed by Pope Boniface.

With a few exceptions, the works for which we now know
Donne best, his poems, were not printed in his lifetime. They
circulated in manuscript, often as copies of copies, amongst those
in the know. In recent years, this kind of circulation has become

known as 'scribal publication', for it was the means by which a writer could make his work known to a socially restricted readership. It had long been a pattern. The court poets of the Tudor age – Wyatt and Surrey, Sidney and Raleigh – wrote only for a select audience, releasing their verse without the vulgarity of entering print. Scribal publications, especially sophisticated or offensive verses, begged attribution. Non-authorial manuscripts of seventeenth-century poems often have the names of their supposed authors added by the owner or transcriber (and often these attributions are wrong).[30] Anonymity gives the satirist opportunity to act the devil.

The most admired and entertaining devil of late seventeenth-century satire was John Wilmot, Earl of Rochester. 'Libertine and wit' is the conventional description, but the wit and the libertinism were connected. An aristocratic rake, Rochester confounded conventional morality in his satirical writings. His occasional rival and foe John Sheffield, Earl of Mulgrave, tried to debunk his reputed devilishness in his 'An Essay upon Satyr' of 1679.

> *Rochester* I despise for his meer want of wit,
> Though thought to have a Tail and Cloven Feet;
> For while he mischief means to all mankind,
> Himself alone the ill effects does find.[31]

The lines convey well enough the sense that it was a kind of flattery to call Rochester a devil. Three years earlier George Etherege's play *The Man of Mode* had ushered onto the London stage, in the character of Dorimant, a poetry-loving rake who was understood by all fashionable theatre-goers to be Rochester by another name. He is a seducer, and suitably seductive. An anxious mother, Lady Woodvill, warns her daughter Harriet about him. 'He is the prince of all the devils in the town—delights in nothing but in rapes and riots.'[32] She is apparently appalled but really thrilled by his appearance amongst the other fashionable strollers in the Mall. 'Oh, he has a tongue, they say, would tempt the angels to a second fall.' The association between Rochester and the Devil was common. Rochester seems to have written his own hellish self-damnation in 'To the Postboy', in which he talks of all his sins. 'Pox on't, why do I speak of these poor things? / I have blasphemed my God, and libeled Kings!' (ll. 13–14).[33] Rochester asks 'the readiest way to Hell' and is told 'The readiest way, my Lord, 's by Rochester' (l. 16). Naturally, attribution of the lines, though now accepted by most scholars, cannot be certain.[34] It is as if the author were daring us to believe that a man could write thus about himself.

Rochester asserted himself through anonymity. His readers were to be privileged to recognize his wit.

> He had a strange Vivacity of thought, and vigour of expression: His Wit had a subtility and sublimity both, that were scarce imitable. His Style was clear and strong: When he used Figures they were very lively, and yet far enough out of the Common Road.[35]

In a dedication to Rochester, who was for a time his patron, the playwright John Crowne expresses his delight 'that I have seen in some little sketches of your Pen, excellent Masteries and a Spirit inimitable'.[36] 'Inimitable' sounds like ordinary hyperbole, but over and over again it was said that Rochester was entirely singular, truly beyond imitation. Crowne has been shown manuscript verse and seen in it his patron's unmistakable wit. In a coterie culture of manuscript it was something to recognize Rochester's:

> he laid out his wit very freely in libels and satires, in which he had a peculiar talent of mixing his wit with his malice and fitting both with such apt words that men were tempted to be pleased with them: from thence his composures came to be

easily known, for few had such a way of tempering those together as he had; so that when any thing extraordinary that way came out, as a child is fathered sometimes by its resemblance, so it was laid at his door as its parent and author.[37]

Burnet's analogy neatly compares the bad Earl's clever compositions to the bastards that a rake leaves behind him.

Rochester himself made mock of the 'discovery' of his authorship in one of his best-known satires. In 'Timon', the speaker is buttonholed in the Mall by some 'dull dining sot' who fancies himself a connoisseur of contemporary satire. The fool assures Rochester's alter ego that he recognizes his authorship of the incompetent verses. (The passage includes a swipe at Rochester's foe Shadwell.)

> He takes me in his coach, and as we go,
> Pulls out a libel of a sheet or two,
> Insipid as the praise of pious queens
> Or Shadwell's unassisted former scenes,
> Which he admired, and praised at every line;
> At last it was so sharp it must be mine. (ll. 13–18)[38]

The speaker denies that he ever writes more than the odd amorous song, adding, with an archness that his companion cannot hear, 'I vowed I was no more a wit than he' (l.19). But it is no good.

> He knew my style, he swore, and 'twas in vain
> Thus to deny the issue of my brain. (ll. 25–6).

There is no choice but to leave him 'to his dear mistake', and soon the dunce has spread the misattribution 'o'er the whole town' (ll. 28–9).

Guessing at a particular author's style was essential to the pleasure of being a reader of satire. Being able to identify Rochester became a test of poetical taste. In the prefatory Advertisement to his own anonymous collection of translations and imitations, *Some New Pieces Never before Publisht* (1681), John Oldham discussed his version of 'The Lamentation for Adonis' by the Greek poet Bion. The first fifteen lines of the translation had been 'begun by another hand . . . but who was the author I could never yet learn'.[39]

> I have been told that they were done by the Earl of *Rochester*, but I could not well believe it, both because he seldom med-dled with such Subjects, and more especially by reason of an uncorrect line or two to be found amongst them, at their first coming to my hands, which never us'd to flow from his excellent Pen.

Oldham was thrusting his work forward at a time when a gentle-man poet would still avoid print. His anonymity was the neces-sary false modesty of a young writer in need of patronage. The brilliant son of a country schoolmaster, he earned his living as a private tutor to the sons of rich men. Yet anonymity also gave him a licence to create devilish characters and voices. His first collection of poems included his 'Satyr against Vertue', inspired by the drunken exploits of the Earl of Rochester. Rochester had, 'in a frolic', destroyed a glass sundial in the King's private garden at Whitehall. According to Aubrey,

> the earl of Rochester, lord Buckhurst, Fleetwood Shephard, etc., comeing in from their revels. 'What!' said the earl of Rochester, 'doest thou stand here to [fuck] time?' Dash they fell to work.[40]

The poem with which Oldham commemorates the episode is 'Suppos'd to be spoken by a Court-Hector' and is indeed a dra-matic monologue by a libertine courtier who celebrates his pleas-ures. 'Happy! whose Lives are merely to Enjoy, / And feel no stings of Sin that may their Bliss annoy' (ll. 22–3).[41] With angry gusto the speaker derides virtue and, for almost three hundred lines, cries up 'Debauchery'. Amongst other brave spirits, he celebrates Satan, the libertine's inspiration. 'He gain'd sufficient Triumph, that he durst Rebell, / And 'twas some Pleasure to be thought the great'st in Hell' (ll. 247–8). The speaker, a 'bold Columbus' of vice, himself expects 'high Preferment' in Hell (l. 263).

The poem's official purpose is irony: a mockery of the amoral code to which it gives a voice. Yet in its anonymity, set free from authorial control, this hymn of praise to vice has a heated relish about it. Though it did not have Oldham's name attached to it in print, even in the pirated edition that had been published without the poet's consent in 1679, its authorship was discoverable by privileged readers. Apparently Rochester himself was so impressed that he and some fellow court wits visited Oldham. The odd consequence of this supposed attack on libertinism was that its author composed a series of poems for Rochester's circle. One of these, 'Upon the Author of a Plat call'd *Sodom*' purports to hold Rochester, 'abandon'd Miscreant', to account for his obscene writings.[42] Yet in fact it adopts exactly the disgusted obscenity that was his stock in trade.

> Sure Nature made, or meant at least't have don't,
> Thy Tongue a Clitoris, thy Mouth a Cunt.
> How well a Dildoe would that place become,
> To gag it up, and make't for ever dumb! (ll. 30–4)

Another, 'A Dithyrambique on Drinking', was 'Suppos'd to be spoken by Rochester' (though this subtitle was removed when the poem was printed). Oldham has the rakish aristocrat orate in praise of 'All mighty Wine ... the World's great Soul' (ll. 29–34).[43] The witty, drunken Earl speaks wittily and drunkenly of wine's inspiring powers. Oldham's mimicry of libertine irreverence is now much like homage.

Oldham used anonymity to unleash his own most substantial

satanic satire. The 'Satyr against Vertue' was printed with his *Satyrs upon the Jesuits*, appearing in 1681, in the wake of national hysteria over the supposed 'Popish Plot' against Charles II. This sequence of four satires was animated by the belief that 'pointed Satyr and the sharps of wit' should be recruited to defeat Catholic conspiracy.[44] In the Prologue the nameless poet vaunts his 'rank envenom'd spleen' and brandishes his 'stabbing Pen', acting out the part of a railer in the style of Juvenal, too indignant to conform to the smoother poetic fashions of his time.[45] The first of the satires is spoken by the ghost of Father Henry Garnet, the Roman Catholic priest executed after being convicted of treason for his involvement in the Gunpowder Plot. This character diabolically addresses a 'private Cabal' of fellow Jesuits (his first words are 'By hell . . .'), rousing them to rebellion against a monarch who stands in the way of returning England to Rome:

> Let rabble Souls of narrow aim and reach
> Stoop their vile Necks, and dull Obedience preach. (ll. 84–5)

He rouses them not only to rebellion, for once let loose this devilish voice, invoking Hell all the way, rants of the pleasure to be taken in all acts of vindictiveness and destruction. To the modern reader the delight in cruelty is sometimes inadvertently comic:

> Brain the poor Cripple with his Crutch, then cry,
> You've kindly rid him of his misery. (ll. 302–3)

Further satires in the collection are spoken in the imagined voice of Ignatius Loyola, imparting 'hidden Rules and Secrets' to those who would practise some 'future Villainy'.[46]

The anti-Catholic satires were a great success, and encouraged Oldham to come up to London to seek his fortune as an author, though soon he was again having to take up a post as a private tutor. He held back from using his name, but he clearly wanted to be known. The two other collections that he published before his death in 1683, aged only thirty, were announced as 'By the Author of the *Satyrs upon the Jesuites*'. Anonymity was officially maintained, but attribution encouraged. The last of these collections, *Poems and Translations*, carried an Advertisement in which the author promised that he would at some future time 'have ready a very Sparkish dedication, if he can but get himself known to some Great Man, that will give a good parcel of Guinnies for being handsomely flatter'd'.[47] If he could only acquire such a patron, his book could bear 'his Head in the Front very finely cut', and plenty of commendatory verses by fellow poets. Without such backing, his volume had to remain 'naked, Undedicated, and Unprefac'd'. Rochester's was a lordly anonymity, one version of an attitude to satire expressed in Dryden's 'Discourse concerning the Original and Progress of Satire'. The satirist who respected the ancient models was entirely different, Dryden argued, from the 'multitude of Scriblers, who daily pester the world with . . . Lampoons and Libels'.[48] The 'Scriblers' were all anonymous, but they were also indistinguishable. In contrast, anonymity allowed the qualities of the best writer to be recognized.

To know what you were reading, especially if it were audacious or abusive, was to belong to a select group. Inside knowledge, especially of the court, allowed special kinds of devilry in the late seventeenth and early eighteenth centuries. A distinct genre of mocking and revealing works called 'secret histories' flourished. They relied a great deal on the mystery, or pseudo-mystery, of their authorship. Such accounts were 'secret' because they came from an insider, revealing what was supposed to be concealed. Naturally, such an author had to stay hidden, though the sense of risk was largely manufactured. The flourishing of secret histories marks a transition between a truly courtly culture of privileged readers, and a public of readers relishing the gossip and scandals of a world to which they did not actually belong. They were also 'secret' because they required decoding, by a reader who was presumed to be at least half-knowing. The most notorious, and therefore successful, of these was Delarivière Manley's 1709 *New Atalantis*, an exposé of hidden machinations and secret peccadilloes of Whig politicians and aristocrats. The book's original title was *Secret Memoirs and Manners of several Persons of Quality, of both Sexes. From the new Atalantis, an Island in the Mediterranean.* The title page gave no author's name but declared that the work was 'Written originally in Italian'. A prefatory dedication to the Duke of Beaufort spoke in the guise of 'an unknown and meer Translator', who had according to the dedication been given the work by a friend who had come upon it in Brussels and wished it to 'Visit the Court, and Great Britain'.[49]

The work is as dull now as it was once incendiary, for its interest is all in the true identities of its fictionalized characters. Two of the three copies of the first edition in the British Library are annotated in a contemporary hand, and there are very few contradictions between them. Both readily, compulsively identify the persons featured. Manley's authorship cannot have been much of a secret. Only days after the provocation of a second volume of her satirical exposé, she was arrested. In the account that she herself gave five years later in the autobiographical *Adventures of Rivella*, she recalled that, under examination by Under-Secretary of State John Hopkins, it was the identity of her informants that most troubled the authorities. 'They used several arguments to make her discover ... from whom she had received information of some special facts, which they thought were above her own intelligence.'[50]

In the eighteenth century, not surprisingly, that addict of anonymity Daniel Defoe became involved in secret histories. In 1715 the former chief minister Robert Harley printed a newspaper advertisement denying authorship of *The Secret History of the White Staff*.[51] Defoe wrote a rejoinder to what was in fact his own work. *The Secret History of the Secret History* cleared Harley of all involvement, and suggested that Defoe himself played a negligible role in the creation of the original *Secret History*. Defoe played dizzying games of self-answering, possible only because of anonymity, and often hardly grasped by biographers and scholars. He would complain often enough about misattribution, but he relied on it too.

> Hymn, Song, Lampoon, Ballad, and Pasquinade,
> My recent Memory invade;
> My Muse must be the Whore of Poetry,
> And all *Apollo*'s Bastards laid to me.[52]

He complained that if a work were anonymous and controversial 'it must be *the Devil or De Foe*', but his very hyperbole indicated a kind of pride.[53]

Defoe's contemporaries Swift and Pope used anonymity for their varieties of what might be called 'the mock-book'. Pope, Swift, John Arbuthnot and John Gay, amongst others, gathered in the Scriblerus Club, producing collective satirical writings which invariably took the form of mock books: *The Memoirs of Martinus Scriblerus* was a pseudo-biography of a character devised to represent every absurdity of contemporary learning; *The History of John Bull* was an account of a character representing the traits of the nation. They were published with the names of their authors removed and peculiar explanations of their manuscripts found their way into print. The authors liked to enact the follies they satirized. 'Mockery' had a double meaning: both making fun of something and parodying it. When *The Dunciad* first appeared in May 1728, its title page claimed (falsely) that it was a London reprint of an earlier Dublin edition. Despite all its evidence of Pope's particular enmities, a well-connected reader could still write to the second Earl of Oxford, one of Pope's circle, asking 'Who is the Author of the *Dunciad*?' though he did next ask 'Is it not Pope?'[54]

The first edition opened with a preface, 'The Publisher to
the Reader', observing that *the town has been persecuted with
Pamphlets, Advertisements, Letters, and weekly Essays, not only
against the Wit and Writings, but against the Character and Person,
of Mr. Pope'.*[55] No one has defended him except 'the Author of
the following Poem'. The preface even jested about the poem's
undeclared author: 'Who he is, I cannot say.'[56] If his style was
reminiscent of Pope's, perhaps 'it might be done on purpose, with
a view to have it pass for his'. Soon Edmund Curll's *Compleat
Key to the Dunciad* was scornfully 'unmasking' Pope: '*Not to keep
the Reader any longer in Suspence, he may be assured the* Alexander
Pope *Esq; is both the* Publisher *and Author of this Patch-Work
Medley.*'[57] The 'Letter to the Publisher' talks of the poem as
'an Orphan', which 'its parent seems to have abandoned from
the very beginning, and suffered to step into the world naked,
unguarded, and unattended'.[58] Pope's withholding of his own
name was a natural joke in a poem that is full of writers' names.
A note added seven years after the poem's first publication right-
eously explained that the 'hired Writers' named and mocked in
The Dunciad were those who had 'aspersed almost all the great
Characters of the Age, and this with impunity, their own Persons
and Names being utterly secret and obscure'. The note was signed
by Pope's abetter, Richard Savage, but was apparently composed
by Pope himself.[59]

Pope took 'some Opportunity of doing good, by detecting
and dragging into light these common Enemies of Mankind'.[60]
Perhaps the loss of their anonymity would spoil their credit
with the booksellers – or even shame them into restraint. The
identification of these hidden authors of 'abusive Falshoods and
Scurrilities' was Pope's first impulse.

This it was that gave birth to the Dunciad, and he thought it
an happiness, that by the late Flood of Slander on himself, he

had acquired such a peculiar right over their Names as was necessary to his Design.

The first edition was the only one that was truly anonymous. When *The Dunciad Variorum* appeared a year later, complete with an elaborate apparatus of mock annotations, it included a prefatory 'Letter to the Publisher', signed by Pope's friend William Cleland (but probably composed by Pope), which names Pope as the poem's author. 'He has laughed, and written the DUNCIAD'.[61] Yet long after it had become a famous, or infamous, work, Pope insisted on the superficial anonymity of his *Dunciad*. When a rewritten version of the poem was published the year before he died, some fifteen years after its first appearance, its title page declared that it was 'printed according to the complete Copy found in the Year 1742'.

Personal satires ('lampoons') went on being written in the eighteenth century, went on being anonymous, and went on being attributed. Pope in his *Epistle to Dr Arbuthnot* (1735) sighed with mock fatalism about the self-appointed *littérateur* Balbus, who dedicates himself to 'discovering' Pope's writing,

> And then for mine obligingly mistakes
> The first lampoon Sir Will or Bubo makes.

The great poet, helpless to teach a fool the true signs of his poetic workmanship, permits himself some pretend self-pity.

> Poor guiltless I! And can I choose but smile,
> When every coxcomb knows me by my *style*?[62]

Just Rochester's weary complaint.

Anonymity in satire could be a sign that the author knew he was going too far. In 1764 the verse satire *The Times* was published anonymously. It was an enraged discovery of the prevalence of homosexuality amongst the poet's luxury-addled contemporaries. The anonymity was teasing, the title page declaring it to be 'A Poem. By' and then a blank space. Yet the disguise was token. At the end of the poem in its first edition, was a short list of works with the heading 'BOOKS written by Mr. CHURCHILL, to be had of all the Booksellers in Town'.[63] Charles Churchill, its author, was by this time a successful professional writer and, thanks largely to his friendship with the politician John Wilkes, a notorious public figure. In *The Times* this clergyman-rake (an associate, with Wilkes, of the libertine Monks of Medmenham) berates his countrymen for a vice 'which but to name / Would call up in my cheeks the marks of shame' (ll. 263–4).[64] The satire begins as an attack on enervating luxury but soon singles out rapacious homosexuality as the dominant vice of 'The Times'. Now 'Woman, the pride and happiness of man . . . is out of date' (ll. 301–19), and the very propagation of the species seems to be threatened. The ruling classes are the most corrupted, with the satire's representative modern aristocrat, Apicius, doting on his male servant Corydon, 'A smooth, smug stripling in life's fairest prime' (l. 421). Men who marry or who keep whores are probably 'Vile Pathicks', merely screening their sodomitical pursuits (l. 555). Any man's son is everywhere in danger from 'this giant sin' (l. 663). Churchill, commemorated as 'the bruiser' by his sworn enemy Hogarth, was not by temperament a man who would fear putting his name to a poem. Indeed, when Wilkes was pursued for his obscene, anonymous *Essay on Woman*, Churchill put himself forward as the author. Anonymity was rather the token reticence required in order to broach such 'disgusting' subject-matter.

Anonymity could also permit some readers to find devilish amusement where they might have taken offence. When the first two volumes of Laurence Sterne's *Tristram Shandy* were published anonymously at the end of 1759, the book was a fashionable hit and a critical success. None of the reviewers complained that the novel began with an extended joke about what went wrong at the very moment (the *very* moment) of its narrator's conception (his father being 'interrupted' by a malapropos question from his wife). However, when Sterne, an Anglican vicar from Yorkshire, appeared in London in the wake of his book, some commentators began to be shocked.[65] The shock was the greater as Sterne insisted on dressing in clerical black, as if refusing to dissociate jester from cleric. When, later the same year, he published his sermons as the *Sermons of Mr. Yorick*, adopting the pseudonym of the Shandy family's local vicar in his now notorious novel, the scandal of his identity could not be ignored. The reviewers turned against him, though his popular success protected him from their power.

Anonymity was a way of releasing devilish thoughts. Why else would William Blake, who usually showed little concern for the sensitivities of possible readers, have published his *The Marriage of Heaven and Hell* anonymously? It was highly unusual for Blake not to inscribe his name, as printer if not as author, on the title page of this work. Its anonymity is only a matter of form. Every plate of the work is shaped by its author's hand, and every copy was printed and coloured for a patron rather than a customer. There was no question of anyone not knowing the author's identity. Yet the mocking devilishness of this work made its anonymity fitting. Is 'The Voice of the Devil' Blake's voice too?[66] When it declares the 'Errors' of 'All Bibles or sacred codes' it certainly sounds like it. Are the 'Proverbs of Hell' authoritative? Some have been taken to be essentially Blakean: 'The road of excess leads to the palace of wisdom.' Yet most are provocative rather than true. 'Sooner murder an infant in its cradle than nurse unacted desires.' 'Without Contraries is no progression,' the book has declared, and being 'contrary' is its undertaking.

For diabolical contrariness, the Romantic age knew only one leader of fashion, and it is not accidental that Byron was its greatest exploiter of mocking anonymity. His first satirical poem,

English Bards and Scotch Reviewers, was written in wounded resentment after his first published collection of poems received condescending reviews. It revenges him on the reviewers, and especially Francis Jeffrey, editor of the hugely influential *Edinburgh Review*, but it also disparages his contemporaries and rivals: Coleridge, Southey, Scott, Wordsworth, and a host of others. 'The simple WORDSWORTH' is mocked for exactly the simplicity that he has attempted to achieve in his *Lyrical Ballads*. Sardonically echoing Wordsworth's Preface to that collection, *English Bards* wonders at the idiocy of a writer 'Who, both by precept and example, shows / That prose is verse, and verse is merely prose' (ll. 241–2). A whole generation of what we would now call Romantic writers is scorned by a poet whose own models are Pope and Dryden. The scorn is ostensibly audacious. 'As to my Satire, I defy the scribblers,' he wrote to his friend Francis Hodgson.[67] If he had feared its effects he would have remained silent. Yet he badly wanted to conceal his name. He wrote to the London bookseller Ben Crosby, 'It must be published (if at all) anonymously, & in such a manner that my name as the author, may never transpire at any future period.'[68] When it was published in March 1809, friends were warned to keep his authorship a secret.[69] Soon the satire was selling well, and Byron's friend Robert Dallas, who acted as his agent for *English Bards*, inquiring at the Piccadilly bookseller Hatchard's, found that 'notwithstanding our precautions, you are pretty generally known to be the author'.[70]

Such anonymity could not withstand a book's success. This was Byron's first taste of how attribution was a consequence of a satire's éclat. 'It is reported that this little volume is the vengeful retort of Lord Byron on the severity of the Edinburgh Review,' the *Cabinet; or Monthly Report of Polite Literature* told its fashionable readers.[71] The reviewer, however, thought that 'the Satire is written with more talent than Lord Byron possesses'.

The reviewer in the *Critical Review* regretted that the author's identity should become known, as if satire were only excusable if the satirist remained unguessable. 'We are not ignorant that the name of a very young man has been whispered about as that of the author—but even should the report be correct, we are unwilling to contribute to the circulation of what, for his sake, we wish had been kept a close secret.'[72] Its offence is its 'personality'.

Assured of his poem's popularity, Byron ensured that the second edition, published later the same year, bore his name and a Postscript in which the author vaunted himself with almost mock bravery. 'Since the publication of this thing, my name has not been concealed; I have been mostly in London, ready to answer for my transgressions.'[73] He even added lines to the poem in which (echoing Prospero's lines about Caliban in *The Tempest*) he rejected any idea that his initial anonymity had been fearful – any idea, indeed, that he had actually been trying to remain hidden.

This thing of rhyme I ne'er disdained to own,
Though not obtrusive, yet not quite unknown:
My voice was heard again, though not so loud;
My page, though nameless, never disavowed. (ll. 1039–42)[74]

The *Antijacobin Review*, which had given an approving review of the first edition, expressed its 'admiration of the resolute temper and spirit' shown by 'the noble satirist'.[75] His satire would inevitably 'make many enemies, and draw down much vulgar abuse on his head'. Byron's friends, the reviewer reported, had 'advised him still to suppress his name, but he rejected their advice, and resolutely followed the bias of his own uncultivated mind'. Anonymity makes trouble, and the more mischief as Byron became a celebrity after the publication of the first two Cantos of *Childe Harold* in 1812. Byron had wanted to publish this poem anonymously.[76] In the event, he compromised with Murray and the title page declared it to be 'By the Author of *English Bards and Scotch Reviewers*'.

Byron amused friends and tormented enemies by holding himself aloof from his creations, as in *Beppo*, the dry run for *Don Juan*, published in 1817. He composed the poem in Venice, and subtitled it 'A Venetian Story': Venetian not just for its setting, but because it tells of the easy-going sexual mores of the city's sophisticated residents. It is spoken by one who seems to know Venice – 'the seat of all dissoluteness', as the poem's mock-censorious epigraph has it – all too well. It is based on a 'true' story, told to Byron by the husband of one of his mistresses. Laura's mariner husband Beppo goes missing for 'several years' (Stanza XXVII). After she has 'waited long, and wept a little', she finds she 'could not sleep with ease alone at night':

> And so she thought it prudent to connect her
> With a vice-husband, *chiefly* to *protect her*. (Stanza XXIX)

Her decision is made the easier by the acceptance in the lands of the 'warm South' that a married woman could take a *cavalier servente*.

> Besides, within the Alps, to every woman
> (Although, God knows, it is a grievous sin)
> 'Tis, I may say, permitted to have *two* men;
> I can't tell who first brought the custom in,
> But 'Cavalier Serventes' are quite common,
> And no one notices, nor cares a pin;
> And we may call this (not to say the worst)
> A *second* marriage which corrupts the first. (XXXVI)

It is a custom alien to the British, with their mingled moralism and appetite for scandal.

But Heaven preserve Old England from such courses!
Or what becomes of damages and divorces? (XXXVII)

After six years of this arrangement, Laura encounters in the
midst of the carnival 'a Turk, the colour of mahogany' (LXX). At
the end of the night's festivities he announces to her and her
cavalier that he is her long-forgotten husband. It being Venice,
wife, lover and husband swiftly adjust to the new situation, with
the two men naturally becoming friends. It is a story told against
the sexual hypocrisy of the English and dares its readers to identify the worldly, amoral narrator with the infamous aristocrat.
Readers are fed their own sense of an author's reputation. Byron
was famous for his verse narratives of the East, and remarks how
easy it would be to supply another 'Grecian, Syrian, or *Assyrian
tale*' (LI). The reader was invited to recognize the former leader
of London fashion, literary and otherwise, recently exiled.

But I am but a nameless sort of person
(A broken Dandy lately on my travels) (LII)

Dispatching it to John Murray, Byron wrote, 'You perhaps had
better publish it anonymously.'[77] The anonymity of *Beppo* allows
for a suppressed sense of scandal – or rather, it is evidence of a
suppression that is itself mildly scandalous, a suppression of the
author's own biography and involvement.

With all its sinful doings, I must say,
That Italy's a pleasant place to me. (XLI)

The tale permits Byron to digress at will about his own doings
and pleasures, his delight at the climate, the language and the
women.

Anonymity enables a kind of flippancy, where every remark
is a throwaway one. Byron's old foe Francis Jeffrey praised the
poem in the *Edinburgh Review* as 'very pleasant, amiable, and
gentleman-like', while insisting on referring to its author as 'the

unknown writer before us'.[78] A month later, Hazlitt, writing in
The Yellow Dwarf, said, 'It is attributed to Lord Byron, and certainly must be the production of some one who has great power
and practice in versification.'[79] By April, the reviewer for the
Edinburgh Magazine was implying that he knew its authorship
because he mingled in the right circles. 'It is attributed, we hear,
to no humbler a pen than that of Lord Byron.'[80] The poem was,
said the reviewer in *The Champion*, 'very generally attributed to
Lord Byron'.[81] Yet the *Literary Journal* in April compared some
of the stanzas to the verse of 'Scott, Byron, or Moore', adding that
'they need not blush at the comparison'.[82] The *Eclectic Review*,
reviewing the fourth edition of the poem in June 1818, gave
no evidence of knowing its authorship.[83] It was the reviewer
in *Blackwood's* who sensed that anonymity somehow made the
poem all the more irresistibly autobiographical. 'We were well
enough disposed to treat you with distant respect, but you have
courted and demanded our gaze . . . You have been the vainest
and most egotisitical of poets. You have made yourself your only
theme.'[84] If reviewers made 'remarks of a personal nature', he
could hardly complain. His name first appeared on the fifth
edition, in April. 'If you think that it will do *you* or the work—or
works any good,—you may—or may not put my name to it—*but
first consult the knowing ones*,' he told Murray.[85]

Byron may have said that he would not anonymously publish
his preface to *Don Juan*, which attacked Southey, but in 1822 he
did anonymously publish a poem mocking the same rival. *The
Vision of Judgment* parodied Southey's laureate poem, *A Vision
of Judgment*, which mourned the death of George III. Southey
had peculiarly provoked Byron by deploring, in his Preface, the
influence of 'immoral writers', chief of whom, though not actually named, was clearly Byron himself. 'The school which they
have set up may properly be called the Satanic school.'[86] Their
writings are 'characterised by a Satanic spirit of pride and

audacious impiety'. The devilish poet responded with a satire in which Satan and the Archangel Michael dispute for the late King's soul. Its eventual title page declared it to be 'By Quevedo Redivivus', a pseudonym that paid homage to the Spanish satirist Quevedo y Villegas, who published a 'Vision of the Last Judgement' in 1607. In front of the celestial gates, a witness against the King is a 'mighty Shadow of a Shade' (l. 651): Junius, the great anonymous satirist of the previous century.[87] 'The Devil himself seem'd puzzled even to guess' (l. 603). The force of satire is inextricable from the power of anonymity. Naturally Southey arrives, borne on the pinions of a devil who has found him labouring on some libel at his Lake District desk. Satan confides that he knows him 'of old' and has 'expected him for some time' (ll. 697–8). Satan wants to know what he has been scribbling, but his recitation of his poetry is enough to drive away all angels and devils, and George III slips into Heaven unnoticed.

When *The Vision of Judgment* appeared in 1822 in the first number of the radical journal *The Liberal*, it aroused what Murray called 'a universal outcry'.[88] In the same letter the publisher confirmed that it was generally attributed to Byron. The publisher of such a work might be at risk, and indeed the Consitutional Association brought a prosecution against John Hunt for publishing a 'gross, impious, and slanderous libel' on George III.[89] Byron, however, was quite safe. His anonymity was not actual protection, but something more like the conventional licence of the satirist. Byron even had the nerve to tell Murray that a publisher should have the gumption to put his name to a book, even where the author cared not to.

> I do not approve of your mode of not putting publisher's names on title pages—(which was unheard of—till *you* gave yourself that *air*)—an author's case is different—and from time immemorial have published anonymously.[90]

The anonymously incendiary satire of Byron's friend Shelley also threw attention on the publisher. Shelley responded to the accession of George IV, and the new King's calumnifying of his wife Caroline, with his comic closet drama *Oedipus Tyrannus. Or Swellfoot the Tyrant. A Tragedy in Two Acts*. It was published anonymously in 1820 by Joseph Johnson, a bookseller with a long history of radical sympathies. It was accompanied by an Advertisement saying that it was 'evidently written by some *learned Theban*'. Shelley had been in exile in Italy for two years, and did not himself need to fear the consequences of the outrage that his play was designed to provoke. It was Johnson who was at risk, and having sold only seven copies, he surrendered his remaining stock on the threat of a prosecution by the Society for the Suppression of Vice.[91] Shelley clearly relished letting it loose, with the confidence that contemporary readers – if he had ever been able to find them – would be able to find all the necessary analogues for its grotesque characters and cameos.

Perhaps he had learnt how useful it was for the satirist to be anonymous from his erstwhile mentor Thomas Love Peacock, a connoisseur of anonymity. In Peacock's witty and allusive tales, representatives of intellectual fashions or contemporary follies meet, usually in a country house, and engage in mutually uncomprehending dialogue. In the first of his tales, *Headlong Hall* (1816), Mr Foster is a 'perfectibilian', determined that 'everything we look on attests the progress of mankind in all the arts of life, and demonstrates their gradual advancement towards a state of unlimited perfection.'[92] Mr Escot, whose company he is frequently forced to keep, is a 'deteriorationist', certain that 'the factitious wants and unnatural appetites' fostered by civilization mean that 'every human being . . . degenerates so rapidly from the primitive dignity of his sylvan origin, that it is scarcely possible to indulge in any other expectation, than that the whole species must at length be exterminated by its own infinite imbecility and vileness.'[93] Foster may be derived from Peacock's friend Shelley, and has a good deal of the philosophy of Shelley's intellectual mentor (and father-in-law), William Godwin. Escot has ladles of Rousseau in his speeches, and some inflections of pessimism from Malthus. They represent current habits of thought recognizable to any of Peacock's readers. Everything proves their different points. However, Peacock also knew the itch of some readers to discover particular people in his satires, so these appear too. His third tale, *Nightmare Abbey* (1818), features several. Coleridge appears as Mr Flosky, who had 'plunged into the central opacity of Kantian metaphysics, and lay *perdu* several years in transcendental darkness, till the common daylight of common sense became intolerable to his eyes'.[94] Byron is Mr Cypress, who is 'on the point of leaving England' after a quarrel with his wife, full of lofty, gloomy quotations from *Childe Harold* and self-dramatizing hyperbole: 'I have no hope for myself or for others. Our life is a false nature; it is not in the harmony of things; it is an all-blasting upas, whose root is earth, and whose leaves are the skies which rain their poison-dews upon mankind.'[95]

For Peacock's first readers, reading meant putting in the names – and wondering about the most important name: the author's. Retrospectively explaining the anonymity of his satires, Peacock wrote that he had 'left them to speak for themselves': 'I thought I might very fitly preserve my own impersonality, having never intruded on the personality of others, nor taken any liberties but with public conduct and public opinions.'[96] There is gentlemanly reticence here. Peacock lived a quiet and genteel life, first on a private income, later supplemented by his salary from the East India Company, where he was an administrator. He was clearly most comfortable as a somewhat removed spectator of literary and intellectual life. There is also a more creative aspect to his self-effacement. Much of Peacock's satire consists of voices 'speaking for themselves' – speaking without the intervention of a judging author. Peacock's approach lets others' arguments run away with themselves, madly accumulating evidence for whatever their prejudices might be. Though a more tolerant parodist, he shares something with Swift. Abandoning your fiction to those whom you satirize is part of the point of anonymity.

Readers of Peacock caught the tang of topicality and tried to identify this clever author, so familiar with the cultural fashions and leading literary characters of the day. Even those who knew everyone did not necessarily know. Leigh Hunt, who assiduously cultivated literary acquaintances, had clearly read and admired *Headlong Hall* without being sure of its author, for Shelley wrote to him in December 1816 to tell him, 'Peacock is the author of Headlong Hall, – he expresses himself much pleased by your approbation.'[97] (More pleased for knowing that he had won this approbation as an unknown, rather than as a friend of a friend.) Amongst hostile reviewers anonymity was a goad – an extra insult. A reviewer of Peacock's second tale, *Melincourt* (1817), nettled by its sustained mockery of the Toryism and Anglicanism of the once-radical Lake Poets – Wordsworth, Coleridge and Southey – detected the satirist's 'cloven foot of infidelity'.[98] He guessed that the author was Sir William Drummond, a free-thinking scholar and antiquarian who had caused some controversy in a book that explained Old Testament stories as astronomical allegories. The irritated attribution was not so wrong: Drummond was a writer whom Peacock and his friend Shelley much admired for his sceptical accounts of different philosophies and religions. Peacock did not own up in print to *Melincourt*, but by the time of *Nightmare Abbey*, his hand seems to have been recognized in the literary world.[99] Yet, for the rest of his intermittent career as a satirist, Peacock kept to his anonymity: 'by the Author of Headlong Hall' was what usually appeared on his title pages. Even with the mischievous potential of secrecy gone, the author refused to involve himself in his mock-making work.

The anonymity of these mocking works now looks exceptional, but would have seemed less so to readers used to the provoking use often made of anonymity in the periodicals of the age. None more so than the monthly *Blackwood's Edinburgh Magazine* (or 'Maga', as its knowing readers liked to call it) with its fictional editor, 'Christopher North', its 'Noctes Ambrosianae', which recording the conversations, loosened by alcohol, of its leading contributors: James Hogg, John Wilson, William Maginn and John Gibson Lockhart. As North comments cheerfully in one of the 'Noctes', 'Why, you know, every body writes books in our days, and nobody owns them.'[100] Blackwood's made its name with the publication of the *Chaldee MS* in 1817, the year in which it was founded. Not only was this libellous, but it courted offence by being written in the style of the Authorized Version of the Bible. When one of its targets, John Graham Dalyell, sued, the public interest in the offending material ensured the magazine's commercial success.

In a gentler vein, Thackeray began his career by developing a style of mockery that exploited the prevailing anonymity of the periodicals like *Fraser's Magazine* for which he wrote. His first success was with the *Yellowplush Papers*, written in the persona of a footman with ideas above his station called Charles Yellowplush (the surname referring to his faded breeches). With his cockney slang and his malapropisms, his delusions of gentility and literary taste, he became the means by which Thackeray satirized the fashionable classes on whom Yellowplush reported. His employer reads his articles in *Fraser's* and is 'very much amused'.[101] Dispatching the first of these to James Fraser, he felt that he had hit on a fertile persona. 'I think I could make half a dozen stories by the same author, if you incline.'[102] For the magazine satirist, an author was a fictional invention.

In the number for August 1838, Yellowplush introduces a guest who asks to be announced as 'Sawedwadgeorgeearllittnbulwig'.[103] This is Edward Bulwer Lytton, his lisp mercilessly replicated through the dialogue that Yellowplush overhears. Mr Bullwig vaunts a new periodical, 'the Litewawy Chwoniocle, of which I have the honour to be the pwincipal contwibutor', and discusses with some perplexity the Yellowplush articles in *Fraser's*. He and the other guests debate 'who *is* Yellowplush?': 'I was given to understand that the name was only a fictitious one, and that the papers were written by the author of the *Diary of a Physician*,' says Bullwig.[104] The Duke of Doublejowl disagrees; 'everybody knows it's Barnard, the celebrated author of "Sam Slick".' Not at all, interjects Lord Bagwig, 'it's the authoress of *High Life*, *Almacks*, and other fashionable novels.' A literary man scorns these attributions and declares that Bullwig is pretending to ask questions because 'It's you yourself.' Only then does Yellowplush's master point to the true author: 'he gave you, my dear Bullwig, your last glass of champaigne.' From the evening's encounter Yellowplush learns a lesson in self-advancement with which he ends his final column: 'I'm about a novvle (having made great progress in spelling), in the style of my friend Bullwig.'

Between May 1839 and February 1840 Thackeray published *Catherine: A Story* in *Fraser's Magazine*. It was announced to be 'By Ikey Solomons, Esq. Junior'. The tale, for which the author provided his own illustrations, was begun in order to satirize the hugely popular 'Newgate Novels' of the time, which told the stories of notorious criminals. 'For our own part, we know what the public likes, and have chosen rogues for our characters.'[105]

We give the reader fair notice, that we shall tickle him with a few such scenes of villainy, throat-cutting, and bodily suffering in general, as are not to be found, no, not in ——; never mind comparisons, for such are odious.[106]

Comparisons with the novels of Bulwer Lytton or Harrison Ainsworth, or even with Dickens's *Oliver Twist*, were Thackeray's point. (Ikey Solomons, Thackeray's pseudonym, was the early nineteenth-century fence on whom Dickens's Fagin was based.)

Set in the early eighteenth century, like several of the most successful Newgate Novels, *Catherine* concerns Catherine Hall, whose exploits Thackeray had found in the notorious Newgate Calendar, a popular collection of criminal tales raided by other novelists before him. Catherine begins as a serving girl in a country inn. An accomplished coquette, she attaches herself to a visiting officer, Count von Galgenstein, and becomes his mistress. When she finds that he is planning to discard her, she tries to poison him and flees, leaving their child behind her. Accomplished in 'wicked coquetries, idlenesses, vanities, lies, fits of anger, slanders, foul abuses, and what not', she is a clever and ruthless survivor.[107] Eventually, married to a money-lender and living conveniently on the road to Tyburn (watching executions is a favourite family entertainment), she meets the Count once more and decides to be rid of her husband. She plans his murder, which is carried out by her illegitimate son and an elderly male admirer; the decapitation and dismembering of the body is described in some detail. All three are caught, tried and executed. Thackeray was clearly attempting to mock the fashion for stories of audacious criminals by making Catherine repellent, yet her cynicism is too often entertaining. Thackeray was to acknowledge privately that he had not resisted a 'sneaking kindness' to his anti-heroine.[108] Though he cannot realize this, she is an early version of an even more alluring and cynical adventuress, Becky Sharp in *Vanity Fair*. Several newspapers of the time commented on *Catherine* without any sense of its authorship. *The Morning Post*, however, did surmise that it came 'from the pen of the author of the "Yellowplush Correspondence" '.[109]

Thackeray had many pseudonyms. He invented Michael

Angelo Titmarsh as a persona for a review of the National
Gallery's annual exhibition, and the alias attached itself to a
sequence of his publications. Titmarsh went from being the
invention of a nameless hack to the alter ego of a successful
writer: he was credited as author of *The Parish Sketch Book*
(1840), a collection of Thackeray's writing about France and the
French, and as the supposed editor of *Comic Tales and Sketches*.
The lengthy review of the former in the *Athenaeum* refers to the
author throughout as 'Mr Titmarsh'.[110] But we have seen in the
previous chapter that several of the reviewers knew Thackeray's
identity perfectly well, and were in communication with him
about these reviews. Anonymity is a fact for the reading public,
not for the literary circles of London. By the time that Thackeray
began publishing his *The Snobs of England* ('By One of Themselves') in *Punch*, he may have declared in the very first number that 'The Writer's Name is Neither Here Nor There', but
those in the know knew that name very well.[111] Some of these
satirical pieces were illustrated by Thackeray, and some of these
illustrations featured the tiny pair of glasses that was his mark
of authorship. The pseudonyms proliferated, most announcing
themselves as pseudonyms: Bashi-Bazouk, Folkstone Canterbury,
George Savage Fitz-Boodle, Dr Solomon Pacigico, Launcelot
Wagstaffe. By 1848 *Vanity Fair* had made Thackeray a 'name'
and in 1849 his *Miscellanies* began appearing, collecting under
his own name many of the satirical writings of the decade before
Vanity Fair. He went on using some of his fictional identities,
especially M. A. Titmarsh. They now signified a certain playfulness, being attached to his *Rebecca and Rowena: A Romance upon
Romance* (1850) or his children's drama *The Rose and the Ring*.
They also signified the creative use that Thackeray had made of
the unavoidable anonymity of the literary hack.

For the last important satirist of the Victorian age, anonymity
began as a personal necessity. Samuel Butler was anxious about

what his religiously orthodox family would think of what he wrote. The son of a clergyman and the grandson of a bishop, Butler was intended for the Church. Working as an assistant to Rev. Philip Perring, a curate at St James' Piccadilly, Butler's religious faith disappeared. He travelled to New Zealand, where he spent five successful years as a sheep farmer. The year after his return he published anonymously *The Evidence for the Resurrection of Jesus Christ as given by the Four Evangelists critically examined*. This concluded that Jesus had not been dead when he was removed from the cross, and that he later simply recovered consciousness. Then, in 1872, he published *Erewhon*, a journey to an imaginary land where the pieties of Victorian culture were paralleled or inverted. *Erewhon* was anonymous and many attributed it to Bulwer Lytton, whose science-fiction novel *The Coming Race* had appeared, also anonymously, the previous year. Lytton's novel also involved the discovery by his hero of an alternative civilization (in this case living underground). It seems likely this intial misattribution of *Erewhon* considerably helped its sales.

The very form of *Erewhon* makes its anonymity look creatively useful. Sometimes reminiscent of Swift's *Gulliver's Travels*, it is a first-person account by a nameless traveller who leaves us to judge the strange land that he visits. 'If the reader will excuse me, I will say nothing of my antecedents, nor of the circumstances which led me to leave my native country.'[112] It is not clear whether Butler himself decided to acknowledge authorship of *Erewhon*, or whether the decision was taken for him.[113] Even when he decided to put his name to the second edition, his father, while not objecting, wrote telling him, 'I shall take your advice and not read the book.'[114] Anonymity enabled the next of Butler's satires, *The Fair Haven*, to be a kind of hoax. If false assumptions about the authorship of *Erewhon* irritated him, this work was designed to trick some readers into wrong guesses about its author, or about his beliefs. It purported to be, as its title page declared,

'A work in defence of the miraculous element in our Lord's ministry upon earth, both as against Rationalistic impugners and certain Orthodox defenders'. It begins with a 'Memoir' of its supposed author, John Pickard Owen, supposedly written by his brother. This explains how he grew to be sceptical about the trustworthiness of the New Testament, and to think that it provided little useful in the way of moral guidance. In a passage of dizzying irresponsibility, the editor quotes his brother quoting Swift's *An Argument against Abolishing Christianity* on the impracticality of any 'true Christianity'.[115]

John Pickard Owen's supposed work seeks 'to establish the Resurrection and Ascension of the Redeemer upon a basis which should satisfy the most imperious demands of modern criticism'. Some of the first reviewers (in *The Rock* and *The Scotsman*) indeed took it to be an orthodox defence of Christianity. But in fact it is a mock-vindication. It will perform a substantiation of the Resurrection 'so clearly and satisfactorily . . . that the question can never be raised hereafter by any candid mind'.[116] The Swiftian false modesty of the speaker should, of course, make the reader suspicious. 'I humbly trust that the reader will feel that I have not only attempted it, but done it.' The reader is to be cast loose on the waters of earnest rational enquiry. 'One thing only is wanted on the part of the reader, it is this, the desire to attain truth regardless of past prejudices.'[117] But this too is a mockery.

Owen is pained to have to present the argument of 'our opponents' about the Resurrection – an argument that takes up over fifty pages and appears to be indistinguishable from Butler's views, as presented in his earlier pamphlet on the Resurrection. 'We are inclined . . . to believe that Jesus Christ really did reappear shortly after the Crucifixion, and that his reappearance, though due to natural causes, was conceived to be miraculous.'[118] The refutation of this argument that Owen promises is a mock refutation, conceding almost everything to his author's true views.

Belief in Christ's divinity is effectively abandoned, leaving only the 'Christ-ideal which . . . is the soul and spirit of Christianity'.[119] Despite his official wishes, Owen is close to accepting the New Testament as 'a work of art, a poem, a pure fiction from beginning to end', to be revered 'for its intrinsic beauty'.[120]

The second edition declared Butler's authorship, and prefaced the work with a mock explanation of his original anonymity. *Erewhon* had been attacked by 'certain ultra-orthodox Christians' for being anti-Christian. If *The Fair Haven* had been seen to have the same author, such critics might have suspected that here too 'something in the way of satire had been intended'.[121] Now he appears 'in my true colours as the champion of orthodoxy', citing with evident pleasure the approbatory, deluded comments of the reviewer in the *Rock*: 'I am not responsible for the interpretations of my readers.'[122] In his *Note-Books*, evidently intended for posthumous publication, he recorded what he was up to.

MYSELF AND *THE FAIR HAVEN*
What did I do in this book other than what the church does? She attacks reasonable conclusions under the guise of defending them, with a view to impose on those who have not wit enough to find her out.[123]

The Fair Haven is a counter-imposition, requiring anonymity to trick those who had readily accepted Christian platitudes. In its quiet and obscure way, mockery reaches an extreme in Butler's work, for it becomes mockery of most of its possible readers.

8

CONFESSION

Why would a work offering the personal history of its author withhold his name? Take one of the best-selling autobiographical narratives of the eighteenth century. *An Authentic Narrative of some Remarkable and Interesting Particulars in the Life of ********* (1764) sounds like a spoof title, all those words telling you exactly nothing about its contents. Yet it would be hard to imagine a more earnest story. Its subtitle stated it to be 'Communicated in a Series of Letters, to The Reverend Mr. Haweis, Rector of Aldwinckle, Northamptonshire, And by him (at the Request of Friends) now made public'. A signed preface by the Rev. Haweis assured the reader that the narrative was 'quite genuine' and that the letters that compose it were no literary artefacts. 'They were written in haste, as letters of friendship, to gratify my curiosity; but the style, as well as the narrative itself, is so plain and easy, that corrections were thought needless.'

If the first readers were not to know who it was about, they were to be clear from the beginning what it was about. It was what we might call an autobiography, but written to show how 'every believer' might discover in 'his own case' the evidence of God's 'providence and grace'.[1] The author tells his story in order to add his own name to the roll of 'eminent sinners' brought to reformation. His actual name, however, is withheld, and the author's reticence on this score enters into his account. He worries religiously about publication, disturbed by 'the ill use which persons of corrupt and perverse minds are often known to make of such instances'. The writer's confidence that his story will necessarily convey the proper Christian lesson clearly needs some bolstering. But it runs deeper than this. When he thought of charting his experiences, he says, he hesitated. 'I was deterred . . . by the great difficulty of writing properly where *Self* is concerned.'[2] Telling your own story might be a kind of self-indulgence. Anonymity is the sinful author's means of holding himself in check.

The *Authentic Narrative* was the spiritual autobiography of John Newton, evangelical clergyman and formerly crew member of a slave ship. (He is best known to us for penning the hymn 'Amazing Grace'.) His worry about 'Self' was present in his private writings too. As he contemplated composing his autobiography he wrote to Haweis expressing his doubts. 'Alas you know not my heart, & how hard I find it to fight against that accursed principle of *Self*.'[3] But Haweis encouraged him to complete his story of an unnamed sinner brought back to God. It tells how, the son of a merchant captain, he becomes a sailor in his teens and eventually joins a ship working the slave trade out of West Africa. Under the influence of an irreligious friend, and of the Deistic philosopher the Earl of Shaftesbury, he renounces 'the hopes and comforts of the gospel'.[4] He becomes a blasphemer, contemptuous of religion. This is the story of a sinner and self-deluder who turns away from God. The account hints that he also became sexually abandoned. But 'the Lord sent from on high and delivered me out of deep waters.' Literally so, for during a storm at sea his ship begins filling with water and, death seeming imminent, he prays to God for mercy. All night he pumps and bails, and while he does so begins thinking of 'my former religious professions, the extraordinary turns in my life; the calls, warnings, and deliverances I had met with, the licentious course of my conversation'.[5] The crisis passes and, for the rest of the voyage, with food and water scarce and his fellow sailors still fearing death, he reads the Bible and Thomas à Kempis's *Imitation of Christ*. Like Robinson Crusoe, danger and surprising 'deliverance' push him to acknowledge 'that wonderful providence which watched over me for good'.[6] Though this sinner has been actively employed in the slave trade, his retrospective concerns, about a pursuit that was 'in many respects, far from eligible', seem notably untormented.[7] 'I was sometimes shocked with an employment that was perpetually conversant with chains, bolts, and shackles' – this is the most offended statement he can manage. His wish for 'a more human calling' is made to sound an incidental aspect of his narrative. Back in England, he devotes himself to religious pursuits while supporting himself and his wife by working as a tide surveyor in Liverpool. He studies the scriptures, teaching himself Hebrew and Greek to read these in the original, and at the end of his story he is awaiting the opportunity to become a minister of the Church.

It is a story of the operation of God's grace, but, unlike Crusoe, this narrator worries about whether his very narration manifests irreligious self-regard.

> Dear Sir,
>
> I almost wish I could recall my last sheet, and retract my promise. I fear I have engaged too far, and I shall prove a mere *Egotist* . . . However, it is some satisfaction that I am writing to yourself only.[8]

We now know that the 'letters' that compose his account were circulated widely in manuscript, and that it was necessary to publish them in order to forestall an unauthorized edition.[9] By the time it reached print, a large number of like-minded Christians knew its authorship. Soon after its publication, John Wesley wrote to Newton approving of his story's designs.[10] It is clear from his own reports that his parishioners at Olney in Buckinghamshire, where he was appointed to a curacy just before the book was published, knew well of his authorship. 'The people stare at me since reading [it],' he wrote in a letter.[11] Newton was something of a celebrity, such a popular preacher that a gallery had to be added to the Olney church the year after his appointment. His former life was well known, not least because of his own habit of recalling it.

By the end of the century Newton's spiritual memoir had reached its ninth English edition and was still being published anonymously. Editions published in Ireland and in America, over which he had no control, all placed his name on the title page. It was a name that had become famous, notably with the publication of *Olney Hymns*, jointly composed with William Cowper, in 1779. Thomas Scott's *The Force of Truth: an Authentic Narrative* (which its author read to Newton while it was still in manuscript) not only echoed Newton's title, it advertised after its preface four of Newton's works, including *Olney Hymns* and a volume of sermons 'preached in the Parish Church of Olney, by JOHN NEWTON'.[12] At the head of these was Newton's *Authentic Narrative*, obstinately anonymous but clearly understood to be Newton's. The Advertisement to an edition of Newton's works published in Edinburgh in 1780 (reprinted in London in 1787) explained that 'The Authentic Narrative being usually ascribed to Mr. Newton, the liberty has been taken to include it in the present collection.'[13] Every sign is that Newton maintained his anonymity as a kind of propriety. It was a conventional self-effacement that became all the more significant when the author's suspicion of his own self-regard was fundamental to his narrative. Paradoxically, the autobiographical particularity made anonymity more desirable.

Cowper himself prepared a spiritual autobiography in 1767. It was read in manuscript by several friends and family members, and Newton published part of it after Cowper's death. Cowper vividly recorded his religious terrors and his long history of what we would call depression. The latter was interpreted by Cowper in religious terms, so the suicidal inclinations that he recalled were interpreted as Satan's final temptation of this wandering sinner.[14] Cowper attempted to hang himself, after which his brother sent him to be cared for by Dr Nathaniel Cotton at an asylum in St Albans – though Cowper described his affliction in theological terms. Cowper's autobiography remained unpublished until after his death, and therefore he did not have to worry about the consequences of publication as Newton did. Newton was a religious zealot, but the struggling with 'Self' is a matter for any confessional narrative. Confessional texts derive their authority from their resistance to self-indulgence. This was recognized by probably the most famous English 'confessions', Thomas De Quincey's *Confessions of an English Opium Eater*, published anonymously in 1821. Its nameless author claims to have agonized about making public such a record of 'errors and infirmities': 'It is not without an anxious review of the reasons for and against this step, that I have, at last, concluded on taking it.'[15]

De Quincey's *Confessions* was one in a wave of 'confessions'. It was preceded by Charles Lamb's *Confessions of a Drunkard*, first published in the *Philanthropist* (No. IX) in 1813. This was reprinted in Basil Montagu's *Some Enquiries into the Effects of Fermented Liquors* in 1814. 'I am a poor nameless egotist, who have no vanity to consult by these Confessions.' It appeared for a third time in the *London Magazine* for August 1822, signed 'ELIA', Lamb's pen-name as an essayist. 'O pause, thou sturdy moralist . . .' It is written in the face of imagined disapproval and impatience. He talks of knowing a man who has struggled painfully to conquer alcohol. 'Why should I hesitate to declare, that the man of whom I speak is myself? I have no puling apology to make to mankind.' His problems began when he tried to appear as a wit in a circle of hard-drinking friends. Next he became addicted to tobacco. Then alcohol. For him there is no hope. 'The waters have gone over me.' A prefatory editorial note in the *London Magazine* described how the 'lucubrations' of Elia were scattered through various periodicals, 'set forth for the most part (such his modesty!) without a name'.[16] Such is the article now recovered in response to 'Messieurs the Quarterly Reviewers', who have speculated that 'the describer . . . partly sate for his own picture'. On the contrary, these were 'imagined experiences', confessed with 'mock fervor, and counterfeit earnestness', and composed out of 'long observations'. 'We deny not that a portion of his own experiences may have passed into the picture (as who, that is not a washy fellow, but must at some times have felt the after-operation of a too generous cup?)—but then how heightened! how exaggerated!' Lamb, realizing that the piece was being pinned to him, wanted to convert it from confession into literature.

In September 1822 the *London Magazine* began *The Memoir of a Hypochondriac*, an account that begins with the narrator saying that he was inspired by reading *Confessions of an English Opium Eater*. He declined to explain just why he was prepared to go into such 'painful detail'. 'There is more to be learned from a man's weakness than from his strength. Some of mine I shall unveil to you (*for what I write is true*), and you will therefore, I am sure, spare me (and yourself) the fruitless trouble of too strict an inquisition.'[17] *Confessions of an English Opium-Eater* had made him see that the important truths were those that men usually like to hide. Part I of De Quincey's *Confessions*, entitled 'Being an Extract from the Life of a Scholar', had appeared in the *London Magazine* of September 1821. It was not only De Quincey's first contribution to the magazine but the opening gambit of his literary career – previously he had only published obscurely in the *Westmoreland Gazette*. While promising to detail the writer's 'fascinating enthralment' to opium, it narrated instead his wanderings as a youth, discontented with his schooling and unwilling to trust in his guardians. Memorably, it told of his penniless existence in the 'mighty wild' of London and his friendship with a prostitute called Ann. The magazine's editor John Taylor must have known he was on to something. By the next month the second part of the *Confessions* was the lead article, and the editorial was puffing 'the deep, eloquent and masterly paper which stands first in our present Number'.[18]

It was calculated to arouse interest and controversy. While warning of opium's pains, it celebrated many of its effects in visionary style. 'Oh! just, subtle, and mighty opium!'[19] The exclamation is in De Quincey's ironically hyperbolical style, but matches much of his account. The writer expected that there might be readers who would take against him. 'Courteous and, I hope, indulgent reader,' begins his section on 'The Pains of Opium', and he adds in parentheses, 'for all *my* readers must be indulgent ones, or else, I fear, I shall shock them too much to count on their courtesy'.[20] He chooses to imagine some readers asking after his health, and hopes that the claret, port or Madeira drunk regularly by his 'good reader' may 'as little disorder your health as mine was disordered by the opium'. He offers his dreams, even the nightmarish ones, as evidence that the drug brings inspiration as well as a kind of bondage.

Opium, readily and legally available to any purchaser, is, he provocatively says, his society's secret pleasure, not just his own. One reason for the anonymity of the *Confessions* is implied in the introductory address 'To the Reader'. The author talks of the men 'of eminent station' whom he has known to be 'opium-eaters: the eloquent and benevolent——, the late dean of——; Lord——; Mr——, the philosopher'.[21] He may himself refuse to acknowledge any guilt, but the identity of the opium addict is to be kept from the world. The names were inserted when De

Quincey revised the work for publication in 1856, when he filled in its many other blanks: the name of his school, his teachers, places he visited. In the original version, he likes to leave things out. His eventually excessive use of opium, for instance, is sparked by 'a very melancholy event' whose nature 'I need not more particularly notice'.[22] He is amusedly aware that there is some irony in publishing confessions – that it is 'the public' 'into whose private ear I am confidentially whispering my confessions'.[23] But anonymity is the very evidence of the work's truthfulness.

The truthfulness was what some reviewers challenged. Provoked by a sceptic writing in the Sheffield *Iris*, De Quincey composed a letter printed in the *London Magazine* of December 1821. Signed 'X. Y. Z.', this rebutted suspicions that the *Confessions* was a work of fiction. It conceded some suppression of interesting details from 'regards of delicacy towards some who are yet living, and of just tenderness to the memory of others who are dead': 'In every thing else I spoke fearlessly, and as if writing private memoirs for my own dearest friends.'[24] The *Confessions* appeared in book form, anonymously, in October 1822. Its publisher was also John Taylor, and 'The *Confessions* were instantly famous.'[25] A second edition appeared in January 1823, another in June 1823, and a fourth in 1826. All these were also anonymous. There was no further edition until 1845, when De Quincey's *Suspiria de Profundis* began appearing in *Blackwood's*, and then in 1853. Even these editions remained anonymous. Only when De Quincey himself revised the work substantially for his collected works of 1856, *Selections Grave and Gay*, published when its author was in his seventies, was the name of that author officially attached to his most famous work. Yet its true anonymity had perished even before it became a book. Henry Crabb Robinson, *a littérateur* and inveterate gossip, records in his diary as early as October 1821 that the *Confessions* is De Quincey's 'best-known' work.[26] A month later De Quincey was talking quite openly to Robinson about how much he had been paid for it.[27] The author was not trying to keep his authorship secret, but its official anonymity was nonetheless steadfastly maintained. The first page of the *Confessions* suggested why. Its author knew that it would put its reader in mind of the notorious *Confessions* of Jean-Jacques Rousseau. Rousseau's *Confessions* were published only post-humously, but the author had given public readings of his self-revelation, referred to in the first paragraph of De Quincey's *Confessions* as 'gratuitous self-humiliation'.[28] This author offered nothing so proudly shameful as Rousseau's display of 'spurious and defective sensibility'.

> Nothing, indeed, is more revolting to English feelings, than the spectacle of a human being obtruding on our notice his moral ulcers or scars, and tearing away that 'decent drapery', which time, or indulgence to human frailty, may have drawn over them.

A review in the *European Magazine* of November 1822 judged De Quincey's *Confessions* to be 'the offspring of an accurate and vigorous pen' and 'a proof of superior genius'.[29] The reviewer 'can make no allowances' for its author's conduct as 'the friend, the companion, and lover of one of the very lowest class of the most abandoned' (even though De Quincey specifically denies a sexual relationship with the prostitute Ann). Yet, despite this 'moral criticism', he is bound 'to bestow very high praise on the work'. The description of opium addiction 'rivets the attention and interests the feelings exceedingly'. A long review in the *New Edinburgh Review* of January 1823 begins, 'Whenever a man prefaces what he is about to say, with the words, "I confess," we are sure that he does not mean to speak in his own disparage-ment.'[30] The reviewer is determined 'to treat the Confessions as altogether fabulous' rather than as 'a piece of authentic biography'.[31] No hint is given that the reviewer might know the author's identity. None of the first reviewers of the *Confessions* seems to have known anything of its author beyond what was told in the work itself.

With one exception. In the *John Bull Magazine* in July 1824, in the first article of a projected series on 'Humbugs of the Age', William Maginn attacked the *Confessions* as fraudulent. To do so he displayed his personal knowledge of the author. In his review, Maginn refers to him as 'Quincey' (claiming that the 'De' is a mere affectation).The Opium-Eater had made himself seem attractive, he said, but in fact had a face of 'utter grotesqueness and inanity'.[32] What is more, his wife was his former servant maid and their first child was conceived before they were ever married. Maginn was a leading contributor to the Edinburgh-based *Blackwood's Magazine*, bitter rival to the *London Magazine*. *Blackwood's* editor was John Wilson, a close friend of De Quincey's, from whom Maginn could have had his information. 'The Opium-Eater' had become a character in the 'Noctes Ambrosianae' series in *Blackwood's* in October 1823, and his appearance there made it clear that the *Blackwood's* men knew exactly who he was. Wilson, presumably regretting the use that Maginn had made of gossip about De Quincey's private life, had Maginn's alter ego 'Odoherty' rebuked in 'Noctes Ambrosianae' for his attack.[33]

So much of what we have come to call Romantic literature consists of forms of autobiography that we may not notice the resistance to self-revelation that writers needed to overcome. This seems to have been true of even the most fearless and iconoclastic of writers. Percy Bysshe Shelley's most autobiographical poems, *Julian and Maddalo* and *Epipsychidion*, were both anonymous. *Epipsychidion* is a tender case because it seemed to speak in favour of free love, whilst containing confessional narrative of the poet's own passions.

> I never was attached to that great sect,
> Whose doctrine is, that each one should select
> Out of the crowd a mistress or a friend,
> And all the rest, though fair and wise, commend
> To cold oblivion, though it is the code
> Of modern morals.[34]

The poet's beliefs are supported by a personal narrative in which one woman is the moon, 'cold' and 'chaste', while another is a comet, 'beautiful and fierce' (l. 368). The poem is dedicated to 'EMILIA V—' and this third woman is directly addressed as 'Emily', 'my heart's sister' (l. 415). She is imagined as sharing some 'Elysian isle' with the poet, where 'Our breath shall intermix, our bosoms bound, / And our veins beat together' (ll. 565–6).

Biographers now know that this was Emilia Viviani, the nineteen-year-old daughter of Count Viviani, the Governor of Pisa, who had been confined in a convent while her parents attempted to arrange her marriage. She had been 'discovered' by Mary Shelley's stepsister Claire Clairmont, and visited regularly by the two women and Shelley himself. The poet confessed himself enchanted and his feelings seemed to come alive in the poem. If we know the background, we can also recognize the cold woman as Shelley's wife Mary, and the comet as Claire Clairmont. Shelley, living in Italy, may have been out of the range of British critics' censoriousness, but he nonetheless wrote to the publisher of *Epipsychidion*, Charles Ollier, on 16 February 1821 to require the poem's anonymity. He devised an Advertisement saying that the poem's author 'died at Florence, as he was preparing for a voyage to one of the wildest of the Sporades', a Greek island where he had planned to live and realize 'a scheme of life, suited perhaps to that happier and better world of which he is now an inhabitant, but hardly practicable in this'.[35] It is an odd distancing device: not only is the author dead, but he is also labelled as an unrealistic dreamer, whose ideas about love might be thought to be above reality.

Including *Epipsychidion* with two shorter pieces that were to be published under his name, Shelley told Ollier, 'The longer poem, I desire, should not be considered as my own; indeed, in a certain sense, it is a portion of me already dead.'[36] He imagined a readership only of 'the esoteric few' and explained, 'I make its author a secret, to avoid the malignity of those who turn sweet food into poison; transforming all they touch into the corruption of their own natures.' He had been bruised by what reviewers had said before – true and false – about his personal life, especially in the wake of his legal battle for custody of his children by his first wife Harriet, after her suicide. Yet it is ironical that a writer who turned private, even intimate, experience into philosophical verse should here wish to erase his authorship. From its dedication onwards, *Epipsychidion* is clearly a poem rooted in real relationships and real passions. It is characteristic of Shelley in confessing feelings that might be thought painful to those close to him, particularly his wife. However, he had come to dread the very biographical interpretation that he made so unavoidable.

The year after De Quincey's *Confessions* appeared in book form saw the publication of another confessional account of obsession and enslavement, William Hazlitt's *Liber Amoris* (1823). Like De Quincey's account, it was an autobiographical tale of humiliation, weakness, and self-destructiveness. Like De Quincey's account, it was published anonymously. In 1820 Hazlitt, separated from his wife, and trying to earn a living through literary journalism, had taken a room in 9 Southampton Buildings, Holborn. His landlady, Mrs Walker, the wife of a tailor, had six children, including a nineteen-year-old daughter called Sarah. Hazlitt became infatuated by her. Over the course of the next year, they spent long hours in each other's company, with Hazlitt's amorous hopes rising and falling. Late in 1821, he sought a divorce from his wife – also called Sarah – to whom he had been married for thirteen years. He had decided that he would only break through Sarah Walker's reserve if he were able to offer her marriage. With his wife's apparent agreement, he travelled to Scotland, where divorce was much easier to obtain than in England. On the way, he began a record of his conversations with her.[37] He had to live in Scotland for three months, and then be witnessed in adultery – which was arranged to take place at a brothel in Edinburgh. All this time he was writing letters to a friend in London, Peter Patmore, and occasionally, without producing anything but a terse and coldly polite response, to Sarah Walker herself.

His divorce was granted on 17 July 1822, and he returned to London. A week later he met Sarah Walker in the street. She was on the arm of John Tomkins, a young lawyer who had also been a lodger in the Walkers' home. All his hopes were dashed. But he decided to make a book out of the whole affair. He produced *Liber Amoris*, published anonymously in May 1823, an exposure of the agonies and follies of unrequited love. Before publication he showed it to some friends; one of these, the painter Benjamin Haydon, said it was written 'in order to ease his soul of this burden'.[38] The Advertisement prefacing the book claimed that its author and subject had recently died in the Netherlands, 'it is supposed, of disappointment preying on a sickly frame and morbid state of mind'. It went to say that the publication of the story of his 'fatal attachment' was undertaken in accordance with his wishes. And though it had been suggested to the 'friend' who organized the publication that 'childish or redundant' passages might be removed, he had kept to his promise that 'not a word should be altered'. Though 'names and circumstances' are disguised, this is the unedited truth.

The 'narrative' itself is a strange combination of fragments in three parts. Part I consists largely of dialogues between 'H.' and

'S.' (which we now know were based on Hazlitt's notebook of conversations between himself and Sarah), a couple of letters to her, an ecstatic inscription 'Written in a blank leaf of Endymion' and a passage copied out from Shakespeare's *Troilus and Cressida*. The latter ends with Troilus's declaration of the 'truth' of his love for Cressida on the night that their love is consummated.

> I am as true as truth's simplicity,
> And simpler than the infancy of truth.

Cressida will of course betray Troilus, for all her matching expressions of fidelity. The fragment epitomizes the self-dramatization that is the method of *Liber Amoris*. It turns a real and, for Hazlitt, mortifying drama of unrequited infatuation into a performance that is happy to borrow its lines from literature. It is also peculiarly self-deluding: on the very evidence of the earlier dialogues, Sarah never reciprocated his expressions of love and certainly never seemed likely to gratify his sexual yearnings.

The dialogues themselves are apparently private fragments, in which 'H.' expresses his love in variously ecstatic ways but gets nothing better than the profession of friendship in return. Or rather, no words better than this, for H.'s occasional requests for kisses appear to be granted. 'One kiss! Ah! ought I not to think myself the happiest of men?'[39] On the evidence of one of the dialogues, Sarah (she is explicitly named) was willing to spend time sitting on H.'s lap ('. . . you were sitting in your old place, on my knee, embracing and fondly embraced . . .').[40] The dialogues are also highly wrought vignettes, given titles ('The Invitation', 'The Message', 'The Quarrel') that make significance from some inconsequential exchange. H. speaks in histrionic fashion – 'Your charms are irresistible as your will is inexorable' – and with the thees and thous taken from some old drama.[41] 'I could almost wish to go mad for thy sake: for then I might fancy that I had thy love in return, which I cannot live without!'[42] This is confessional, publishing the evidence of an infatuation. It is also stagey, even comically so. One of the dialogues is actually entitled 'The Confession', and has Sarah admitting that she is still in love with a young man who broke off their 'intimacy' because of her lowly social status. H. appears to be gratified that she has told him this secret. 'How can I thank you for your condescension in letting me know your sweet sentiments?'[43] Hazlitt seems determined to show just how enslaved, how absurdly self-tormenting he was. He does so by making himself into a dramatic character.

Part II is made up of letters, mostly to his friend 'C. P——, Esq.' (We now know they were edited by Hazlitt from real letters to Peter Patmore.) In these he vents his suspicions that his beloved is 'an arrant jilt', 'a little artful vixen', and Othello-like claims that he would be contented if he but 'knew she was a mere abandoned creature'.[44] 'If you can give me any consolation on the subject of my tormentor, pray do.'[45] His friend defends her, bringing effusive gratitude. 'Your reproofs of me and your defences of her are the only things that save my soul from perdition.'[46] He is dizzy with the thought that Sarah might become his bride. And then in the very next letter he is experiencing 'the eternity of punishment in this life' and she is 'the false one' who 'hardens herself against me'.[47] The letters enact his swoops of feeling in flurries of exclamation marks and quotations from *Othello*: 'Wretched being that I am! I have thrown away my heart and soul upon an unfeeling girl!' But 'she's gone, I am abused, and my revenge must be to *love* her!'[48] He even regrets that, after 'exciting her wayward desires by the fondest embraces', he 'did not proceed to gratify them, or follow up my advantage'.[49] With what must have seemed shocking earnestness, he calls himself a 'credulous fool' for not having 'made the experiment' – for not having sexually forced himself on her.

As he feels madness approaching, he thinks himself like King

Lear. 'I must break off here; for the *hysteria passio* comes upon me, and threatens to unhinge my reason.'[50] He says he has contemplated suicide. Sarah has thrown herself at another. Yet immediately there is a letter to her begging for forgiveness and asking 'may I come back, and try to behave better?'[51] His friend writes to tell him, 'She is still to be won by wise and prudent conduct on your part.' So now he is back to adoration. 'She is an angel from Heaven, and you cannot pretend I ever said a word to the contrary!'[52]

Part III of *Liber Amoris* is composed of three long letters addressed to a friend, J. S. K—— (the Scottish dramatist James Sheridan Knowles). These letters seem not to have been based on any real correspondence, but Hazlitt needs letters because he wants somehow to chart the ebbing of hope into despair and back into hope again. He writes after the event, knowing it all has come to nothing, but in order to recreate the feelings that possessed him. The final letters narrate his return to London from Scotland and the coldness of Sarah's reception of him. But still the smallest evidence revives his hopes. Each meeting with 'my inhuman betrayer and my only earthly love' promises to be the end to his illusions.[53] When she confirms that she has no affection for him he responds with characteristic grandiloquence. 'She started up in her own likeness, a serpent in place of a woman. She had fascinated, she had stung me, and had returned to her proper shape, gliding from me after inflicting the mortal wound.'[54] Sarah is Lamia, the alluring, deadly snake-woman of Keats's poem, first published in 1820. But then all it takes is for Sarah's mother to assure H. that her daughter has gone to great lengths to mend his favourite bust of Napoleon (which he has smashed in a temper), and his heart is melted again.

Throughout his book of love, the would-be lover toils with female stereotypes: 'witch', 'sorceress', 'demon', 'angel', 'good girl'. He veers from one to another. Only when, by chance, he finally meets Sarah in the street with her beau, the very former lodger whom H. accused her of loving, is he finally rid of his illusions. Now she is something less exotic than a vampiric serpent-woman: 'She is a practised, callous jilt, a regular lodging-house decoy, played off by her mother upon the lodgers.'[55] The last 'letter' ends in a posture of superiority that is at once absurd and entirely credible. 'I am afraid she will soon grow common to my imagination, as well as worthless in herself.'[56] Hazlitt had made his disappointed passion into a drama of infatuation that was believable because its protagonist was so foolish, so self-deceiving.

The first review came in the *Examiner*, a liberal journal for which Hazlitt had himself written. It was edited by Leigh Hunt, who knew Hazlitt well, and whilst professing ignorance of the work's authorship ('Who this extraordinary person is, it is for our readers to guess . . .') is likely to have been written in full knowledge.[57] It praises 'the eloquence of soul and of passion' with which *Liber Amoris* transforms 'trite and by no means exalted events', and provides long passages of quotation to exemplify the book's merits. It is peculiar that Hazlitt should have believed that his authorship might remain secret from his many journalistic enemies. He had been busy telling anybody willing to listen about his passion, and had published a strange little essay inspired by it in the *New Monthly Magazine* in 1821. Called 'On Great and Little Things', it celebrated the allure of 'humble beauties, servant-maids and shepherd-girls', and addressed itself to one of these, 'my Infelice', who, Hazlitt hoped, might one day 'grace my home with thy loved presence, as thou hast cheered my hopes with thy smile'.[58] The essay was reprinted in 1822, under his own name, in his collection *Table-talk*.

Only eight days after *Liber Amoris* was published, a review in the *Literary Register* announced its authorship to the world. The reviewer declared that he wished to give the public

every opportunity of seeing what materials go to the composition of these liberal and radical rapscallions, who take upon
them the airs of philosophers, poets, and politicians, dis-
seminators of truth, improvers of taste, reformers of abuses,
and ameliators of mankind, as they call themselves.[59]

Sarah Walker was described, in the same article, as 'an artful,
shameless, trumpery, common strumpet – the common servant
in a common lodging house – the creature and the property of
every inmate who might chance to become ... the object of
lascivious fancy'. *The Times* a week later published a short notice
ranking the book 'among the curiosities of literature' and praising it for the accuracy of its depiction of 'a man under the
influence of a degrading infatuation'.[60] It did not name the
author, but said he had 'done a real service to the cause of sound
sense and rational affection' by dramatizing 'the drivelling imbecility and impotent dotage' of the 'senseless lover'. The author
and his character were, it seems, to be regarded as distinct.

The reviewer in the *Literary Gazette* the next day took delight
in reporting that 'this matchless conjunction of vulgar sensuality
and Cockney affectation' had been 'cruelly ascribed by some
malignant enemy to Mr. Hazlitt'.[61] He was only surprised that
the aforementioned Mr. Hazlitt had not 'leaped forth to disclaim
the foul reproach'. For the attribution would be 'absolute
slaughter' to its reputed author. The whole review is mocking
quotation and mocking commentary. Never has there been 'a
greater blockhead or sillier creature' than this author. J. G. Lockhart's review in *Blackwood's*, in contrast, began as if sympathetically, calling it a 'simple story', unfolded in 'soul-harrowing
fullness of detail'.[62] By the end of the review, however, it was
clear that it was deriding a 'disgusting' tale, an 'abomination'
written by 'a COCKNEY and "a LIBERAL" '.[63] Lockhart, who had
attacked Hazlitt before, was indicating that he knew the author

well enough. His friends were 'puffing him as a new Rousseau', wrote Lockhart scornfully, and indeed more than one reviewer drew the analogy with Rousseau's *Confessions*. The *Globe* did so while praising the book for describing 'sentiments and sensations which the common race of mankind seek most studiously to mystify or conceal'.[64]

Hazlitt's exposure did not end with his identification. On 8 June 1823 the rabidly Tory *John Bull* (the same journal that had named De Quincey as the 'opium-eater') mentioned, in the course of an assault on the supposedly Whig *Times*, that newspaper's support for 'the beastly trash of BILLY HAZLITT'.[65] The writer had been alerted to this by 'a puff from the fellow himself, in the Cockney journal'. In the next issue, the *John Bull* duly weighed in to *Liber Amoris* and Hazlitt's 'struggles against taste, decency, and morality'.[66] The 'imagined character', it declared, was none other than the author. 'Having made every effort which a very ill-looking middle-aged man could make to undermine the principles of SALLY, he took to the resolution of writing *a book about her*'. The attack ran on into the next issue, where 'this nasty little book' was condemned by having one of its letters set against a real letter written to Sarah from Scotland.[67] The journal had procured a love letter that he had written to Sarah from Scotland the previous year. Even by the codes of the bitterly partisan journalism of the day, the unlicensed printing of private correspondence was highly improper. But the confessional account of sexual infatuation was itself improper. If Hazlitt objected to having a private letter made public, he should recall 'that it is he himself who has given publicity to the affair altogether'.

Hazlitt was ridiculed in conservative journals from then on – frequently appearing in *Blackwood's* as 'Mr. H. of the *Liber Amoris*, who, for his drivelling, was despised, even by the daughter of a tailor'. This was part of the magazine's constant attack on the 'Cockney school' to which he supposedly belonged (along with Keats and Leigh Hunt). Derision was the price that Hazlitt paid for his attempt, via anonymous publication, to turn the personal into the fictional. As an alternative to Rousseau's stern confessional 'truth', Hazlitt had foolishly attempted something very unusual. He had used anonymity to catch the self unawares. He had written his book as if there could be a gap between the author and the person whose blunderings he describes – himself in a state of infatuation. The book's very subtitle, 'or, The New Pygmalion', alerts the reader to self-mockery. Pygmalion is the sculptor who falls in love with his own creation, and who prays to the Gods to give life to the product of his own imagination. H. is similarly caught by his fantasies. Hazlitt's anonymity was his attempt to convert a private story into this representative drama. (Thus the choice of a Latin title, impersonal and eternal.) He freed himself to show himself as ridiculous. No wonder his enemies were so delighted.

This might explain a natural relationship between confession and anonymity: the writer reveals himself but steps back from his own absurdity. So it was with Robert Browning's first published work, the anonymous *Pauline: A Fragment of a Confession*, which appeared in 1833. Addressed to the woman named in the title, whom the poet loves ('Pauline, mine own, bend o'er me – thy soft breast / Shall pant to mine'), it appears to follow the life and frustrated hopes of a young poet.[68] It begins with his rebellion against the values with which he is brought up. Self-absorbed to the point of frequent obscurity, it goes on to describe the loss (and later rediscovery) of religious belief and the dwindling of youthful political idealism, to be replaced by a more mature faith in himself and humanity. It describes the influence of music, theatre, painting and books – especially the work of Shelley (though he is never actually named). In its fervour, which often becomes feverishness, it is consciously imitative of Shelley. Browning would go on to make his name as a 'dramatic' poet, whose best poems are, in the words of his note to his early collection *Dramatic Lyrics* (1842), 'so many utterances of so many imaginary persons, not mine'.[69] Browning later suppressed *Pauline*, apparently because the author was identified by some reviewers with the speaker of the confession. When he reluctantly reprinted the poem late in his life he prefaced it with the claim that it was 'dramatic in principle' – nothing to do with himself.[70] Some of the first readers knew better. 'The author is in the confessional, and acknowledges to his mistress the strange thoughts and fancies with which his past life has been crowded,' said one reviewer.[71] 'We have never read anything more purely confessional,' said another. This latter, writing anonymously in the *Monthly Repository*, was in fact Browning's friend and mentor W. J. Fox.[72] Fox was also guardian to Sarah and Eliza Flower, two sisters whom Browning knew well and on one of whom the character of Pauline was based.

Hazlitt and Browning might later have regretted their confessional texts, but confession was not inevitably rash. Probably the most admired book of poems of the Victorian age, Tennyson's *In Memoriam A. H. H.*, was confessional. It made the name of its author, but it was published anonymously, and remained officially anonymous throughout its author's life. *In Memoriam* was written in grieving memory of the poet's friend Arthur Henry Hallam, his identity preserved in the initials of the original title. Hallam, whom Tennyson had met when the two of them were fellow students at Trinity College, Cambridge, had died in 1833, aged twenty-two. He had been Tennyson's dearest friend, and was engaged to the poet's sister Emily. Tennyson contemplated writing a memoir of his friend soon after his death, but felt unable 'to do him justice'.[73] As a different kind of tribute, the sequence of poems that became *In Memoriam* grew over the next fifteen years. Friends were aware of this; sometimes Tennyson would read aloud some of his 'elegies', as they were often called. He would show it 'even to casual acquaintances'.[74] Before they were eventually published in 1850, they had a private life. Indeed, Tennyson made them public in part because some friends had put pressure on him to do so.

Tennyson clearly felt some reticence about the publication of *In Memoriam*. He told his friend Aubrey de Vere that he would print a small number, and send him a copy that should be either returned or destroyed. 'I shall print about 25 copies and let them out among friends under the same condition of either return or cremation.'[75] Initially he had a private edition of only six copies printed.[76] 'Give none away and retain none yourself,' he told his printer Edward Moxon. We know that the work's anonymity was merely official, because the first commercial announcement of the poem's publication included the author's name by error. The first reviews, in the *Examiner* and the *Spectator*, baldly told their readers the author's identity. Despite the apparent mystery of the book's title page, the *Spectator* informed its readers, 'it is well known to be from the pen of Alfred Tennyson.'[77] The reviewer went on to identify Arthur Hallam and to infer that 'the deceased was betrothed to a sister of Tennyson, while the friend-ship on the poet's part has "passed the love of women"'. A week later the *Athenaeum* confidently declared that the volume, 'though published anonymously, bears such intrinsic proof of Mr. Tennyson's authorship that we hazard nothing in at once assuming the fact'.[78] Perhaps the attribution derived from critical acumen alone, but it is more likely that the reviewer's confidence was based on report rather than stylistic analysis.

Only the *Literary Gazette*, reviewing the work on the same day as the *Athenaeum*, seemed in the dark. 'If by a female hand, as it purports to be, we welcome to the Muse's banquet, melancholy though the music be, one of their sweetest minstrels.'[79] Presum-ably the reviewer takes the poem's voice to be female because it speaks of 'love' for a young man. The false guess was made despite the *Literary Gazette* having listed *In Memoriam* as by Tennyson in its new books column a fortnight earlier.[80] In an anonymous review written some three months after its publication, Charles Kingsley declared,

> All the world, somehow or other, knows the author. His name has been mentioned unhesitatingly by several reviews already, whether from private information, or from the certainty which every well-read person must feel, that there is but one man in England possessed at once of poetic talent and artistic experience sufficient for so noble a creation.[81]

Kingsley agonized about whether to name the author.

> Critics cannot in general be too punctilious in their respect for an *incognito*. If an author intended us to know his name, he would put it on his title-page. If he does not choose to do that, we have no more right to pry into his secret than we have to discuss his family affairs or open his letters.

However, he did feel licensed to break a gentlemanly convention and 'ignore an incognito which all England has ignored before us'. He duly attributed *In Memoriam* 'to the pen of the author of *The Princess*' (which had been published under Tennyson's name in 1847).

It was received with acclaim, enthusiastic reviews appearing throughout the national and periodical press. In November 1850 Tennyson was offered and accepted the post of Poet Laureate, vacant since the death of Wordsworth. Eighteen months after its first appearance, *In Memoriam* had already reached its fifth edition. Anonymous it might have been, but it made its author famous. Yet Tennyson made sure that none of the editions published in his lifetime had his name upon it (though, beginning in 1870, it did appear in collected editions of Tennyson's work). In

1867, when he wrote giving permission for Emma Wood to use attributed extracts from his work in a poetry anthology, he made an exception of *In Memoriam*: 'In Memoriam is an anonymous work and not to be meddled with.'[82] T. S. Eliot described *In Memoriam* as 'the concentrated diary of a man confessing himself'.[83] Unlike any memoir that Tennyson might have contemplated, it is a work about its author rather than his dead friend. 'Let Love clasp Grief lest both be drowned,' declares section I.[84] Those capital letters for 'Love' and 'Grief' make the thought a generality, but the clasping of grief is always personal in the poem. It includes many personal details. Section IX of the sequence names the poet's friend for the first time and imagines the ship that brings his body back to England (Hallam had died in Vienna).

> Fair ship, that from the Italian shore
> Sailest the placid ocean-plains
> With my lost Arthur's loved remains,
> Spread thy full wings, and waft him o'er.

Fragments of autobiography are detectable: a trip to France together when they were students (LXXI), Hallam's planned marriage to Emily Tennyson (LXXXIV). The poem has become famous for speaking for its culture: enacting the Victorians' death-drawn doubts, their grappling for religious consolation. It also lets us overhear a private torment. Tennyson's direct expressions of loss and love are perhaps the more disconcerting for the modern reader, unused to one man addressing another as 'dearest' (LXXIV, l. 5; CXXII, l. 1) or 'my lost desire' (CXXIX, l. 1). The poet does not hesitate to draw an analogy between himself and a deserted lover (VIII): 'So seems it in my deep regret, / O my forsaken heart.' Post-Victorian readers have been prone to a kind of embarrassment in the face of the poet's peculiar intimacy with his dead friend – 'My Arthur, whom I shall not see / Till all my widowed race be run' (IX, ll. 17–18). It is symptomatic that one of the several aphorisms now famous from *In Memoriam* has been transformed from an affirmation of faith in the face of a friend's death into a vainglorious Romantic truism. ''Tis better to have loved and lost / Than never to have loved at all' (XXVII, ll. 15–16).

It is not as if Tennyson felt a need to disguise what was personal, let alone to make his mourning poetry impersonal. He refuses to believe that the commonness of his loss would make his grief less individually sharp.

> That loss is common would not make
>   My own less bitter, rather more:
>   Too common! Never morning wore
> To evening, but some heart did break. (VI, ll. 5–8)

Yet there is the thought that there is something wrong in turning his bereavement into poetry.

> I sometimes hold it half a sin
>   To put in words the grief I feel;
>   For words, like Nature, half reveal
> And half conceal the Soul within. (V, ll. 1–4)

The reader is to take it that the verses 'enfold' his feelings rather than expressing them – that his grief is 'given in outline and no more' (ll. 11–12). The use for the poet of putting things 'in measured language' is, perhaps, only anaesthetic: 'The sad mechanic exercise, / Like dull narcotics, numbing pain' (ll. 7–8). You have to say 'perhaps' because the sequence form, like the sequence of Shakespeare's sonnets that it sometimes recalls, allows Tennyson to stage a drama of different moods and arguments. One section even acknowledges that if the work 'closed / Grave doubts and answers here proposed', it might deserve scorn (XLVIII, ll. 2–3). Instead it flits from one small verse drama to another: 'Short swallow-flights of song, that dip / Their wings in tears, and skim away.' It performs the honest variety of feelings (XLVIII, ll. 15–16).

Queen Victoria herself turned to *In Memoriam* in the months after Prince Albert's death.[85] Many Victorian readers found in it, if not consolation, at least an eloquent echo of their own struggles for consolation. It was the telling meeting of faith and dismay that made the work so powerful for many of its first readers. In his 1897 memoir of his father, Hallam Tennyson quoted a letter from Brooke Westcott, Bishop of Durham, on the impact that *In Memoriam* had made on him as a young Cambridge fellow in the 1850s. 'As I look at my original copy of "In Memoriam," I recognise that what impressed me most was your father's splendid faith (in the face of the frankest acknowledgement of every difficulty) in the growing purpose of the sum of life.'[86] According to Hallam Tennyson, his father wrote a note more than thirty years after the poem's first publication recalling that he did not originally write the different sections 'with any view of weaving them into a whole, or for publication'.[87] Tennyson usually put his name to his work, and we might think that his anonymity here signified something singular about *In Memoriam*: that it was the published form of a private exercise. One of the early reviewers thought that the poet's only motive for anonymity could be 'that delicate bias which, in raising so solemn and tender a memorial, would not obtrude on the tablet even the name of its founder'.[88] Yet, in the very same note, Tennyson also removes his elegiac sequence from its private origins. ' "I" is not always the author speaking of himself, but the voice of the human race speaking thro' him.' He said something similar to his friend James Knowles in the early 1870s when reading the poem to him. 'It is rather the cry of the whole human race than mine. In the poem altogether private grief swells out into thought of, and hope for, the whole world.'[89]

It is as if the making public of what was once private requires the author's withdrawal. This was also the case with one of the most famous personal accounts of a Victorian childhood, Edmund Gosse's *Father and Son.* Gosse's memoir was written in the early years of the twentieth century when its author was in his fifties and an established man of letters. It tells of his early life and of his relationship with his father, who was both a notable naturalist and a devoted member of the fundamentalist Plymouth Brethren sect. The book was published anonymously in 1907, and Gosse himself initially hoped that his anonymity could be maintained: 'I hope the secret of the authorship will be kept as long as possible.'[90] Friends were sent copies by his publisher, William Heinemann, 'with the author's regards', but no mention of Gosse's name. Gosse wrote to his friend Thomas Hardy to tell him that a copy of an anonymous book called *Father and Son* was being sent to him, and that he would 'take it as a kind of favour' if he were to read it. Even here he was declining to acknowledge the book as his own. Hardy wrote back ten days later to say that he was reading 'your spiritual autobiography', which 'took me completely by surprise'.[91] It is clear from the rest of Hardy's letter that he was surprised simply by the 'extraordinary' nature of Gosse's childhood experiences. The two men knew each other well, but Hardy had not realized the sheer 'narrowness' of his friend's upbringing.

Gosse's memoir is sometimes treated, often alongside Samuel Butler's *The Way of All Flesh,* as an Edwardian debunking of Victorian values, and in particular as an anatomy of the intellectual and emotional tyranny of the Victorian patriarch. In truth, however, Gosse's upbringing was peculiar, not representative. Membership of their religious sect sealed his parents off from wider society. After his mother's death when he was seven years old, painfully narrated in the book, he was schooled by his father in a Calvinistic Puritanism that would have been thought

extreme, even fanatical, by most of his contemporaries. Looking
back in the early twentieth century, Gosse supposed that not
even his older readers would recognize 'the puritanism of which
he was perhaps the last surviving type'.[92] His father belonged to
the seventeenth century, not the nineteenth.

We say 'Gosse's memoir', but *Father and Son* did not at first
present itself as this. Its author was nameless. The removal of the
author from his own memoir was explained in the declaration
made by its first sentence: 'This book is the record of a struggle
between two temperaments, two consciences and almost two
epochs.'[93] The author was standing aside in order to see some
larger pattern in his upbringing. The first chapter begins by
talking disinterestedly of the 'two persons' of its title, and it
ends, in a chapter called 'Epilogue', by returning to this style,
reflecting on the future destinies of 'the son' and 'the father'. In
between this beginning and this end, it is a first-person narrative, though something different from an autobiography. Finding himself recalling some of the most important facts about his
education, the author stops himself. 'But this is not an autobiography, and with the cold and shrouded details of my
uninteresting school life I will not fatigue the reader.'[94] Not an
autobiography because it is an account of his relationship with
his father, and will miss out many of the mere facts of his life.
But also not an autobiography because it is a kind of confession,
a reckoning with the truth about his own often ignoble inclinations as a boy and an adolescent. The Preface declares the
account to be 'scrupulously true', but it is the truth not of names
and dates, but of memories brought into the light. This confessional narrative method was urged on Gosse by the man who had
suggested writing the book in the first place, his friend and confidante George Moore. Moore advised Gosse not to be diverted
into careful research amongst his father's notes about members
of his Plymouth Brethren congregation. 'You are writing about

yourself and your father, and your memory should be much better than these little realistic patches.'[95]

It is strange that Gosse should have talked of the 'the secret of the authorship', for within the narrative, apart from the omission of his and his father's names, he made little attempt at actual secrecy. As one reviewer noted, there was 'no attempt at concealment'.[96] His father was the author of many books on natural history, a Fellow of the Royal Society, and an acquaintance of some of the leading scientists of the age. Edmund Gosse had already written a biography of him, published in 1890. On its title page both their names were declared: 'The Life of Philip Henry Gosse FRS by his son Edmund Gosse'. Father and Son may have held back his father's name, but the first edition had a photograph of Gosse père and fils as its frontispiece. Throughout the book the titles of Philip Henry Gosse's books are given without disguise. When the son praises his father's The Romance of Natural History as 'the most picturesque, easy and graceful of all his writings' and says that it is 'even now a sort of classic', he seems to expect readers to recognize his father's published work.[97] It is not quite clear whether it was the author's wish or the publisher's that Heinemann's New York representative was voicing when he told the book's American publisher, 'Will you please remember that the book is to be published anonymously, although the name of the author is to leak out at once'.[98] Father and Son does, however, seem to be another version of that anonymity without actual disguise that we find so often.

Gosse's most recent biographer, Ann Thwaite, thinks the anonymity a publicity trick: 'It seems to have been a ploy to arouse curiosity and increase comment.'[99] There is no particular evidence for this. For early reviewers there was no question of curiosity because they were confident about the work's authorship. A month after its publication, the reviewer in The Academy was able to say, 'The secret has not been kept for long, and we understand that Mr. Edmund Gosse does not deny that he is the writer of the book.'[100] His next sentence might take us closer to Gosse's reasons for anonymity. 'It is a great book, but for our part we scarcely like this close anatomisation by a son of a father.' *Father and Son* was fascinating for its improper scrutiny of a father by a son, for its making public of a familial relationship hidden from the world. 'It is idle to pretend ignorance of the identity of the distinguished author,' began the review in the *Athenaeum* just over a month later. It declared that no apology was needed for using Gosse's name because it had been mentioned so often by 'the "rapid" reviews'.[101] This reviewer gives us a taste of what some commentators might have said against *Father and Son.*

> In spite of what has been said on the question of taste, we cannot see that the writer is to be blamed for this account of his father; it seems to us neither disrespectful nor untender, but eminently delicate and fair; nor do any of the jokes seem to us ungenerous. In the minds of some, it was clearly wrong for a son to bare the relationship between himself and his father. Given this resistance, anonymity liberated the author to write of his father and his young self with the book's peculiar, melancholy intimacy.

In his earlier and more conventional life of his father, Edmund Gosse had described the clash between Philip Gosse's religious convictions and the growing scientific – and especially geological – knowledge of the age. There the son regretted that his father had 'left his own field of research, that field in which he was gathering such thick and clustering laurels, to adventure in a province of scientific philosophy which lay outside his sphere, and for which he was fitted neither by training, nor by native aptitude, nor by the possession of a mind clear from prejudice'.[102] Being a noted naturalist, Philip Gosse attempted the reconciliation of religious fundamentalism and science in print, publishing a book,

Omphalos, in which he argued that the story of the Creation in Genesis was true, but that the world that God created 'presented, instantly, the structural appearance of a planet on which life had long existed'.[103] Or, as a scornful press would paraphrase it, 'God hid the fossils in the rocks in order to tempt geologists into infidelity.' The responses of many are characterized in the *Life* by a long letter from Charles Kingsley, in which he explains why he cannot accept his account of how God has deceived men by natural appearances. But almost immediately Philip Gosse is happily engrossed once again in his researches among the Devon rock pools. In *Father and Son* the episode is narrated differently. The scornful or neglectful response to his work drives the author's father to near-despair. In his disappointed hopes he infers God's punishment.

> In those brooding tramps round and round the garden, his soul was on its knees searching the corners of his conscience for some sin of omission or commission, and one by one every pleasure, every recreation, every trifle scraped out of the dust of past experience, was magnified into a huge offence.[104]

As often in *Father and Son*, the intellectually impossible, self-punishing father becomes a curious focus of our sympathies.

Gosse's *Life* of his father does not omit to characterize his Christian fundamentalism, but it does not dramatize the testing of his faith as his later, anonymous account would do. The years in Devon between 1857 and 1864 are covered in a chapter headed 'Literary Work in Devonshire', which consists almost entirely of an account of his researches and writings. There is no mention of what takes up most of the space in *Father and Son*: the customs of the local Plymouth Brethren, of whom the author's father is the leading spirit, and the unrelenting spiritual demands made of the son by the father. Apart from his useful factual recollections, the son is almost absent from Gosse's *Life*.

He is there to testify to his father's character – 'I have never met with a man, of any creed, of any school of religious speculation, who was so invulnerably cased in fully developed conviction upon every side' – but the influence of that intransigence on himself is never measured.

Father and Son is the story of the author's loss of faith, pushed to extremity by his father's intense, unwavering concern for his son's spiritual condition. In an extraordinary passage originally designed to end the book, he recollected one late summer afternoon of unusual calm when he addressed God through the open window of his Devon school, declaring that he was at that moment ready to be taken away from the 'wicked world' and admitted to Paradise. 'Oh, come, now, now, and take me before I have known the temptations of life.'[105] He waited for 'the glorious apparition', at 'the apex of my striving after holiness'. As the ordinary sounds of life rose around him, 'in my heart the artificial edifice of extravagant faith began to totter and crumble.' However singular this boy's upbringing, it also seems a representative confession. The book ran through four impressions in less than six months. The last of these, published in March 1908, bore a new title page with Gosse's name (and academic honours) duly declared. A prefatory note explained, 'It is indicated to me that the slight veil of anonymity which I originally drew over this narrative was long ago torn to tatters, and that to pretend to preserve it would now be an affectation.'[106] Gosse had been identified. His anonymity, as in so many of the examples described in this book, had encouraged readers to find the author. The liberation from himself that had allowed him to write his confessional narrative had only been temporary.

9

EPILOGUE

When I began working on this book, I imagined that it would be possible to write a brief history of literary anonymity. If no such book already existed, this must be due to the collective oversight of academics and critics. Now I realise that there are other, better reasons for the absence of any historical survey of anonymity. Delve into the uses of anonymity over the last five centuries of English literature and you find that anonymity does not exactly have a history. There is no possible grand narrative of the changing conventions of anonymous and pseudonymous publication because, at any given time, there are different reasons for it. The same author will sometimes publish anonymously, and sometimes not. Latter-day expectations are often upset: a female author will sometimes use her name while a male contemporary does not; an author will attach his name to a controversial work and keep it off a facetious one. Even within a particular genre at a particular time, there are rarely fixed rules.

There is, however, one historical pattern. Anonymity became much less common in the twentieth century, and few leading literary authors made much use of it. The first obvious reason for this is that the convention of genteel reticence about making your name public had been eroded away. Many of the authors I have looked at in this book were not really either shy or modest, and some used anonymity or pseudonymity precisely in order to excite curiosity. But the convention of reticence allowed them to play their games. Authors hoping to make their names by winning critical or popular approval might begin their careers anonymously, conforming to a pattern of tentativeness that, amongst novelists, was still common in the nineteenth century. If a book were successful, the writer could then declare him- or herself on the title pages of subsequent books. Even late in the nineteenth century we can see the traces of this convention. R. D. Blackmore in the 1860s and Thomas Hardy and Samuel Butler in the 1870s, for instance, published their first novels anonymously. Yet the anonymity of the first-time novelist was already much less common than it had been. Anthony Trollope (in 1847), Wilkie Collins (1850), George Meredith (1855) and George Gissing (1880), for example, all published their first novels with their names on the title pages.

A second reason for the withering of anonymity is that the business of selling authors became inextricable from the business of selling books. Of course this was well under way in the Victorian age: Thackeray toured and lectured in order to promote his own books; Dickens's public performances of highlights from his fiction put even the self-promotional efforts of today's writers into the shade. Yet it was in the twentieth century that newspapers and magazines, and later radio and television, made it impossible to imagine the marketing of a book without the promotion of its author. Pseudonymity, while still common, became largely unmysterious. In the twentieth and twenty-first centuries, it has rarely been a kind of anonymity. Our shelves are still thick with pseudonyms, but these do not excite the curiosity of readers as 'Currer Bell' or 'George Eliot' once did. Certain popular genres generate pseudonyms: romance, crime, science fiction. The compiler of a recent dictionary of literary pseudonyms notes that embarrassment is an unlikely motive for camouflage, 'given the respectability attaching to much popular fiction'.[1] When Julian Barnes calls himself 'Dan Kavanagh' in order to write detective fiction, there is nothing shamefaced about the gesture. It has become an acknowledged way of labelling a sub-genre. Edith Pargeter called herself 'Ellis Peters' on the title pages of her popular 'Brother Cadfael' historical mysteries, in order to distinguish these from her serious historical novels. The prolific popular novelist Harry Patterson began publishing under his own name, but then developed a series of pseudonyms for different categories of his fiction, including 'Jack Higgins', which first appeared on *The Eagle Has Landed* in 1974. The huge sales of this novel encouraged the author to re-use the pseudonym, but no concealment was involved. Disguise has become mock-disguise, advertising the adaptability of the author rather than concealing his or her identity. We may no longer be used to literary anonymity, but we are used to the cultivation of multiple authorial personalities. When Ruth Rendell publishes as Barbara Vine, there is no puzzle about her identity. For the purchaser there is simply the sense of getting something different from the last, perhaps recent, Ruth Rendell novel.

In the 1980s, however, there was a case of a famous author using pseudonymity with a real intent to conceal herself, even from potential publishers. While the five volumes of her science fiction *Canopus in Argos* series were being published between 1979 and 1983, Doris Lessing wrote a novel called *The Diary of a Good Neighbour*. It could hardly have been further away from the futuristic allegories that she had been writing. Narrated in the first person, it is the account by a recently widowed young career woman, Janna, of her surprising friendship with an old woman, Maudie, whom she meets in a chemist's shop. It is 'realistic' in a demanding way – attentive to the grubbiness of Maudie's life and the physical indignities of old age. Over the closing pages, we watch with Janna as Maudie, once a 'furious bundle of energy', grimly and resentfully dies.[2] And it ends with the old woman's anger against life somehow transferred to Lessing's narrator. Through Lessing's agent, who was in on the scheme, this new work was submitted to her usual publishers, Jonathan Cape and Granada, under the name of 'Jane Somers'. Jonathan Cape turned it down rapidly; Granada thought about it for longer, but then also declined, saying, according to Lessing, that it was 'too depressing to publish'.[3] The publishers Michael Joseph did agree to publish – their reader remarking, with an accuracy of discernment that few academic critics of literature could manage, that the book 'reminded him of Doris Lessing'.

Once the publishers had taken on the novel, they were let in to the secret. When the book was published in 1983, the dust jacket made it clear that 'Jane Somers' was some kind of pseudonym, describing the author, inaccurately, as 'a well-known woman journalist' (in the novel Janna edits a 'glossy and sleek and slick' women's magazine).[4] It was treated quite generously by reviewers, though none guessed its true authorship, and sold almost three thousand copies in America, and fifteen hundred in Britain – respectable for a literary first novel in hardback, if only a fraction of what a new Doris Lessing novel would sell. The next year, still as 'Jane Somers', Lessing published a sequel: *If the Old Could* . . . In her own account, she says this: 'Predictably, people who had liked the first book were disappointed by the second. And vice versa. Never mind about the problem of publishers: the main problem of some writers is that most reviewers and readers want you to go on writing the same book.'[5]

Friends were indiscreet, Lessing reported, and though the publishers kept the secret, news of her authorship began to circulate. Later in 1984, both books were republished under Lessing's own name as *The Diaries of Jane Somers*, with a Preface in which she gave her account of the books' first publication. She claimed to have been delighted by the fact that under its false name, her original novel earned adjectives that were not usually given to her work, and descriptions that utterly contradicted each other.

One of my aims has more than succeeded. It seems I am like Barbara Pym! The books are fastidious, well-written, well crafted. Stylish. Unsparing, unsentimental, and deeply felt. Funny, too. On the other hand, they are sentimental, and mawkish. Mere soap opera. Trendy.

I am going to miss Jane Somers.

Lessing's trick asked how reading might depend on the pre-conceptions attached to an author's name. To what extent do we *need* that author's name in order to read? Lessing said that she had published pseudonymously in order 'to be reviewed on merit' and 'to cheer up young writers'. Her third reason, more sympathetically and convincingly, was a tincture of malice. Nettled by the reception of her science fiction she itched for some revenge on reviewers who complained that she did not 'write realistically, the way I used to do before'. 'Jane Somers' would allow her to escape the preconceptions of her critics (and some of her readers). 'I wrote in ways that Doris Lessing cannot.' If a writer is not allowed different voices, what is she allowed? It is as if she were rediscovering that escape from herself permitted to so many writers of earlier centuries.

There have been more famous literary pseudonyms in the twentieth century, but rarely has pseudonymity implied anonymity. When Cecily Fairfield gave herself the pen-name 'Rebecca West' at the age of nineteen, she was declaring rather than concealing herself. 'Rebecca West' was the dangerously liberated heroine of Ibsen's play *Rosmersholm* – a suitable model for a feminist writer. The most famous English literary pseudonym of the twentieth century was less forthright. Eric Blair adopted the pseudonym 'George Orwell' for his first published book, *Down and Out in Paris and London*. After having it rejected by Jonathan Cape and Faber and Faber, he sent it to a literary agent, Leonard Moore, stipulating authorial disguise. 'If by any chance you *do* get it accepted, will you please see that it is published pseudonymously, as I am not proud of it.'[6] In a letter to Moore three months later, after Victor Gollancz had agreed to publish it, he again urged his pseudonymity. 'I have no reputation that is lost by doing this and if the book has any kind of success I can always use the same pseudonym again.'[7] Victor Gollancz advocated 'X', but Orwell wanted a re-usable nom de plume.[8] Even after he had returned a corrected proof of the book this was still not decided. He suggested four names to Moore: P. S. Burton, Kenneth Miles, George Orwell, and H. Lewis Allways. 'I rather favour George Orwell.'[9] Absolute secretiveness was not a possibility, for he had already published parts of it under his own name. 'The Spike' had appeared in the *Adelphi* and 'Hop Picking' and 'Common Lodging Houses' in the *New Statesman and Nation*, all as written by Eric Blair. He told his sister Avril that he was publishing under a pseudonym because he thought his parents might be shocked.[10] But there is not much evidence of concealment. When advance copies arrived in the small Suffolk town of Southwold, where his parents lived, Orwell was soon distributing them amongst friends and relatives. His mother read it. When he wrote to *The Times* to respond to complaints by a French hotelier he signed his letter 'George Orwell', with the name in inverted commas to indicate that it was a pseudonym.

There is no mention in surviving correspondence of what might now seem the most likely reason for anonymity, the fact that this account of life as a kitchen porter in a Paris hotel and a vagrant in London was actually penned by an Old Etonian. The incongruity was noted by an American reviewer. James Farrell in the *New Republic* told his readers, 'Orwell is an Eton graduate,' though he drew no lesson from the fact.[11] There are details in the book that imply some of Orwell's background. One night in a lodging house a fellow vagrant with 'an educated, half-drunken voice' recognizes him from his accent as 'An old public school boy, what?'[12] The drunkard announces himself to be an Old Etonian and begins to sing the Eton boating song, 'not untunefully'. Yet Orwell's narrative sometimes gains its force from avoiding the facts of his own life. In the book, he returns from Paris to find himself penniless and destitute.[13] In fact, in 1930–1, when he was gathering some of the experiences of vagrancy that went into his book, he was based at his parents' genteel Suffolk home. The pattern of Orwell's two-part narrative was artificial: many of his London experiences had been gathered in 1927–8, before he ever went to Paris. The pseudonym was Eric Blair's way of escaping autobiographical accuracy; within a couple of years, which also saw the publication of *Burmese Days* and *The Clergyman's Daughter*, it had become his universally acknowledged identity.

Eric Blair's professed anxiety about his family's reactions to his writing looks a little unconvincing. Such a concern was rather more pressing in the case of Sylvia Plath, who made what we might think an old-fashioned use of disguise when she published *The Bell Jar* in 1963 under the pseudonym 'Victoria Lucas'. She had written this inescapably autobiographical novel in the spring of 1961. Its narrator, clever, ambitious Esther Greenwood, begins the novel having won a writing competition set up by a fashion magazine, as Plath herself did a decade earlier. The prize, in the novel as in reality, is a month's work as an editor in the magazine's New York office, a tenure satirically rendered in the novel. She returns to her New England home and, discouraged by her rejection for a creative writing course, she falls into depression. She sees a psychiatrist and is given ECT treatment. Later she tries to kill herself. The events of the novel closely follow those of Plath's life. Aged twenty, on her own return from New York, she had failed to gain a place on a summer writing course at Harvard and made a serious suicide attempt.[14] Like the author, Esther is taken into psychiatric hospital. At the end of the novel, she faces release into the world, 'patched, retreaded and approved for the road'.[15] A month after its appearance, Plath committed suicide.

Any reader of any of the biographies of Plath will know that the critical reception of her work mattered hugely to her. Only a fortnight before her death she was showing a neighbour the complimentary review of *The Bell Jar* by Anthony Burgess in the *Observer* and explaining that she was the true author.[16] (She also told him that the poem by Ted Hughes in the same paper was by her husband.) She wanted to be known, yet had taken measures not to be. She told some friends about her authorship of the novel, apparently saying that it would be published under a pseudonym because it was a potboiler rather than the serious work of a poet.[17] She was at this time hardly known as a poet, or indeed as any kind of writer. In the *Listener*, Laurence Lerner, ignorant of the author's true identity, perceptively praised the book's 'almost poetic delicacy of perception'.[18] In the *TLS*, the reviewer said that 'Miss Lucas can certainly write'.[19] 'It reads so much like the truth that it is hard to disassociate her from Esther Greenwood.' Those who knew the author best would know how 'much like truth' the novel was.

In *The Bell Jar* Esther decides to write a novel as a vengeful act.

Then I decided I would spend the summer writing a novel.
That would fix a lot of people.[20]

For biographers, the resentful depiction of the narrator's mother, who calls her 'honey' and always reasons with her 'sweetly', but whom Esther fantasizes about strangling, would be evidence of Plath's feelings towards her mother, Aurelia.[21] The story, while told with a brilliant chilliness, is hardly a likely best-seller. However, it does seem much like those confessional narratives whose author wanted to shield particular individuals, but also to turn private experiences into some universal narrative. The sense that *The Bell Jar* touched personal bruises was confirmed by Aurelia Plath's efforts to prevent the novel from being published in the USA until 1971, when it was finally published under Plath's name. (Her name had appeared on the cover of the second British edition, published by Faber and Faber in September 1966.)

The playfulness that often attached to anonymity in the past is hardly understood any more, as the *Primary Colors* episode demonstrates. Thus the fate of Anthony Burgess when he adopted the trick of self-reviewing once played by Walter Scott. In 1963, his novel *Inside Mr. Enderby* was published under the pseudonym 'Joseph Kell'. It was the second novel to have this name on its title page: *One Hand Clapping* by Joseph Kell had been published in 1961. Having completed his *Malayan Trilogy* in 1959, he had published two novels under his own name in each of the next three years (including *A Clockwork Orange* in 1962). His editor at Heinemann had persuaded him that his prolific rate of production might begin to attract critical scorn. He had the same perceived problem as Anthony Trollope in the nineteenth century: he wrote too fast. In the mid-1860s, Trollope, sensitive to charges of over-production, decided to publish some of his work anonymously. When *Nina Baltka* appeared, only one reviewer, in the *Spectator*, spotted the author. 'If criticism be not delusion from the very bottom, this pleasant little story is written by Mr. Anthony Trollope.'[22] But other reviewers did not echo the atrribution.

Like some of his modern antecedents, Trollope explained his self-disguise in creative rather than commercial terms. He did it, he said, in order to 'test' the justice of critical verdicts – 'in order that I might see whether I could succeed in obtaining a second identity,—whether as I had made one mark by such literary ability as I possessed, I might succeed in doing so again'.[23] Unfortunately (as Lessing found out), without the right name sales were disappointing, and his publishers persuaded him to drop the disguise.

Burgess was a regular and well-remunerated contributor to the *Yorkshire Post*, for whom he wrote a weekly column on new fiction. He was sent his own novel for review and review it he duly did, though within a survey of recent fiction. Later he was to claim that he had believed that his editor at the *Yorkshire Post*, Kenneth Young, was in on the secret. In a 1976 interview with Robert Robinson for BBC2's *The Book Programme*, printed in the *Listener*, he said, 'I assumed that the editor wanted a bit of a joke – wanted me to review this, but didn't want to make this request in writing.'[24] (He might have noted that the *Daily Telegraph* of 19 April 1963 had identified Joseph Kell as Burgess almost a month before his review appeared.) The novel, he wrote, was 'a quiet and cunning female monologue that fell from the presses unnoticed'.[25] After a rapid, droll plot resumé, Burgess solemnly told his readers that it was 'in many ways, a dirty book'. 'It is full of bowel-blasts and flatulent borborygms' ('borborygm' is defined by the *OED* as 'rumbling noise in the guts'). He phrased complaint as covert praise. 'It turns sex, religion, the State into a series of laughing-stocks. The book itself is a laughing-stock.' There was no denying the novel's 'gross richness'. When his editor Kenneth Young found out about the trick, he appeared on Granada TV's news bulletin to sack Burgess. Burgess was to complain in his *Book Programme* interview that his *jeu d'esprit* had a 'respectable ancestry', citing Scott, though inaccurately asserting that he had reviewed *Waverley* in the *Edinburgh Review*.

The attribution of literary works is nowadays the habitual activity only of a few academic specialists. In one particular area they do sometimes make headlines: the 'discovery' of previously unidentified works by Shakespeare. Probably the best-known such specialist in the English-speaking world, Professor Don Foster, began his career by claiming 'A Funerall Elegye', a poem by 'W. S.' published in 1612, as Shakespeare's.[26] Outside the Shakespeare industry, the study of attribution, and the discussion of literary anonymity, tends to be minutely focused on particular texts. Yet anyone interested in literary history will find that anonymity is ubiquitous. It is a feature, of course, of English literature from before the world of print. The author of *Beowulf* is nameless. So is the poet who wrote *Sir Gawain and the Green Knight* in the late fourteenth century. Most medieval literature is anonymous, and scholars usually agree that, before the age of print, 'the author' had none of the status that he or she would later acquire. The preservation and circulation of literature depended on scribes, and only occasionally did these scribes record or show interest in the identity of the author of what they were transcribing.[27] The very word 'anonymous', used to describe a literary text, dates only from the sixteenth century, as if it took print to make the absence of an author's name an important fact.[28] Print gave books and their producers ways of making anonymity 'visible'. From the mid-sixteenth century, title pages became common.[29] The absence of an author's name was now marked, a decisive omission. With the possibility of this omission came an interest in attribution. For much of the history of English literature, this interest shaped readers' interpretations.

Looking at the different stories of anonymity helps us to think about the extraordinary currency of that phrase which has migrated from literary theory into popular culture: 'The Death of the Author', from Roland Barthes's 1967 essay of that title. For in the past the author was often not present to the reader of the work. And we can see what usually happened. Barthes's essay offered a thought that provides a clue to the effects of anonymity on the first readers of many of the works of literature that I have discussed. Barthes observes, as if it were a complaint, that '*explanation* of the work is still sought in the person of its pro-ducer'.[30] An author, in other words, is a kind of short cut to interpretation. The long history of anonymity shows how vari-ously the appetite for such explanation works among readers. Any interesting or controversial work that appears without its true author's name, and marks that absence, sends not just critics but ordinary readers off in search of the author. That is the way it has always been. And that is why a book about ano-nymity is a book about the importance of authors, and about how and why readers need them.

NOTES

Place of publication is London unless otherwise stated.

INTRODUCTION

1 Alexander Pope, *The Rape of the Lock and Other Poems*, ed. Geoffrey Tillotson (1940), p. 142
2 See Geoffrey Tillotson, introd., ibid., p. 89
3 *The Spectator*, 523 (30 October 1712)
4 *A Dictionary of the Anonymous and Pseudonymous Literature of Great Britain*, ed. Samuel Halkett and John Laing, rev. James Kennedy, 7 vols. (1926–34), I, p. xi

1 MISCHIEF

1 Letter of 8 August 1726, in *The Correspondence of Jonathan Swift*, ed. Harold Williams, 5 vols. (Oxford, 1963–5), III, p. 153. See Irvin Ehrenpreis, *Swift. The Man, His Works and the Age*, 3 vols. (1962, 1967, 1983), III, pp. 493–5
2 Pope to Swift, 16 November 1726, *The Correspondence of Jonathan Swift*, III, p. 181
3 Letter of 17 November 1726, ibid., p. 182
4 Letter of 5 November 1726, ibid., p. 179
5 Pope to Swift, 16 November 1726, ibid., p. 181
6 The Earl of Peterborough to Swift, 29 November 1726, ibid., pp. 191–2
7 Viscountess Bolingbroke to Swift, 1 February 1727, ibid., p. 197
8 Swift to Mrs Howard, 1 February 1727, ibid., p. 196
9 'Lemuel Gulliver' to Mrs Howard, 28 November 1726, ibid., pp. 190–1
10 Sir Walter Scott, 'Memoirs of Jonathan Swift D.D.', in *The Works of Jonathan Swift*, vol. I (Edinburgh, 1814), p. 347

11 See David Nokes, *Jonathan Swift, A Hypocrite Reversed* (Oxford, 1985), p. 310

12 *The Complete Letters of Lady Mary Wortley Montagu*, ed. Robert Halsband, 3 vols. (Oxford, 1965–7), II, p. 71

13 *A Letter from a Clergyman to his Friend, with an Account of the Travels of Capt. Lemuel Gulliver: and a Character of the Author* (1726), p. 11

14 Ibid., p. 8

15 Ehrenpreis, *Swift*, II, p. 407

16 Ibid., II, p. 331

17 *The Prose Works of Jonathan Swift*, ed. Herbert David et al., 14 vols. (Oxford, 1939–68), XII, p. 111

18 Ibid., XII, p. 118

19 *Gulliver's Travels*, ed. Robert DeMaria (2001), Part IV, ch. vii, p. 237

20 Ibid., IV, viii, p. 243

21 Ibid., IV, xii, pp. 266–7

22 Ibid., II, i, p. 83 and II, viii, p. 139

23 *The School for Scandal*, Act 1, sc. 1, ll. 254–9, in Richard Brinsley Sheridan, *The School for Scandal and Other Plays*, ed. Michael Cordner (Oxford, 1998)

24 Pope's ways with anonymity are succinctly described in Pat Rogers, 'Nameless Names: Pope, Curll, and the Uses of Anonymity', *New Literary History*, 33:2 (Spring 2002), pp. 233–45

25 Pope to Jonathan Richardson, 2 March 1733, in *The Correspondence of Alexander Pope*, ed. George Sherburn, 5 vols. (1956), III, p. 352

26 J. V. Guerinot, *Pamphlet Attacks on Alexander Pope 1711–1744* (New York, 1969), p. 192

27 John Barnard (ed.), *Pope. The Critical Heritage* (1973), p. 279

28 Alexander Pope, *The Dunciad in Four Books*, ed. Valerie Rumbold (1999), p. 65

29 The soubriquet was coined by Scott's printer James Ballantyne, one of those who was in the know. See J. G. Lockhart, *Memoirs of the Life of Sir Walter Scott, Bart.* (Edinburgh, 1837), vol. IV, p. 166.

30 Sir Walter Scott, *Waverley*, ed. Claire Lamont (Oxford, 1986), p. 341

31   *The Edinburgh Review*, November 1814, p. 167

32   In *Waverley*, ed. Lamont, p. 344

33   [John Leycester Adolphus,] *Letters to Richard Heber, Esq: containing critical remarks on the series of novels beginning with "Waverley" and an attempt to ascertain their author* (1821), p. 2

34   Ibid., pp. 3–4

35   Ibid., p. 10

36   From the Contents pages, ibid., p. vi

37   Ibid., p. 19

38   Ibid., p. 22

39   Walter Scott, *The Fortunes of Nigel*, ed. Frank Jordan (Edinburgh, 2004) pp. 8–9

40   *The Letters of Sir Walter Scott*, ed. H. Grierson, 12 vols. (1932–7), VII, p. 86

41   Ibid., IX, p. 345

42   Lockhart, *Memoirs*, V, pp. 293–4

43   Ibid., p. 300

44   Ibid., p. 301

45   Ibid., pp. 301–2

46   Edgar Johnson, *Sir Walter Scott: The Great Unknown*, 2 vols. (1970), p. 438

47   William St Clair, *The Reading Nation in the Romantic Period* (Cambridge, 2004), p. 510

48   Lockhart, *Memoirs*, IV, p. 201

49   Walter Scott, *Chronicles of the Canongate*, ed. Claire Lamont (Edinburgh, 2000), p. 10

50   Lockhart, *Memoirs*, IV, p. 201

51   Ibid., IV, p. 200

52   Ibid., IV, p. 32

53   See Johnson, *Sir Walter Scott*, p. 457

54   Lockhart, *Memoirs*, III, p. 334

55   Walter Scott, *The Heart of Midlothian*, ed. Tony Inglis (1994), ch. 2, p. 27

56   Ibid., ch. 8, p. 75

57   *Waverley*, ed. Lamont, p. 13

58   Letter of 28 July 1814, in *Letters*, III, p. 479

59   *Chronicles of the Canongate*, ed. Lamont, p. 3

60 Ibid., p. 10
61 General Preface to the *Waverley Novels* (1829), in *Waverley*, ed. Lamont, p. 355
62 Ibid., p. 356
63 Michael Lewis in *New York Times*, 28 January 1996
64 *Primary Colors* (New York, 1996), p. 3
65 Ibid., p. 8
66 Ibid., p. 247
67 *New York Times*, 19 July 1996
68 Lockhart, *Memoirs*, X, p. 343
69 Anthony Trollope, *The Claverings*, ed. David Skilton (Oxford, 1986), ch. XIV, p. 139
70 It appeared in *The Quarterly Review*, April 1817
71 We do not know exactly who wrote which parts of what is a long article. Martin Lightfoot has argued convincingly that Scott was responsible for the deprecatory parts of the review, Erskine for the laudatory parts. See 'Scott's Self-Review: Manuscript and Other Evidence', in *Nineteenth-Century Fiction*, 23 (September 1968), pp. 150–60
72 John O. Hayden, ed., *Scott. The Critical Heritage* (1970), p. 113
73 Gordon S. Haight, *George Eliot. A Biography* (Oxford, 1968), pp. 212–16
74 Ibid., p. 252
75 *The George Eliot Letters*, ed. Gordon S. Haight, 9 vols. (New Haven, 1954–5, 1978), II, p. 436
76 Swift, *The Drapier's Letters*, ed. Herbert Davis (1935; rpt. Oxford, 1965), V, 'Directions to the Printer'. See also Ehrenpreis, *Swift*, III, pp. 308–9
77 Frances Burney, *Memoirs of Dr. Burney*, 3 vols. (1832), II, p. 126
78 John Sutherland, *The Life of Walter Scott: A Critical Biography* (Oxford, 1995), p. 172
79 Scott, *Chronicles of the Canongate*, ed. Lamont, pp. 3–4
80 See *The Letters of Lewis Carroll*, ed. Morton N. Cohen, 2 vols. (1979), II, pp. 1038–9

2 MODESTY

1 Letter to Catherine Laing, 30 November 1880; *The Letters of Lewis Carroll*, ed. Morton N. Cohen, 2 vols. (1979), I, p. 395

2 Letter to Catherine Laing, 14 June 1881; ibid., I, p. 433

3 By his death in 1898, *Alice's Adventures in Wonderland* and *Through the Looking-Glass* had between them sold more than a quarter of a million copies. See Morton N. Cohen, *Lewis Carroll. A Biography* (1995), p. 134

4 *Letters of Lewis Carroll*, see letters to Catherine Laing, 14 June 1881, I, pp. 395–6; to Falconer Madan, 8 December 1880, I, p. 396; and to E. W. B. Nicholson (Bodley's Librarian), 25 April 1882, I, p. 457. See also K. A. Manley, 'Dodgson v Carroll' in *TLS*, No. 3773, 28 June 1974

5 *Letters of Lewis Carroll*, II, pp. 811–12

6 See Cohen, *Lewis Carroll*, p. 297

7 Letter to Mrs C. A. Heartley, 11 May 1883: *Letters of Lewis Carroll*, I, p. 446

8 Letter to Alexander Macmillan, 9 May 1879: ibid., I, p. 337

9 Letter to Catherine Laing, ibid., I, p. 95

10 Ibid., II, p. 692

11 Ibid., II, p. 888

12 See Cohen, *Lewis Carroll*, pp. 161–2

13 Letter to Francis Atkinson, 10 December 1881: *Letters of Lewis Carroll*, I, p. 445

14 Letter to Frederick Langbridge, 13 November 1896: ibid., II, p. 1103

15 Letter to Lydia Becker, 24 January 1877: ibid., I, p. 267

16 See letter to Florence Balfour, 5 February 1877: ibid., I, p. 268

17 Ibid., I, p. 375

18 Ibid., I, p. 433

19 Letter to Mary Manners, 7 February 1895: ibid., II, p. 1051

20 See letter to Mrs. W. Hunter, 27 November 1888: ibid., pp. 721–2

21 Letter to Ellen Knight, 1 September 1888: ibid., p. 717

22 Letter to B. P. Lascelles, 8 March 1890: ibid., p. 780

23 Letter to Mary Manners, 18 July 1889: ibid., p. 751

24 Letter to Edith Blakemore, 22 December 1889: ibid., p. 770

25 Letter to Mrs. N. H. Stevens, 4 May 1891: ibid., p. 838

26 Letter to Mary Manners, 5 December 1885: ibid., I, p. 607
27 See Roger Lancelyn Green, introduction to *Alice's Adventures in Wonderland* and *Through the Looking-Glass* (Oxford, 1971), pp. xi–xv
28 Ibid., p. 247
29 The original title page is photographically reproduced in *The Yale Edition of the Shorter Poems of Edmund Spenser*, ed. William A. Oram et al. (New Haven, 1989), p. 2. All quotations from *The Shepheardes Calender* are taken from this edition.
30 George Puttenham, *The Arte of English Poesie*, ed. G. D. Willcock and A. Walker (Cambridge, 1936), pp. 21–3
31 Ibid., p. 2
32 *Shorter Poems of Edmund Spenser*, ed. Oram et al., p. 14
33 Ibid., p. 16
34 Ibid., pp. 32–3
35 Ibid., p. 70
36 R. M. Cummings, ed., *Spenser: The Critical Heritage* (1971), p. 57
37 Ibid., p. 60
38 Puttenham, *Arte, of English Poesie*, p. 63
39 The classic analysis of this is J. W. Saunders, 'The Stigma of Print. A Note on the Social Bases of Tudor Poetry', *Essays in Criticism*, 1 (1951)
40 *Eliza's Babes: or, The Virgins-Offering* (1652)
41 Germaine Greer, *Slip-Shod Sybils. Recognition, Rejection and the Woman Poet* (1995), p. 154
42 Many other examples are to be found in the biographical headnotes of Roger Lonsdale's *Eighteenth-Century Women Poets. An Oxford Anthology* (Oxford, 1989). They include 'Cotswouldia' (Elizabeth Thomas, née Amherst)
43 *The Gentleman's Magazine*, February 1745
44 *The Complete Letters of Lady Mary Wortley Montagu*, ed. Robert Halsband, 3 vols. (Oxford, 1965–7), III, p. 37
45 The comment is the Duke of Buckingham's. See Isobel Grundy, *Lady Mary Wortley Montagu. Comet of the Enlightenment* (Oxford, 1999), p. 196
46 Ibid., p. 197
47 See Robert Halsband, ' "The Lady's Dressing-Room" explicated

by a contemporary', in *The Augustan Milieu*, ed. H. K. Miller et al. (Oxford, 1970), pp. 225–31

48   In Lady Mary Wortley Montagu, *Essays and Poems and Simplicity, a Comedy*, ed. Robert Halsband and Isobel Grundy (Oxford, 1993)

49   Grundy, *Lady Mary Wortley Montagu*, pp. 338–40

50   Ibid., pp. 507–8

51   Thomas Gray to Horace Walpole, *Correspondence of Thomas Gray*, ed. Paget Toynbee and Leonard Whibley, corr. H. W. Starr, 3 vols. (Oxford, 1971), p. 283

52   See Robert L. Mack, *Thomas Gray. A Life* (New Haven, 2000), pp. 412–13

53   *Correspondence of Thomas Gray*, p. 341

54   In *The Poems of Thomas Gray, William Collins, and Oliver Goldsmith*, ed. Roger Lonsdale (1969), p. 111

55   See James Raven, *British Fiction, 1750–1770, A Chronological Checklist* (Newark, N.J., 1987), and Peter Garside and James Raven, eds., *The English Novel, 1770–1829: A Bibliographical Survey of Prose Fiction Published in the British Isles* (Oxford, 2000)

56   *The Monthly Review*, 5 (1751), p. 394

57   *The Early Journals and Letters of Fanny Burney 1768–1791*, ed. Lars E. Troide and Stewart J. Cooke, 3 vols. (Oxford, 1988–94), III, p. 32

58   See Claire Harman, *Fanny Burney. A Biography* (2000), p. 169

59   See Fanny Burney, *Evelina*, ed. Edward A. Bloom (Oxford, 1982), pp. 3–9

60   *Early Journals*, II, p. 129

61   Ibid., II, p. 131

62   Ibid., III, p. 28

63   *Evelina*, p. 25

64   *Early Journals*, III, pp. 6 and 59

65   *Diary & Letters of Madame D'Arblay*, ed. Charlotte Barrett, preface and notes Austin Dobson, 6 vols. (1904–5), II, p. 320

66   *Early Journals*, III, p. 5

67   *Evelina*, p. 179

68   *Early Journals*, III, pp. 89–90

69 Ibid., pp. 20–1

70 Ibid., pp. 44–5

71 Ibid., pp. 45–6

72 Ibid., p. 52

73 Ibid., p. 7

74 Ibid., p. 37

75 Fanny Burney, *The Witlings*, ed. Peter Sabor and Geoffrey Sill (Peterborough, Ontario, 2002), p. 65, Act II, ll. 1–12

76 William Austen-Leigh and Richard Arthur Austen-Leigh, *Jane Austen. A Family Record*, rev. Deirdre Le Faye (1989), pp. 170–1

77 *Jane Austen's Letters*, ed. Deirdre Le Faye (1995; rpt. Oxford, 1997), p. 201

78 *Early Journals*, III, p. 202

79 Ibid., p. 193

80 See *Diary and Letters*, ed. Barrett, II, p. 173

81 James Edward Austen-Leigh, *A Memoir of Jane Austen*, ed. R. W. Chapman (1926; rpt. Oxford, 1951), p. 122

82 Her niece Anna Lefroy was to recollect, almost seventy years later, hearing the early version of *Pride and Prejudice* being read aloud to a family group. Anna Lefroy, 'Recollections of Aunt Jane' (1864), in Kathryn Sutherland, ed., J. E. Austen-Leigh, *A Memoir of Jane Austen and Other Family Recollections* (Oxford, 2002)

83 *Letters*, p. 174

84 Park Honan, *Jane Austen. A Life* (1987), p. 284

85 See David Nokes, *Jane Austen: A Life* (1997), pp. 383–90

86 *Jane Austen. A Family Record*, p. 167

87 Ibid., p. 168

88 *Letters*, p. 52

89 *Jane Austen. The Critical Heritage*, ed. B. C. Southam (1968), p. 41

90 *Jane Austen. A Family Record*, p. 175

91 David Gilson, *A Bibliography of Jane Austen*, corrected edition (1997), p. 25

92 Ibid., pp. 175–6

93 Ibid., pp. 185–6

94 See W. A. W. Jarvis, JA Society *Report* for 1986

95 *Letters*, p. 250

96   *The Works of Jane Austen*, ed. R.W. Chapman (Oxford, 1954), vol. VI, *Minor Works*, p. 435

97   *Letters*, p. 231

98   Ibid., p. 262

99   See Nokes, *Jane Austen*, p. 477

100 *Jane Austen. A Family Record*, pp. 198–9

101 See *Letters*, p. 287. In a letter from London, dated 30 November 1814, to her niece Fanny Knight, Austen says, 'We are to see Egerton today.' It is possible that Austen met Egerton, with her brother, on one of two previous visits to London that year.

102 See the article by H. J. Jackson in *TLS*, no. 5375, 7 April 2006. When the Queen's library was auctioned at Christie's after her death in 1818, the sale catalogue listed them as Austen's works.

103 *Letters*, p. 234

104 Austen-Leigh, *Memoir*, p. 102

105 *Jane Austen. A Family Record*, pp. 187–8

106 Austen-Leigh, *Memoir*, p. 103

107 Ibid., p. 115.

108 Honan, *Jane Austen*, pp. 352–3

109 *Letters*, p. 265

110 *Evelina*, p. 7

111 *Letters*, p. 335

3 WOMEN BEING MEN

1   See Jenny Uglow, *Elizabeth Gaskell* (1993), p. 182

2   Letter of 17 November 1847, quoted ibid., p. 183

3   *The Letters of Mrs Gaskell*, ed. J. A. V. Chapple and Arthur Pollard (1966), letter 29

4   *The Examiner*, 4 November 1848, p. 708

5   Letter of 27 December 1848, in *Elizabeth Gaskell. The Critical Heritage*, ed. Angus Easson (1991), p. 89

6   'Biographical Notice', in Emily Brontë, *Wuthering Heights*, ed. Ian Jack (Oxford, 1981), p. 359

7   *The Letters of Charlotte Brontë*, ed. Margaret Smith, vol. I: *1829–1847* (Oxford, 1995), p. 459

8   Letter of 23 July 1846: ibid., p. 487

9   Letter of 6 October 1846: ibid., p. 501

10 Juliet Barker, *The Brontës* (1994), p. 499

11 See Miriam Allott, ed., *The Brontës. The Critical Heritage* (1974), p. 59

12 Ibid., p. 63

13 See letter to Smith & Elder, 15 July 1847, in *The Letters of Charlotte Brontë*, ed. Margaret Smith, vol. II: 1848–1851 (Oxford, 2000), p. 533

14 Charlotte Brontë, *The Professor*, ed. Margaret Smith and Herbert Rosengarten (Oxford, 1987), ch. xii, p. 89

15 Harold Orel, ed., *The Brontës. Interviews and Recollections* (1997), p. 90. Smith's memoir of Charlotte Brontë was first published in *Cornhill Magazine*, New Series 9 (December 1900), pp. 778–95

16 Letter to Messrs Smith, Elder and Co., 12 September 1847: *Letters*, ed. Smith, I, p. 540

17 *Letters of Lewis Carroll*, ed. Morton N. Cohen, 2 vols. (1979), I, pp. 82–3

18 Letter of 28 January 1848, in *Letters*, ed. Smith, I, p. 579

19 *The Examiner*, 27 November 1847, in Allott, *Critical Heritage*, p. 77

20 *Era*, 14 November 1847: ibid., pp. 78–9

21 Letter of 17 November 1847 in *Letters*, ed. Smith, I. p. 564

22 *Fraser's Magazine*, December 1847, in Allott, *Critical Heritage*, p. 84

23 *The Letters and Private Papers of William Makepeace Thackeray*, ed. Gordon N. Ray, 4 vols. (1945), II, pp. 318–19

24 Letter of October 1848, ibid., p. 441. Procter is Brian Waller Procter, better known by his pseudonym, Barry Cornwall. He was a successful writer of songs and popular verses, as well as of biographies

25 Elizabeth Gaskell, *The Life of Charlotte Brontë*, ed. Alan Shenston (1975), pp. 325–6

26 Charlotte Brontë, *Jane Eyre*, ed. Michael Mason (1996), vol. I, ch. 9, p. 91

27 Ibid., I, ch. 12, p. 126

28 Ibid., I, ch. 12, p. 124

29 Ibid., II, ch. 1, p. 336

30 Ibid., III, ch. 9, p. 459

31 Ibid., I, ch. 12, p. 125

32   Review of April 1848, in Allott, *Critical Heritage*, p. 89
33   Gaskell, *Life*, p. 326
34   *Jane Eyre*, I, ch. 4, p. 36
35   *North American Review* 141 (October 1848), in Allott, *Critical Heritage*, p. 98
36   See Allott, *Critical Heritage*, pp. 218, 226–7, 230
37   *Letters*, ed. Smith, I, p. 587, note 1
38   *Jane Eyre*, ed. Mason, p. 9
39   Barker, *The Brontës*, p. 557
40   George Smith, *A Memoir* (1902), p. 89
41   Letter to Mary Taylor, 4 September 1848, in *Letters*, ed. Smith, II, p. 112
42   *Jane Eyre*, ed. Mason, pp. 6–7
43   *Letters*, ed. Smith, II, p. 22
44   See *Letters of Thackeray*, II, p. 759
45   Gordon N. Ray, *Thackeray. The Age of Wisdom 1847–1863* (1958), p. 11
46   See E. M. Delafield, ed., *The Brontës. Their Lives Recorded by Their Contemporaries* (1935; rpt. 1979), p. 165
47   See Ann Monsarrat, *An Uneasy Victorian. Thackeray the Man* (1980), p. 255
48   Letter of November 1848, in Delafield, *The Brontës*, pp. 162–3
49   *Letters*, ed. Smith, II, pp. 242–5
50   The recollection is in a manuscript annotation to her privately printed but suppressed edition of Charlotte Brontë's letters. See *Letters*, ed. Smith, II, p. 82
51   Letter to Ellen Nussey, 28 April 1848, in *Letters*, ed. Smith, II, p. 56
52   Letter of 3 May 1848: ibid., p. 62
53   Barker, *The Brontës*, p. 552
54   Gaskell, *Life*, p. 342
55   *Letters*, ed. Smith, II, p. 82. This is from the same annotation mentioned in note 50, above
56   Letter to Ellen Nussey, 26 June 1748: ibid., p. 81
57   Gaskell, *Life*, p. 343
58   Letter to W. S. Williams, 31 July 1848, in *Letters*, ed. Smith, II, p. 94
59   See Barbara Whitehead, *Charlotte Brontë and her 'Dearest Nell'* (1993), pp. 271–2

60 Barker, *The Brontës*, p. 608
61 *Letters*, ed. Smith, II, p. 261, n. 3
62 Barker, *The Brontës*, p. 609
63 Letter of 5 December 1749, in *Letters*, ed. Smith, II, p. 301
64 George Smith, *Cornhill Magazine* 9 (December 1900)
65 Gaskell, *Life*, p. 392
66 Barker, *The Brontës*, p. 928
67 *Letters*, ed. Smith, II, p. 304
68 Substantial extracts from the letter were published in *Brontë Society Transactions*, 19:1 & 2, and are reprinted as a footnote in *Letters*, ed. Smith, II, pp. 304–5
69 Ibid., p. 287
70 Harriet Martineau, *Autobiography*, ed. Maria Weston Chapman, 3 vols. (1877), II, p. 324
71 Ibid., p. 288
72 Ibid., p. 305
73 Ibid., p. 325
74 Gaskell, *Life*, p. 392
75 Martineau, *Autobiography*, II, p. 325
76 Ibid. p. 326
77 *Letters of Mrs Gaskell*, letter 60
78 D. J. Taylor, *Thackeray* (1999), p. 289
79 Letter of 17 November 1849, in *Letters*, II, ed. Smith, p. 288
80 Letter of November 1849, probably to Catherine Winkworth, *Letters of Mrs Gaskell*, letter 57
81 Ibid., letter 55. Though the standard edition of Gaskell's letters dates this 26 November 1849, this is open to doubt. See Margaret Smith's footnote in her *Letters of Charlotte Brontë*, II, p. 289
82 Letter to James Taylor, 6 November 1849, *Letters*, ed. Smith, II, p. 280
83 Letter of 16 August 1849, ibid., p. 235
84 Allott, *Critical Heritage*, p. 162
85 See *Letters*, ed. Smith, II, p. 279
86 Letter of 19 January 1850, ibid., II, pp. 332–3
87 CB to Ellen Nussey, 5(?) February 1850, ibid., p. 340. See Barker, *The Brontës*, pp. 626–7
88 CB to W. S. Williams, 22 February 1850, in *Letters*, ed. Smith, II, p. 350

89 Quoted in Barker, *The Brontës*, p. 629
90 Anne Thackeray Ritchie, *Chapters from Some Memoirs* (1894), pp. 60–2
91 Charles and Frances Brookfield, *Mrs Brookfield and her Circle* (1906), p. 304
92 Barker, *The Brontës*, p. 623
93 In *Letters*, ed. Smith, II, p. 742
94 Barker, *The Brontës*, p. 703
95 Brontë's real name was used, for instance, in reviews in the *Critic* and *Putnam's Monthly Magazine*. See Allott, *Critical Heritage*, pp. 190 and 212
96 Letter of 20 April 1848, in *Letters*, ed. Smith, II, p. 51
97 Charlotte Brontë, *Villette*, ed. Mark Lilly (1979), ch. 4, p. 94
98 Ibid., ch. 40, p. 577
99 Letter of 19 September 1849, *Letters*, ed. Smith, II, p. 256
100 Elizabeth Gooch, Preface to *Sherwood Forest* (1804), quoted in Peter Garside, 'Historical Introduction', *The English Novel 1770–1829*, II, p. 66
101 Rosemary Ashton, *George Eliot. A Life* (1996), p. 125
102 Gordon S. Haight, *George Eliot. A Biography* (Oxford, 1968), pp. 213–14
103 Ibid., p. 215
104 *The George Eliot Letters*, ed. Gordon S. Haight, 9 vols. (New Haven, 1954–5, 1978), II, p. 292
105 J. W. Cross, *George Eliot's Life as Related in her Letters and Journals*, 3 vols. (1885), I, p. 431
106 Letter to John Blackwood, 14 March 1857, in *Letters*, ed. Haight, II, pp. 309–10
107 Letter to John Blackwood, 11 June 1857, ibid, pp. 347–8
108 William Blackwood to John Blackwood, 14 June 1859: ibid., III, p. 85
109 'Amos Barton' in *Scenes of Clerical Life*, ed. Thomas A. Noble (Oxford, 1988), pp. 5–8
110 Haight, *George Eliot*, p. 219
111 Letter of 22 November 1848, in *Letters*, ed. Smith, II, p. 142
112 Haight, *George Eliot*, p. 269
113 Letter of 5 November 1858, in *Letters*, ed. Haight, II, p. 494
114 Letter of 12 February 1859: ibid., III, p. 13

115   Review of *Adam Bede, Westminster Review,* April 1857
116   Letter to Charles Bray, 24 June 1859, in *Letters,* ed. Haight, III, p. 91
117   Elizabeth Gaskell to George Eliot: ibid., June 1857, ibid. p. 74
118   In Haight, *George Eliot,* p. 282
119   Letter of 2 June 1857, in *Letters,* ed. Haight, II, p. 337
120   Haight, *George Eliot,* pp. 283–4
121   *Letters,* ed. Haight, IX, p. 279
122   Ibid., II, p. 505
123   An excellent brief account is Troy J. Bassett, 'T. Fisher Unwin's Pseudonym Library: Literary Marketing and Authorial Identity', *English Literature in Transition* 47:2 (2004)
124   Philip Unwin, *The Publishing Unwins* (1972), p. 42
125   John Sutherland, *The Longman Companion to Victorian Fiction* (1988), p. 285
126   Lanoe Falconer, *Mademoiselle Ixe* (1891), p. 30
127   Ibid., pp. 134–5
128   Ibid., pp. 121–2
129   Ibid., p. 161
130   Bassett, 'T. Fisher Unwin's Pseudonym Library', p. 155
131   Ibid., p. 152
132   *Novel Review,* 1 August 1892, p. 399
133   George Egerton, *Keynotes* (1893), pp. 17–18
134   Ibid., pp. 20–1
135   Ibid., p. 119
136   Ellen Thorneycroft Fowler, *Concerning Isabel Carnaby* (6th edn., 1898), VI, p. 88
137   Ibid., XV, p. 217
138   Ibid., XX, p. 306
139   Ibid., XXI, p. 312
140   Ibid., XXII, p. 327
141   Ibid., VIII, p. 117

4 MEN BEING WOMEN

1   Rahila Khan, *Down the Road, Worlds Away* (1987)
2   See *Guardian,* 10 November 1987
3   *Guardian,* 7 November 1987

4   *London Review of Books*, 4 February 1988

5   Daniel Defoe, *Moll Flanders*, ed. G. A. Starr (Oxford, 1971), p. 7

6   Ibid., p. 214

7   Ibid., pp. 221–2

8   Ibid., p. 241

9   *The History of Laetitia Atkins, vulgarly called Moll Flanders* (London, 1776), p. v

10   *The History of Mademoiselle de Beleau; or, The New Roxana* (1775), p. 9

11   Ibid., p. 1. Thomas Southerne (1659–1746) was a successful dramatist. There is no record of any contact between him and Defoe

12   Ibid., p. 4

13   See Maximilian Novak, *Daniel Defoe. Master of Fictions* (Oxford, 2001), p. 540

14   See John Mullan, introd., Daniel Defoe, *Memoirs of a Cavalier*, ed. James T. Boulton (Oxford, 1991), pp. ix–xii

15   *Moll Flanders*, p. 343

16   Ibid., p. 247

17   Ibid., pp. 86–7

18   Daniel Defoe, *Roxana*, ed. John Mullan (Oxford, 1996), p. 176

19   Samuel Richardson, *Pamela*, ed. Thomas Keymer and Alice Wakely (Oxford, 2001), p. 4

20   Letter of 13 December 1740, in *The Letters of Doctor George Cheyne to Samuel Richardson (1733–1743)*, ed. Charles F. Mullett (Columbia, Missouri, 1943), p. 64

21   T. C. D. Duncan Eaves and Ben D. Kimpel, *Samuel Richardson: A Biography* (Oxford, 1971), pp. 119–20

22   Henry Fielding, *Joseph Andrews* and *Shamela*, ed. Douglas Brooks-Davies and Martin C. Battestin, rev. Thomas Keymer (Oxford, 1999), p. 318

23   See Martin Battestin, *Henry Fielding. A Life* (1989), pp. 301–2

24   Thomas Keymer, Introduction, *The Pamela Controversy: Criticisms and Adaptations of Samuel Richardson's* Pamela *1740–1750*, 6 vols., ed. Thomas Keymer and Peter Sabor (2001), I, p. liii

25   Samuel Richardson, *Clarissa*, ed. Angus Ross (1985), p. 35

26   See James Raven, 'Historical Introduction', *The English Novel*

1770–1829: A Bibliographical Survey of Prose Fiction Published in the British Isles, ed. Peter Garside and James Raven, 2 vols. (2000), I, pp. 41–3

27 *Critical Review*, August 1759, in Alison Adburgham, *Women in Print: Writing Women and Women's Magazines from the Restoration to the Accession of Victoria* (1972), pp. 114–15

28 Roger Lonsdale, introd., *Eighteenth-Century Women Poets. An Oxford Anthology* (Oxford, 1989), p. xxxvi

29 James Raven, 'The Anonymous Novel in Britain and Ireland, 1750–1830', in Robert J. Griffin, ed., *The Faces of Anonymity: Anonymous and Pseudonymous Publication from the Sixteenth to the Nineteenth Century* (Basingstoke, 2003), p. 145

30 Ibid., p. 155

31 Raven, *The English Novel 1770–1829*, I, p. 42

32 Garside, ibid., II, p. 66

33 Troy J. Bassett, 'T. Fisher Unwin's Pseudonym Library: Literary Marketing and Authorial Identity', p. 160

34 See Waldo Dunn, *R. D. Blackmore* (1956), p. 112

35 R. D. Blackmore, *Clara Vaughan* (1872), Preface

36 *The Saturday Review*, 30 April 1864, quoted in Kenneth Budd, *The Last Victorian. R. D. Blackmore and his Novels* (1960), p. 33

37 *Athenaeum*, no. 1905, 30 April 1864

38 R. Rooksby, *A. C. Swinburne: A Poet's Life* (1997), p. 227

39 See R. G. Cox, ed., *Thomas Hardy. The Critical Heritage* (1970), p. 1

40 Fiona MacLeod, *Pharais* (Edinburgh, 1894), p. x

41 Ibid., pp. 44 and 170

42 Ibid., p. 43

43 Ibid., p. 171

44 Elizabeth Sharp, *William Sharp (Fiona MacLeod): A Memoir* 2 vols. (1910; rpt. 1912), II, p. 18

45 Ibid., p. 19

46 Ibid., p. 22

47 'Dream Fantasy', in Fiona MacLeod, *From the Hills of Dream* (Edinburgh, [1897]), p. 41

48 'The Voice Among the Dunes', ibid., p. 35

49 'The Rune of the Passion of Women', ibid., p. 81

50 Fiona Macleod, *Wind and Wave. Selected Tales* (Leipzig, 1902), pp. 7–8

51 Elizabeth Sharp, *William Sharp (Fiona MacLeod)*, II, p. 58

52 Flavia Alaya, *William Sharp—"Fiona MacLeod" 1855–1905* (Cambridge, Mass., 1970), p. 135

53 Ibid., Preface

54 Elizabeth Sharp, *William Sharp (Fiona MacLeod)*, II, p. 208

55 Ibid., I, Preface

56 Ibid., II, p. 119

57 Ibid., II, pp. 62–3

58 *Uncollected Prose by W. B. Yeats*, vol. II, ed. John P. Frayne and Colton Johnson (1975), pp. 44–5

59 See William F. Halloran, 'W. B. Yeats, William Sharp, and Fiona Macleod: A Celtic Drama, 1897', in Warwick Gould, ed., *Yeats and the Nineties* (2001), pp. 159–208

60 *Daily Chronicle*, 28 January 1899. See the article in *ODNB* by Murray Pittock

61 Alaya, *William Sharp*, p. 138

62 Elizabeth Sharp, *William Sharp (Fiona MacLeod)*, II, p. 332

5 DANGER

1 *An Exact Narrative of the Tryal and Condemnation of John Twyn, for Printing and Dispersing of a Treasonable Book* (1664), p. 27

2 Ibid., p. 73

3 Ibid., p. 74

4 Ibid., p. 20

5 Ibid., p. 22

6 See F. S. Siebert, *Freedom of the Press in England 1476–1776* (Urbana, Illinois, 1965), p. 267

7 *An Exact Narrative*, pp. 19–20

8 Henry R. Plomer, *A Dictionary of the Booksellers and Printers Who Were at Work in England from 1641 to 1667* (1907), p. 43

9 *An Exact Narrative*, p. 21

10 Ibid., p. 30

11 Ibid., pp. 44–5

12 Ibid., p. 72

13   See Cyndia Susan Clegg, *Press Censorship in Elizabethan England* (Cambridge, 1997), pp. 93–4

14   Siebert, *Freedom of the Press*, p. 268

15   Clegg, *Press Censorship in Elizabethan England*, p. 27

16   See David Daniell, *William Tyndale. A Biography* (New Haven, 1994), p. 134

17   Ibid., p. 157

18   Paul L. Hughes and James F. Larkin, eds., *Tudor Royal Proclamations*, 3 vols. (New Haven, 1964–9), I, p. 375

19   John Guy, *Tudor England*, (Oxford, 1988) pp. 219–229

20   D. M. Loades, 'The Theory and Practice of Censorship in Sixteenth-Century England', *Transactions of the Royal Historical Society*, 24, Series 5 (1974), p. 103

21   See Cyndia Susan Clegg, *Press Censorship in Jacobean England* (Cambridge, 2001), p. 20

22   *A Book containing all such proclamations as were published during the reign of the late Queene Elizabeth* (1618), no. 191

23   William Camden, *Annales* (1625), Book III, p. 10

24   Siebert, *Freedom of the Press*, p. 92

25   Patrick Collinson, *The Elizabethan Puritan Movement* (1967), p. 120

26   C. H. Timperley, *Encyclopædia of Literary and Typographical Anecdote*, first published 1839, 2nd edn. (1842), p. 405

27   Clegg, *Press Censorship in Elizabethan England*, p. 196

28   *The Marprelate Tracts* [*1588–1589*]. A Scolar Press Facsimile (Menston, 1967), *The Epistle*, p. 1

29   Ibid., pp. 4 and 17

30   Ibid., p. 9

31   Ibid., p. 20

32   Ibid., p. 9

33   Ibid., p. 23

34   J. Dover Wilson, 'The Marprelate Controversy', in *The Cambridge History of English Literature*, vol. III, ed. A. W. Ward and A. R. Waller (Cambridge, 1909), p. 381

35   *Marprelate Tracts, The Epitome,* unnumbered

36   *Marprelate Tracts, Hay any worke for Cooper,* unnumbered

37   *Marprelate Tracts, The protestatyon of Martin Marprelate,* unnumbered

38 William Pierce, *An Historical Introduction to the Marprelate Tracts* (1908), p. 197

39 Ibid., p. 206

40 Leland H. Carlson, 'Martin Marprelate: His Identity and His Satire', in *English Satire. Papers Read at a Clark Library Seminar, January 15, 1972* (Los Angeles, 1972), p. 34

41 See Collinson, *Elizabethan Puritan Movement*, p. 393

42 Dover Wilson, 'The Marprelate Controversy', p. 383

43 Everett H. Emerson, *English Puritanism from John Hooper to John Milton* (Durham, N.C., 1968), p. 138

44 As well as works already cited, see Donald J. McGinn, *John Penry and the Marprelate Controversy* (New Brunswick, N.J., 1966) and Leland H. Carlson, *Martin Marprelate, Gentleman* (1981)

45 See Hughes and Larkin, eds., *Tudor Royal Proclamations*, III, pp. 233–4

46 William Cobbett, ed., *A Complete Collection of State Trials*, 33 vols. (1809–26). III (1809), pp. 383–4

47 Ibid., p. 385

48 Mark Rose, *Authors and Owners. The Invention of Copyright* (Cambridge, Mass., 1993), p. 22

49 C. H. Firth and R. S. Rait, eds., *Acts and Ordinances of the Interregnum*, 2 vols. (1911), I, p. 1022

50 See *A Chronology and Calendar of Documents Relating to the London Book Trade 1641–1700*, ed. D.F. McKenzie and Maureen Bell, 3 vols. (Oxford, 2005), I, pp. 19, 26, 29, 31, 45 and *passim*

51 *The Complete Prose Works of John Milton*, vol. II (1643–1648), ed. Ernest Sirluck (New Haven, 1959), p. 569

52 *Poems on Affairs of State. Augustan Satirical Verse, 1660–1714*, vol. I, ed. George de F. Lord (New Haven, 1963), p. xxxiii

53 A succinct account of the legal position is given by Robert J. Griffin in his Introduction to *The Faces of Anonymity*, pp. 5–6

54 Alastair J. Mann, *The Scottish Book Trade 1500–1720* (East Linton, 2000), p. 182

55 Harold Love, *English Clandestine Satire 1660–1702* (Oxford, 2004), p. 151.

56 *Mercurius Anglicus*, 17–20 December 1679

57 Edward L. Saslow, 'The Rose Alley Ambuscade', *Restoration*, 26:1

(Spring 2002), p. 27. See James M. Osborn, *John Dryden: Some Biographical Facts and Problems* (1965), pp. 144–5 for documents relating to the attack.

58 See Paul Hammond's note in his edition of *The Poems of John Dryden*, vol. II (1995), p. 53.

59 *Poems on Affairs of State*, I, p. xxxvi

60 *Poems on Affairs of State*, vol. II (New Haven, 1965) ed. Elias F. Mengel Jr., p. 425

61 *Poems on Affairs of State*, I, p. 46

62 *The Diary of Samuel Pepys*, ed. Robert Latham and William Matthews, 11 vols. (1970–83), VII, p. 407

63 Entry for 20 January 1667, ibid., VIII, p. 21

64 See Love, *English Clandestine Satire*, p. 105

65 *The Poems and Letters of Andrew Marvell*, ed. H. M. Margoliouth, rev. Pierre Legouis and E. E. Duncan-Jones (Oxford, 1971), 2 vols., I, p. 348

66 Annabel Patterson, *Marvell: The Writer in Public Life* (2000), p. 77

67 See Elizabeth Story Donno, ed., *Andrew Marvell. The Critical Heritage* (1978), pp. 36 and 40

68 *The Rehearsal Transpros'd* and *The Rehearsal Transpros'd. The Second Part*, ed. D. I. B. Smith (Oxford, 1971), p. xxii

69 Donno, *Andrew Marvell*, p. 64

70 Letter of July 1 1676 in *Poems and Letters*, II, p. 346

71 See ibid., p. 394, for an example of a contemporary who knew that Marvell was the author

72 *An Account of the Growth of Popery and Arbitrary Government in England* (1677), p. 3

73 Ibid., p. 14

74 Letter of 10 June 1678, in *Poems and Letters*, II, p. 357

75 The advertisement is reproduced in Hilton Kelliher, *Andrew Marvell: Poet and Politician*, Catalogue of British Library Exhibition (1978), p. 113

76 *An Account of the Growth of Knavery* (1678), pp. 4–5

77 Ibid., p. 6

78 Maurice Cranston, *John Locke. A Biography* (1957; rpt. Oxford, 1985), pp. 323–4

79 John Locke, *Two Treatises of Government*, ed. Peter Laslett (1960; rpt. Cambridge, 1989), p. 137

80 Laslett, Introd., *Two Treatises*, p. 6

81 Ibid., p. 9

82 Letter to Richard King, 25 August 1703, in *The Correspondence of John Locke*, ed. E. S. de Beer, 8 vols. (Oxford, 1976–89), VIII, p. 58

83 Letter of *c.* 19 December 1689, *Correspondence*, III, p. 764

84 Letter of 18 March 1690, *Correspondence*, IV, p. 36

85 Letter of 9 August 1692, ibid., IV, p. 495

86 Letter of 27 August 1692, ibid., IV, p. 508

87 See *Two Treatises*, pp. 62–5. Laslett's lengthy introduction includes detailed discussion of the dating of the *Two Treatises*

88 John Locke, *Epistola de Tolerantia*, ed. Raymond Klibansky (Oxford, 1968), Preface, p. xviii

89 Ibid., p. xxiii

90 John Dunn, *Locke* (Oxford, 1984), p. 14

91 John Locke, *A Letter concerning Toleration in Focus*, ed. John Horton and Susan Mendus (1991), p. 18

92 Ibid., pp. 16–17

93 John Locke, *The Reasonableness of Christianity as delivered in the Scriptures*, ed. John C. Higgins-Biddle (Oxford, 1999), ch. 15, p. 170

94 Ibid., p. 169

95 Letter of 10 May 1695, *Correspondence*, V, p. 371

96 Locke, *Reasonableness*, Introd., p. xxxix

97 Ibid., pp. xlvi–xlix

98 Ibid., p. xlix

99 *Two Tracts on Government*, ed. and trans. Philip Abrams (Cambridge, 1967), p. 118

100 See *Correspondence*, VIII, pp. 425–6

101 See Cranston, *John Locke*, p. 387

102 Daniel Defoe, *The Shortest Way with Dissenters*, in *Political and Economic Writings of Daniel Defoe*, vol. III, ed. W. R. Owens (2000), p. 104

103 *The Shortest Way with Dissenters . . . Consider'd* (1703), p. 26

104 Maximilian Novak, *Daniel Defoe. Master of Fictions* (Oxford, 2001), pp. 178–9

105 Paula R. Backscheider, *Daniel Defoe. His Life* (Baltimore, Md., 1989), pp. 100–1

106 Novak, *Daniel Defoe*, p. 183

107 Ibid., pp. 425–6

108 Daniel Defoe, *An Essay on the Regulation of the Press*, in *Political and Economic Writings*, vol. VIII, p. 155

109 Ibid., p. 156

110 Novak, *Daniel Defoe*, p. 330

111 Joseph Spence, *Anecdotes, Observations and Characters of Books and Men, Collected from the Conversation of Mr. Pope* (1820), pp. 267–8

112 Leslie Stephen, *English Men of Letters: Alexander Pope* (1880), p. 130. See also James Sutherland, introd., *The Dunciad* (1953), p. xxii

113 *House of Lords Journals*, XIX, p. 634

114 George A. Aitken, *The Life of Richard Steele* (1889), 2 vols., II, p. 15

115 'The Author upon Himself', ll. 59–62. I take my text of this and other poems by Swift from Jonathan Swift, *The Complete Poems*, ed. Pat Rogers (1983)

116 Irvin Ehrenpreis, *Swift. The Man, His Works and the Age*, 3 vols. (1962, 1967, 1983), III, p. 128

117 See *The Correspondence of Jonathan Swift*, ed. Harold Williams, 5 vols. (Oxford, 1963–5), II, pp. 359, 365 and 380

118 Jonathan Swift, *The Drapier's Letters*, ed. Herbert Davis (1935; rpt. Oxford, 1965), p. 14

119 Letter of 28 April 1724, *Correspondence*, III, pp. 11–13

120 See Davis, introd., *Drapier's Letters*, pp. xliv–xlv

121 Ehrenpreis, *Swift*, II, p. 272

122 Ibid. II, p. 276

123 Ibid. III, p. 316

124 See David Nokes, *Jonathan Swift. A Hypocrite Reversed* (Oxford, 1985), p. 289

125 *Drapier's Letters*, p. 111

126 *Correspondence*, III, p. 234

127 See *Complete Poems*, p. 751

128 'Verses on the Death of Dr Swift, D. S. P. D.' in *Complete Poems*, ll. 351–4

129 Ibid., ll. 355–8

130 See Pat Rogers's notes to the poem in *Complete Poems*, pp. 846–9

131   Jonathan Swift, *Journal to Stella*, ed. Harold Williams, 2 vols. (1948; rpt. Oxford, 1986), 7 Oct. 1710, I, p. 47

132   Cobbett, ed., *State Trials*, XIV, p. 1095

133   Siebert, *Freedom of the Press*, p. 382

134   Cobbett, ed., *State Trials*, XVII, p. 672

135   Lewis M. Knapp, *Tobias Smollett. Doctor of Men and Manners* (1949), pp. 213–14

136   Adam Sisman, *Boswell's Presumptuous Task* (2000), p. 43

137   See V. G. Kiernan, *The Duel in European History. Honour and the Reign of Aristocracy* (Oxford, 1988), p. 208

138   P. B. Ellis and S. Mac A'Ghobhainn, *The Scottish Insurrection of 1820* (1970), p. 284

139   Andrew Steinmetz, *The Romance of Duelling in All Times and Countries*, 2 vols. (1868), I, p. 317

140   Ibid., p. 318

141   See his instructions to John Murray in a letter of 25 January 1819, in *Byron's Letters and Journals*, ed. Leslie A. Marchand, 13 vols., VI (1976), pp. 94–5

142   Letter to Douglas Kinnaird, 6 March 1819, ibid., p. 101

143   Letter of 6 April 1819, ibid., p. 105

144   Letter of 6 May 1819, ibid., p. 123

145   Letter of 24 August 1819, ibid., p. 216

146   Letter of 22 June 1820, ibid., VII (1977), p. 121

147   Letter of 3 November 1821, ibid., IX (1979), p. 54

148   See Thomas Moore, Memoirs, *Journal and Correspondence of Thomas Moore*, ed. Lord John Russell, 8 vols. (1853–4), pp. 199ff.

149   *English Bards and Scotch Reviewers*, ll. 1047, in Lord Byron, *The Complete Poetical Works*, ed. Jerome J. McGann (Oxford, 1980–93), vol. I, p. 262

150   Letter of 3 July 1808, in *Byron's Letters and Journals*, I, p. 167

151   *Complete Poetical Works*, I, p. 263

152   Leonidas M. Jones, 'The Scott–Christie Duel', in *Texas Studies in Literature and Language*, 12:4 (Winter 1971), p. 609

153   Stanley Jones, *Hazlitt: A Life* (Oxford, 1989), p. 288

154   *Glasgow Chronicle*, 12 and 13 May 1818

155   *Fraser's Magazine*, January 1837, p. 134

6 REVIEWING

1   *TLS*, 29 January 1999
2   *London Review of Books*, 18 March 1999
3   Ibid., 1 April 1999
4   Ibid., 15 April 1999
5   See Frank Donoghue, 'Colonizing Readers. Review Criticism and the Formation of a Reading Public', in Ann Bermingham and John Brewer, eds., *The Consumption of Culture 1600–1800. Image, Object, Text* (1995), pp. 54–74
6   See James Raven, 'The Anonymous Novel in Britain and Ireland, 1750–1830', in *The Faces of Anonymity. Anonymous and Pseudonymous Publication from the Sixteenth to the Twentieth Century*, ed. Robert J. Griffin (Basingstoke, 2003), pp. 155–6
7   In Lewis M. Knapp, *Tobias Smollett. Doctor of Men and Manners* (1949), p. 171
8   See Walter Graham, *English Literary Periodicals* (1930), p. 212
9   Knapp, *Tobias Smollett*, p. 175
10 Samuel Richardson, *Pamela*, ed. Thomas Keymer and Alice Wakely (Oxford, 2001), p. 7. See also T. C. D. Duncan Eaves and Ben D. Kimpel, *Samuel Richardson: A Biography* (Oxford, 1971)
11 Isobel Rivers, ed., *Books and their Readers in Eighteenth-Century England* (Leicester, 1982), p. 115
12 See Frederick A. Pottle, *James Boswell. The Earlier Years 1740–1769* (1966), p. 106
13 Derek Roper, *Reviewing before the Edinburgh 1788–1802* (1978), p. 31
14 See Eudo Mason, *The Mind of Henry Fuseli* (1951), pp. 32, 354, 358–9
15 Roger Lonsdale, *Dr Charles Burney* (Oxford, 1965), pp. 106–7
16 Ibid., p. 109
17 Ibid., p. 121
18 Ibid., p. 180
19 Ibid., p. 310
20 Ibid., p. 344
21 Samuel Taylor Coleridge, *The Watchman*, ed. Lewis Patten (1970), no. I, 1 March 1796, p. 15
22 Samuel Taylor Coleridge, *Biographia Literaria*, ed. James Engell and W. Jackson Bate, 2 vols. (1983), I, ch. 1, p. 13

23   Ibid., I, ch. 2, p. 42

24   Ibid., I, ch. 3, p. 50

25   Coleridge's original articles were in *The Courier* of 29 August and 7, 9, 10 and 11 September 1816. See Engell and Bate, *Biographia*, Editors' Introduction, p. lxiii

26   *Biographia*, I, ch. 3, p. 53

27   Ibid., I, p. 52

28   Ibid., II, ch. 22, p. 157

29   See Graham, *English Literary Periodicals*, p. 240

30   See *The Wellesley Index to Victorian Periodicals 1824–1900*, vol. I, ed. Walter E. Houghton (1966), p. 419

31   William Hazlitt, *The Spirit of the Age*, ed. E. D. Mackerness (1969), p. 214

32   Unpublished letter, 12 May 1812, quoted in Leslie A. Marchand, *Byron: A Biography*, 3 vols. (1957), I, p. 346

33   See Elisabeth W. Schneider, 'Tom Moore and the *Edinburgh Review* of *Christabel*', *PMLA* 77 (1962), pp. 71–6

34   From *The Young Romantics and Critical Opinion 1807–1824* (1973), ed. Theodore Redpath, pp. 342–7

35   *The Letters of Percy Bysshe Shelley*, ed. Frederick L. Jones, 2 vols. (1964), II, p. 203

36   Stanley Jones, *Hazlitt: A Life* (Oxford, 1989), p. 300

37   See Redpath, ed., *The Young Romantics*, p. 468

38   Quoted in Houghton, ed., *The Wellesley Index*, I, p. 7

39   From a letter to Robert Baldwin, 24 January 1819, quoted in Leonidas M. Jones, 'The Scott–Christie Duel', *Texas Studies in Literature and Language*, 12:4 (Winter 1971), p. 605

40   Walter Scott, *Chronicles of the Canongate*, ed. Claire Lamont (Edinburgh, 2000), p. 8

41   See Martin Lightfoot, 'Scott's Self-Reviewal: Manuscript and Other Evidence', *Nineteenth-Century Fiction*, 23, (September 1968) p. 154

42   In *Scott. The Critical Heritage*, ed. John O. Hayden (1970), p. 114

43   *Fraser's Magazine* (January 1835)

44   Patrick Leary, '*Fraser's Magazine* and the Literary Life, 1830–1847', *Victorian Periodicals Review*, 27:2 (Summer 1994), p. 112

45 *Fraser's Magazine*, vol. XIII (January 1836), pp. 80–1

46 'On the Anonymous in Periodicals', *The New Monthly Magazine*, part III (1833), p. 5

47 Letter to John Carlyle, 18 September 1830, in *The Collected Letters of Thomas and Jane Welsh Carlyle*, ed. C. R. Sanders, Clyde de L. Ryals et al., 32 vols. (Durham, N.C., 1976–93), V, p. 164

48 *Fraser's Magazine*, vol. XV (January 1837), p. 137

49 *Blackwood's Edinburgh Magazine*, 27 (May 1830), pp. 711–16, in *The Novels and Selected Works of Mary Shelley*, vol. II (1996), ed. Pamela Clemit, pp. 201–9

50 *The Letters of Mary Wollstonecraft Shelley*, ed. Betty T. Bennett, 3 vols. (Baltimore, 1983–8), II, p. 109

51 Gertrude Reese Hudson, *Robert Browning's Literary Life* (Austin, Tex., 1992), pp. 1–5

52 Edward Balwer Lytton, *England and the English* (1833), vol. II, p. 18. See also, from this period, Macaulay's attack on puffery in the *Edinburgh Review*, April 1830, pp. 193–210

53 *England and the English*, p. 19

54 Ibid., p. 21

55 Ibid., p. 18

56 'On the Anonymous in Periodicals', *The New Monthly Magazine*, Part III (1833), p. 3

57 'Anonymous Publications', in *Fraser's Magazine*, 11 (May 1835), pp. 549–51

58 W. M. Thackeray, *Pendennis*, ed. John Sutherland (1994), ch. xxxv, pp. 443–4

59 Ibid., p. 440

60 Laurel Brake, 'Literary Criticism and the Victorian Periodicals', *Yearbook of English Studies*, 16 (1986), p. 107

61 Letter of 12 July 1840, in *The Letters and Private Papers of William Makepeace Thackeray*, ed. Gordon N. Ray, 4 vols. (1945), I, pp. 455–6

62 Ibid., p. 455

63 Ibid., p. 453

64 J. Don Vann, 'Unrecorded Reviews of Thackeray's *Paris Sketch-Book*', *Papers of the Bibliographical Society of America*, 71:3 (1977), p. 345

65 W. M. Thackeray, *Letters and Private Papers*, I, p. 457

66 Letter of 20 April 1843, ibid., II, p. 105

67 Letter of 11 January 1847, ibid., II, p. 267

68 Robert Bernard Martin, *Tennyson. The Unquiet Heart* (1980), p. 265

69 *Edinburgh Review*, 77 (April 1843), in *Tennyson. The Critical Heritage*, ed. John Jump (1967), p. 146

70 The editors of *The Wellesley Index* have calculated that, before 1865, more than ninety-six per cent of all articles (and stories) in periodicals were anonymous or pseudonymous. For the period from 1865 to 1900 the figure falls to fifty-seven per cent. See *Wellesley Index*, II, p. xvi

71 Letter of 22 September 1856, in *The George Eliot Letters*, ed. Gordon S. Haight, 9 vols. (New Haven, 1954–5, 1978), II, p. 264

72 Letter of 16 July 1855, ibid., II, p. 209

73 Letter of 19 February 1856, ibid., II, p. 228

74 Letter of 26 January 1857, ibid., II, pp. 289–90

75 Letter of 15 October 1855, ibid., II, p. 218

76 Letter of 13 October 1855, quoted in Rosemary Ashton, *George Eliot. A Life* (1996), p. 146

77 In George Eliot, *Selected Essays, Poems and Other Writings*, eds A. S. Byatt and Nicholas Warren (1990), p. 161

78 Ibid., pp. 141–2 and pp. 148–9

79 See Leslie A. Marchand, *The Athenaeum. A Mirror of Victorian Culture* (1941), pp. 105–6

80 Ibid., p. 98

81 See Frederick Karl, *George Eliot. A Biography* (1995), p. 205. She reviewed, for instance, Charles Kingsley's *Westward Ho!* in the *Leader*, 19 May 1855, and then in the *Westminster Review* in July 1855

82 *The Critic*, 11 (1852), p. 114

83 Leary, '*Fraser's Magazine*', p. 114

84 *George Eliot Letters*, II, p. 289

85 *The Leader*, no. 293, 3 November 1855, p. 1058. Such partiality is subtle compared to the case of Walt Whitman in America. On the publication of the first edition of his *Leaves of Grass* in 1855 there appeared a series of anonymous reviews which he had written himself. 'An American bard at last!' begins the first of

these. See *Whitman. The Critical Heritage*, ed. Milton Hindus (1971)

86   Anthony Trollope, *An Autobiography*, ed. Michael Sadleir and Frederick Page (1980), p. 130

87   Ibid., p. 264

88   *Edinburgh Review*, 106 (July 1857), in *Dickens. The Critical Heritage*, ed. P. Collins (1971), pp. 367–8

89   *Household Words*, 1 August 1857, in *The Dent Edition of Dickens' Journalism*, vol. III, ed. Michael Slater (1999), p. 420

90   Oscar Maurer, 'Anonymity vs. Signature in Victorian Reviewing', *Texas University Studies in English*, 28:1 (June 1948), p. 4

91   Trollope, *Autobiography*, p. 189

92   Anthony Trollope, 'On Anonymous Literature', *Fortnightly Review*, 1 (July 1865), pp. 493–7

93   Review of William Lecky's *The Influence of Rationalism*, *Fortnightly Review*, 15 May 1865

94   Robert H. Tener, 'Breaking the Code of Anonymity: The Case of the *Spectator*, 1861–1897', *Yearbook of English Studies*, 16 (1986), p. 65

95   Thomas Hardy, *A Pair of Blue Eyes*, ed. Roger Ebbatson (1986), ch. 1, p. 52

96   Ibid., ch. 7, p. 113

97   Ibid., ch. 15, p. 200

98   Ibid., p. 202

99   Ibid., ch. 16, p. 205

100 Anthony Trollope, *The Way We Live Now*, ed. John Sutherland (1982), vol. I, ch. 1, p. 6

101 Ibid., vol I, ch. 2, p. 17

102 Ibid., p. 7

103 Ibid., vol I, ch. 11, pp. 95–6

104 Trollope, *Autobiography*, pp. 192–4

105 Ibid., p. 192

106 *New Review* (November 1889), pp. 514–15

107 *New Review* (March 1890), p. 270

108 Ibid., p. 276

109 Quoted in Tener, 'Breaking the Code', p. 25

110 George Gissing, *New Grub Street*, ed. Bernard Bergonzi (1968), ch. 36, p. 533

111 Ibid., ch. 7, p. 111

112 Marchand, *The Athenaeum*, p. 108

113 *The Athenaeum*, 20 June 1919, p. 491

114 Jeremy Treglown, 'Bateson and the *TLS*', *Essays in Criticism*, 51:1 (January 2001), pp. 148–9

115 Nicolas Barker, *Stanley Morison* (1972), p. 407

116 Hermione Lee, *Virginia Woolf* (1996), p. 216

117 Derwent May, *Critical Times. The History of the Times Literary Supplement* (2001), p. 313

118 Letter of 4 August 1906, in *The Letters of Virginia Woolf*, ed. Nigel Nicolson, 6 vols. (1975–80), I (1975), p. 234

119 Letter of 20 October 1924, in *Letters*, ed. Nicolson, vol. III, (1975), p. 135

120 *The Diary of Virginia Woolf*, ed. Anne Oliver and Andrew McNeillie, 5 vols. (1977–84), 1, 18 April 1918, p. 142

121 Ibid., 18 March 1918, p. 129

122 Quoted in Deborah McVea and Jeremy Treglown, 'The *TLS* and its Contributors', in May, *Critical Times*, pp. 416–17

123 May, *Critical Times*, p. 125

124 *TLS*, no. 2916, 17 January 1958

125 May, *Critical Times*, pp. 416–17

126 *TLS*, no. 3130, 23 February 1962

7 MOCKERY AND DEVILRY

1 *The Whipping of the Satyre*, ed. Arthur Davenport (Liverpool, 1951), p. 10

2 Ibid., p. 23

3 Ibid., p. 6

4 Ibid., p. 22

5 See Richard McCabe, 'Elizabethan Satire and the Bishops' Ban of 1599', *Yearbook of English Studies*, 11 (1981), p. 188

6 Ibid., p. 189

7 *The Poems of Joseph Hall*, ed. Arthur Davenport (Liverpool, 1969), p. xxxv

8   Lib. I, Sat. vii, ll. 11–12, ibid., p. 18

9   I. i, ll. 11–12, ibid.

10 *The Metamorphosis of Pigmalions Image and Certaine Satyres* (1598), pp. 29, 42, 50

11 *The Poems of John Marston*, ed. Arnold Davenport (Liverpool, 1961), p. 247

12 Ibid., p. 106, Satyre II, ll. 7–8

13 'Satyre Preludium', ll. 9–14, in *Skialetheia*, ed. D. Allen Carroll (Chapel Hill, N. C., 1974), p. 59

14 Satire I, l. 2, ibid., p. 63

15 Evelyn Simpson, *A Study of the Prose Works of John Donne* (Oxford, 1948), p. 316

16 John Donne, Satyre I, ll. 4 & 52, in *Donne Poetical Works*, ed. Herbert J. C. Grierson (1933; rpt. Oxford, 1979), pp. 129–30

17 Juvenal, *The Sixteen Satires*, trans. Peter Green (1974), pp. 66–7

18 *Skialetheia*, p. 84, Satire V, l. 66

19 Ibid., p. 87, Satire V, ll. 171–2

20 Ibid., p. 65, Satire I, ll. 85–8

21 John Harington, *A New Discourse of a Stale Subject Called the Metamorphosis of Ajax*, ed. Elizabeth Story Donno (New York, 1962), p. 204

22 George Puttenham, *The Arte of English Poesie* ed. G. D. Willcock and A. Walker (Cambridge, 1936), p. 31

23 John Marston, *The Dutch Courtesan*, ed. David Crane (1997), Act III, sc. 1, ll. 42–5. Manuscript circulation of abusive personal satires became common. See Andrew McRae, *Literature, Satire and the Early Stuart State* (Cambridge, 2004)

24 John Donne, *Ignatius His Conclave*, ed. T. S. Healy (Oxford, 1969), pp. 2–3

25 Ibid., p. xxix

26 Ibid., p. 7

27 Ibid., p. 29

28 Ibid., p. 31

29 Ibid., p. 43

30 See Harold Love, *Scribal Publication in Seventeenth-Century England* (Oxford, 1993), pp. 235–6

31 In David M. Vieth, *Attribution in Restoration Poetry. A Study of Rochester's Poems of 1680* (New Haven, Conn., 1963), p. 189

32 George Etherege, *The Man of Mode*, ed. John Barnard (1979; rpt. 1997), III.3, ll. 105–15

33 *The Complete Poems of John Wilmot, Earl of Rochester*, ed. David M. Vieth (New Haven, Conn., 1968), p. 131

34 See Vieth, *Attribution*, pp. 200–3

35 Gilbert Burnet, *Some Passages of the Life and Death of the Right Honourable John Earl of Rochester* (1680), p. 7

36 John Crowne, Dedication to *The History of Charles VIII of France*, in *Dramatic Works*, ed. J. Maidment and W. H. Logan (1873), I, p. 127

37 Burnet, *Some Passages*, p. 14

38 Rochester, *Complete Poems*, ed. Veith, pp. 65–6

39 *The Poems of John Oldham*, ed. Harold F. Brooks and Raman Selden (Oxford, 1987), pp. 89–90

40 Ibid., p. 400

41 Ibid., p. 58

42 Ibid., pp. 341–4

43 Ibid., pp. 260–4

44 'Satyrs upon the Jesuits', Prologue, l. 26, ibid., p. 5

45 ll. 57–8, ibid., p. 6

46 'Satyr III', ll. 10–13, ibid., p. 26

47 Ibid., p. 161

48 John Dryden, *Selected Criticism*, ed. James Kinsley and George Parfitt (Oxford, 1970), p. 212

49 *Secret Memoirs and Manners of several Persons of Quality, of both Sexes* (1709), pp. i–iii

50 Delarivière Manley, *The Adventures of Rivella*, ed. Katherine Zelinsky (Peterborough, Ontario, 1999), p. 110

51 John Richetti, *The Life of Daniel Defoe* (Oxford, 2005), p. 183

52 Defoe, *An Elegy on the Author of the True-born Englishman* (1704), II, pp. 105–8

53 *London Post*, 9 April 1705

54 Quoted by Pat Rogers in 'Nameless Names: Pope, Curll, and the Uses of Anonymity', *New Literary History*, 33:2 (Spring 2002), p. 237

55 Alexander Pope, *The Dunciad. An Heroic Poem* (1728), pp. iii–iv

56 Ibid., p. v

57 Edmund Curll, *A Compleat Key to the Dunciad* (1728), p. iv

58 Alexander Pope, *The Dunciad in Four Books*, ed. Valerie Rumbold (1999)

59 See Samuel Johnson, *The Lives of the Most Eminent English Poets*, ed. Roger Lonsdale, 4 vols. (Oxford, 2006), IV, p. 32

60 Alexander Pope, *The Dunciad*, ed. Rumbold, p. 364

61 Ibid., p. 32

62 *An Epistle to Dr Arbuthnot*, ll. 279–82, in *The Poems of Alexander Pope*, ed. John Butt (1963; rpt. 1977), p. 607

63 *The Times. A Poem* (1764), p. 33

64 *Selected Poems of Gray, Churchill and Cowper*, ed. Katherine Turner (1997), p. 79

65 See Alan B. Howes, *Yorick and the Critics. Sterne's Reputation in England, 1760–1868* (1958; rpt. Hamden, Conn., 1971), p. 5

66 William Blake, *The Marriage of Heaven and Hell*, ed. Geoffrey Keynes (Oxford, 1975), Plate 4

67 Letter of 21 March 1809, in *Byron's Letters and Journals*, ed. Leslie A. Marchand, 13 vols. (1973–94), I, p. 198

68 Letter of 22 December 1807, ibid., I, p. 141

69 Leslie A. Marchand, *Byron: A Biography*, 3 vols. (1957), I, p. 171

70 Ibid., I, p. 175; see Robert Dallas, *Recollections of the Life of Lord Byron* (1824), p. 36

71 *Cabinet*, 2nd series, I (June 1809), in Donald Reiman, ed., *The Romantics Reviewed*, 9 vols. (New York, 1972), Part B, vol. II, p. 512

72 *Critical Review*, 3rd series, XVII (May 1809), ibid., p. 611

73 Byron, *The Complete Poetical Works*, ed. Jerome J. McGann, 7 vols. (Oxford, 1980–93), I, p. 263

74 Ibid., p. 262

75 *Antijacobin Review*, 37 (September 1810), in Reiman, *The Romantics Reviewed*, Part B, Vol. I, p. 8

76 See letter to Robert Charles Dallas, 21 August 1811, in Marchand, ed., *Letters and Journals*, II, p. 75

77 Letter of 23 October 1817, in Marchand, ed., *Letters and Journals*, V, p. 269

78 Issue of February 1818, in Theodore Redpath, ed., *The Young Romantics and Critical Opinion 1807–1824* (1973), pp. 225–6

79 Ibid., p. 226

80 *Edinburgh Magazine*, 2nd series, 2 (April 1818), in Reiman, *Romantics Reviewed*, Part B, vol. V, p. 2175

81 *Champion*, 29 March 1818, ibid., vol. II, p. 533

82 *Literary Journal*, 5 April 1818, ibid., vol. IV, p. 1475

83 *Eclectic Review*, 2nd series, IX (June 1818), ibid., vol. II, p. 753

84 *Byron. The Critical Heritage*, pp. 128–9

85 *Letters and Journals*, ed. Marchand, VI, p. 25

86 Redpath, ed., *Young Romantics*, pp. 275–6

87 Byron, *Complete Poetical Works*, ed. McGann, vol. VI, p. 337

88 Letter of 29 October 1822, in Marchand, *Byron*, p. 1040

89 Ibid., p. 1041

90 Letter of 4 October 1821, in *Letters and Journals*, ed. Marchand, VIII, p. 232

91 Richard Holmes, *Shelley: The Pursuit* (1974), p. 611

92 David Garnett, ed., *The Novels of Thomas Love Peacock* (1948), p. 11

93 Ibid., p. 12

94 Ibid., p. 360

95 Ibid., p. 410

96 Preface to volume LVII of Bentley's 'Standard Novels' (1837), ibid., p. xxi

97 *The Letters of Percy Bysshe Shelley*, ed. Frederick L. Jones, 2 vols., (1964), I, p. 518

98 *The British Critic*, VIII, p. 430

99 See for instance *The Literary Gazette*, II, no. 99 (12 December 1818), p. 787. 'The author of this work, and of several similar productions, is, we understand, a Mr. Peacock.'

100 *Blackwood's Edinburgh Magazine*, 11 (May 1822), p. 601

101 *Fraser's Magazine*, 17 (January 1838), p. 39

102 Letter of October 1837, in *The Letters and Private Papers of William Makepeace Thackeray*, ed. Gordon N. Ray, 4 vols. (1945), I, p. 349

103 *Fraser's Magazine*, 18 (August 1838), p. 196

104 Ibid., p. 198

105 *Catherine: A Story*, ed. Sheldon F. Goldfarb (Ann Arbor, Mich., 1999), p. 19

106 Ibid., p. 2

107 Ibid., p. 35

108 *Letters*, ed. Ray, I, p. 421

109 *Catherine*, ed. Goldfarb, p. 253

110 *The Athenaeum*, no. 665, 25 July 1840, pp. 589–90

111 *Punch*, 10 (1846), p. 101

112 Samuel Butler, *Erewhon*, ed. Peter Mudford (1981), p. 39

113 Peter Raby, *Samuel Butler. A Biography* (1991), p. 120

114 Ibid., p. 121

115 *The Fair Haven* (1873), 'Memoir of the Author', p. 54

116 Ibid., p. 5

117 Ibid., p. 22

118 Ibid., p. 165

119 Ibid., p. 199

120 Ibid., pp. 212–13

121 *The Fair Haven*, 2nd edn. (1873), p. iii

122 Ibid., p. viii

123 *The Note-Books of Samuel Butler*, vol. I: 1874–1883, ed. Hans-Peter Breuer (Lanham, Md., 1984), p. 81

8 CONFESSION

1 [John Newton], *An Authentic Narrative of some Remarkable and Interesting Particulars in the Life of ******** (1764), pp. 5, 9

2 Ibid., p. 11

3 Letter of 7 January 1763, in D. Bruce Hindmarsh, *John Newton and the English Evangelical Tradition between the Conversions of Wesley and Wilberforce* (Oxford, 1996), p. 33

4 *Authentic Narrative*, p. 47

5 Ibid., pp. 113–14

6 Ibid., p. 152

7 Ibid., p. 192

8 Ibid., p. 170

9 See Hindmarsh, *John Newton*, p. 32

10 Ibid., p. 34

11   Ibid., p. 187

12   Thomas Scott, *The Force of Truth: an Authentic Narrative* (1779), p. viii

13   John Newton, *Letters, Sermons, and a Review of Ecclesiastical History* (Edinburgh, 1780)

14   See *The Letters and Prose Writings of William Cowper*, ed. James King and Charles Ryskamp, 5 vols. (Oxford, 1979–86), I, pp. 17–21

15   Thomas De Quincey, *Confessions of an English Opium-Eater and Other Writings*, ed. Grevel Lindop (Oxford, 1985), p. 1

16   *London Magazine*, 6:32 (August 1822), p. 99

17   *London Magazine*, 6:33 (September 1822), p. 249

18   *London Magazine*, vol. IV (October 1821), p. 351

19   *Confessions*, ed. Lindop, p. 49

20   Ibid., p. 50

21   Ibid., p. 3

22   Ibid., p. 52

23   Ibid., p. 61

24   *London Magazine*, vol. IV (December 1821), p. 585

25   Grevel Lindop, *The Opium-Eater. A Life of Thomas De Quincey* (1981), p. 248

26   *Diary, Reminiscences and Correspondence of Henry Crabb Robinson*, ed. Thomas Sadler (1869), II, p. 216

27   Ibid., p. 218

28   *Confessions*, ed. Lindop, p. 1

29   *European Magazine*, 82 (November 1822), p. 459

30   *New Edinburgh Review*, 4 (January 1823), p. 253

31   Ibid., pp. 254–5

32   *John Bull Magazine and Literary Recorder*, 1 (July 1824), p. 22

33   See Lindop, *The Opium-Eater*, p. 270

34   *Epipsychidion*, ll. 149–54, in *Shelley. Poetical Works*, ed Thomas Hutchinson, rev. G. M. Matthews (Oxford, 1970), p. 425

35   Ibid, p. 411

36   *The Letters of Percy Bysshe Shelley*, ed. Frederick L. Jones, 2 vols. (1964), II, pp. 262–3

37   Stanley Jones, *Hazlitt: A Life* (Oxford, 1989), p. 320

38 Ibid., p. 337
39 William Hazlitt, *Liber Amoris*, introd. Michael Neve (1985), p. 11
40 Ibid., p. 26
41 Ibid., p. 9
42 Ibid., p. 2
43 Ibid., p. 18
44 Ibid., pp. 52, 80, 55
45 Ibid., p. 56
46 Ibid., p. 57
47 Ibid., p. 64
48 Ibid., pp. 83, 95
49 Ibid., pp. 81–2
50 Ibid., p. 91
51 Ibid., p. 98
52 Ibid., pp. 108, 112
53 Ibid., p. 149
54 Ibid., pp. 155–6
55 Ibid., p. 176
56 Ibid., p. 182
57 *The Examiner*, 11 May 1823
58 In *Liber Amoris*, p. 254
59 Jones, *Hazlitt*, pp. 337–8
60 *The Times*, 30 May 1823
61 *The Literary Gazette and Journal of Belles Lettres, Arts, Sciences, etc.*, 31 May 1823, p. 339
62 *Blackwood's Magazine*, June 1823, p. 640
63 Ibid., p. 645
64 Jones, *Hazlitt*, p. 338
65 *John Bull*, 8 June 1823, p. 180
66 Ibid., 15 June 1823, p. 188
67 Ibid., 22 June 1823, pp. 197–8
68 *Pauline; A Fragment of a Confession*, ll. 1–2. Quotations are taken from Robert Browning, *The Poems*, vol. I, ed. John Pettigrew, rev. Thomas J. Collins (1981)
69 Ibid., p. 347
70 William Clyde DeVane, *A Browning Handbook* (1935; rpt. New Haven, Conn., 1955), p. 48

71 In Gertrude Reese Hudson, *Robert Browning's Literary Life* (Austin, Tex., 1992), p. 12

72 DeVane, *Browning Handbook*, p. 45

73 Letter to Henry Hallam, 14 February 1834, in *The Letters of Alfred Lord Tennyson*, ed. Cecil Y. Lang and Edgar F. Shannon, 3 vols. (Oxford, 1982–90) I, p. 108

74 Robert Bernard Martin, *Tennyson. The Unquiet Heart* (1980), p. 325

75 Letter of February 1850, in Lang and Shannon (eds.), *Letters*, I, p. 321

76 Letter to Edward Moxon, March 1850, ibid., p. 322

77 *The Spectator*, 33, 8 June 1850, p. 546

78 *The Athenaeum*, 15 June 1850, pp. 629–30

79 *Literary Gazette*, 15 June 1850, p. 407

80 See E. F. Shannon, *Tennyson and the Reviewers* (Cambridge, Mass., 1952), pp. 141–2

81 Review in *Fraser's Magazine* (September 1850) in John Jump, ed., *Tennyson. The Critical Heritage* (1967), p. 173

82 Letter to Mrs Steele, 20 April 1867, in Lang and Shannon (eds.), *Letters*, II, p. 460

83 T. S. Eliot, *Selected Essays* (1951), p. 291

84 I, l. 9. The text is taken from *Tennyson. A Selected Edition*, ed. Christopher Ricks (1989) and referenced, as here, by section and line number

85 Martin, *Tennyson*, p. 442

86 Hallam Tennyson, *Alfred Lord Tennyson: A Memoir*, 2 vols. (1897), I, p. 300

87 Ibid., I, p. 304

88 *The Athenaeum*, 15 June 1850, p. 629

89 In Ricks (ed.), *Tennyson*, p. 339

90 Ann Thwaite, *Edmund Gosse: A Literary Landscape 1849–1928* (1984), p. 433

91 Letter of 3 November 1907, in *The Collected Letters of Thomas Hardy*, ed. Richard Little Purdy and Michael Millgate, 7 vols. (Oxford, 1978–88), III, p. 282

92 Edmund Gosse, *Father and Son*, ed. Michael Newton (Oxford, 2004), p. 176

93   Ibid., p. 5
94   Ibid., p. 157
95   Letter of 22 February 1906, in Charles Burkhart, 'George Moore and *Father and Son*', *Nineteenth-Century Fiction*, 15:1 (June 1960), p. 74
96   *The Dial*, 16 February 1908, p. 96
97   Gosse, *Fathers and Son*, p. 130
98   Thwaite, *Edmund Gosse*, p. 434
99   Ibid., p. 433
100 *The Academy*, 73, 30 November 1907, p. 188
101 *The Athenaeum*, no. 4184, 4 January 1908, p. 6
102 Edmund Gosse, *The Life of Philip Henry Gosse* (1890), p. 276
103 Ibid., p. 63
104 Gosse, *Father and Son*, p. 66
105 Ibid., p. 172
106 Edmund Gosse, *Father and Son* (1908), p. xi

EPILOGUE

1   T. J. Carty, *A Dictionary of Literary Pseudonyms in the English Language* (1995), Preface
2   Doris Lessing, *The Diaries of Jane Somers* (1984), p. 242
3   Ibid., Preface
4   Ibid., p. 26
5   Ibid., Preface
6   Letter of 26 April 1932, in *The Collected Essays, Journalism and Letters of George Orwell*, ed. Sonia Orwell and Ian Angus, 4 vols. (1968), vol. I, *An Age Like This, 1920–1940*, pp. 77–8
7   Letter of 6 July 1932, ibid., p. 85
8   Michael Shelden, *Orwell: The Authorised Biography* (1991), p. 180
9   Letter of 19 November 1932, in Orwell and Angus, eds., *Collected Essays, Journalism and Letters*, I, p. 106
10 Peter Stansky and William Abrahams, *Orwell: The Transformation* (1979), p. 7
11 Jeffrey Meyers, ed., *George Orwell: The Critical Heritage* (1975), p. 46

12 George Orwell, *Down and Out in Paris and London* (2001), ch. 29,
    p. 160

13 Ibid., ch. 24, p. 128

14 See Anne Stevenson, *Bitter Fame. A Life of Sylvia Plath* (Boston,
    Mass., 1989), pp. 43–7

15 Sylvia Plath, *The Bell Jar* (1966), p. 257

16 Ronald Hayman, *The Death and Life of Sylvia Plath* (1991),
    pp. 2–3

17 Stevenson, *Bitter Fame*, p. 285

18 *Listener*, 31 January 1963

19 *TLS*, No. 3178, 25 January 1963

20 Plath, *The Bell Jar*, p. 126

21 Ibid., pp. 129–30

22 John Hall, *Trollope: A Biography* (Oxford, 1991), p. 288

23 Anthony Trollope, *An Autobiography*, ed. Michael Sadleir and
    Frederick Page (1980), p. 204

24 *Listener*, 30 September 1976

25 *Yorkshire Post*, 16 May 1963. The auto-review is reproduced in
    Andrew Biswell, *The Real Life of Anthony Burgess* (2005), pp.
    274–6

26 See Don Foster, *Author Unknown. On the Trail of Anonymous*
    (2001), ch. 1, for his own version of this. It is an attribution from
    which he has since retreated

27 One important example is William Langland, author of *Piers
    Plowman*. His name and all that we know of him come from the
    note made by a scribe at the end of one transcription of his
    poem. See A. V. Schmidt, introd., William Langland, *The Vision of
    Piers Plowman* (1995), pp. xx–xxi

28 Anne Ferry, 'Anonymity: The Literary History of a Word', *New
    Literary History*, 33 (2002), pp. 193–214

29 Lucien Febvre and Henri-Jean Martin, *The Coming of the Book*
    (1958; trans. 1976), p. 261

30 Roland Barthes, 'The Death of the Author', in *The Rustle of
    Language*, trans. Richard Howard (Oxford, 1986), p. 50

BIBLIOGRAPHY

Place of publication is London unless otherwise stated.

An Account of the Growth of Knavery (1678)

An Account of the Growth of Popery and Arbitrary Government in England (1677)

Adburgham, Alison, *Women in Print: Writing Women and Women's Magazines from the Restoration to the Accession of Victoria* (1972)

[Adolphus, John Leycester] *Letters to Richard Heber, Esq: containing critical remarks on the series of novels beginning with "Waverley" and an attempt to ascertain their author* (1821)

Aitken, George A., *The Life of Richard Steele*, 2 vols. (1889)

Alaya, Flavia, *William Sharp—"Fiona MacLeod" 1855–1905* (Cambridge, Mass., 1970)

Allott, Miriam, ed., *The Brontës. The Critical Heritage* (1974)

Ashton, Rosemary, *George Eliot. A Life* (1996)

Austen, Jane, *The Works of Jane Austen*, ed. R. W. Chapman (Oxford, 1954)

– *Jane Austen's Letters*, ed. Deirdre Le Faye (1995; rpt. Oxford, 1997)

Austen-Leigh, James Edward, *A Memoir of Jane Austen*, ed. R. W. Chapman (1926; rpt. Oxford, 1951)

Austen-Leigh, William, and Richard Arthur Austen-Leigh, *Jane Austen. A Family Record*, rev. Deirdre Le Faye (1989)

Backscheider, Paula R., *Daniel Defoe. His Life* (Baltimore, Md., 1989)

Barker, Juliet, *The Brontës* (1994)

Barker, Nicolas, *Stanley Morison* (1972)

Barnard, John, ed., *Pope. The Critical Heritage* (1973)

Barthes, Roland, 'The Death of the Author', in *The Rustle of Language*, trans. Richard Howard (Oxford, 1986)

Bassett, Troy J., 'T. Fisher Unwin's Pseudonym Library: Literary Marketing and Authorial Identity', *English Literature in Transition*, 47:2 (2004)

Battestin, Martin, *Henry Fielding. A Life* (1989)

Bermingham, Ann, and John Brewer, eds., *The Consumption of Culture 1600–1800. Image, Object, Text* (1995)

Biswell, Andrew, *The Real Life of Anthony Burgess* (2005)

Blackmore, R. D., *Clara Vaughan* (1872)

Blake, William, *The Marriage of Heaven and Hell*, ed. Geoffrey Keynes (Oxford, 1975)

A Book containing all such proclamations as were published during the reign of the late Queene Elizabeth (1618)

Brake, Laurel, 'Literary Criticism and the Victorian Periodicals', *Yearbook of English Studies*, 16 (1986)

Brontë, Charlotte, *The Professor*, ed. Margaret Smith and Herbert Rosengarten (Oxford, 1987)

– *Jane Eyre*, ed. Michael Mason (1996)

– *Villette*, ed. Mark Lilly (1979)

– *The Letters of Charlotte Brontë*, ed. Margaret Smith, 3 vols. (Oxford 1995–2004)

Brontë, Emily, *Wuthering Heights*, ed. Ian Jack (Oxford, 1981)

Brookfield, Charles and Frances, *Mrs Brookfield and her Circle* (1906)

Browning, Robert, *The Poems*. vol. I, ed. John Pettigrew, rev. Thomas J. Collins (1981)

Budd, Kenneth, *The Last Victorian. R. D. Blackmore and His Novels* (1960)

Bulwer Lytton, Edward, *England and the English*, 2 vols. (1833)

Burkhart, Charles, 'George Moore and *Father and Son*', *Nineteenth-Century Fiction*, 15:1 (June 1960)

Burnet, Gilbert, *Some Passages of the Life and Death of the Right Honourable John Earl of Rochester* (1680)

Burney, Frances, *Evelina*, ed. Edward A. Bloom (Oxford, 1982)

– *Memoirs of Dr. Burney*, 3 vols. (1832)

– *The Early Journals and Letters of Fanny Burney 1768–1791*, ed. Lars E. Troide and Stewart J. Cooke, 3 vols. (Oxford, 1988–94)

– *Diary & Letters of Madame D'Arblay*, ed. Charlotte Barrett, preface and notes Austin Dobson, 6 vols. (1904–5)

– *The Witlings*, ed. Peter Sabor and Geoffrey Sill (Peterborough, Ontario, 2002)

Butler, Samuel, *The Note-Books of Samuel Butler*, vol. I: 1874–1883, ed. Hans-Peter Breuer (Lanham, Md., 1984)

– *Erewhon*, ed. Peter Mudford (1981)

[Butler, Samuel,] *The Fair Haven* (1873)

Byron, George Gordon, Lord, *The Complete Poetical Works*, ed. Jerome J. McGann, 7 vols. (Oxford, 1980–93)

– *Byron's Letters and Journals*, ed. Leslie A. Marchand, 13 vols. (1973–94)

Camden, William, *Annales* (1625)

Carlson, Leland H., 'Martin Marprelate: His Identity and His Satire', in *English Satire. Papers Read at a Clark Library Seminar, January 15, 1972* (Los Angeles, 1972)

– *Martin Marprelate, Gentleman* (1981)

Carlyle, Thomas, *The Collected Letters of Thomas and Jane Welsh Carlyle*, ed. C. R. Sanders, Clyde de L. Ryals et al., 32 vols. (Durham, N.C., 1976–93)

Carroll, Lewis, *Alice's Adventures in Wonderland* and *Through the Looking-Glass*, introd. Roger Lancelyn Green (Oxford, 1971),

– *The Letters of Lewis Carroll*, ed. Morton N. Cohen, 2 vols. (1979)

Carty, T. J., *A Dictionary of Literary Pseudonyms in the English Language* (1995)

Cheyne, George, *The Letters of Doctor George Cheyne to Samuel Richardson (1733–1743)*, ed. Charles F. Mullett (Columbia, Mo., 1943)

[Churchill, Charles,] *The Times. A Poem* (1764)

Clegg, Cyndia Susan, *Press Censorship in Elizabethan England* (Cambridge, 1997)

– *Press Censorship in Jacobean England* (Cambridge, 2001)

Cobbett, William, ed., *A Complete Collection of State Trials*, 33 vols. (1809–26)

Cohen, Morton N., *Lewis Carroll. A Biography* (1995)

Coleridge, Samuel Taylor, *The Watchman*, ed. Lewis Patten (1970)

– *Biographia Literaria*, ed. James Engell and W. Jackson Bate, 2 vols. (1983)

Collins, P., ed., *Dickens. The Critical Heritage* (1971)

Collinson, Patrick, *The Elizabethan Puritan Movement* (1967)

A Compleat Key to the Dunciad (1728)

Cowper, William, *The Letters and Prose Writings of William Cowper*, ed. James King and Charles Ryskamp, 5 vols. (Oxford, 1979–86)

Cox, R. G., ed., *Thomas Hardy. The Critical Heritage* (1970)

Crabb Robinson, Henry, *Diary, Reminiscences and Correspondence of Henry Crabb Robinson*, ed. Thomas Sadler (1869)

Cranston, Maurice, *John Locke. A Biography* (1957; rpt. Oxford, 1985)

Cross, J. W., *George Eliot's Life as Related in her Letters and Journals*, 3 vols. (1885)

Crowne, John, *Dramatic Works*, ed. J. Maidment and W. H. Logan (1873)

Cummings, R. M., ed., *Spenser: The Critical Heritage* (1971)

Curll, Edmund, *A Compleat Key to the Dunciad* (1728)

Dallas, Robert, *Recollections of the Life of Lord Byron* (1824)

Daniell, David, *William Tyndale. A Biography* (New Haven, Conn., 1994)

Defoe, Daniel, *The Shortest Way with Dissenters*, in *Political and Economic Writings of Daniel Defoe*, vol. III, ed. W. R. Owens (2000)

– *Memoirs of a Cavalier*, ed. James T. Boulton, introd. John Mullan (Oxford, 1991)

– *Moll Flanders*, ed. G. A. Starr (Oxford, 1971)

– *Roxana*, ed. John Mullan (Oxford, 1996)

– *An Essay on the Regulation of the Press*, in *Political and Economic Writings of Daniel Defoe*, vol. VIII, ed. W. R. Owens (2000)

– *An Elegy on the Author of the True-born Englishman* (1704)

Delafield, E. M., ed., *The Brontës. Their Lives Recorded by Their Contemporaries*, (1935; rpt. 1979)

De Quincey, Thomas, *Confessions of an English Opium-Eater and Other Writings*, ed. Grevel Lindop (Oxford, 1985)

DeVane, William Clyde, *A Browning Handbook* (1935; rpt. New Haven, Conn., 1955)

Dickens, Charles, *The Dent Edition of Dickens' Journalism*, vol. III, ed. Michael Slater (1999)

Donne, John, *Ignatius His Conclave*, ed. T. S. Healy (Oxford, 1969)

– *Poetical Works*, ed. Herbert J.C. Grierson (1933; rpt. Oxford, 1979)

Donno, Elizabeth Story, ed., *Andrew Marvell. The Critical Heritage* (1978)

Dryden, John, *The Poems of John Dryden*, ed. Paul Hammond, vol. II (1995)

– *Selected Criticism*, ed. James Kinsley and George Parfitt (Oxford, 1970)

Dunn, John, *Locke* (Oxford, 1984)

Dunn, Waldo, *R. D. Blackmore* (1956)

Easson, Angus, ed., *Elizabeth Gaskell. The Critical Heritage* (1991)

Eaves, T. C. D. Duncan, and Ben D. Kimpel, *Samuel Richardson: A Biography* (Oxford, 1971)

Egerton, George, *Keynotes* (1893)

Ehrenpreis, Irvin, *Swift. The Man, His Works and the Age*, 3 vols. (1962, 1967, 1983)

Eliot, George, *Scenes of Clerical Life*, ed. Thomas A. Noble (Oxford, 1988)

– *The George Eliot Letters*, ed. Gordon S. Haight, 9 vols. (New Haven, Conn., 1954–5, 1978)

– *Selected Essays, Poems and Other Writings*, eds A. S. Byatt and Nicholas Warren (1990)

Eliot, T. S., *Selected Essays* (1951)

Eliza's Babes: or, The Virgins-Offering (1652)

Ellis, P. B., and S. Mac A'Ghobhainn, *The Scottish Insurrection of 1820* (1970)

Emerson, Everett H., *English Puritanism from John Hooper to John Milton* (Durham, N.C., 1968)

Etherege, George, *The Man of Mode*, ed. John Barnard (1979; rpt. 1997)

An Exact Narrative of the Tryal and Condemnation of John Twyn, for Printing and Dispersing of a Treasonable Book (1664)

Falconer, Lanoe, *Mademoiselle Ixe* (1891)

Febvre, Lucien, and Henri-Jean Martin, *The Coming of the Book* (1958; trans. 1976)

Ferry, Anne, 'Anonymity: The Literary History of a Word', *New Literary History*, 33 (2002)

Fielding, Henry, *Joseph Andrews* and *Shamela*, ed. Douglas Brooks-
    Davies and Martin C. Battestin, rev. Thomas Keymer (Oxford, 1999)
Firth, C. H., and R. S. Rait, eds, *Acts and Ordinances of the Interregnum*,
    2 vols. (1911)
Foster, Don, *Author Unknown. On the Trail of Anonymous* (2001)
Fowler, Ellen Thorneycroft, *Concerning Isabel Carnaby* (6th edn., 1898)

Garside, Peter, and James Raven, eds., *The English Novel, 1770–1829: A
    Bibliographical Survey of Prose Fiction Published in the British Isles,*
    2 vols. (Oxford, 2000)
Gaskell, Elizabeth, *The Life of Charlotte Brontë*, ed. Alan Shenston
    (1975)
– *The Letters of Mrs Gaskell*, ed. J. A. V. Chapple and Arthur Pollard
    (1966)
– *Mary Barton*, ed. Edgar Wright (Oxford, 1987)
Gilson, David, *A Bibliography of Jane Austen*, corrected edn. (1997)
Gissing, George, *New Grub Street*, ed. Bernard Bergonzi (1968)
Gosse, Edmund, *Father and Son*, ed. Michael Newton (Oxford, 2004)
– *Father and Son* (1908)
– *The Life of Philip Henry Gosse* (1890)
Graham, Walter, *English Literary Periodicals* (1930)
Gray, Thomas, *Correspondence of Thomas Gray*, ed. Paget Toynbee and
    Leonard Whibley, corr. H. W. Starr, 3 vols. (Oxford, 1971)
Greer, Germaine, *Slip-Shod Sybils. Recognition, Rejection and the
    Woman Poet* (1995)
Griffin, Robert J., ed., *The Faces of Anonymity. Anonymous and
    Pseudonymous Publication from the Sixteenth to the Nineteenth
    Century* (Basingstoke, 2003)
Grundy, Isobel, *Lady Mary Wortley Montagu. Comet of the
    Enlightenment* (Oxford, 1999)
Guerinot, J. V. *Pamphlet Attacks on Alexander Pope 1711–1744*
    (New York, 1969)
Guilpin, Everard, *Skialetheia*, ed. D. Allen Carroll (Chapel Hill, N. C.,
    1974)
Guy, John, *Tudor England* (Oxford, 1988)

Haight, Gordon S., *George Eliot. A Biography* (Oxford, 1968)

Halkett, Samuel, and John Laing, eds., *A Dictionary of the Anonymous and Pseudonymous Literature of Great Britain*, rev. James Kennedy (1926–34)

Hall, John, *Trollope: A Biography* (Oxford, 1991)

Hall, Joseph, *The Poems of Joseph Hall*, ed. Arthur Davenport (Liverpool, 1969)

Halloran, William F., 'W. B. Yeats, William Sharp, and Fiona Macleod: A Celtic Drama, 1897', in Warwick Gould, ed., *Yeats and the Nineties* (2001), pp. 159–208

Hardy, Thomas, *A Pair of Blue Eyes*, ed. Roger Ebbatson (1986)

– *The Collected Letters of Thomas Hardy*, ed. Richard Little Purdy and Michael Millgate, 7 vols. (Oxford, 1978–88)

Harington, John, *A New Discourse of a Stale Subject Called the Metamorphosis of Ajax*, ed. Elizabeth Story Donno (New York, 1962)

Harman, Claire, *Fanny Burney. A Biography* (2000)

Hayden, John O., ed., *Scott. The Critical Heritage* (1970)

Hayman, Ronald, *The Death and Life of Sylvia Plath* (1991)

Hazlitt, William, *Liber Amoris*, introd. Michael Neve (1985)

– *The Spirit of the Age*, ed. E.D. Mackerness (1969)

Hindmarsh, D. Bruce, *John Newton and the English Evangelical Tradition between the Conversions of Wesley and Wilberforce* (Oxford, 1996)

Hindus, Milton, ed., *Whitman. The Critical Heritage* (1971)

The History of Laetitia Atkins, vulgarly called Moll Flanders (1776)

The History of Mademoiselle de Beleau; or, The New Roxana (1775)

Holmes, Richard, *Shelley: The Pursuit* (1974)

Honan, Park, *Jane Austen. A Life* (1987)

Houghton, Walter E., ed., *The Wellesley Index to Victorian Periodicals 1824–1900*, vol. I (1966)

Howes, Alan B., *Yorick and the Critics. Sterne's Reputation in England, 1760–1868* (1958; rpt. Hamden, Conn., 1971)

Hudson, Gertrude Reese, *Robert Browning's Literary Life* (Austin, Tex., 1992)

Hughes, Paul L., and James F. Larkin, eds., *Tudor Royal Proclamations*, 3 vols. (New Haven, Conn., 1964–9)

Johnson, Edgar, *Sir Walter Scott: The Great Unknown*, 2 vols. (1970)

Johnson, Samuel, *The Lives of the Most Eminent English Poets*, ed. Roger Lonsdale, 4 vols. (Oxford, 2006)

Jones, Leonidas M., 'The Scott–Christie Duel', *Texas Studies in Literature and Language*, 12:4 (Winter 1972)

Jones, Stanley, *Hazlitt: A Life* (Oxford, 1989)

Jump, John, ed., *Tennyson. The Critical Heritage* (1967)

Juvenal, *The Sixteen Satires*, trans. Peter Green (1974)

Karl, Frederick, *George Eliot. A Biography* (1995)

Kelliher, Hilton, *Andrew Marvell: Poet and Politician*, Catalogue of British Library Exhibition (1978)

Keymer, Thomas, and Peter Sabor, eds., *The Pamela Controversy: Criticisms and Adaptations of Samuel Richardson's* Pamela *1740–1750*, 6 vols. (2001)

Khan, Rahila, *Down the Road, Worlds Away* (1987)

Kiernan, V. G., *The Duel in European History. Honour and the Reign of Aristocracy* (Oxford, 1988)

[Klein, Joe,] *Primary Colors* (New York, 1996)

Knapp, Lewis M., *Tobias Smollett. Doctor of Men and Manners* (1949)

Leary, Patrick, '*Fraser's Magazine* and the Literary Life, 1830–1847', *Victorian Periodicals Review*, 27:2 (Summer 1994)

Lee, Hermione, *Virginia Woolf* (1996)

Lessing, Doris, *The Diaries of Jane Somers* (1984)

A Letter from a Clergyman to his Friend, with an Account of the Travels of Capt. Lemuel Gulliver: and a Character of the Author (1726)

Lightfoot, Martin, 'Scott's Self-Review: Manuscript and Other Evidence', *Nineteenth-Century Fiction*, 23 (September 1968)

Lindop, Grevel, *The Opium-Eater. A Life of Thomas De Quincey* (1981)

Loades, D. M., 'The Theory and Practice of Censorship in Sixteenth-Century England', *Transactions of the Royal Historical Society*, 24, Series 5 (1974)

Locke, John, *Two Treatises of Government*, ed. Peter Laslett (1960; rpt. Cambridge, 1989)

– *Two Tracts on Government*, ed. and trans. Philip Abrams (Cambridge, 1967)

– *Epistola de Tolerantia*, ed. Raymond Klibansky (Oxford, 1968)

- *A Letter concerning Toleration in Focus*, ed. John Horton and Susan Mendus (1991)
- *The Reasonableness of Christianity as delivered in the Scriptures*, ed. John C. Higgins-Biddle (Oxford, 1999)
- *The Correspondence of John Locke*, ed. E. S. de Beer, 8 vols. (Oxford, 1976–89)

Lockhart, J. G., *Memoirs of the Life of Sir Walter Scott, Bart.*, 7 vols. (Edinburgh, 1837)

Lonsdale, Roger, ed., *Eighteenth-Century Women Poets. An Oxford Anthology* (Oxford, 1989)
- ed., *The Poems of Thomas Gray, William Collins, and Oliver Goldsmith* (1969)
- *Dr Charles Burney* (Oxford, 1965)

Lord, George de F., ed., *Poems on Affairs of State. Augustan Satirical Verse, 1660–1714*, vol. I (New Haven, Conn., 1963)

Love, Harold, *Scribal Publication in Seventeenth-Century England* (Oxford, 1993)
- *English Clandestine Satire 1660–1702* (Oxford, 2004)

McCabe, Richard, 'Elizabethan Satire and the Bishops' Ban of 1599', *Yearbook of English Studies*, 11 (1981)

McGinn, Donald J., *John Penry and the Marprelate Controversy* (New Brunswick, N.J., 1966)

McKenzie, D.F., and Maureen Bell, eds., *A Chronology and Calendar of Documents Relating to the London Book Trade 1641–1700*, 3 vols. (Oxford, 2005)

Mack, Robert L., *Thomas Gray. A Life* (New Haven, Conn., 2000)

MacLeod, Fiona, *Pharais* (Edinburgh, 1894)
- *From the Hills of Dream* (Edinburgh, [1897])
- *Wind and Wave. Selected Tales* (Leipzig, 1902)

McRae, Andrew, *Literature, Satire and the Early Stuart State* (Cambridge, 2004)

[Manley, Delarivière,] *Secret Memoirs and Manners of several Persons of Quality, of both Sexes* (1709)

Manley, Delarivière, *The Adventures of Rivella*, ed. Katherine Zelinsky (Peterborough, Ontario, 1999)

Manley, K. A., 'Dodgson v Carroll', *TLS*, 28 June 1974

Mann, Alastair J., *The Scottish Book Trade 1500–1720* (East Linton, 2000)

Marchand, Leslie A., *Byron: A Biography*, 3 vols. (1957)

– *The Athenaeum. A Mirror of Victorian Culture* (1941)

The Marprelate Tracts [*1588–1589*]. A Scolar Press Facsimile (Menston, 1967)

Marston, John, *The Poems of John Marston*, ed. Arnold Davenport (Liverpool, 1961)

– *The Dutch Courtesan*, ed. David Crane (1997)

Martin, Robert Bernard, *Tennyson. The Unquiet Heart* (1980)

Martineau, Harriet, *Autobiography*, ed. Maria Weston Chapman, 3 vols. (1877)

Marvell, Andrew, *The Poems and Letters of Andrew Marvell*, ed. H. M. Margoliouth, rev. Pierre Legouis and E. E. Duncan-Jones (Oxford, 1971)

– *The Rehearsal Transpros'd* and *The Rehearsal Transpros'd. The Second Part*, ed. D. I. B. Smith (Oxford, 1971)

Mason, Eudo, *The Mind of Henry Fuseli* (1951)

Maurer, Oscar, 'Anonymity vs. Signature in Victorian Reviewing', *Texas University Studies in English*, 28: 1 (June 1948)

May, Derwent, *Critical Times. The History of the Times Literary Supplement* (2001)

The Metamorphosis of Pigmalions Image and Certaine Satyres (1598)

Mengel, Elias F. Jr., *Poems on Affairs of State*, vol. II

Meyers, Jeffrey, ed., *George Orwell: The Critical Heritage* (1975)

Miller, H. K., et al, ed., *The Augustan Milieu* (Oxford, 1970)

Milton, John, *Areopagitica*, in *The Complete Prose Works of John Milton*, vol. II (1643–1648), ed. Ernest Sirluck (New Haven, Conn., 1959)

Monsarrat, Ann, *An Uneasy Victorian. Thackeray the Man* (1980)

Montagu, Lady Mary Wortley, *Essays and Poems and Simplicity, a Comedy*, ed. Robert Halsband and Isobel Grundy (Oxford, 1993)

– *The Complete Letters of Lady Mary Wortley Montagu*, ed. Robert Halsband, 3 vols. (Oxford, 1965–7)

Moore, Thomas, *Memoirs, Journal and Correspondence of Thomas Moore*, ed. Lord John Russell, 8 vols (1853–4)

Newton, John, *Letters, Sermons, and a Review of Ecclesiastical History* (Edinburgh, 1780)

[Newton, John,] *An Authentic Narrative of some Remarkable and Interesting Particulars in the Life of* ******** (1764)

Nokes, David, *Jonathan Swift, A Hypocrite Reversed* (Oxford, 1985)

– *Jane Austen: A Life* (1997)

Novak, Maximilian, *Daniel Defoe. Master of Fictions* (Oxford, 2001)

Oldham, John, *The Poems of John Oldham*, ed. Harold F. Brooks and Raman Selden (Oxford, 1987)

Orel, Harold, ed., *The Brontës. Interviews and Recollections* (1997)

Orwell, George, *The Collected Essays, Journalism and Letters of George Orwell*, ed. Sonia Orwell and Ian Angus, 4 vols. (1968)

– *Down and Out in Paris and London* (2001)

Osborn, James M., *John Dryden: Some Biographical Facts and Problems* (1965)

Patterson, Annabel, *Marvell: The Writer in Public Life* (2000)

Peacock, Thomas Love, *The Novels of Thomas Love Peacock*, ed. David Garnett (1948)

Pepys, Samuel, *The Diary of Samuel Pepys*, ed. Robert Latham and William Matthews, 11 vols. (1970–83)

Pierce, William, *An Historical Introduction to the Marprelate Tracts* (1908)

Plath, Sylvia, *The Bell Jar* (1966)

Plomer, Henry R., *A Dictionary of the Booksellers and Printers Who Were at Work in England from 1641 to 1667* (1907)

Pope, Alexander, *The Dunciad in Four Books*, ed. Valerie Rumbold (1999)

– *The Dunciad*, ed. James Sutherland (1953)

– *The Rape of the Lock and Other Poems*, ed. Geoffrey Tillotson (1940)

– *The Poems of Alexander Pope*, ed. John Butt (1963; rpt. 1977)

– *The Correspondence of Alexander Pope*, ed. George Sherburn, 5 vols. (1956)

[Pope, Alexander,] *The Dunciad. An Heroic Poem* (1728)

Pottle, Frederick A., *James Boswell. The Earlier Years 1740–1769*
    (1966)
Puttenham, George, *The Arte of English Poesie*, ed. G.D. Willcock and
    A. Walker (Cambridge, 1936)
[Puttenham, George,] *The Arte of English Poesie* (1589)

Raby, Peter, *Samuel Butler. A Biography* (1991)
Raven, James, *British Fiction, 1750–1770, A Chronological Checklist*
    (Newark, N.J., 1987)
Ray, Gordon N., *Thackeray. The Age of Wisdom 1847–1863* (1958)
Redpath, Theodore, ed., *The Young Romantics and Critical Opinion
    1807–1824* (1973)
Reiman, Donald, ed., *The Romantics Reviewed*, 9 vols. (New York, 1972)
Richardson, Samuel, *Clarissa*, ed. Angus Ross (1985)
– *Pamela*, ed. Thomas Keymer and Alice Wakely (Oxford, 2001)
Richetti, John, *The Life of Daniel Defoe* (Oxford, 2005)
Ritchie, Anne Thackeray, *Chapters from Some Memoirs* (1894)
Rivers, Isobel, ed., *Books and their Readers in Eighteenth-Century
    England* (Leicester, 1982)
Rochester, John Wilmot, Earl of, *The Complete Poems of John Wilmot,
    Earl of Rochester*, ed. David M. Vieth (New Haven, Conn., 1968)
Rogers, Pat, 'Nameless Names: Pope, Curll, and the Uses of
    Anonymity', *New Literary History*, 33:2 (Spring 2002), pp. 233–45
Rooksby, R., *A. C. Swinburne: A Poet's Life* (1997)
Roper, Derek, *Reviewing before the Edinburgh 1788–1802* (1978)
Rose, Mark, *Authors and Owners. The Invention of Copyright*
    (Cambridge, Mass., 1993)

St Clair, William, *The Reading Nation in the Romantic Period*
    (Cambridge, 2004)
Saslow, Edward L., 'The Rose Alley Ambuscade', *Restoration*, 26:1
    (Spring 2002)
Saunders, J. W., 'The Stigma of Print. A Note on the Social Bases of
    Tudor Poetry', *Essays in Criticism*, 1 (1951), pp. 139–64
Schneider, Elisabeth W., 'Tom Moore and the *Edinburgh* Review of
    Christabel', *PMLA*, 77 (1962), pp. 71–6
Scott, Thomas, *The Force of Truth: an Authentic Narrative* (1779)

Scott, Walter, *Chronicles of the Canongate*, ed. Claire Lamont, (Edinburgh, 2000)
– *The Fortunes of Nigel*, ed. Frank Jordan (Edinburgh, 2004)
– *The Heart of Midlothian*, ed. Tony Inglis (1994)
– *The Letters of Sir Walter Scott*, ed. H. Grierson, 12 vols. (1932–7)
– 'Memoirs of Jonathan Swift D.D.', in *The Works of Jonathan Swift*, vol. I (Edinburgh, 1814)
– *Waverley*, ed. Claire Lamont (Oxford, 1986)
Shannon, E. F., *Tennyson and the Reviewers* (Cambridge, Mass., 1952)
Sharp, Elizabeth, *William Sharp (Fiona MacLeod): A Memoir*, 2 vols. (1910; rpt. 1912)
Shelden, Michael, *Orwell: The Authorised Biography* (1991)
Shelley, Mary, *The Novels and Selected Works of Mary Shelley*, vol. II (1996), ed. Pamela Clemit
– *The Letters of Mary Wollstonecraft Shelley*, ed. Betty T. Bennett, 3 vols. (Baltimore, Md., 1983–8)
Shelley, P. B., *The Letters of Percy Bysshe Shelley*, ed. Frederick L. Jones, 2 vols. (1964)
– *Poetical Works*, ed. Thomas Hutchinson, rev. G.M. Matthews (Oxford, 1970)
Sheridan, Richard Brinsley, *The School for Scandal and Other Plays*, ed. Michael Cordner (Oxford, 1998)
The Shortest Way with Dissenters . . . Consider'd (1703)
Siebert, F. S., *Freedom of the Press in England 1476–1776* (Urbana, Ill., 1965)
Simpson, Evelyn, *A Study of the Prose Works of John Donne* (Oxford, 1948)
Sisman, Adam, *Boswell's Presumptuous Task* (2000)
Smith, George, *A Memoir* (1902)
Southam, B. C., ed., *Jane Austen. The Critical Heritage* (1968)
Spence, Joseph, *Anecdotes, Observations and Characters of Books and Men, Collected from the Conversation of Mr. Pope* (1820)
Spenser, Edmund, *The Yale Edition of the Shorter Poems of Edmund Spenser*, ed. William A. Oram et al. (New Haven, Conn., 1989)
Stansky, Peter, and William Abrahams, *Orwell: The Transformation* (1979)

Steinmetz, Andrew, *The Romance of Duelling in All Times and Countries*, 2 vols. (1868)

Stephen, Leslie, *English Men of Letters: Alexander Pope* (1880)

Stevenson, Anne, *Bitter Fame. A Life of Sylvia Plath* (Boston, Mass., 1989)

Sutherland, John, *The Longman Companion to Victorian Fiction* (1988)

– *The Life of Walter Scott: A Critical Biography* (Oxford, 1995)

Sutherland, Kathryn, ed., J. E. Austen-Leigh, *A Memoir of Jane Austen and Other Family Recollections* (Oxford, 2002)

Swift, Jonathan, *The Prose Works of Jonathan Swift*, ed. Herbert David et al., 14 vols. (Oxford, 1939–68)

– *The Correspondence of Jonathan Swift*, ed. Harold Williams, 5 vols. (Oxford, 1963–5)

– *Journal to Stella*, ed. Harold Williams, 2 vols. (1948; rpt. Oxford, 1986)

– *The Complete Poems*, ed. Pat Rogers (1983)

– *The Drapier's Letters*, ed. Herbert Davis (1935; rpt. Oxford, 1965)

– *Gulliver's Travels*, ed. Robert DeMaria (2001)

Taylor, D. J., *Thackeray* (1999)

Tener, Robert H., 'Breaking the Code of Anonymity: The Case of the *Spectator, 1861–1897*', *Yearbook of English Studies*, 16 (1986)

Tennyson, Alfred Lord, *Tennyson. A Selected Edition*, ed. Christopher Ricks (1989)

– *The Letters of Alfred Lord Tennyson*, ed. Cecil Y. Lang and Edgar F. Shannon, 3 vols. (Oxford, 1982–90)

Tennyson, Hallam, *Alfred Lord Tennyson: A Memoir*, 2 vols. (1897)

Thackeray, William Makepeace, *Pendennis*, ed. John Sutherland (1994)

– *Catherine: A Story*, ed. Sheldon F. Goldfarb (Ann Arbor, Mich., 1999)

– *The Letters and Private Papers of William Makepeace Thackeray*, ed. Gordon N. Ray, 4 vols. (1945)

Thwaite, Ann, *Edmund Gosse: A Literary Landscape 1849–1928* (1984)

Timperley, C. H., *Encyclopædia of Literary and Typographical Anecdote*, first published 1839, 2nd edn. (1842)

Treglown, 'Bateson and the *TLS*', *Essays in Criticism*, 51:1 (January 2001)

Trollope, Anthony, *The Claverings*, ed. David Skilton (Oxford, 1986)
– *The Way We Live Now*, ed. John Sutherland (1982)
– *An Autobiography*, ed. Michael Sadleir and Frederick Page (1980)
– 'On Anonymous Literature', *Fortnightly Review*, 1 (July 1865)
Turner, Katherine, ed., *Selected Poems of Gray, Churchill and Cowper* (1997)

Uglow, Jenny, *Elizabeth Gaskell* (1993)
Unwin, Philip, *The Publishing Unwins* (1972)

Vann, J. Don, 'Unrecorded Reviews of Thackeray's *Paris Sketch-Book*', *Papers of the Bibliographical Society of America*, 71:3 (1977)
Vieth, David M., *Attribution in Restoration Poetry. A Study of Rochester's Poems of 1680* (New Haven, Conn., 1963)

The Whipping of the Satyre, ed. Arthur Davenport (Liverpool, 1951)
Whitehead, Barbara, *Charlotte Brontë and her 'Dearest Nell'* (1993)
Wilson, J. Dover, 'The Marprelate Controversy', in *The Cambridge History of English Literature*, vol. III, ed. A.W. Ward and A.R. Waller (Cambridge, 1909)
Woolf, Virginia, *The Diary of Virginia Woolf*, ed. Anne Oliver and Andrew McNeillie, 5 vols. (1977–84)
– *The Letters of Virginia Woolf*, ed. Nigel Nicolson, 6 vols. (1975–80)

Yeats, W. B., *Uncollected Prose by W.B. Yeats*, vol. II, ed. John P. Frayne and Colton Johnson (1975)

INDEX

Abbotsford, near Melrose 24, 25, 26
Abbott, Chief Justice 179
Abinger, Lord 180
Academy, The 282–3
Act of Union of England and Scotland
      (1907) 168
Adelphi 291
Admonition to the Parliament
      (anonymous pamphlet) 145
Adolphus, John Leycester 20
   meets Scott 24–5
   sets out to identify author of
      'Waverley novels' 20, 22–4
   Letters to Richard Heber, Esq.:
      containing critical remarks on the
      series of novels beginning with
      "Waverley" and an attempt to
      ascertain their author 22–4
Ainsworth, Harrison 249
Albermarle, Duchess of 155
Albermarle, George Monck, Duke of 155
Albert, Prince Consort 279
All the Year Round 207
Allen, Grant 132–3
Ambrose's Tavern, Edinburgh 191
Anders (a clergyman) 107
Anderton, William 142
Anglesey, Earl of 156
Anglicanism 246
Anne, Queen 168
anonymity
   absence of the author's name as a
      decisive omission 296
   acknowledges author's humble status
      47, 48
   authorial 'motive' 4
   author's willingness to lie when
      identified 29, 35, 36–7, 56
   common in novel-writing 36, 57
   concealment of the author's
      handwriting 25, 29, 39–40, 42
   and dedications to patrons 47–8
   defensiveness about 'identifications'
      74–5
   Defoe argues against it 166–7
   Defoe's *Moll Flanders* and *Roxana*
      presented as anonymous
      memoirs by women 118–19
   Dodgson's horror of being known by
      sight 42, 43–4
   gives the satirist opportunity to act
      the devil 225
   Henry VIII's proclamation (1546)
      143
   initial deception of publishers and
      family members 29
   intending to declare him/herself after
      an anonymous career start 286–7
   makes trouble 239
   male novelists pretending to be
      female (18th century) 126–8
   Marprelate tracts (1588–9) 146–50
   medieval literature 296
   much less common in twentieth
      century 286
   natural relationship between
      confession and anonymity 273
   permits devilish amusement 236–7
   prevailing anonymity of lampoons
      154
   Richardson's *Pamela* as an
      anonymous book written in a
      female voice 123
   seen as a special threat 143
   seen by Fanny Burney as an enjoyable
      game 63

365

sinful author's means of holding
    himself in check 255
sometimes outlawed 143
Tennyson's motivation for *In
    Memoriam*'s anonymity 279
used to provoke speculation about
    authorship 20, 30, 36, 55, 286
writers able to arrange promotion of
    their work 183–4
Anti-Corn Law Circular 198
Antijacobin Review 239
Apostles 200
Arbuthnot, John 10, 11, 13, 233
'Ardelia' *see* Finch, Anne, Countess of
    Winchelsea
Athenaeum magazine 79, 82, 84, 93, 129,
    130, 198, 204, 210, 212, 250, 275,
    283
Atlas 93
attribution
    Adolphus's urge for 22, 24
    of Austen's novels 68–9, 71
    of *Evelina* 63, 64
    Halkett and Laing's dictionary 3
    modern attribution of literary works
        295–6
    of 'Ode on a Distant Prospect of Eton
        College' 55–6
    rapid attribution of *Pamela* to
        Richardson 128
    readers' attempts to attribute
        Gulliver's Travels 10–11
    in satires 221
    scribal publications 225
    of *Waverley* 21, 36
Aubrey, John 156, 228
*Aurulia: or the victim of sensibility. A
    novel, by a young lady* 57
Austen, Anna 65
Austen, Caroline 72, 73
Austen, Cassandra 65, 67, 69, 74
Austen, Frank 69
Austen, Reverend George 66
Austen, Henry 66, 68, 70, 71
Austen, James 67
Austen, Jane
    becomes reconciled to discovery 69,
        70

family involvement in her literary
    career 70
meets her publisher 71
novels finally attributed to her in
    print 69
'personal obscurity' 73–4
protective role of anonymity 74
success of the novels 68, 69
tests out unsuspecting acquaintances
    with her fiction 65
use of 'A Lady' pseudonym 50, 57, 67,
    68
her writing desk 72–3
'Elinor and Marianne' 67
Emma 71, 72
'First Impressions' 66, 68
Mansfield Park 69, 70–71, 72
Northanger Abbey 67, 71
Persuasion 71, 72
Pride and Prejudice 2, 65, 66, 68–9, 70
Sense and Sensibility 50, 57, 67–8, 70
'Susan' 66–7
Austen, Mary 68
Austen-Leigh, James Edward 72, 73–4
authors
    author as a short cut to interpretation
        297
    computer analysis of writing styles
        34–5
    exiled authors of suppressed Catholic
        texts 144
    importance of 297
    medieval scribes and 296
    modern promotion of 30
    printers executed when authors
        untraceable 138–42
Aylmer, John, Bishop of London 146, 147
Aytoun, William 199

Bacon, Sir Francis 146
Baillie, Joanna 187
Ballantyne, James 26, 38, 39
Ballantyne, John 25, 26
Bancroft, Richard, Bishop of London 218
Barber, John 168
Barber, Mrs Mary 124
Baretti, Giuseppe 62
Barker, Juliet 91, 93

Barnes, Julian ('Dan Kavanagh') 287
Barthes, Roland: 'The Death of the
    Author' 296–7
Bateson, F. W. 215
Bathurst, Lord 167, 168
BBC Radio 115
BBC2 295
Beaufort, Duke of 232
Behn, Aphra 51
'Belinda': 'To the Author of Pamela' 53
Bell, Currer, Ellis and Acton *see* Brontë
Bell, Vanessa 213
Bellamy, Edward 166
Beowulf 296
Berkeley, Craven 179
Berkeley, Grantley 179–80
    Berkeley Castle 179
Bewley, William 185, 186
Bion: 'The Lamentation for Adonis' 228
Birstall, near Dewsbury, Yorkshire 90
Blackmore, R. D. 287
    Clara Vaughan 129
Blackwood, John 38–9, 101–4, 106, 107
Blackwood, William 107, 179, 191, 195, 198
Blackwood's Edinburgh Magazine
    ('Maga'; later *Blackwood's
    Magazine*) 102, 178, 179, 190, 192,
    194, 195, 199, 204, 242, 261, 271–2
    'Noctes Ambrosianae' series 191, 247,
    263
Blair, Eric *see* Orwell, George
Blake, William 216, 237
    The Marriage of Heaven and Hell 237
Blakemore, Edith 45
'bluestockings' 58
Bodleian Library, Oxford 42, 164
Bolingbroke, Henry St John, Viscount
    10, 12
Book of Common Prayer 146
Book Programme, The (BBC2) 295
Boringdon, Lady, of Saltram 69
Boswell, Alexander 174–5
Boswell, James 174
    *Letters between the Hon. Andrew
    Erskine and James Boswell* 184
Boyle, Robert 159
Bradbrook, M. C. 215–16
Bradford, Yorkshire 97

Bradford Observer 97
Brake, Laurel 198
Bray, Charles 201–2
Brewster, Thomas 141
Bridges, John, Dean of Salisbury 147
Bright, Mary Chavelita (née Dunne) *see*
    Egerton, George
British Critic 68
British Library, London 114
British Museum, London 3, 73
Brontë, Anne
    as Acton Bell 78–80, 87
    visits Smith, Elder & Co. 88
    Agnes Grey 87, 88
    Poems (with Charlotte and Emily) 78,
        79
    The Tenant of Wildfell Hall 88
Brontë, Branwell 79
Brontë, Charlotte 108
    celebrity in London 74
    creates new possibilities for women
        writers 111
    as Currer Bell 76, 78–82, 86, 88, 89, 90,
        92–101, 115, 117, 130, 287
    experiences as a teacher in Brussels
        99
    identity announced in *Bradford
        Observer* 97
    stays with George Smith in London
        92–4, 97
    use of a pseudonym gives her
        freedom 98–9, 113
    visits Smith, Elder & Co. 88
    visits Thackeray 97–8
    'Biographical Notice of Ellis and
        Acton Bell' 99
    Jane Eyre 74
        accepted by Smith, Elder & Co.
            80–81
        author's eagerness for reviews 82–3
        author's removal of herself from
            the novel 99–100
        'An Autobiography' subtitle 81–2
        Charlotte declines to confess her
            authorship 90–95
        dedication of second edition to
            Thackeray 88–9
        Jane the narrator 84–6

and Newby's unscrupulous
    behaviour 88
  publication of 78
  speculation about authorship of 76,
    81, 82–4, 86–7, 89, 91, 94–8, 105,
    106, 117
  success of 81, 82, 84, 87, 99
  Poems (with Emily and Anne) 78,
    79
  The Professor 80
  Shirley 90, 92, 94, 96–7, 99, 100
  Villette 80, 99–100
  'A Word to the "Quarterly"' 90
Brontë, Emily
  as Ellis Bell 78–80, 87, 88, 92
  Poems (with Charlotte and Anne) 78,
    79
  Wuthering Heights 78, 87, 88
Brontë, Reverend Patrick 79, 97
Brooke, Richard: *New and Accurate
    System of Natural History* 184
Brookfield, William 83
Brougham, Henry 189
Brown, Martha 97
Browning, Robert
  Dramatic Lyrics 274
  Pauline: A Fragment of a Confession
    195, 273–4
Brunton, Mary
  Discipline 72
  Self-Control 72
Brussels 99
Buckhurst, Lord 228
Buckingham, James Silk: *Autobiography*
    201
Bulwer (later Bulwer Lytton), Edward
    196, 248
  The Coming Race 251
  England and the English 195–6
Bunyan, John 11
Burgess, Anthony 293, 294, 295
  A Clockwork Orange 294
  Inside Mr. Enderby 294
  Malayan Trilogy 294
  One Hand Clapping 294
Burghley, Lord 47, 48, 149–50
Burnet, Gilbert 226–7
Burney, Charles 38, 59, 60

Burney, Dr Charles 58–9, 63, 184–6
  Account of the Commemoration 186
  *A General History of Music from the
    Earliest Ages to the Present Period*
    39, 185–6
  German Tour 185
  Italian Tour 185
Burney, Charlotte 58
Burney, Edward 60
Burney, Fanny 184, 185
  *Evelina; Or, A Young Lady's Entrance
    into the World*
    defensiveness about
      'identifications' 74–5
    Dr Burney's acknowledgement of
      58–9
    Fanny disguises her handwriting 39
    Fanny enjoys collecting
      unsuspecting readers' comments
      63–4
    Fanny's efforts to keep her identity
      hidden 38, 59–60
    George III intrigued by the secrecy
      surrounding it 61–2
    its author revealed in a satirical
      pamphlet 65
    and Reverend Austen 66
    snobbery in 62–3
    success of 60, 62, 65
    written in the letters of the heroine
      61
  The Witlings 64
Burney, Richard 63
Burney, Susanna 58, 64, 185
Burton, Robert 223
Butler, Samuel 250–53, 287
  Erewhon 251, 253
  *The Evidence for the Resurrection of
    Jesus Christ as given by the Four
    Evangelists critically examined*
    251
  The Fair Haven 251–3
  Note-Books 253
  The Way of All Flesh 280
Byron, Ada, Lady Lovelace 177
Byron, George Gordon, Lord 68, 176–8,
    189, 237–43, 244
  Beppo 240–42

Childe Harold 189, 239–40, 245
Don Juan 176–7, 240, 242
English Bards and Scotch Reviewers
     177, 178, 237–9, 240
Hours of Idleness 178, 189
The Vision of Judgment 242–3
Byron, Lady 176

Cabinet, or Monthly Report of Polite
     Literature 238
Cadell, Thomas 66
Calvert, Elizabeth 140
Calvert, Giles 140
Cambridge, George 65
Cambridge University 200
Cambridge University Library 60
Camden, William: *Annales* 145
Carlyle, Jane 199
Carlyle, John 193
Carlyle, Thomas 193–4
Caroline, Queen 244
Carroll, Lewis *see* Dodgson, Charles
Cartagena, West Indies 174
Carter, Elizabeth 52
Carter, William 141
Carteret, Lord 169–70, 171–2
Cash, Mrs John 202
Catholic texts 144
CBS News 36
Cecil, Sir Robert 218
Chaldee MS 247
Chalk Farm, London 177, 178
Champion, The 242
Chandos, Duke of 18
Chapman, Edward 76
Chapman, John 101–2, 105–6
Charles Edward Stuart, Prince ('Bonny
     Prince Charlie') 28
Charles I, King 138, 141
Charles II, King 138, 152, 153, 154, 156, 157,
     161, 230
Charlotte, Princess 68
Charlotte, Queen 71
Chatterton, Thomas: Rowley poems 116
Chawton, Hampshire 72, 73, 74
Cheltenham, Gloucestershire 68
Cheyne, George 123
Chomet, Serweryn 216

Chorley, Henry 198–9
Christ Church, Oxford 42, 43, 223
Christian Remembrancer 86, 200
Christie, John 178–9
Church of England 102, 145, 146
Church of England Journal 82
Churchill, Awnsham (Locke's publisher)
     161
Churchill, Charles 236
     The Times 235–6
circulating libraries 57, 65, 91, 120–21, 127
Clairmont, Claire 264
Clarke, Edward 160
Clarke, Hewson 178
Cleland, John: *Memoirs of a Woman of*
     Pleasure ('Fanny Hill') 126
Cleland, William 235
Clinton, Bill 30, 31, 32
Clinton, Hillary 31
Cloth Fair, near Smithfield, London 139
CNN 32
Cockburn, Henry 188
'Cockney school' 190, 273
Colburn, Henry 198
Coleridge, John Taylor 190
Coleridge, Samuel Taylor 186–8, 189, 193,
     238, 246
     Biographia Literaria 186–7, 191
     'Christabel' 189
     Lyrical Ballads (with Wordsworth)
          187–8, 238
     Zapolya 187
College, Stephen: *A Raree Show* (attrib.)
     154
Collins, Wilkie 287
Colman, George 186
Combe, George 201
Committee for Printing, parliamentary
     152
Commonwealth 157
confessions
     alcoholic 258–9
     Browning's first published work 274
     Cowper's spiritual biography 257–8
     De Quincey's confession of taking
          opium 258, 259–65
     Gosse's *Father and Son* 280–85
     Hazlitt's *Liber Amoris* 265–73

natural relationship between
    confession and anonymity 273
Newton's spiritual autobiography
    254–7
Shelley's autobiographical poems
    263–5
Conrad, Joseph: *Almayer's Folly* 109
Constable, Archibald 21, 29
Constitutional Association 243
Contemporary Review 207
Cooper, Bishop, of Winchester 148
Cornbury, Lord 53
Cotton, Dr Nathaniel 258
Cottrell, Sir Charles 51
Courier, The 187
Coussmaker, Miss (admirer of *Evelina*)
    60, 61
Covenanters 153
Cowper, William 257–8
    Olney Hymns (with John Newton)
    257
Craftsman 173
Craigie, Pearl Mary-Teresa *see* Hobbes,
    John Oliver
Crisp, Samuel 61, 63, 185
Critic 79, 204
Critical Review 68, 174, 182, 183, 184, 186,
    239
Croker, J. W. 190
Cromwell, Oliver 140, 156, 157
Croome, George 166
Crosby, Ben 238
Crosby & Co. 67
Cross, John Walter 101, 103
Crowne, John 226
Cumberland, Richard 188
Cumming, Dr John 202
Cuomo, Mario 31
Curll, Edmund 53–4
    Compleat Key to the Dunciad 234
    Court Poems (pub.) 54

Daily Chronicle 136
Daily News 96
Daily Telegraph 209, 295
Dallas, E. S. 206
Dallas, Robert 238
Dalyell, John Graham 247

Davies, Eliza Rhyl (pseud. of William C.
    Russell)
    A Dark Secret 130
    The Mystery of Ashleigh Manor 130
De Quincey, Thomas 272
    Confessions of an English Opium Eater
    258, 259–65
    Selections Grave and Gay 261
    Suspiria de Profundis 261
de Vere, Aubrey 275
Declaration of Indulgence for Catholics
    and Dissenters 156
dedications 47–8, 88–9, 232, 264
Defoe, Daniel
    appearance 166
    argues against anonymity 166–7
    bowdlerized versions of his work
        name him 119–20
    charged with libel and imprisoned
        166
    goes into hiding 165
    handwritings 166
    literary style 121–2
    rescued from prison by Robert Harley
        166
    reward for his apprehension 166
    and secret histories 232–3
    threatened with murder 167
    Essay on the Regulation of the Press
        166–7
    A Journal of the Plague Year 121
    Memoirs of a Cavalier 121
    Moll Flanders 118–19, 121, 122
    Robinson Crusoe 4, 121
    Roxana 118–22
    The Secret History of the Secret History
        232–3
    The Secret History of the White Staff
        232, 233
    The Shortest Way with the Dissenters
        165–6
Delesert's English Library, Florence
    190
Denham, Henry 156
Dennis, John 167
devilry
    anonymity gives the satirist
        opportunity to act the devil 225

anonymity permits devilish amusement 236–7
Byron's diabolical contrariness 237
diabolical purpose of the satirist to exciting curiosity 222
Donne's diabolical vision in *Ignatius His Conclave* 223–4
and inside knowledge 231
Oldham creates devilish characters and voices 228
Oldham's most substantial satanic satire 229–30
Rochester 225, 226
Southey on the 'Satanic school' 242–3
Dickens, Charles
and increasing frequency of 'signed' contributions to journals 207
public performances of highlights from his fiction 287
rewards a favourable review 206
victim of a reviewer's partiality 206
Little Dorrit 206
Oliver Twist 249
Our Mutual Friend 206
Dickinson, Violet 213
Dilke, Sir Charles Wentworth 84, 204
Dodgson, Charles
conceals his handwriting 40
concerned with privacy rather than concealment 41–3
eagerness for reviews 82
horror of being known by sight 42, 43–4
passion for photography 43
his pseudonym 40, 41, 42, 44–5, 46
reasons for his 'shyness' 45–6
Alice books 42
Alice's Adventures in Wonderland 46
Euclid and His Modern Rivals 45
Symbolic Logic 45
Through the Looking-Glass 42, 46
Dodsley, Robert: *A Collection of Poems* 56
Donne, John 220, 222–5
Ignatius His Conclave 222–4
Pseudo-Martyr 223
'To Mr. E. G.' 220

Dorset, Mrs Catherine: *The Peacock at Home* 68
Dryden, John 153, 154, 238
'Discourse concerning the Original and Progress of Satire' 231
Du Plessis Mornay, Philippe: *Discourse de la vie et de la mort* 51
Dublin University Magazine 79–80
Duckworth, Robinson 46
duels, literary 177–9
Dusautoy family 74

East India Company 245
'Ebony' *see* Blackwood, William
Eclectic Review 242
Economist, The 82, 181
Edgeworth, Maria 77
Edinburgh 20–21, 27, 28, 179
Whig literati 191
Edinburgh Review 21, 96, 177, 187, 188, 189, 194, 199, 200, 206, 210, 238, 241, 242, 295
Edward VI, King 143
Egerton, George (Mary Chavelita Bright)
Keynotes 110–111
'A Cross Line' 111
'An Empty Frame' 111
'A Little Grey Glove' 111
Egerton, Thomas 67, 68, 71
Ehrenpreis, Irvin 14
'E.K.' (commentator on Spenser) 48, 49
'Elia' *see* Lamb, Charles
Eliot, George (Mary Anne Evans) 287
anonymous editing of *Westminster Review* 102, 203
choice of pseudonym 103
cohabits with George Henry Lewes 101, 102, 103
communicates indirectly with her publisher 38–9
creates new possibilities for women writers 111
a free-thinker and religious sceptic 104
marries John Walter Cross 101
problem of her 'true' name 101

her pseudonym becomes her name 108
and reviewing 200–205
speculation about her true identity 104–7
translations 101, 102
use of a pseudonym gives her freedom 113
uses her incognito against Blackwood 103–4
Adam Bede 39, 105–6, 107
Middlemarch 108
The Mill on the Floss 107
'The Sad Fortunes of the Rev. Amos Barton' 102, 104–5
Scenes of Clerical Life 102–5, 107, 203
'Silly Novels by Lady Novelists' 203–4
Eliot, T. S. 215, 277
Poems 212
Elizabeth I, Queen 51, 144–6, 149, 150, 217
English College, Douai 141
'Ephelia': *Female Poems on Several Occasions* 52
Epps, Dr. 95–6
Erskine, Andrew 184
Erskine, William 26, 37, 192
Espinasse, Francis ('Herodotus Smith') 204
Essay in Defence of the Female Sex, An... Written by a Lady 51
Essays in Criticism 215, 216
Essex, Earl of 162
Etherege, George: *The Man of Mode* 225–6
'Ettrick Shepherd, The' *see* Hogg, James
European Magazine 262
Evans, Harold 32, 38
Evans, Isaac 103
Evans, Mary Anne *see* Eliot, George
Examiner, The 10, 77, 82, 93, 194, 198, 270, 275

Faber and Faber 290, 294
Fairfield, Cecily *see* 'West, Rebecca'
Falconer, Lanoe (Mary Hawker): *Mademoiselle Ixe* 109–110
Farrell, James 291
Faulkner, George 172

female pseudonyms
celebrated case of William Sharp 131–7
female Asian name used by a white male vicar 114–18
odd examples of male Victorian writers adopting female pseudonyms 129–30
preponderance of male pseudonyms over female 128
R. D. Blackmore suspected of being a female 128–9
Ferguson, John 26–7
Fermor, Arabella 1, 2
Feuerbach, Ludwig: *Das Wesen des Christenthums* (The Essence of Christianity) 102
Field, John 145
Field, Richard 48
Fielding, Henry
Joseph Andrews 2
Shamela 124–5
Fielding, Sarah 125
Filmer, Sir Robert 161
Finch, Anne, Countess of Winchelsea 52
Miscellany Poems, on several occasions. Written by a Lady 52
Fitzgeoffrey, Charles 218
Flaubert, Gustave 117
Flower, Eliza 274
Flower, Sarah 274
Flowers, Gennifer 31
Ford, Charles 39
Forster, John 77, 198, 199, 213
Fortnightly 207, 210
Forward, Reverend Toby 114–18
an Anglican vicar 115, 117
cites Charlotte Brontë as his model 115
claims to target a certain habit of reading 117
pseudonym as a creative strategy 115, 116
a white man writing as an Asian woman 115–16
Down the Road, Worlds Away (as Rahila Khan) 114–15, 117
'Winter Wind' 114–15
Foster, Professor Donald 34, 35, 296

Four Days' Battle (1666) 155
Fowler, Ellen Thorneycroft: *Concerning Isabel Carnaby* 111–13
Fox, Tottie 95
Fox, William Johnson 195, 274
Francis, Duke of Alençon and Anjou 144
Franklin, Richard 173
Fraser, James 179, 180, 247
Fraser's Magazine 83, 179, 193, 194, 196, 199, 200, 205, 247, 248
Frederick, Prince, Duke of York 68
French Conquest, neither desirable nor practicable, A (Jacobite pamphlet) 142
French Revolution 175
Fry, Roger 213
Fuseli, Henry: *Remarks on Rousseau* 184
Füssli, Johann Kaspar: *Archives of Etymology* 184

Galsworthy, John 181
Galt, John 196
'Ganconagh' *see* Yeats, W. B.
Garnet, Father Henry 230
Garnier, Robert: *Marc Antoine* 51
Garrick Club, London 95
Gaskell, Elizabeth
    and authorship of *Adam Bede* 106
    and Charlotte Brontë's self-concealment 82, 86–7, 92, 95–6
    masculine pseudonyms 76–7
    short-lived anonymity 77–8
    The Life of Charlotte Brontë 84, 86–7, 92, 101
    Mary Barton 76–7
    Ruth 77–8
Gay, John 13
    and the authorship of *Gulliver's Travels* 9, 10, 11
    and *Court Poems* 54
    mock books 233
Geddes, Patrick 135
Gentleman's Magazine 53
George I, King 170
George II, King (and as Prince of Wales) 12, 28
George III, King 28, 61–2, 71, 173, 242, 243

George IV, King (and as Prince Regent) 28, 36, 71, 244
George's bookshop, Bristol 42
Gifford, Arthur: *Omen* 127
Gifford, William 192
Gilbert, Sandra M. and Gubar, Susan: *The Madwoman in the Attic* 84
Gissing, George 181, 287
    New Grub Street 211
Gladstone, William Ewart 110
Glasgow *Evening News* 136
Glasgow Sentinel 174
Globe, The 272
Glorious Revolution (1688) 159, 161
Godwin, William 245
    Cloudesley 194–5
Goethe, Johann Wolfgang 205
Goldsmith, Oliver 126–7, 183, 184
Gollancz, Victor 291
Gosse, Sir Edmund 211
    Father and Son 280–85
    The Life of Philip Henry Gosse, FRS 282, 283, 284
Gosse, Philip Henry 280–85
    Omphalos 284
    The Romance of Natural History 282
Granada 289
Granada TV 295
Grand Jury of Middlesex 164, 171
Gray, Thomas
    'Elegy Written in a Country Church-yard' 56–7
    'Ode on a Distant Prospect of Eton College' 55–6
Greer, Germaine: *Slip-Shod Sibyls* 52
Gregg's Coffee House, Covent Garden, London 60
Greville, Frances 63
Griffiths, Ralph 183, 185
Gros, Eugene 216
Gross, John 216
Gubar, Susan *see* Gilbert, Sandra M.
Guilpin, Everard 217–18, 219–20
    Skialetheia. Or, A Shadow of Truth, in certaine Epigrams and Satyres 219, 220, 221
Guizot, François: *Washington* 212
Gunpowder Plot 230

Guthrie, James and Johnston, Archibald:
  Causes of God's Wrath (attrib.)
  152–3

Hales, Lady 60, 61
Halifax, Yorkshire 97
Halkett, Samuel and Laing, John:
  *Dictionary of the Anonymous and
  Pseudonymous Literature of
  Great Britain* 2–4, 41, 42, 44
Hall, Joseph 220
  Virgidemiae 218, 219
Hallam, Arthur Henry 274, 275, 277
Hamilton, Elizabeth: *The Cottagers of
  Glenburnie* 68
handwriting
  analysis 35, 39
  concealment of 25, 29, 39–40, 42
  Defoe's handwritings 166
  the truest proof of authorship 40
Harding, John 16, 171
Harding, Mrs: 'On Wisdom's Defeat in a
  Learned Debate' 171
Hardy, Thomas 27, 111, 280, 287
  Desperate Remedies 130
  A Pair of Blue Eyes 208
Harley, Sir Edward 157
Harley, Robert 166, 232–3
Harvey, Gabriel 150
Hatchard's bookshop, Piccadilly,
  London 238
Haweis, Rev. 254, 255
Hawker, Mary *see* Falconer, Lanoe
Haworth, Yorkshire 80, 91, 97
Haworth Mechanics' Institute 97
Haworth Parsonage 97
Haydon, Benjamin 266
Haywood, Eliza 118
  History of Miss Betsy Thoughtless 57–8
Hazlitt, Sarah 265, 266
Hazlitt, William 189, 190, 242, 274
  Lectures on the English Comic Writers
  190
  Liber Amoris 265–73
  'On Great and Little Things' 270
  The Spirit of the Age 188, 192
  Table-talk 270
Heber, Richard 22, 24

Heinemann, William (publisher) 280,
  282, 294
Hennell, Sara 107, 201
  Christianity and Infidelity 205
Henry VIII, King 142, 143
Herbert, Mary, Countess of Pembroke
  51
Hervey, Lord 55
Heyward, Andrew 36
'Higgins, Jack' *see* Patterson, Harry
Higginson, Henry 110
High Church 165
Highland News, The 136
Hill, Aaron 123–4
Hobbes, John Oliver (Pearl Mary-Teresa
  Craigie): *Some Emotions and a
  Moral* 110
Hobhouse, John Cam 176
Hodgkin, John 149
Hodgson, Francis 238
Hogarth, William 236
Hogarth Press 212
Hogg, James ('The Ettrick Shepherd')
  191, 247
Honan, Park 74
Hood, Thomas 198
Hopkins, John 232
Hopkins, Tighe 210–211
Horne, Richard Henry 205
*Hortensia: or, the distressed wife. A novel,
  by a lady* 57
House of Commons 165, 166, 175
House of Lords 168
Household Words 206, 207
Howard, Henrietta, Countess of Suffolk
  12, 13
Howlitt, William 76
Howlitt's Journal 76
Hughes, Ted 293
Humphries, Miss (Fanny Burney's
  cousin's nurse) 61, 63
Hunt, John 243
Hunt, Leigh 190, 191–2, 246, 270, 273
Hunt, Thornton 103
Huxley, Aldous 181
Huxley, Thomas 43
Hyde, Lord Chief Justice 139, 140–41
Hyde Park, London 175

Ibsen, Henrik: *Rosmersholm* 290
Inns of Court, London 220, 221

Jacobite Rebellion (1745) 28
Jacobitism 28, 142
James, Henry
  The American Scene 213
  The Golden Bowl 213
James I, King 223
James II, King (previously Duke of
  York) 142, 155, 157, 159–62
James Francis Edward Stuart, Prince
  (the Old Pretender) 142
Jape, Jonathan 289
Jeffrey, Francis 21, 177, 178, 187–8, 189,
  238, 241–2
Jeffreys, Judge 154
Jesuits 222, 230
John Bull Magazine 194, 263, 272
Johnson, Esther (Stella) 173
Johnson, Joseph 244
Johnson, Dr Samuel 58, 62
Johnston, Archibald *see* Guthrie, James
Jonson, Ben 217
'Junius' 173
Juvenal 230
  First Satire 220

'Kavanagh, Dan' *see* Barnes, Julian
Keats, John 190–91, 273
  Endymion 190, 267
  Lamia 269
'Kell, Joseph' *see* Burgess, Anthony
Kelly, J. B. 216
Kennedy, James 3
Kerr, Lady Robert 70
Khan, Rahila *see* Forward, Reverend
  Toby
King, Archbishop 169, 170
King, Larry 32
King's Bench Prison, London 174
King's College, Cambridge 56
Kingsley, Charles 276, 284
'Kinsayder, W.' *see* Marston, John
Klein, Joe
  a columnist with *Newsweek* magazine
    34
  resigns from CBS News 36

suspended by *Newsweek* 35
Primary Colors 294
  anger at Klein's behaviour 35–6
  Foster's computer analysis 34, 35
  implicit boast of 33
  Klein admits authorship 35
  Klein strongly denies authorship
    35, 36
  modelled on the Clintons 30–32
  narrator 31–3
  promises real secrets 34
  a *roman-à-clef* 30
  speculation about author's identity
    32, 34
  subtitled 'A Novel of Politics' 3
  success of 30–31, 32, 34
Knight, Fanny 67, 75
Knowles, Admiral Charles 174
Knowles, James Sheridan 269, 279

Laing, Catherine 3, 41, 42, 44
Laing, Rev. John *see* Halkett, Samuel
Lake Poets 246
Lamb, Charles: *Confessions of a*
  Drunkard 258–9
Lane, John 111
Leader, The 205
Lee, Hermione 213
legislation
  Elizabethan statutes forbidding anti-
    monarchy writing 144
  Henry VIII's proclamation (1546) 143
  law of seditious libel 150, 165
  licensing laws 142, 143–4, 151, 158, 165
  measures to control printing and
    publishing (1799) 175–6
  names of author, printer and licenser
    to be given on publications 151–2
  Printing Act (1662) 152
  Star Chamber Decree (1637) 151
  Treason Act (1661) 152
  treason laws extended to cover
    printed material 144
Leigh, Percival 199
Leighton, Alexander 151
  An Appeal to the Parliament; or Sion's
    Plea against the Prelacie 151
Lerner, Laurence 293

Lessing, Doris 288–90, 295
  Canopus in Argos series 288
  The Diaries of Jane Somers 289
  The Diary of a Good Neighbour (as 'Jane Somers') 288–9
  If the Old Could … (as 'Jane Somers') 289
l'Estrange, Sir Roger 139, 140, 154–5, 156, 167
  An Account of the Growth of Knavery 158–9
Lewes, Agnes 103
Lewes, George Henry
  cohabits with George Eliot 101, 102, 103
  edits the *Fortnightly* 207
  and Eliot's anonymity 105, 106
  go-between with Eliot's publisher 38–9
  initialed reviews 200–201
  productivity 204–5
  puffing by 205
  review of *Jane Eyre* 83
  review of *Shirley* 96–7
  reviewing style 204
  Life and Work of Goethe 205
Liberal, The (radical journal) 243
Liddell, Alice 46
Liddell, Edith 46
Liddell, Ina 46
Liggins, Joseph 107
Limborch, Philip van 162, 163
Listener 293, 295
Literary Gazette 271, 275–6
literary hoaxes 116–17
Literary Journal 242
Literary Register 270
Locke, John 159
  anxious to preserve his anonymity 159, 160–61, 163–4
  his associates 162
  in exile in Holland 162
  and loss of his anonymity 162–3
  more audacious and cautious than Marvell 159
  his part in abandonment of state censorship of published materials 164–5
  renowned throughout England and Europe 159
  watched by government spies 162
  De Morbo Gallico (On the French Disease) 162
  An Essay concerning Human Understanding 159, 164
  Letter concerning Toleration 161, 162, 163
  The Reasonableness of Christianity as delivered in the Scriptures 163–4
  Two Treatises of Government 159–62
Lockhart, John Gibson 36, 89, 178, 191, 247, 271–2
  Memoirs of the Life of Sir Walter Scott 24, 27
London Chronicle 174, 184
London Gazette 158, 166
London Magazine 178, 258, 259, 261, 263
London Review 188
London Review of Books 115, 181
Lonsdale, Roger 127, 184–5, 186
Lowndes, Thomas 38, 59, 60
Loyola, Ignatius 230
Lubbock, Percy 213
'Lucas, Victoria' *see* Plath, Sylvia

MacCarthy, Desmond 213–14
MacCarthy, Molly: *A Nineteenth Century Childhood* 213
Mackenzie, Margaret 68
'MacLeod, Fiona' *see* Sharp, William
Maclise, Daniel 193
Macmillan, Alexander 42
Macpherson, James: Ossian epics 116, 133
McVea, Deborah 181, 182
Maginn, William 179, 194, 205, 247, 263
Mallet, David 124
Malthus, Thomas 245
Manchester 76, 77
Manley, Mrs Mary Delariviere 118
  Adventures of Rivella 232
  New Atalantis (previously *Secret Memoirs and Manners of several Persons of Quality, of both Sexes. From the new Atalantis, an Island in the Mediterranean*) 232
Manners, Mary 45

'Manners, Mrs Horace' *see* Swinburne, Algernon

Marchand, Leslie 212

Marprelate tracts (1588–9) 146–50, 218
  The Epistle 147
  The Epitome 148
  Hay any worke for Cooper 148
  More work for the Cooper 149
  The protestatyon of Martin Marprelate 148, 149

Marston, John 217–18, 220
  The Dutch Courtesan 222
  The Metamorphosis of Pigmalions Image and Certaine Satyres 218, 219
  The Scourge of Villanie 218, 219

Martin, Gregory: *A Treatise of Schisme* 141

Martin, Samuel 175

Martineau, Harriet 94, 95

Martineau, James 102

Martineau, Lucy 94

Marvell, Andrew 176
  drawn to dangerous publications 156
  great circumspection 156
  and John Locke 159
  Second Advice to a Painter (attrib.) 155–6
  strong religious and political convictions 156
  successful politician 156
  successfully dodges identification 158
  An Account of the Growth of Popery and Arbitrary Government in England 157, 158
  Mr Smirke: Or, The Divine in Mode 157
  The Rehearsal Transpros'd 156
  The Rehearsal Transpros'd: The Second Part 156–7
  Short Historical Essay touching General Councils, Creeds, and Imposition in Religion 157
  Third Advice to a Painter (attrib.) 155–6

Mary, Queen 144

Mary II, Queen 159

masculine pseudonyms
  Brontës' choice of ambiguous Christian names 78
  construction of Mary Hawker's pseudonym 109
  Gaskell's belated request 76–7
  George Eliot's reasons for retaining her pseudonym 101, 103–4
  preponderance of male pseudonyms over female 128
  use changes from a sign of modesty to one of boldness 110–111
  within a novel 111–13

Mather, Cotton 76

Matthews, John 142

Maturin, Charles: *Bertram* 187

medieval literature 296

Memoir of a Hypochondriac, The 259

Menaker, Daniel 32

Meredith, George 132, 287

Middleton, Thomas 35
  Micro-cynicon 221

Milbanke, Arabella (later Lady Byron) 68

Mill, John Stuart 200

Millais, Sir John Everett 43

Milton, John: *Areopagitica; For the Liberty of Unlicenc'd Printing* 152

Mist's Weekly Journal 173

Mitford, Mary Russell 68–9, 71

mock books 233

mockery
  Donne's mocking account, *Ignatius His Conclave* 223
  double meaning 233
  of the followers of the age's literary fashions 218
  'hired Writers' named and mocked in *The Dunciad* 234
  law students speak of frustrated ambitions 221
  London's mockable variety of character types 220
  Rochester makes mock of the 'discovery' of his authorship 227
  satire mocks the age offended by its misanthropy 221
  Thackeray's style 247

modesty
  as an alibi as well as an obligation 52
  Austen's literary modesty 72, 74, 75
  Burney's debut as a writer 58
  Dodgson's sense of the privacy of his
    authorship 46
  mixed with some more teasing
    motivation 78
  modesty of anonymous authors
    commonly false 64
  tradition of 'modest' anonymity and
    pseudonymity in English
    literature 46
  a virtue associated with female
    authors 50–51, 55, 57
Monks of Medmenham 236
Montagu, Basil: *Some Enquiries into the
  Effects of Fermented Liquor* 258
Monthly Repository 195, 274
Monthly Review 182–6
Moore, George 281–2
Moore, Leonard 290–91
Moore, Tom 177–8, 189, 242
  Odes and Epistles 177
More, Hannah 52
Morison, Stanley 212
Morning Herald 59
Morning Post, The 249
Morphew, John 168
Morrice, Bezaleel: *An Essay on the
  Universe* 19
Morritt, John 26, 28
Motte, Benjamin 9, 11, 17, 38
Moxon, Edward 275
Mulgrave, John Sheffield, third Earl of
  225
  An Essay upon Satire 153–4, 225
Murray, John 27, 71, 176, 177, 240, 241, 242
Murray, John Middleton: *The Critic in
  Judgement* 212

Napier, Macvey 188
Napoleon Bonaparte 269
Nashe, Thomas 50, 150
National Gallery, London 250
Nesbit, Edith 111
New Edinburgh Review 262
New Monthly Magazine 198, 270

New Review 211
New Statesman and Nation 291
New Testament 142–3, 252
New York magazine 34
New York Times 35–6
Newby, Thomas 88
Newcastle, Lord 170
Newgate Calendar 249
Newgate Novels 248, 249
Newgate Prison, London 138, 166
Newsweek magazine 34, 35, 37
Newton, Sir Isaac 159
Newton, John 255, 256–7
  'Amazing Grace' 255
  *An Authentic Narrative of some
    Remarkable and Interesting
    Particulars in the Life of* ********
    254–7
  Olney Hymns (with William Cowper)
    257
Nichols, Mike 34
Nicolson, William, Bishop of Derry
  170–71
Nineteenth Century 207
Noble, Francis 119–21
  *The History of Laetitia Atkins, vulgarly
    called Moll Flanders*
    (bowdlerized version of *Moll
    Flanders* pub. by Noble) 119–20
  *The History of Mademoiselle de
    Beleau; or, The New Roxana*
    (pub. by Noble) 120
Nonconformists 156
'North, Christopher' *see* Wilson, John
North American Review 105
North Briton journal 175
Northumberland, John Dudley, Duke of
  144
Novel Review 110
novels
  anonymity and pseudonymity
    common in novel-writing 36, 57,
    128
  'by a lady' 57
  circulating libraries 57
  lists of 57
  popular subjects (18th-19thC) 57
Nussey, Ellen 90–93

Oath of Supremacy and Allegiance 223
Observator journal 173
Observer 96, 293
Old Testament 143, 246
Oldham, John 228–31
   'A Dithyrambique on Drinking' 229
   'The Lamentation for Adonis' (trans.) 228
   Poems and Translations 231
   'Satyr against Vertue' 228, 230
   Satyrs upon the Jesuits 230, 231
   Some New Pieces Never before Publisht 229
   'Suppos'd to be spoken by a Court-Hector' 228–9
   'Upon the Author of a Plat call'd *Sodom* 229
Ollier, Charles 264, 265
Olney, Buckinghamshire 256–7
'Opium Eater, The' (a member of Blackwood's circle) 191
'Ordnance for the Regulation of Printing' (1643) 152
Orwell, George (Eric Blair) 290–92
   Burmese Days 292
   The Clergyman's Daughter 292
   Down and Out In Paris and London 290, 291–2
Otway, Thomas 154
Owen, Agnes 105
Oxford, Edward Harley, 2nd Earl of 233
Oxford, Robert Harley, 1st Earl of 10
Oxford English Dictionary (*OED*) 108, 295

Page, William 145
Paget, Lady Augusta 68
'paid paragraphs' 198
Paine, Adelaide 44
Pall Mall Gazette 134
Pargeter, Edith ('Ellis Peters'): 'Brother Cadfael' historical mysteries 288
Parker, Maynard 35
Parker, Samuel 156, 157
Patmore, Peter 266, 268
patronage 47, 228
Patterson, Harry ('Jack Higgins'): *The Eagle Has Landed* 288

Peacock, Thomas Love 244–7
   Headlong Hall 244–5, 246
   Melincourt 246
   Nightmare Abbey 245, 246
Penn, Admiral Sir William 155
Penry, John 149
Perring, Rev. Philip 251
Peterborough, Earl of 12
'Peters, Ellis' *see* Pargeter, Edith
Petrarch: *Trionfo della Morte* 51
Petre, Lord 1
Philanthropist 258
Philips, Katherine (the 'Matchless Orinda') 51–2
   Poems by the Incomparable Mrs K.P. 52
Phillipson, Caroline 201
'Philomela' *see* Rowe, Elizabeth
pirating of published work 56
Pitt, William, the Younger 175
Plath, Aurelia 293, 294
Plath, Sylvia 292–4
   The Bell Jar 292–4
Plymouth Brethren sect 280, 281, 284
Pope, Alexander 10, 20, 52, 238
   and authorship of *Gulliver's Travels* 9, 11–12, 13
   and *Court Poems* 54
   his foes 13, 19, 55
   'reclaiming' of his own work 18
   threatened with violence 167–8
   uses anonymity to provoke 168
   The Dunciad 19, 167, 233–5
   The Dunciad Variorum 235
   Epistle to Burlington 18
   Epistle to Dr Arbuthnot 235
   An Essay on Man 18–19
   A Full and True Account of a Horrid and Barbarous Revenge by Poison, On the Body of Mr. Edmund Curll 54
   The Rape of the Lock 1–2
Popple, William 156, 157, 162, 163
pornography 4, 126
Portsmouth, Duchess of 153
Pound, Ezra 212
Primary Colors (film) 34

printers
    blamed for printing without author's
        consent 51–2
    execution for printing materials
        139–43, 154
    fined 142
    imprisoned 142, 157, 169, 171
    physical evidence against them 142
    put in the pillory 142, 154
    see also legislation
Printing Act (1662) 152
Private Eye 181
Privy Council 142, 170, 218
Procter, Bryan Waller 198
Protestant texts 144
Pryce-Jones, Alan 213, 215
Pseudonym Library 108–9, 110, 128
pseudonymity
    ambiguous Christian names 78
    becomes largely unmysterious 287
    Charlotte Brontë's pseudonym
        becomes a sign of creative
        defiance 100
    common in novel-writing 36
    distinction between pseudonymity
        and anonymity 4
    due to characters being based on
        family members 130
    a matter of privacy rather than
        concealment to Dodgson 41,
        44–5
    names that announce themselves as
        fictional 128
    popular genres 287
    standard pseudonym for women
        writers ('A Lady') 50, 51, 52, 54,
        55, 57, 67, 68, 126–7
    Thackeray's many pseudonyms 4, 198,
        248, 249–50
    see also female pseudonyms;
        masculine pseudonyms
Public Advertiser 173
publishers
    Austen meets her publisher 71
    as co-conspirators with authors 38
    duped by a vicar 114–17
    go-betweens with 38–9, 59–60, 66–7,
        68, 102

    Newby's unscrupulous behaviour 88
    puffing 54, 198–9, 204, 205, 210, 272
Punch 250
Puritan publications 145, 147
Puritanism 145, 146, 149, 150, 280–81
Puttenham, George 50
    The Arte of English Poesie 47, 222
Pygmalion 273
Pym, Barbara 290

Quarterly Review 71, 89, 188, 189, 190, 192,
        194, 200
Quinn, Sally 35

Rackett, Magdalen (Pope's half-sister)
        167
Raine, Kathleen 216
Raleigh, Sir Walter 225
Random House (publishers) 32, 35
Rather, Dan 36
Raven, James 127
Reeve, Henry 212
Remarks upon the present confederacy
        and late revolution in England
        (Jacobit pamphlet) 142
Rendell, Ruth ('Barbara Vine') 288
Restoration 152, 153
reviewing
    advantages of anonymity 182
    anonymity in the TLS 212–16
    anonymous reviewing as a matter for
        debate 196, 215
    authors mistaken about reviewers'
        identities 189–90
    Bulwer opposes anonymity 195–6
    criticism of anonymous critics 186–8
    demands for identity of authors of
        offensive reviews 190–91
    by Dickens 206–7
    Dilke's view of anonymity 204
    Eliot and 200–205
    ensuring a charitable reception to
        books 184–6
    Fraser's relishes critical mischief 193
    gentlemanly convention of
        anonymity for reviewers 182–3
    identification of anonymous
        reviewers 205–6

increasing frequency of signed
reviews 207, 210, 211
intimacy issue 213–15
misattribution as a response of
victims 191–2
most reviewing remains anonymous
208, 210
moves against anonymous reviewing
200–201
partiality discovered 206
pretending to a status as outsider 212
and promotion of work 183–4
puffing 53, 198–9, 204, 205, 210, 272
reviewers writing for rival reviews 204
self-reviewing 212
small number of reviewers write
much of the copy 183, 188–9
Thackeray's cameo of the life of a
periodical 197
TLS proposals to identify anonymous
reviewers 181–2
Rhodes, Dennis 3
Richardson, Samuel 58
letter-writing form 125–6
persistent anonymity 125
a successful businessman 123
Clarissa 125
Pamela
advertising 183–4
and Fielding *Shamela* 124–5
influence of 61, 123, 126
novel-in-letters form 61, 123
preface 123
rapid attribution to Richardson 128
Richardson regrets his name
becoming public 124
speculation about its authorship
124
success of 123, 124
Richmond, Bruce 213, 214, 215
Rigby, Elizabeth 89–90
Robbins, Kathy 32
Robinson, Henry Crabb 261–2
Robinson, Robert 295
Rochefort, France 174
Rochester, Bishop of 149
Rochester, John Wilmot, Earl of 225–31,
235

asserts himself through anonymity
226
commonly associated with the Devil
226
drunken exploits 228
libertine and wit 225
lordly anonymity 231
the most admired and entertaining
devil of late seventeenth century
satire 225
his style 226, 227
visits John Oldham 229
'Timon' 227
'To the Postboy' 226
Rock, The 252, 253
Roman Catholicism 145
Romantic age 237, 238
Romantic literature 263
Ross, Alexander 208
Rossetti, Dante Gabriel 131
Rousseau, Jean-Jacques 245, 273
Confessions 262, 272
Rowe, Nicholas 52
Roye, William 143
Rupert, Prince 155
Ruskin, John 43
Russell, William C. 130
see also Davies, Eliza Rhyl
Rye House Plot 162

St Albans, Hertfordshire 258
St James's Chronicle 175
St Paul's Churchyard, London: sign of
the Spread Eagle 140
Salisbury Crags, Edinburgh 27
Sand, George 103
Sandwich, Lord 155
satire
anonymity gives the satirist
opportunity to act the devil 225
anonymity in 235–6
anti-Catholic 230
attribution 221
banned (1599) 150, 218, 222
burning of 218
exciting curiosity 222
flourish in a special domain 219
hostility to 217–18

offends by its misanthropy 221
personal satires (lampoons) 235
proliferation of verse satires in
    Charles II's reign 153–4
Puttenham's explanation of its
    original naming 222
requires private manuscript
    circulation or anonymity 221
satire as a generic malcontent 219
vogue for formal verse satires 218
Satirist, The 178
Saturday Review, The 129, 210
Savage, Richard 234
'scandal narratives' 118
Scotsman, The 252
Scott, Anne 26
Scott, John 178–9, 191–2
Scott, Lady 26
Scott, Sir Walter 20–30, 191, 238, 242, 294
    his anonymous review of Old
        Mortality 37–8
    biography of Swift 13
    concealment of his handwriting 25,
        29, 39–40
    finds anonymity congenial 25, 26,
        29–30
    flattered and intrigued by Adolphus's
        book 24
    'the Great Unknown' 21, 26
    a highly successful poet 21
    initial deception of publishers and
        family members 25–6, 29
    meets Adolphus at Abbotsford 24–5
    reviews Emma 71
    'Waverley novels' 20–30
        best-selling novels 20
        speculation about their author's
            identity 20–21
        Scottish settings 21, 25
        Scott named as the possible author
            from the first 21
        Scott teases his readers about their
            anonymity 21
        construction of elaborate plots
            about their origins 21
        described by Adolphus 23
        plays founded upon some of them
            25

Scott willing to lie about
    authorship 27, 29, 36–7
Scott owns up to his fiction 26,
    28–9, 192
controversial history in 28
The Antiquary 37
The Bride of Lammermoor 23
Chronicles of the Canongate 29, 192
The Fortunes of Nigel 24
Guy Mannering 37
The Heart of Midlothian 20, 27
Ivanhoe 20, 21
Marmion 22, 23
Old Mortality 21–2, 27, 37
Rob Roy 20, 26
Tales of My Landlord 27, 192
Waverley 20, 21, 25, 26, 28, 29, 36, 295
Scott, Thomas: The Force of Truth: an
    Authentic Narrative 257
scribal publications 225
scribes 296
Scriblerians 10, 11
Scriblerus Club 233
    The History of John Bull 233
    The Memoirs of Martinus Scriblerus
        233
secret histories 231–3
seditious libel 150, 165, 173
Settle, Elkanah: A Session of the Poets 154
Seward, Anna 52
Seymour, William 66
'Shadowe of truthe in Epigrams and
    Satyres, The' 218
Shadwell, Thomas 227
Shaftesbury, Anthony Ashley-Cooper,
    3rd Earl of 161–2, 164
Shakespeare, William 35, 278, 296
    and 'A Funerall Elegye' 296
    Shakespeare studies 34–5
    Othello 268
    The Tempest 239
    Troilus and Cressida 267
Sharp, Elizabeth 135
    Memoir 132
Sharp, William 131–7
    admiring study of Rossetti 131
    admits being 'Fiona MacLeod' on his
        death 137

begins writing as 'Fiona MacLeod' 131
carefully keeps the secret of his dual
  identity 134
publicly denies authorship 135–7
taken over by the invented personage
  135
*From the Hills of Dream: Mountain
  Songs and Island Runes* 133–4
The Mountain Lovers 133
Pharais 131–3
The Sin Eater 133
The Washer at the Ford 133
Sharpe, Henry 149
Sheffield Iris 82, 261
Shelley, Harriet 177, 265
Shelley, Mary 195, 264
  Frankenstein 2
Shelley, Percy Bysshe 177, 245, 263–5, 273,
  274
  Epipsychidion 263–4, 265
  Julian and Maddalo 263
  'Lines to a Critic' 189
  *Oedipus Tyrannus. Or Swellfoot the
    Tyrant. A Tragedy in Two Acts*
    244
  Preface to *Adonais* 190
  The Revolt of Islam 189–90
Shephard, Fleetwood 228
Sheridan, Richard Brinsley: *A School for
  Scandal* 18
'Shirley' *see* Skelton, John
Sidney, Algernon 162
Sidney, Sir Philip 47, 51, 225
Simoni, Anna 3
Singer, Elizabeth ('Philomela'; later
  Rowe) 52
Singleton, Hugh 145
Sir Gawain and the Green Knight 296
Skelton, John 129–30
  A Campaigner at Home (as 'Shirley')
    129
  Nugae Criticae (as 'Shirley') 129
  Thalatta! Or the Great Commoner 130
Smith, Charlotte 68
Smith, Elder & Co. 80, 88, 92
Smith, Francis 154
Smith, George Murray 80–81, 88, 92, 93,
  97, 98

'Smith, Herodotus' *see* Espinasse,
  Francis
Smith, Sydney 189
Smith Williams, William 80–83, 88, 89,
  92, 96, 99, 105
Smollett, Tobias 174, 183
  The Complete History of England 184
'Snarlinge Satyres' 218
Society for the Suppression of Vice 244
'Solomons, Ikey' *see* Thackeray, William
  Makepeace
Solomons, Ikey (an early nineteenth-
  century fence) 249
'Somers, Jane' *see* Lessing, Doris
Southey, Robert 187, 189, 190, 193, 238,
  242, 246
  A Vision of Judgment 242
Southwold, Suffolk 291
Spectator, The 2, 93, 208, 210, 275, 294
Spedding, James 200
Spencer, Herbert 105
  Principles of Psychology 205
Spender, Stephen 215
Spenser, Edmund
  The Faerie Queene 49
  The Shepheardes Calender
    anonymity 47, 48, 49
    archaisms 48–9
    author's identity guessed at 49–50
    dedication to Philip Sidney 47
    E.K.'s commentary 48–9
    prologue by 'Immerito' 47, 49
    self-promotional 49
    sets out to remake English poetic
      language 49
    stanza forms and metrical patterns
      48
    typography 48
Standard 194, 205
Star Chamber 146, 150–51
  Decree (1637) 151
Stationers' Company 144, 146, 151, 218
Steele, Richard: *The Crisis* 168
Stephanopoulos, George 32
Stephen, James Fitzjames 206
Stephen, Sir James 206
Sterling, Edward 199
Sterling, John 200

Sterne, Laurence 182–3, 237
  Sermons of Mr. Yorick 237
  Tristram Shandy 182, 236–7
Steventon, Hampshire 74
Strachey, Lytton: *Eminent Victorians* 214
Strauss, David Friedrich: *Life of Jesus* 101,
  102
Stuart, James 174–5
Stubbs (Stubbe), John: *The Discoverie of
  a Gaping Gulf Whereinto
  England is like to be swallowed
  by another French marriage*
  144–5
Sturrock, John 181–2
Surrey, Henry Howard, Earl of 225
Sutcliffe, Matthew 150
Swift, Jonathan 52, 176, 246
  concerned about his advancement in
    the church 172–3
  criticism of 13–14
  Dean of St Patrick's Cathedral,
    Dublin 9
  a former political controversialist 10
  Gulliverian jokiness 12–13
  likes to make trouble 14
  loyalty of his important friends 168
  mock books 233
  his printers 168–9, 171
  reasons for his anonymity 14, 20
  rewards offered to identify him 168,
    171–2
  a Scriblerian 10
  sermons 17
  subterfuge with publisher Motte 9
  *An Argument against Abolishing
    Christianity* 252
  'The Author upon Himself' 168
  The Drapier's Letters 169–72
  The Examiner (periodical) 10
  Gulliver's Travels 38, 251
    Swift's efforts to ensure
      anonymous publication 9, 10, 14,
      17, 39
    political readings 10
    success of 10, 13
    speculation on its authorship 10–11,
      13
    creation of alternative worlds 12

Gulliver as object of the satire 16
Gulliver as 'the author' 16–17
'The Lady's Dressing Room' 54
Miscellanies in Prose and Verse 10
Modest Proposal 14–15, 17
Proposal for Irish Manufacture 169
The Publick Spirit of the Whigs 168, 172
Seasonable Advice to the Grand Jury
  171
A Tale of a Tub 172–3
'To the Shopkeepers, Tradesmen,
  Farmer and Common People of
  Ireland' 169, 170
'Verses on the Death of Dr Swift' 172
Works (ed. Faulkner) 172
Swinburne, Algernon: *A Year's Letters*
  (later *Love's Cross-Currents*)
  (published under the name 'Mrs
  Horace Manners') 130

Taylor, Joe 92
Taylor, John 260, 261
Taylor, Mary 91, 92
Tennyson, Alfred, Lord 43, 199–200,
  274–9
  In Memoriam A. H. H. 274–9
  Poems 199, 200
  The Princess 276
Tennyson, Emily 274, 277
Tennyson, Hallam 279
Thackeray, Anne 97–8
Thackeray, William Makepeace 193
  anonymous literary journalism 196
  Brontë's dedication of *Jane Eyre*
    causes rumours 88–9, 90
  cameo of the life of a periodical 197
  Charlotte visits 97–8
  first meets Charlotte Brontë 93
  gossips about dining with Jane Eyre
    95
  pseudonyms 4, 198, 248, 249–50
  seeks favourable reviews 198–9
  speculates about sex of *Jane Eyre*'s
    author 83–4
  tours and lectures to promote his own
    books 287
  Catherine: A Story 248–9
  Comic Tales and Sketches 199, 250

Irish Sketch Book 199
Miscellanies 250
The Paris Sketch Book 198, 250
Pendennis 197
Rebecca and Rowena: A Romance upon Romance 250
The Rose and the Ring 250
The Snobs of England 250
Vanity Fair 88, 198, 199, 249, 250
Yellowplush Papers 247–8
Theatre Royal, Drury Lane, London 187
Thomas à Kempis: *Imitation of Christ* 256
Thrale, Hester Lynch 63, 65
Throckmorton, Job 150
Thwaite, Ann 282
Tickell, Thomas 170
Times, The 93, 106–7, 181, 194, 206, 210, 271, 272, 291
Times Literary Supplement (*TLS*) 181, 212–16, 293
    Centenary Archive 181
title pages 296
'To the Lady W-y M-e, Upon Her Poems Being Publish'd without a Name' 54
Tomkins, John 266
'Tommy Tickler' (a member of Blackwood's circle) 191
Tooke, Benjamin 173
Toryism 246
Tower of London 149, 162
Treason Act (1661) 152
Treatise of the Execution of Justice, A (anonymous pamphlet) 138
Treglown, Jeremy 181, 182, 212
Trinity College, Cambridge 274
Trollope, Anthony 206, 210, 287, 294–5
    Autobiography 207
    Nina Baltka 294
    The Claverings 37
    The Way We Live Now 208–210
Tutchin, John 167, 173
Twining, Thomas 186
Twyn, John
    admits to correcting the *Treatise's* printed sheets 139
    execution 138, 139, 141, 152
        prints *A Treatise of the Execution of Justice* 138
        refuses or unable to name the pamphlet's author 138–41
        trial of 139, 140–41
Tyburn, London 142
Tyndale, William 142–3
Tyrrell, James 160–61
    Patriarcha non Monarcha 161

Udall, John 150
Unwin, Thomas Fisher 108, 109
Upton, William 127

Vanity Fair 43
Venice 240
Victoria, Queen 279
Vilvorde, Belgium 143
'Vine, Barbara' *see* Rendell, Ruth
Virago 114–17
'Virago Upstarts' series 114
'Vivian' *see* Lewes, George Henry
Viviani, Count 264
Viviani, Emilia 264
Vox Populi Vox Dei (pro-Jacobite pamphlet) 142

Waldegrave, Robert 147–8, 149
Walker, Joseph 139
Walker, Mrs (Hazlitt's landlady) 265
Walker, Sarah 265–72
Waller, Edmund: *Instructions to a Painter* 155
Walpole, Horace 55, 56
Walpole, Robert 10, 169
Walton, Izaak: *Life of Dr. John Donne* 223
Warburton, William 1
Ward, Leslie 43
Warner Books 32
Washington Post 35
Watchman, The (periodical) 186
Waters, Edward 168–9
Webbe, William: *A Discourse of English Poetrie* 49–50
Webster, William 183
Weekly Miscellany 183–4
Wellesley Index to Victorian Periodicals, The 188–9

Welsted, Leonard 19
Wesley, John 256
'West, Rebecca' (Cecily Fairfield) 290
Westcott, Brooke, Bishop of Durham
    279
Westminster Review 101–2, 105, 133, 188,
    200–203
Westmoreland Gazette 259
Wharton, Edith 181
Whipping of the Satyre, The (pamphlet
    by 'W. I.') 217
Whitgift, John, Archbishop of
    Canterbury 145, 146–7, 150, 218
*Whole Duty of a Woman, The ... Written
    by a Lady* 50–51
Who's Who 135
Wilcox, Thomas 145
Wildman, James 75
Wilkes, John 175, 236
    Essay on Woman 236
William III, King 142, 159, 161
Wilson, James 198
Wilson, John ('Christopher North') 191,
    247
Wolsey, Cardinal 143
women
    'bluestockings' 58
    Elizabeth and Jacobean writers 51
    high-ranking writers 51, 52
    as likely readers and possible authors
        of novels 57–8
    'literary ladies' 58
    modesty associated with female
        authors 50–51, 55, 57
the 'new woman' 110–111
non-aristocratic writers 52–3
as prodigies of humanist learning 51
'women's poetry' becomes
    fashionable 127
Women's Press, The 116
Wood, Anthony: *Athenae Oxonienses*
    156
Wood, Emma 277
Wood, William 169, 170, 171
Woodfall, Henry 173
Woolf, Leonard 212
Woolf, Virginia 72, 212, 213–14
Wordsworth, William 187, 191, 238, 246,
    276
    Lyrical Ballads (with Coleridge)
        187–8, 238
Worms, Germany 143
Wortley Montagu, Lady Mary 13,
    53–5
    *The Dean's Provocation for Writing the
        Lady's Dressing Room* 54–5
    Embassy to Constantinople 53
    'town eclogues' 54
    *Verses Address'd to the Imitator of the
        First Satire of the Second Book of
        Horace* 55
Wroth, Lady Mary: *Urania* 51
Wyatt, Sir Thomas 225

Yeats, W. B. 110, 136
Yellow Dwarf, The 242
Yorkshire Post 295
Young, Kenneth 295